PAWNS
OF
PLEIKU

MONTY DARRYL VOGEL

II

Grateful acknowledgement is made to include my own quotes in Newsweek magazine in May of 1971, plus Newsweek's information other than the reconsolidation work in Pleiku Province.

ISBN 9781090939517

CHAPTERS

INTRODUCTION

The United States was involved in the war in Vietnam long before most Americans realize; the U.S. employed advisory 'Deer Teams' in Vietnam as early as 1945, immediately after the removal of the Japanese in World War II. The American involvement began with advisory teams and it ended with them.

The Army, Navy, Marines, and Air Force all supplied advisers. Some worked with large Vietnamese units, some small. Some worked in comfort and safety, others in filth and danger, with little U.S. support. This story is about an Army Infantry **M**obile **A**dvisory **T**eam, or **MAT**. A MAT consisted of five men at full strength; usually a captain or first lieutenant team leader, a lieutenant assistant leader, and three non-commissioned officers, or sergeants. One sergeant was a heavy weapons adviser, one a light weapons adviser, and one a medic. The MAT team's job consisted of living with, advising, training, and joining in infantry operations with indigenous soldiers of a given area. 'Vietnamization of the War' began in late 1969. Special Forces teams were replaced with smaller advisory teams resuming their duties, just as Special Forces had resumed similar jobs of early advisers several years before.

Indigenous soldiers of Pleiku province consisted of both Vietnamese and Montagnard troops. These troops were not in the South Vietnamese **A**rmed **R**epublic of **V**iet **N**am regular army, or **ARVN**. Comprised of **R**egional **F**orce and **P**opular **F**orce militia, they were referred to as **RF-PF**s, or "Ruff-Puffs". Lightly armed and often poorly equipped, they were assigned to protect the provincial and district areas in which they lived. Regional Force units, usually the better equipped of the two, covered a Province area, what Americans might think of as a county in their state. The Popular Force units covered the village area, or town where they lived.

There were also **People's Self Defense Forces, PSDF**s. These were not soldiers, but outgunned villagers provided with WW II weapons, given the duty or opportunity to protect their villages and crops from the Viet Cong. Their survival was typically less likely than all others.

No Americans saw the war from Vietnamese civilians' and soldiers' views as did men on MAT teams, as well as the progress or lack thereof in winning this war. The U.S. military divided the country of South Vietnam into four Corps. I Corps was the northern quarter, where Marines made up the majority of U.S. personnel in the field. II Corps, including Pleiku was south of that, the largest and least populated. Further south was III Corps, and the Delta IV Corps made up the southern quarter. Every part of the country and every year was a different war, with personal memories burning forever in the minds of soldiers and sailors who served there.

South Vietnam was split into county-like provinces. Pleiku Province borders Cambodia, which lies south of the Laotian border. In the Central Highlands, Pleiku's geography is a mixture of old Appalachian-like Annamite mountains and flat plateaus, muddy streams, and small rivers. The soil in the area is relatively poor for agriculture. Red laterite sandy-clayish soil, rich in iron and aluminum, made life hard for the Montagnard and Vietnamese rural villagers. The fact that this province was classified as the "least pacified" in the country in 1970-71, made life no easier for civilians and soldiers alike.

Most Pleiku Province village and hamlet names began with "Plei", the Bahnaar Montagnard tribe name for village. Montagnards (pronounced mountain-yards) are an ethnic people who sparsely populate the rural mountainous Highlands. Descended centuries before from traders of the Kingdom of Champa, India, their skin was a medium bronze. They bore dark facial features and prominent, rugged cheekbones and prominent brows. Though most were not over five and a half feet tall, their bodies were usually strong and chiseled. Of nine tribes of Montagnards that populated the Highlands during the war, three inhabited the Pleiku area: Jarai, Rhade (Rah-day) and Bahnaar (Bah-naar, with a rolling R). The Montagnard name was given to them by the French during the French Indonesian war. They were not truly 'mountain people', but were driven to the highlands by the Vietnamese, who typically scorned them and stole their lands, in a manner reminiscent of Europeans in America two centuries before. A Vietnamese term for them was "moi", meaning savages. In later years, they would be collectively called the Degar, meaning mountain people. Their lifestyle was very primitive, similar to that of native Americans in the 1700s. The women were usually topless, the men wore loin cloths. Crossbows, sharpened bamboo and machetes were their weapons until supplied by others. Simple rectangular houses were made of bamboo and straw, on stilts to keep domestic animals out and the floor dry. Grass roofs effectively shed the rain and allowed cooking smoke out.

In 1971, as part of the Vietnamization effort, only two percent of Americans remaining in Vietnam were in the field. Consisting mostly of advisers and those who manned remaining artillery outposts, they were also disappearing. The majority of U.S. personnel left in the country were stationed in large U.S. compounds in the cities along the coast, where little action occurred. By now the war had militarily been a victory for the allies, in spite of a plethora of cynical reports from the media. *"We want the facts to fit the preconceptions. When they don't it is easier to ignore the facts than to change the preconceptions."* This quote by Jessamyn West seemed to epitomize journalists' reports at the time. The Viet Cong were laying low, captured, or dead. North Vietnamese units were shabby, poorly outfitted, and utilized many very young and old men, conscripted by a bleeding North. With a changing U.S. policy, the North was allowed to rebuild for another war, after suffering disastrous losses in 1968-1969, much of it due to their colossal defeat in the Tet offensive and Nixon's renewed bombing of the Ho Chi Minh Trail.

GLOSSARY

AK-47	Kalashnikov Automatic Assault Rifle
AO	Area of Operations
Arc Lite	B-52 Bombing Missions
Article 15	Non-judicial punishment. Can be given by a commander, unlike a court martial.
ARVN	Armed Republic of Vietnam. Regular South Vietnamese Soldiers.
Azimuth	Direction, usually a compass direction.
B-40	Rocket propelled grenade, or RPG, shoulder fired. Launch tube made of wood and steel.
Chuck	Viet Cong, phonetically 'Victor Charles', or 'Charles', or 'Chuck'
C.I.B.	Combat Infantryman's Badge. Though requirements varied, commonly awarded when under enemy fire a minimum of six times.
CIDG	Criminal Investigation Division Group
Claymore	Above ground anti-personnel mine
C-Ration	Small cardboard boxes packed with individual field rations. Date back to WW II.
Dai-uy	Captain in Vietnamese military

DT, Delta Tango	Defensive Targets, artillery
DF, Delta Foxtrot	Defensive Fires, artillery
DEROS	Date Estimated Return Over Seas: Return to the states.
Dust-off	Medical evacuation by helicopter, usually Hueys
ETS	Estimated Time of Separation. Discharged from the military.
FNG	Fucking New Guy
FO	Forward Observer
Four Deuce	4.2 Inch diameter mortar
Gunship	Combat helicopter, usually a Huey, armed with mini-guns, rockets, or grenade launchers.
Gook	G.I. derogatory term for enemy Vietnamese.
H & I	Harrassment and Interdiction fires. Random artillery or mortar fires to harass potential enemy locations.
HE	High Explosive artillery rounds. If "Quick" was added to a fire mission, it would be "Quick detonating", from immediate impact.
Hootch	Small one-room homes, a GI term.

X

KIA	Killed In Action
Klick	Kilometer
LP	Listening Post, usually 2 or 3 men outside a defensive perimeter to listen for the enemy.
LZ	Landing Zone, or Lima Zulu
M-16	Standard automatic assault rifle.
M-79	Grenade launcher. Shoulder fired, 40 mm round.
MACV	Military Assistance Command Vietnam
MAT	Mobile Advisory Team. At full strength, a 5-man team, assigned to live and work with RF, PF, PSDF, and R.D. Cadre Vietnamese and Montagnards.
Medevac	Medical Evacuation, normally via Helicopter
Meter	One meter = 39.37 inches. 1,000 meters = 1 kilometer, or 'klick'.
Mikes	Phonetic 'Mike' for Minutes
Minigun	Electronically fired 7.62 mm rotating barrel Gatling gun, 2,000 rounds per minute. Usually aircraft mounted.
MP	Military Police

MOS	Military Occupational Specialty, assigned as an enlisted job description.
NCO	Non Commissioned Officer. Various grades of Sergeant Rank
NDP	Night Defensive Position. A perimeter set up for the night while on a patrol.
Number Ten	Number (Num-bah) 10 is bad, the worst.
Number One	Number 1 is good, the best.
OCS	Officer Candidate School

Ong, Ong Charles, Mister Mister Viet Cong.

PAVN	Peoples Army of Vietnam (Enemy of the South Vietnbamese government)
P.C.P.T.	Physical Combat Proficiency Test. A series of physical events designed to test strength, speed, coordination and endurance. All soldiers were required to be tested. A maximum score was 500 points.
PF	Popular Forces. Soldiers not assigned to regular ARVN units, assigned to protect home towns and villages.
Phoenix	Program to kidnap or assassinate Viet Cong Infrastrure.
PRC-25	Portable Radio Communications, model 25, or "Prick 25". A backpack FM radio used for short distance communications.

PSDF	Peoples Self Defense Force. Civilian militia
RF	Regional Forces. Same as a PF, but assigned to protect their home province, or "county".
REMF	Rear Echelon Mother Fucker. A G.I. term for those not in combat roles.
RTO	Radio Telephone Operator. Can be in a fixed position in a base or carrying a radio in the field.
Spec 4	Specialist Fourth Class. Same enlisted rank as a corporal, or E-4.
Spec 5	Specialist Fifth Class. Same enlisted rank as a Buck Sergeant, or E-5.
Thieu-ta	Vietnamese Major
Thieu-uy	Vietnamese Second Lieutenant.
Trung-si	Vietnamese Sergeant.
Trung-uy	Vietnamese First Lieutenant.
V.C.	Viet Cong, or phonetically Victor Charlie, Charlie, Chuck
VN	Vietnam
White Mice	VN Military Police, Wore white helmets.
WIA	Wounded In Action
WP	White Phosphorus, or "Whiskey Papa" or "Willie Peter". Intense burning chemical.

Produces copious amounts of white
marking smoke.

XIV

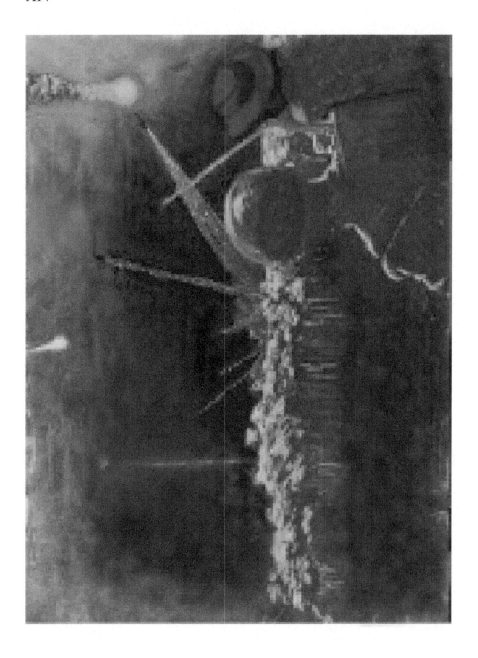

SOUTH VIETNAM

ADMINISTRATIVE DIVISIONS
AND MILITARY REGIONS
JUNE 1967

VIETNAM PROVINCES

**MAT 57 AREA OF OPERATIONS
NORTHERN PLEIKU PROVINCE**

I STARTING POSITION

"Initial Starting Position at the Beginning of a Chess Game"

It was January of 1968, the Tet Offensive in Vietnam was just beginning. A month earlier, at 23 years old, he was struggling to keep his Engineering grade average at the state University above failing; to fail meant the draft and an unknown future. His first years of academic success took a turn south with a variety of burdens that are not uncommon at the age, and a 2F deferment morphed to 1A. Then came the inevitable letter from the draft board: "Greetings……".

Darryl Wagner walked into the Portland, Maine recruiting office on Forest Avenue. Wagner knew he was being drafted, so 'why not enlist and get it over with'. He was twenty three now, not your typical eighteen year old draftee. Deciding to make the best of it, he inquired about Officer Candidate School. The smiling, polite recruiting sergeant in his strack dress uniform greeted him with all the fervor of a lion sizing up its kill. After the formalities and promises of great opportunities and careers available in that magnificent U.S. Army, Sergeant Williamson told Wagner, "The Army has dropped the requirement to have a college degree to go to Officer Candidate School. If you enlist, after Basic and Advanced Individual Training, you will attend 6 months of OCS, with a two year commitment as a lieutenant after." The problem: The Army, in its deficiencies of communications, never got the word about the change in requirements.

Leading into the draft, Wagner had seen his goals and his future melt away with a variety of despairs, including no place to call home, not enough money to continue college...

Working as an entry level draftsman was the only skill he knew, and at $2.00 per hour it didn't pay enough. Loading trucks and working with a logging crew in summers helped reduce the student loans, but now, with the inevitable draft, everything and everybody familiar to him was vanishing. He had never felt so alone and depressed. It made the decision easier to enlist rather than wait. Sergeant Williamson had neglected to give the reason the Army dropped the degree requirement---they were finding it difficult to replace the mounting casualty list of combat officers from a high mortality rate.

In twenty-eight months of Army stateside duty, Wagner had spent half of it in training. Basic Training at Ft. Dix was followed by Camp Roberts and Hunter Liggett Military Reservation in California with an MOS 51M20 assignment as a fireman. As in a putting-out-fires fireman. He hadn't asked for it, it was simply assigned. Wagner didn't want to tell his children someday – if he ever decided to marry – that he put out fires in the war. Months of repeatedly requesting Infantry OCS brought nothing but blunt refusals, due to an erroneous requirement of needing a college degree. Nobody knew or cared to take the five minutes to look into it. The weight of those lax attitudes meant nothing to the negligent NCOs and officers responsible, an attitude that very much permeated a strung-out Army in the middle of the war. But it was huge to Wagner and his future, in ways he could not yet know. As a last resort, his letter to Maine's Congressman Peter Kyros resulted in a reprimanded Colonel at Fort Ord and Wagner's abrupt orders for OCS in Ft. Benning, Georgia. The Colonel, fuming mad, sent a Master Sergeant to the P.C.P.T physical test course to personally thwart Wagner however possible, allowing no rest between events. Instead, he maxed each one.

Graduation from OCS found Wagner serving as a company commander in Aberdeen Proving Ground, Maryland. Several months later, orders came for Special Forces Advisory and Vietnamese Language Schools. They weren't requested, just mysteriously assigned. It seemed nobody ever knew who the gods were who decided these things, they just happened, part of the Green Machine. It may have been as simple as a Specialist Fourth Class company clerk spewing out typewritten orders randomly as they came down the system spillways, simply completing his tasks. Now Vietnam lay ahead. Only stories and one's imagination could form a picture in a soldier's mind what the coming year would bring.

In stateside Army Special Forces Vietnamese Advisory

School group at Fort Bragg, N.C., there were perhaps a hundred lieutenants, all assigned to MACV, Military Assistance Command Vietnam. Throughout the MACV training, each young officer envisioned his coming assignment. The plan was to be attached as a U.S. counterpart to an ARVN Vietnamese unit, probably company sized, maybe battalion. Darryl Wagner could only guess what limb Uncle Sam was putting them on, sent out with ARVN units with few Americans in support. He'd heard the stories of shabby Vietnamese units with a lack of commitment and poor morale. He had no idea where, or even in what section of the country he was headed.

II GAME DEVELOPMENT

*"Process of Bringing Your Pieces Into Play in the
Opening to Get Ready For the Middle Game"*

The World Airways 707 flight from Oakland was much longer than he'd imagined, via Hawaii and Clark Air Force Base in the Philippines. It took over 21 hours, the time changes passing slowly with endless tiny whitecaps below. The World Airways commercial jet was loaded with soldiers, sailors, Air Force, Marines. Soldiers, mostly. They were quiet, ponderous. The stewardesses were older than average, seemingly irritable and frazzled on their long and routine schedule.

Wagner considered the contrast with a civilian commercial flight. Most of the men were young, between 18 and 25, heading for their first tour in Vietnam, but a few were older vets trying their damnedest to look the part.

"Take a good look, the last good lookin' round eyes you'll see in a year of goddamn gooks," he heard a cigar-chomping warrant officer behind him say to another heavy sergeant beside him. They were vets of this war or wars past, khaki shirts sporting rows of ribbons. Most of them were torturing their tight seats of the 707, long past their days of military fitness.

There weren't many senior Officers or Non Commissioned Officers going to Nam for the first time on the plane. Not now, in May of 1970. A lot of lieutenants, PFCs, and Specialists fourth class. A few buck sergeants. Most didn't know exactly what or where their job would be any more than Wagner did. They would all initially stay briefly in Tan Son Nhut, the massive air base outside of Saigon.

He spent most of the flight day-dreaming of the girl he somehow lost, the college coed that filled his mind and heart for years since their breakup. It had been his fault, really, he knew it was. Immaturity, academic failure and family problems were part of the blame. He always thought that she might still love him, but doubtful. More likely, she was angry and hated him. He deserved it. He really did. He hadn't been himself, and he caused it. She was beautiful and smart, a high school Valedictorian. Intelligence, he had come to learn, was as important in a girl as anything else... and a nice ass. She had that, too. He never felt he could live without her, but it was all irrelevant.. she was married now, and a mother. It was over, but far from forgotten.

The plane landed at O-four hundred in the morning. Like Wagner, they were all tired, anxious, and wondering. The big jet coasted to a stop. They stood to open overhead doors while Wagner ducked swinging gear bags and searched for space to breathe between two overweight NCOs around him. The air still reeked of cigars and cigarettes from a cabin full of nervous GIs. Wagner's parents were chain smokers, as were most people of that World War II vintage, and he detested the smell of tobacco all his life. As he approached the door, he was surprised that he wasn't met with a rush of furnace-like hot air, as was the common perception. It was a damp, warm and quiet night, save for a remote rumbling of jet engines in some distant corner of the sky. Jet fuel mingled with sweet tropical air, a welcome respite from the flight's tobacco cloud.

"All MACV people over here" bellowed a large sergeant in jungle fatigues, subdued black and olive rank patches on his rolled up sleeves. The sign on a large wooden building said *Military Assistance Command Vietnam.* Above the words was a 5' high painted MACV unit patch, bright red with a gold border and gold castle-turrets bracketing a vertical white sword. No 9th or 25th Infantry, no 101st or 82nd Airborne, no Big Red One, or any of the other famous unit names Darryl had heard for years. Just MACV. It just didn't have that ring of a unit name. No fame, tradition or glory, not even a comradery or sense of pride. Even their MACV shoulder patch was unfamiliar, though it was worn by much of the top brass in Vietnam, including the commanding General William Westmoreland.

Several days were spent in MACV headquarters orientations, waiting for assignments, standing in line to pick up combat clothing and equipment and to learn some new ambush and defense techniques passed on by previous advisers. Wagner filed through the line, receiving jungle fatigues, Vietnam bush hat, jungle boots, M-16 rifle and field gear. Their khaki uniforms wouldn't be needed again until leaving for R & R, if they were still alive. Wagner fondled his brand spanking new, black M-16. It looked like a Mattel toy, small, light and new. It even smelled new. Training taught soldiers to adopt their weapon. It was your best friend, your most important friend, you always kept it close.

On the last day of a three-day orientation period, Wagner was directed to the holding barracks where assignments were to be given the next day. The building was filled with 'cherry' lieutenants, wearing newly issued unfaded green jungle fatigues, bush hats and jungle boots. Their clothes presented a new and unfamiliar appearance just as did this entire country and war. Each man personalized his bush hat; the cavalry look, folded up in front, Australian look, folded on one side, and the cowboy look, folded on both sides parallel to each side or narrowed toward the front with the side brims in a roll. Finally, the beat look, the brim angling down in a circle all the way around.

Wagner felt the suspense building while they awaited assignments. It filled every discussion. Many in this group were his friends, having shared the last twelve weeks of advisory and language schools. Some went back to the beginning of OCS, Officer Candidate School, a year and a half earlier. They had turned from 2nd to 1st lieutenants after one year as an officer, but the new rank didn't change a thing regarding results of 'dream sheets'-- the forms soldiers filled out to specify preferences for assignment types and locations. Throughout the Army, receiving a desired choice was such a rarity it was regarded as a joke.

Jerry Roux, a friend from Ft. Benning said, "Darryl, you lookin' for a MAT team?

"A what?" Wagner replied.

"MAT team. Mobile Advisory Team. Guess nobody wants it."

"What the hell is it? Never heard of it."

"I looked into it. 5-man team. A captain, lieutenant, 3 sergeants. Called mobile because you move around, work with different units. I hear you only work with Ruff Puffs. Sounds crazy."

"You mean you're not with a company? What the hell is a Ruff Puff?"

Roux moved his eyes a little closer to Wagner. "Ruff Puffs. RFs and PFs. They're the Regional Force and Popular Force troops. They work, live, and fight out of their own province or village. Not regular ARVN Army guys."

"They told us about RFs and PFs. But not much. Where are they?" Wagner asked.

"All over the country, I guess. Under-strength, under-equipped. Not much support. You don't want a MAT team."

Wagner asked around, the other men corroborating Roux's views. Filling out the form, Wagner emphasized he didn't want a Mobile Advisory Team and he didn't want the hot, miserable, often muddy and water-covered Delta. I Corps constituted the north end of Vietnam, where mostly Marines were located. South of that was II Corps and III Corps, where the Annamite Mountain chain channeled down the central and westerly side of the country, forming the Central Highlands.

The Delta was IV Corps, the southern end of the country where flat, low ground, created long ago by the Mekong River formed a fertile, wet, rice breadbasket of Vietnam.

The next morning right after breakfast, Wagner's results came back--a MAT team in II Corps. Wagner looked at the orders with a mixture of mild shock, nerves, and yet excitement. "Goddam dream sheets. At least they didn't give me the Delta," he grumbled, still pondering this new assignment. The recipients of MAT assignments were separated and sent to a classroom for their orientation. A young captain was giving the presentation. "Good morning gentlemen. I am Captain Corson, welcoming you to your MAT assignments. To most of you, this is a new awakening, to be sure, but we will try to enlighten you to your new world. MAT teams are 5-man teams that are assigned to advise, support, and train RF and PF---Regional Force and Popular Force companies and platoons and Peoples Self Defense Forces, or PSDFs in small villages. There are just under three hundred MAT teams currently in operation in South Vietnam. Many of these units that you will live and work with were previously trained by your predecessors, Special Forces A-teams. Some were not. You will find these units more isolated, with less firepower, less support, more out-on-a-limb, so to speak. Basically, it is your country's wish to 'Vietnamize' the war. We wish to give the Vietnamese more and more responsibility in fighting this war as our U.S. involvement is correspondingly reduced." He went on to explain that it meant living in small villages, sometimes eating diseased and disgusting food, fighting beside soldiers of small units of RF, PF, and PSDF soldiers, along with only one to four other Americans. "You will access these small units via Jeep, helicopter, or by foot. Hence the term 'Mobile'".

Since arriving, not until now did Wagner's anticipation turn to a gnawing concern, like butterflies before the kickoff in a football game; "I got a MAT team. Shit." The future was spinning in his head. What were his chances? If entire American units were sometimes overrun, how would a 5-man team fare?

He could only imagine scenarios of small hamlets deep in the jungle, like some scene from childhood books he had read long ago of *Bomba the Jungle Boy*. "These natives have serious weapons," he mused. He tried to envision lying in a strange grass hootch at night, looking through grass walls at a dark jungle a few feet away, wondering how close were these nasty little natives. The old marching song of OCS came to mind, to the tune of *Poison Ivy*: *"You're thinking of your family; Your children and your wife; You better think of Charlie, or he'll stab you with his kni-i-i-ife; In VI-ET NA-A-A-AM! VI-ET NA-A-A-AM! Late at night while you're sleepin' Charlie Cong comes a-creepin' all arou-ow-ow-ow-ound!"*

Orientation period was over, and now that MAT assignments were a given, all that remained was where in II Corps they would be consigned. Most of these lieutenants were about the same age, twenty two to twenty six. Most weren't married, and they all had at least one year, maybe a little more, left in the Army...if the enemy cooperated.

"One good thing about this Army was there were plenty of friends, like me, who were twenty-five and still single," Wagner pondered. Back home, in Portland, Maine, all of his old friends were married. He hardly knew anyone who ever had to go in the service, let alone any close friends. And all those crying babies! So now, these new good friends from this very different, very intense and very momentous era, were splitting up and heading to their assignments. It's possible that they would never see or speak to one another again, even if they made it back. They would rotate back into "the world" as the states were called, and back to a semblance of normality, whatever the hell that is. *Getting on with their lives.* How different would they be then? In spite of the camaraderie and brotherhood that grows in young men sharing the fears and strains of one of the most dangerous, underpaid, and unappreciated jobs on Earth, augmented by an ostracizing of their country, would they still feel the same once they were out? How would he interact with the old world he knew, or would he want to? *We may want to leave all of this so far behind, that perhaps we won't care to see each other again.* These thoughts hung in his brain like cobwebs as he opened a beer from a case being passed around the room. The scent of beer was a welcome distraction from the smells of Vietnam that permeated the air even here, in this large U.S. Saigon compound.

A senior sergeant appeared on a small podium at the front of the room. "May I have your attention sirs!" he yelled in a loud voice. "I have four lists, arranged per your new geographical Corps, as assigned. There are now three sets of these four lists posted on the wall of the MACV reception room, upstairs opposite the HQ S-1 office. These will inform you of your individual MAT team number designations and the Province or town in which you will reside in this beautiful war and tropical vacation paradise. Sergeant Daly will take you upstairs and try to answer your questions."

Wagner found his name, the words *Cam Ranh Bay* popping out below it, along with its MACV HQ advisory team number. Gordon Bailey was standing behind him. Gordon, a friend from their stateside schools, had trimmed down a good 30 lbs. from the start of OCS, as did many from constant motion and tension. After the last several months of decreased activity and stress-free responsibilities in advisory and language schools, he was beginning to pork up again. Gordon loved to eat, earning his nickname 'Grog' from the B.C. comic strip. His added weight had been torturing his tailored uniforms of late, but the loose jungle fatigues hid it. He wasn't a macho wanna-be. Gordon had a considerate, compassionate style, always contemplating, always considering what might work well for others before himself.

"Whatja get, Darryl?"

"Cam Ranh Bay! Can you believe that shit?" Wagner said. Cam Ranh Bay was a relatively safe, beautiful coastal area, just south of Nha Trang. Almost an in-country R & R center. "How about you?" Wagner asked.

"I'm going up to Pleiku. Central Highlands. Not good.

It's rated the least pacified province in the whole damn country. Nothing but bad guys and primitive Montagnard tribesmen we heard about." Gordon was still smiling and upbeat, in his methodical and take-what-comes way. Like Wagner, he had enlisted with an imminent draft coming. He had not chosen Air Force or Navy for a relatively safe service, he chose the Army. Coming from Burbank, California outside of LA, and having 'I Dream of Jeannie' Barbara Eden for a neighbor --- Holy shit, *who would move??*--- he left for Alaska, where he taught Spanish and Bush Pilot Safety to Yupik Eskimos. Gordon relished his rather primitive society there, where they had to ship out their sewer and ship in their water due to six hundred feet of permafrost in their soil. He ate fish eyes, lived on fresh salmon, wild meat and seal parts. He wore sealskin mukluks and a Musk Ox-hair parka, hand made by local Yupiks. It seemed like the Montagnard life style was meant for him.

"Geez, Gordon, that's rough," Darryl said. "I'm sorry, not too considerate of me. Feel like I'm gloating. You okay with this?"

"Well, it is what it is, Darryl. It may not be so bad, I just don't know what we're supposed to be doing. We weren't exactly educated for this job. I mean, this is nothing like what we were trained for. I think the Advisory School mentioned something about Montagnards, and the RF-PFs, but I don't remember much. You have any idea?"

"Nope. Sounds ominous….should get interesting."

It was early the next day in the MACV Annex, Bailey and Wagner were finishing an orientation class. Gordon Bailey had just heard that another close friend from the Ft. Bliss language school was living in Saigon. He'd arrived there two weeks earlier and was living in a BOQ Bachelors Officers Quarters on Tu Do Street in Saigon. Ron Hewitt was assigned as an adviser as well, but as a Military Police lieutenant working with Vietnamese military police. Bailey called him from HQ to get together.

"Darryl, we've got nothing for the rest of the day. We

can hop the MACV bus in town. Chance to see Saigon."

"Fantastic. I've got to hit the latrine, meet you back here in a few minutes?"

They caught the bus shuttle in front of the Annex for downtown. Boarding the bus, Bailey asked what the cyclone fence wire was doing on the windows.

"It's to keep anyone from tossing grenades in." someone said.

"Okay," he replied.

The twenty minute bus ride into the city was an eye opener. Market smells and thick diesel exhaust fumes grew stronger approaching the city. Traffic was chaotic, busy streets completely cluttered with vehicles of all types, mostly motor scooters and mopeds. Larger Lambretta taxis and a few Citroens from French days filled any void as quickly as it opened up., Bailey yelled, "Look at that," pointing to six vehicles all passing one another at the same time. "SIX!", he laughed. "I've never seen that before." A cacophony filled the streets from a roar of unmuffled motor bikes and trucks mixed with horns beeping and blaring as drivers shuffled for position. They disembarked at Tu Do street to look for Ron's BOQ. A short walk past a multitude of small shops brought them to Ron's three story building. His dull green M-151 Jeep was parked in front.

Before they could knock, Ron Hewitt walked out the front door, grabbing them both in each arm with a big dimpled grin, welcoming them to his AO.

"Great to see you guys! Never thought we'd see each other again after Bragg and Bliss."

"So this is it? You're living in a damn BOQ hotel for the war?" Darryl asked.

"Yep. This is what it's all about. Winning the war for those oppressed. Right here." Ron never lost his big grin. He was married before he left his last post at Fort Gordon, Georgia just prior to being assigned to the Special Forces MACV Advisory School and Defense Language Institute Schools in Fort Bragg and Fort Bliss along with the others. He had little time to spend as a married man before his trip to the vacationland of Southeast Asia.

They rode through horribly congested traffic in Ron's Jeep to see what the famous Tu Do strip was all about, famous for its array of strip joints and night clubs. Pulling into an official Vietnamese MP parking zone, his Jeep was relatively safe from theft. They walked a short ways, politely dodging street vendors trying to snag sales for various goods and services. Brightly lit color arrays of flashing fluorescent signs adorned the front of a relatively modern bar. They entered to see a score of soldiers sitting at tables and standing by the bar, amidst as many beautiful young bar girls. A few wore traditional silky, form-fitting Ao Dai (Ow-Yie) dresses that flowed with the breeze and movements graciously down to ankles. Most had scantier, seductive short dresses barely below the crotch, but they were all beautiful and shapely. Credence Clearwater Revival's *Green River* was blaring from overhead speakers. One of the girls approached for the usual "Buy me drink" routine.

"Chao, Co Dep. Co manh goi, khong?" (*Hello pretty girl, how are you?*) asked Wagner. It brought an instant smile and a *"Choi oi"*, literally meaning blue sky in Vietnamese, but translating roughly to 'Good Heavens'.

"Trung uy dep trai lam, ong biet noi tieng Viet?" (*First Lieutenant very handsome, you speak Vietnamese?*) she asked.

"It thoi, toi muon tap duoc." (*A little, I want to practice*) Wagner answered.

She quickly turned, calling to several of her friends hustling GIs at the bar. A half dozen turned and joined them. "Wow, gold strike" he thought. Gordon joined in the conversation, while Ron just smiled and watched the rest of the GIs in the room who were staring, wondering what the hell these guys had that they didn't. Paul Newman waving a wad of bills could not have done better. The language classes were already worth it.

There were thirty bunks in a one-room wooden single floor barracks at the MACV compound in Saigon. It was getting hotter, close to 100°, relieved only by a sudden Monsoon rain, sending torrents of water cascading off a metal corrugated roof. The men stripped off their clothes and ran out to shower in the warm deluge. It ended as quickly as it began, washing not only the men but the sickly smells emanating from street markets of Saigon and Cholon not far away. The markets were alive with vendors selling fruits, rice, monkey brains, fish, chickens, skinned dogs, roasted rats, whatever. But olfactory-wise, it was the fish. All of these blended with a smell of exhaust from poorly tuned diesel and gas scooters, Lambrettas, Hondas, and trucks. It is said that smell is the most memorable of our senses and it became ingrained in anyone who spent time there.

In the late evening, Wagner had just swung his legs onto his steel framed cot, separated from twenty nine other cots by four feet on each side. He pulled a puffy camouflaged poncho liner over his body, soon finding it too warm.

A small wiry lieutenant named Lovak jumped out of his cot to steal one of four floor fans three beds away. With a grin, he placed it by his cot, the fan pointing his way. This might have been amusing but for a stocky, ill-tempered lieutenant named Lucci, who Wagner knew to be an intimidating hot-head back at Ft. Bliss. Lucci arrived shortly after, and demanded to know who "stole his fucking fan". Though Lovak confessed and good-naturedly apologized, Lucci could not let it go. It was quickly developing into a war of its own, the entire room watching. Seconds from Lovak becoming the groups' first casualty of the war, Wagner stepped between them.

"Lucci. He apologized. Let it go."

"That was a cheap fucking trick. To another soldier! You don't do that! This asshole doesn't have a fucking clue. He was stealing, the asshole needs a lesson."

"Lucci," Wagner continued, "Okay, he did an asshole thing, I agree. He apologized. No big deal. Let it go."

Lucci was shouting, still ready to take Lovak apart.

Now Wagner was in his face, between Lucci and Lovak. Wagner's high school idol, like so many teenagers in the 60s, was Steve Reeves of 'sword and sandals' Hercules movies. He had a movie poster of Hercules tacked up in his basement weight room, where he spent countless hours since he was thirteen. Wagner had become a smaller model of his former 'no-steroids' Mr. America hero. Years of football, competitive swimming, wrestling and boxing, augmented by working with a logging crew in the woods of Maine had shaped him. Now he stood between Lucci and Lovak in only his O.D. boxer shorts in an atavistic pose, anticipating Lucci's next move. "I said *let it go*! Do you understand? We've got bigger worries over here than a goddam fan. *Do you understand*?" Lucci recalculated his position, but didn't want to show surrender with thirty men staring. "This is what we're gonna do," Wagner yelled as he pointed locations. "The four fans *will* be placed at equal distances, two on one side, two on the other, all blowing clockwise, horizontal, not down on anybody. We'll get more air flow, we'll all get some relief. We share. Agreed?"

With that, the situation was defused, and Lucci let it go with a glare and a grunt. The room fell quiet, and the men, tired from the day's anxiety, laid down to ponder their assignments and wait for sleep.

In the excitement and noise, nobody noticed a silhouette watching from the darkened entrance door at the end of the room.

III HANGING PIECE

"Unprotected Piece, Attacked By Your Opponent"

It was late in the day, and the temperature had risen again to oppressive levels. The wind direction had shifted, sending changing smells along with it. Tropical vegetation merging with jet fuel and turbine exhausts was relatively sweet compared to smells of the city.

Wagner and Bailey carried their gear onto a C-130 cargo plane. It would fly their now divided numbers to Nha Trang, the coastal city that was home to II Corps headquarters. The C-130 was empty inside, straps along the sides for human cargo seated facing inward. Its turboprops were loud, the whole plane vibrating tediously on the hop to Nha Trang. It was almost dark, and red tracers periodically streamed across the landscape a few thousand feet below, adding to the tension and imagination of newbies arriving in Vietnam.

Two more days would be spent at Nha Trang, with more orientations and more waiting. This was II Corps MACV headquarters, and like Saigon, the post was huge. War birds and helicopters came and went. The noise and smells were an improvement from Tan Son Nhut in Saigon, but not much. The heat and humidity was nearly as oppressive. What once was jungle were now wooden structures, connected by power lines and wires overhead everywhere. Long fields of flat, treeless land, all bare from Agent Orange and levelled with giant Rome plow bulldozers years before, surrounded the base.

The third day at morning chow, Wagner and Bailey were finishing greasy SOP Army pancakes when a Spec 4 walked into the mess hall and yelled, "Is there a Lieutenant Darryl Wagner here?"

Startled, Wagner answered, "Right here."

"Sir, you're Lt. Darryl Wagner?"

"Oh crap. Who wants to know?"

"Sir, I've been instructed to give these orders to you."

As Wagner read, his inquisitive look changed into one of concern and disbelief. The orders read:

DEPARTMENT OF THE ARMY
MILITARY ASSISTANCE COMMAND VIETNAM
SPECIAL ORDERS NUMBER 291   EXTRACT
57 CVN Fol rsg dir. VN P1422
WAGNER, DARRYL M 1LT INF O-2
ASSIGNED TO: ADVISORY TEAM 36, PLEIKU, II CORPS, VIETNAM
SPECIAL INSTRUCTIONS: Officer will rept to HQ, MACV, PLEIKU
NLT 1600 hrs................

Wagner didn't finish reading the rest of the form gibberish, he just sat staring, wondering what the hell had just happened. The Pacific shores of Cam Ranh Bay dried up before his eyes.

"What's up, Darryl?" asked Gordon.

"I don't know. What the hell? I just got my orders changed. Same as yours. Looks like I'm going to Pleiku."

"Holy. How'd that happen? What's it say?"

"Nothing. Just orders to report."

"Darryl, didn't they tell you? We're just pawns, you know that," Gordon said with a shy grin.

"Darryl, you got new orders?" asked Craig Rondell, another friend from the language classes at Ft. Bragg.

"Yeah, I didn't expect this."

"You were going to Cam Ranh Bay, right? I just came back from S-1. Heard your name. You remember Porter Richards? Blonde, scrawny guy, douchebag, from Bragg and Bliss?

"Yeah?"

"He just got his orders changed too. From Pleiku to Cam Ranh Bay. He was bragging about his old man taking care of him. Privileged bastard. His old man is a Colonel back in D.C. I think some friend of Colonel Hallard here."

"You mean he got his orders switched with mine?"

"What else? I went to Basic and AIT with the Spec 4 here in S-1, Rashon Johnson. Old friend. He's the battalion clerk in S-1 Personnel.

"Where's S-1?"

"In the MACV HQ, upstairs. Just came from there."

"Johnson there now?"

Rondell nodded yes, and said, "Black guy, tall, I guarantee a big smile. What are you going to do?"

"Not sure. But I think I'll try to see what happened. I'm pissed."

Wagner walked into S-1 and approached the clerk. "Excuse me Specialist, are you Johnson?"

"Yes, sir, so's my Dad." Big smile, as Rondell said.

Wagner didn't smile, just bent closer and said, "I just got a change in orders, I'm a tad curious. These came from a Colonel, I understand?"

"Yes, sir. Colonel Hallard."

"Is he here now?" Wagner asked, with a hint of anger.

"Yes, sir, right behind that door."

"Rondell was in training with you. Says you were friends. Anything you can tell me about the Colonel?"

With a short chuckle, Johnson said, "Well, the Colonel's only been here a couple weeks. Replaced the previous Full Bird Colonel, like overnight. Came from Ft. Myers, Virginia. I came in one morning, the Full Bird was gone, and Colonel Hallard was in his place. Even the First Sergeant wondered what happened. All I know is he digs into everybody's shit and don't say much."

"What do you mean?"

"I mean, he looks into every FNG's files, like his job is real serious and all that shit, sir. Like he's buckin' for a promotion, from all this serious work, and he's gonna win the war for us. Like he could really make a difference as a REMF. He doesn't talk much, kind of has his own row to hoe."

"REMF?" asked Wagner.

"Rear Echelon Motherfucker", Johnson said with a laugh. "Yeah, this Colonel, he don't talk to me much, don't even talk to the Fus' Sergeant. Fus' Sergeant thinks he's strange, too, I can tell. I don't think he's been in combat. Not much for ribbons for a Colonel, his picture's right there," he said, pointing to the orderly room wall.

Wagner thought he looked distantly familiar. Then he realized he was one of the men on the C-130 flight from Saigon. Without a hat, he saw the balding head. Grayish hair along the sides, and a somewhat stocky frame.

"He just don't say much," Johnson continued. "Unless he's on the phone. Always keeps his door shut, but every time I see him, he's on that damn phone. Then he's always talkin'. Talkin' all the time. When I do go in there, he shuts right up. Puts whoever on hold, and looks at me like, "What the hell do you want?" I don't know much more than that, sir."

Wagner struggled with the injustice of it, but he was discovering a lot of that. All through nine-plus enlisted months before the beginning of OCS, he believed that the soldiers he served with were an even representation of a cross section of America. How could it possibly be anything else? Only during OCS did he begin to learn the truth about the percentages of draftees coming from lower socio-economic classes. The officer candidates he spent six months with were nearly all college graduates. Though some were drafted, most enlisted. They were older, of course, but most were also a hell of a lot more savvy and educated than the average teenage GI coming from the slums of cities, hills of Appalachia and potato fields of northern Maine. Now he was seeing another example, right here inside the officer corps. The 'privileged' Lt. Richards was from Fairfax, VA, outside of D.C., a wealthy neighborhood. It didn't help that this lieutenant whose orders were switched with Wagner's had been universally disliked by other classmates. In fact, no one understood how Richards made the cut to graduate from OCS. He had been recycled from a previous company to give him one last chance at graduating. 40% did not.

The injustice of it all kept boiling up. Wagner decided to

do the unthinkable. He would confront this Colonel and at least get an explanation. Not that it would make a difference, no chance, but he couldn't just drop it. His very life or death might well be decided in the coming months from this one conniving event. After all, *what were they gonna do, send him to Vietnam?* Really, it was the damn principal that it boiled down to.

Wagner thanked Johnson and turned toward the Colonel's door. Johnson started to say something, then thought what the hell. He walked stiffly past the protesting WAC secretary behind Johnson and the First Sergeant who was engrossed in his papers and never bothered to look up. Without waiting for a response to his quick knock, he opened the Colonel's door. The Colonel looked up from his desk, surprised. The room reeked of cigar smoke, and a plume was slowly rising from a half-gone White Owl in the ashtray.

"Yes?" he said with an annoyed expression.

With a salute, Wagner began, "Sir, my name is Lt. Darryl Wagner. I'd like a word with you if I may, sir."

The Colonel looked at him as though he knew what this was about, and leaned back in his chair. "Go ahead Lieutenant."

"I had orders for a MAT team in Cam Ranh Bay. It appears those orders were switched to Pleiku."

"And?"

"And it also appears a Lt. Richards somehow finagled that switch with some parental influence. I believe you know his father?"

Colonel Hallard sat back in his cushioned chair, holding his pen to his lips. Clearly, he hadn't expected to be defending his decision with a lieutenant. Just for a moment, he looked like a kid getting caught cheating in class. Smiling, he leaned forward again and pointed the pen towards Wagner. Pleiku isn't so bad, you know. You'll be up there with Montagnard troops. They'll take care of you up there."

"This is pretty damn poor, sir," Wagner continued, not trying to hide his anger. He had never talked to a field grade officer, or for that matter, any other higher-ranking officer this way. You learn that very early on in this Army. And this was a

Colonel.

"Sir, I enlisted for this Army. *My choice.* The friggin' MOS they gave me was a 51M20 fireman as a Private. I fought this crazy Army for nine and a half months just to get into Infantry and OCS. Had to write my congressman to get Infantry. Crazy! I'm not afraid. I'll go anywhere in this country they send me, that's not the point. As long as it's a fair shake. Luck of the draw. *This* clearly isn't."

Colonel Hallard didn't pull rank. Wagner had a point, maybe even a legal one, or at least enough to possibly warrant an inquiry. If Wagner had, indeed, written his Congressman to get into the Infantry, might he make an issue of this as well? In the states, Hallard had known another senior officer who had had such an experience, and it didn't end well. The Army does not like Congressional Hearings. It often ends up poorly for the initiator, unless he has damn good reasons. As a minimum it could end up as a red mark in his files. The military has a way of screwing with things, and with its people. Particularly the lower ranks, including lieutenants. ***But it also can reflect poorly on the officer in charge.*** A blemish can mean years of waiting for a promotion, if it comes at all. The competition for higher ranks is intense, and it grows with every promotion. The Colonel also knew that pulling rank wouldn't make the situation less precarious, and he saw something in this lieutenant that told him it wasn't going to go away. There really was something to the argument: *What are they gonna do, send me to Vietnam?* And Wagner's complaint wasn't unwarranted. But Colonel Hallard was smooth, he had a knack for dissuading emotions of the moment, manipulating people for an end. In the short two weeks in his position in Nha Trang, he already had a reputation for it. "Again, Lieutenant, you'll be working with the Montagnards up in Pleiku Province. They're a fine bunch of fierce, dedicated fighters, and I'm sure you'll appreciate the experience. They're dedicated and tough. Looking at you, I can tell you're tough, aggressive. They'll appreciate your style. Play any sports in school?"

"Uh...yes, sir."

"Football? What?" the Colonel asked, puffing on his White Owl.

"Yes sir. Wrestling, swimming. A little boxing."

"Good. You're a tough man. I can see that. You'll do well. I can see you've pumped some iron in your day. They'll look up to you. Respect you. They're not like some of the Vietnamese units around here, the Montagnards like Americans and vice-versa. They'll take care of you. I also understand you're the first Officer Candidate to win his C.I.B before going to war," he continued.

The C.I.B., or Combat Infantryman's Badge, was the wreathed musket device earned after being under enemy fire at least six times. In OCS, the senior candidates were enjoying the traditional party just before the sixth month school graduation. Dates were traditionally acquired and bussed in from surrounding southern colleges, the girls supplied with motel rooms in downtown Atlanta. Some drunken soldiers had been causing a multitude of problems when one tried to break in to Wagner's date's room, while he waited outside with friends. Wagner grabbed the man by the collar and slung him around, sending him careening into the upstairs balcony steel railing, knocking out a tooth. Dressed in class A uniform, with his first date in months, Wagner in no way wanted trouble. Not to mention any form of misbehavior could send the entire six months of OCS down the drain, he would never become an officer. Wagner tried to talk the drunken soldier out of it, to no avail. The soldier grabbed him by the lapels and slammed him against the brick wall, which was answered with three rapid punches, the last spinning the soldier around, smacking his head on the concrete walkway when he fell. Wagner left with his date to report the incident to the front desk, the soldier bleeding and unconscious. The clerk grinned at the news, later informing the police that he had been getting calls all evening regarding drunken soldiers causing a variety of semi-serious problems. Because the scuffle was between two soldiers and no civilians, it was dismissed. Six police cars and an ambulance arrived after Wagner and the others departed, and the unconscious soldier didn't awake until the next day. Wagner prayed the fracas would never get back to his OCS cadre. That following Monday, the entire 220-man company was seated in an outside stadium-seat facility, at a Recoilless Rifle range. Opening the class, the Captain instructor said, "Before we begin, will Candidate Wagner post front and center?"

A quizzical Wagner stood up, descended the bleachers, and marched to the Captain to report. The Captain held a giant six-foot cardboard mock-up of a C.I.B. Presenting it to Wagner, he said, "This is the first time in history any Officer Candidate has been awarded the Combat Infantryman's Badge before actually going to war!"

Wagner thought news of the incident had never gotten back to Fort Benning and had long been forgotten.

Colonel Hallard was smiling.

"Oh my God," gasped a stunned Wagner, "How the...."

"I do my homework, Lieutenant. I need a man like you. You think this is all luck of the draw?" I saw the way you handled the fan issue. I want leaders."

When it was over, Wagner recognized the compliments were a schmooze, a means the Colonel used to redirect the focus. Whatever it was, it was at least in part effective. Yes, smooth. "But how in hell did that C.I.B. story get out? It was over a year ago."

Though it all changed nothing, and in reality Wagner expected nothing more, he had said his peace and wondered if there was any way to report this assignment switch, and to who? In any case, he felt somewhat betrayed again by the Army, as he had as a Private, turned down for Officer Candidate School for months, when promised otherwise. But he had kept his cool, didn't lose his show of respect for the rank, and didn't go to jail.

Before leaving for new assignments the next day the group said their goodbyes and good lucks. Wagner wondered how many of them would return. Already, three close friends from his OCS platoon had been killed, some others wounded, before he and the rest even arrived in country. Their deaths were reported in the *Stars and Stripes* Army newspaper, and when it was someone they knew the word spread like wildfire.

Wagner and Bailey boarded a camouflaged C-123 to the Air Force strip in Pleiku Province. Along with a dozen Air Force personnel, they were the only soldiers on board. Their new green jungle fatigues shouted "FNG", and Gordon leaned to Darryl to say he thought they were being stared at. The "Fuckin' New Guys" syndrome has never changed since men evolved with hormones, and never will. Descending past the highest mountains of the Central Highlands near the end of

the trip, Wagner could see the area was far less populated than the coast. Small villages were few and far between. Occasional streams or rivers were terraced into rice paddies near the villages, and some fields and plains occasionally divided the jungle below. Landing at Pleiku Air Base, the loud vibrating cargo plane taxied to a halt. They walked out to a bright midmorning sun that pinched their eyes. Wagner noticed the air was temperate and pleasant, like a day in mid-June in Maine, in sharp contrast to the daytime oppressive temperatures and humidity of the coast. The altitude in the Central Highlands, along with wind currents channeled by the Annamite mountains created a surprisingly familiar environment. The air was cooler

and dryer, and there were noticeable changes in the vegetation. This base looked emptier, far less busy than expected. Nothing like Tan Son Nhut in Saigon, or Nha Trang, where hundreds of C-131s, C-130s, C-123s, and various fighters and F4 Phantom fighter-bombers arrived and departed like bees.

From a figure approaching the plane came a shout, "Darryl! Gordon!" It was Doug Hanson, another friend from Fort Benning days they hadn't seen for over a year. Doug trotted up the tarmac to welcome them to Pleiku.

"My Christ, Doug! I can't believe it. What the hell are you doing here?" Bailey asked.

"Welcome to your new home. I was really surprised when I got the word you guys were coming in"

"*You* were surprised!" said Wagner. "Our old joke was that you'd be seeing us off in San Francisco, not meeting us here! Glad you could make it to beautiful downtown Vietnam!" He slung his duffle bag over his shoulder as Doug gestured toward the Jeep just off the runway. "Are all people here from our old company?" Wagner joked.

Doug's branch of service was Adjutant General Corps, or AG. Considered the cushiest choice, the rest of the class figured he wouldn't even go to 'Nam'. As the top graduate in the 220-man Infantry class, he had his choice of branch.

"He laughed, "No, I couldn't escape it. I'm the S-1 Personnel Officer. I arrived in country two weeks ago. I think you'll like it okay here. Well as can be expected, anyway."

"Yeah, that's easy for you to say, chairborne ranger.'"

"Well, it's not so damn hot here anyway." Hopping in Doug Hanson's M-151 Jeep, they drove a short way on paved Highway QL 14 to Sector headquarters near the center of Pleiku City. The main highways, QL 14 and QL 19 were the width of a rural road in the states. On the way in, Wagner told Doug how his great assignment in Cam Ranh Bay was switched to Pleiku.

"Really! The same thing happened to me!" Doug said. "I was supposed to stay in Nha Trang, on the coast! A couple days later, I learned I was moving to the middle of another freakin' planet! No reason given. Was I pissed!"

Wagner thought for a moment and said, "Ever hear of a Colonel Hallard? A lieutenant colonel?"

"Hallard?....Yeah. Stocky, balding. A touch of gray? I met him in Nha Trang." Doug, graduating top in his class, was an outstanding leader and administrator type. He held a high-level position in a major clothing company before he was drafted. "I hear Colonel Bern talking to him sometimes….and to Colonel Robichaud every day. Our HQ clerk tells them Hallard's on the phone, that's how I know. Always closes the door to take the call."

"Who's Colonel Bern?" Wagner asked.

"Full Bird Colonel. He's the commanding officer. West Pointer. You'll probably meet him this morning. First you'll see

Colonel Robichaud, he's a Light Colonel...Bern's assistant. Nice enough guy. I'll bring you in after you go through your MAT orientation. Bern's been here a couple of months, but he was here in Pleiku on his previous tour, only a year or so ago. He knows the ropes pretty well, knows the area, seems to know the Montagnard villages, where they are, their chiefs, whatever. West Pointer, all business guy. He's really into Psyops, psychological operations stuff, like Viet Cong infrastructure, Phoenix programs, whatever. Seems really on top of things. He works closely with General Ngo, a Vietnamese two-star. I think he's a II Corp counterpart to Bern, a bit of a hard ass. He's definitely the commander, doesn't like anybody questioning progress. Robichaud got here a few weeks ago, came up from Saigon. So Robichaud reports to Bern, I report to Robichaud.

"What's Phoenix?" Wagner asked.

"Program for taking out the V.C. infrastructure." Hanson continued. "They use Vietnamese assassins, basically. When they're convinced they've got an enemy element in a ville or unit, they'll actually send a team in to snatch him, middle of the night. Next day he's gone, never heard from again. When the North did their all-out Tet offensive in '68, it exposed most of the Viet Cong leaders. After that, they were 'removed', so to speak, and it really broke their infrastructure. The V.C. were sapped, now it's mostly NVA."

"I think they told us something about that." Wagner said. "So how does Hallard figure into this? I think he was a West Pointer, too."

Hanson thought for a moment, looking out the window of their concrete-and-block building, still pocked from bullet holes and shrapnel from any of several attacks of the last several years. "I don't know. We're just mushrooms in the dark, getting fed shit. But Robichaud is on the phone a lot with Hallard."

"Personally," said Wagner, "I've only known one West Point officer in this good Army that seemed decent. I'm guessing it has something to do with being raised an Army brat or something. I never expected that. The rest couldn't lead a horse to water. There was one in Indiantown Gap in

Pennsylvania…he was a complete joke. I was sent there TDY, training ROTC cadets. The cadets constantly made jokes about him, did impersonations. He had no respect from them or the officers. The guy was nuts."

"What were you doing there?"

"TDY. Temporary duty. Wassle and I were sent there from Aberdeen Proving Ground. We were supposed to be part of a ROTC training group. I was a company Executive Officer, the CO was a Major. Big difference from OCS, we had forty percent canned."

"Yeah. Wassle was there too?"

"Yep. This ROTC summer camp--everybody graduates. But in our company, one didn't, only because I pleaded with the Major to get this guy out. He literally cried whenever I chewed his ass. Stood there crying. And he had a combat branch, Artillery. Can you imagine? Your firebase gets overrun, and this guy would stand there and cry. The Major listened to me and canned him. But how many made it that weren't much better? If I hadn't been there, he'd probably be here in some firebase today.

"Yeah, you wonder," said Hanson, shaking his head.
If the troops deserve nothing else out of this damn Army, I would hope they deserve decent leadership. It's scary,"

Wagner spent two more days in Pleiku headquarters, when Doug Hanson met him for lunch in the HQ mess hall.

"Darryl, I saw your orders. You're going to be the assistant team leader of a MAT team at another old Special Forces camp on the outskirts of a small village named Le Quon."

"Have you been there?" Wagner asked.

Hanson laughed, "I haven't been anywhere except on a chopper mail run, and that was only once."

Wagner listened as Hanson recapped the makeup of the MAT assignment. "By design, a MAT team consists of a captain as team leader, a first lieutenant assistant and three non-commissioned officers, or NCOs, ranging in rank from Sergeant

First Class E-7, Staff Sergeant E-6, to Buck Sergeant E-5. At full strength, those NCOs consist of a heavy weapons advisor, a light weapons advisor and a medic. There may be a radio telephone operator RTO, but he's not a team member, stationed at some compounds to receive and relay messages." In his briefings, Wagner found his team had the largest area of operations, or AO in the country, embracing the northern two-thirds of Pleiku Province. He was also reminded it was in the least pacified province in the country, and had the most enemy activity. The vanished Cam Ranh Bay assignment was looking more desirable by the minute.

Wagner walked into Pleiku headquarters, where a congenial Master Sergeant greeted him with a smiling "Good afternoon, sir. I'm Sergeant Husky. Colonel Robichaud is expecting you, you can go ahead in."

Wagner saw a fiery, fast-talking, pull-no-punches Colonel with a Dallas accent. Gordon Bailey was already there. Another man stood behind him, in civilian clothes. The civilian barely turned to acknowledge them.

"Welcome to Pleiku." I'm Colonel Robichaud. Lieutenants, you're in for an interesting year. I'm going to apologize for being brief and to the point, but the fact is, I don't have a lot of time right now. You each scored near the top in your language school. Lt. Wagner, you were the only man I've ever personally known to max the PCPT." Turning to the civilian, he said, "Physical Combat Proficiency Test. Perfect score." He turned back to Wagner and Bailey, then looked down at the papers he held in his hands. "Your AFQT tests were very impressive. Nearly every one maxed out. Lt. Wagner, I also see your course was Engineering. You both enlisted."

"Yes sir," they both answered, impressed with the individual attention.

"The Colonel had done his homework, as had Col. Hallard, in Nha Trang," Wagner thought. Not typical military, in Wagner's Limited experience.

"Your team will be MAT Five Seven," he said, looking

at Wagner, "and Four Six," looking at Bailey. Lt. Wagner, your team leader will be Lt. Robinson," the Colonel continued, turning his back to Wagner. His hands were folded behind his back in Parade Rest fashion, as he paced behind his desk. "You'll be his assistant." Lt. Bailey, your team leader just DEROSed, you'll be the team leader. Normally a captain's slot, but you're taking over. I'm gonna tell you both flat out, this Army is expecting a lot from you. You'll be out there without a lot of American interaction. Limited support at times. We've got a job to do. Contrary to what the goddamn press is pushing, we're winning this goddamn war. We're setting Charlie on his ass, and we are *winning* this war. Not a lot of Viet Cong left, or at least active, we're mainly fighting the North Vietnamese Army NVA now. And winning, hands down. But with this Vietnamization of the war, we're going to let the little people win it eventually. You'll be living and operating with Montagnard and Vietnamese units, mostly RFs and PFs. You know you aren't here to command them, only advise them, right?"

"Yes, sir," they both nodded, quietly. Bailey was still trying to absorb the part about being the team leader.

The Colonel was pacing again as he spoke, looking down, then back at them without missing a beat. His words came fast and furious, as if he had to lay out months of facts before he vanished into some foggy, surreal mist within minutes. "II Corps is the largest and least populated of the four Corps. It encompasses thirty thousand square miles, almost half of South Vietnam, but only eighteen percent of the population. About the size of South Carolina. Half of that population is Montagnard, the other half Vietnamese. The western border of II Corps is Cambodia for 175 miles," he said, running his fingers along the map. "Then 65 miles of Laos to the north. Lt. Wagner, your area of operations is the northern two thirds of the Province," he said, now waving his hands over the wall map, outlining the boundaries of the AO. "Kontum Province borders your district to the north, Binh Dinh District to the East, and Phu Nhon District to the South. Lt. Bailey, your AO is the

southern third, running down to Phu Nhon District. The Annam
Corderilla Mountain Range runs pretty much north-south on the
eastern side of your AOs, and it gets pretty unpopulated all
through that area, only a few small and sparse Montagnard
hamlets here and there. Somewhere around three quarters of a
million Montagnards have died in this war or before, and the
maps aren't all that accurate where the villages were and are
now. A lot of them have been abandoned." Wagner and Bailey
were trying to keep up, a lot to absorb in a short time. "Pleiku
Province is the least pacified province in the country. Has been
for most of the war. Pleiku City is here," he continued, pointing.
Your team's purpose is to advise and assist the indigenous
troops in your areas of operations. That includes night and day
operations, search and destroy, screwin' up the NVAs' night
movement, collecting information where you can, and village
protection. Some of the units can use training, others don't need
a hell of a lot, if any. I can tell you a good part of your job when
you're on operations is to call in American artillery. The
Vietnamese artillery here stinks. It's slow and inaccurate. If
you're with a Montagnard outfit, the Vietnamese just damn well
might drop it on you as the enemy. No shit, Lieutenants, that's
the way it is. A lot of Vietnamese hate the 'Yards. The units
you'll be with can't call for American arty. They'll love having
you along for support, believe me!" He paused to think for a
minute, as if to choose his words carefully. "Lieutenants, we're
being pushed to use Vietnamese arty instead of our own, as part
of the 'Vietnamization of the war'. As far as I'm concerned, it's
a good idea for anyone's ass in Saigon. As far as you're
concerned, it's some asshole's idea in Saigon. Or Washington.
When it's your ass on the line, you want the fastest and the best.
Nothing but. But this may be out of your hands soon. It's out of
mine, now. They want you to use Vietnamese arty first, then
American if nothing's available. The last thing they'll want is for
you to call for gunships. Huey helicopters. Only in extreme
situations. By that time, it'll be too late, so learn to depend on
your artillery and yourselves. There aren't any U.S. troops
around to help you. Another thing. Helicopter pilots as a rule

are top notch. They're nuts, they'll go anywhere, anytime. But Camp Holloway, our local helicopter base, has some idiot of late who won't let his pilots fly if there's just a damn low ceiling, let alone foul weather. Been that way for a few months, expect it to continue. At least until he DEROSes or gets his ass sent out of here. That's not likely to happen, he may be here for a while. Now, you'll have four Regional Force companies, or RFs and twelve Popular Force platoons, or PFs in your Areas of Operations. The Montagnard companies and most of the platoons are crackerjack. They'll take good care of you and they will love to have you with them. Your Vietnamese units are 'subject to scrutiny'. There are a couple of damn good ones. Fine leadership, fine troops. Aggressive, energetic. It depends on their leadership. They want to kill the enemy. Period. Some of the others are pathetic. Lousy commanders. It isn't the soldiers' fault. The Vietnamese can be as good as any soldier. But they've got no real future. Nothing to fight for. No light at the end of the tunnel. I can't fault them entirely for bad morale. We'd most likely be the same damn way. The major problem is leadership. They pick most of their leaders from the economically elite, and they're getting about what you'd expect....shit. Now listen, Lieutenants, if it gets deep out there and they run, you run, too. The biggest problem is getting their raggedy asses up and moving on any operation whatsoever. If they don't get out and look for Charlie, and don't keep their goddam area policed up killin' V.C. and the NVA outside their perimeters, Charlie just walks in and chews 'em up, while they're thinking about what they're gonna eat for lunch that day. Understand, Lieutenants?"

"Yes, sir."

"Now, I know I'm filling you in on an awful lot of hog feed in a damn short time, but the truth is, Lieutenants, I don't want to see a lot of good men's time and blood wasted over here. I want to see the good work that's been done continued. For the most part, this war is won. If it's ever lost, it'll be lost by the Vietnamese, not us. But history will say *we* lost it. I don't want all this work and blood thrown away....wasted.

Understand?"

"Yes, sir."

"One important thing. The Montagnards. They're good people. The most honest, decent little people on this good Earth. Been screwed blue by everybody. By the South Vietnamese, the Viet Cong, and now the NVA, the North Vietnamese Army....and by us, too. It's wrong, but a fact. The 'Yards were treated good by the French, but they used them, nonetheless. We've treated them good, for the most part. We used them because they're goddam good fighters, and they love Americans. And Americans love them. They're great little people. They're honest, brave, fair, and tough people, who you can beat over the head with a Texas pine tree and they'll still smile at ya. I'm afraid with this pacification and Vietnamization stuff, turning the war back to the Vietnamese--not that I'm against the idea--the 'Yards are gonna get the shaft. From both sides, if we're not here to help them. They're losing everything. I'm afraid they don't have a chance."

Colonel Robichaud stood silent for a moment, staring into Wagner's eyes. He looked a little sad, like a man without hope, a man who had reached the end of a lifelong task--that failed. Then he took a deep breath, and slowing his pace, he became more serious. His words were quieter, more personal. "Lieutenants, I want you to kick ass and take names out there, for sure. But be goddamn careful. For you and your men. Depend on your good counterpart units, and be damn careful of the shitty ones. If they run, you run too. Don't be left holding the bag. It ain't worth it. You don't have enough numbers with you to win this war yourself. Do your job, finish your year, and get home safe, men."

"Yes, sir." Wagner stared at the Colonel, once again trying to absorb the senior officer's full intent and meaning in this new, perplexing world.

Extending his hand to both, he articulated his words, "I want to wish you all of God's help. Good luck to you, men."

After the briefing, Wagner joined Doug Hanson again at

the mess area for lunch. He told Hanson, "I met Colonel Robichaud. He's an impressive guy. You were right. At the end of his briefing, he seemed sad. Like he was worried, or depressed or something."

"Yes," said Doug, with a concerned look. "I can't quite figure what the hell's going on yet. He seems like a straight shooter to me. He's a workaholic, and no-nonsense. He's on top of everything. He doesn't put up with screw-offs, American or Vietnamese. I know that for a fact. Not sure, but there seems to be a little friction between him and Colonel Bern."

As they talked and ate, they were joined by another acquaintance Wagner knew from language school. He had recently arrived as well and was also stationed at Sector headquarters with Hanson. It was Jerry Dulane, a lieutenant who made no effort to suppress his anti-war feelings. Wagner could never figure why a person who had so disagreed with the war had decided to become an officer, a leader. On several occasions at Ft. Bliss, Wagner and Dulane had debated the war. Wagner had mixed feelings, but saw both good and bad. The end of the Second World War, after all, was only twenty four years ago, the United States was still in a cold war with Russia. The real or perceived threat of Communism was far more intense than a generation in the future would remember. 'Kneel down in the hallway with your hands covering your heads' school air raid drills for a nuclear attack were only a dozen years in the past. McCarthyism anti-Communist paranoias, which didn't seem so crazy at the time, fed the domino theory. It was likely the leading cause for American involvement, as early as 1945. That would gradually convert to a chaotic mixture of establishment lies for many, and would be all but forgotten in the debates and movies of the future. But the past is a place that cannot be revisited. Decades later, the media and documentaries would focus on bad politics, atrocities, and economical demons that surely did occur, leaving little room for debatable truths of another side to the war.

Dulane had only arrived a few days before Wagner, and had just minutes before received his assignment. He had a background that was perfect for the job he had requested, and miraculously, he got it. It was in PSYOPS, or Psychological operations, which was sometimes translated into "propaganda department".

When Wagner asked him about it, Dulane elatedly said, "Darryl! A desk job! I got a desk job! Are you kidding me? I'm not gonna complain the whole year over here. I'm gonna write my wife right now and tell her. Boy, did I luck out! Yo, Babeeee!" Then he paused, hunched his slightly overweight frame forward, and looking Wagner in the eyes said quietly, "You don't think that's backing out do you? I mean, trying to get out of going to the field. Think that's okay?"

Wagner grinned. "Damn straight. I'm amazed this crazy Army is finally making use of some training and education its people have for a change. This is probably the first time I've seen it. I'm really happy for you, Jer."

"Hey, I'm sorry I'm sitting here gloating over this while you've got humpin' the boonies ahead. Not too considerate of me."

"No problem, Jer. I'm excited about what I'm doing, and after over two years of expecting it, I guess I'm mentally up for it. No sweat. We aren't that far away, so I'm sure I'll see you a lot."

"Okay. Look, I've gotta write my wife. I'll be living right here in the headquarters at Sector here in town, so drop by and tell me what it's like out there, alright?"

"Sure will, Jer. I'm leaving in a while for my new home, Le Quon. Take it easy, Buddy." Wagner liked Dulane, but he couldn't help but reflect on how Jerry had slammed U.S. policies on the war and how his relief was so apparent when finding he nailed a safe desk job. His fears were the motive for his sentiments, the same as for most dissenting and draftable people 'back in the world'. He was genuinely happy for him, though. Dulane didn't even have Infantry for a branch of service. In fact, he didn't even have a 'combat arms branch', Infantry, Artillery, or Armor.

Wagner was told to report to Colonel Bern at 1400 hours. Colonel Bern was tall and thin, a serious man with a thin face but strong jaw. Even with a fresh shave the Colonel had a dark shadow. Thin, piercing brown eyes and dark lashes and eyebrows presented a no-nonsense look that begged respect. When Wagner entered his office, Bern wasn't alone. Beside him, inspecting a large topographical map of Pleiku, was the same man in civilian clothes who had been with Colonel Robichaud, named David Friedman. The map had black and red grease pencil circles drawn around rectangular patterns of black squares along the two main Highways QL 19 and QL 14. There were more along the jungle 'Jeep trails' and numerous dashed lines that designated foot trails that interweaved through jungles and streams in remote reaches of the province. Tiny black squares designated individual hootches in villages kilometers apart, more prevalent and numerous near east-west Highway QL 19 and north-south highway QL 14. Generally, the farther from QL 19 or QL 14, the smaller and fewer were the villages. Some had only a dozen or less hootches. QL 19 ran from Pleiku, east about 20 kilometers through the famous and dangerous Mang Yang Pass, and on to the coast. QL 14 connected the city of Kontum , 47 kilometers, or 28miles to the north and Ban Me Thuot, 203 kilometers, or 122 miles to the south of Pleiku.

Friedman was average height with a middle-age spread, somewhat pear shaped, with the beginnings of a double chin. The white shirt and tan baggy civilian pants he always wore looked out of place over here on an American. In military surroundings, his slightly graying curly hair and sideburns made him even more incongruous. He had a large, oblique nose and wire-rimmed glasses that were a little small for his face.

The Colonel looked over to Wagner and said, "Come in, Lieutenant." He introduced Friedman, who was polite enough in the formalities, but Wagner sensed perhaps a condescension as though he and Bern had more important fish to fry than bother with another young officer "rotating through", so to speak. Bern explained that Friedman was with the CIDG, or Criminal

Investigation Division Group.

 The meeting lasted no more than ten minutes, ending with Colonel Bern dismissing him with a simple "Thank you, Lieutenant, that will be all."

 Soon after lunch, Wagner received word that the helicopter mail run would take him as well as Gordon Bailey to their respective MAT teams. Bailey's home compound would be Plei Do Rom, an old Special Forces Compound and Montagnard village where Barry Sadler helped write the famous song, "*Ballad of the Green Berets*". Wagner's new home would be the compound at Le Quon. It was twenty klicks, or kilometers, north of Bailey's, and half way east to Mang Yang Pass, the eastern boundary of his AO. Flinging their gear on, Bailey and Wagner were wished luck by their friend Doug Hanson before lifting off for a whirlwind ride to various other locations and artillery outposts, where the chopper dropped cargo nets of supplies and mail to each. Wagner might have been the pilot of the Huey he was in had he not been refused flight school after a vision test. The Huey pilot either sensed his appreciation for the craft or just wanted to give the FNGs a thrill ride. They kissed the treetops at 120 knots, diving and rising abruptly as the Huey paralleled drops and rises in the terrain below, following ridges, tree lines and valleys. The pilot varied his elevations at times to avoid a pattern. Each time they dropped down, the M-60 machine gunners in the open sides massaged their double vertical handles, watching for enemy tracers or muzzle flashes. The rotors barely missed tree limbs as they occasionally skimmed the ground below the tree line, dangerously close. As they flew over the first Montagnard village, Wagner stretched his head out the open side to see his first topless Montagnard women, walking single file, evenly spaced, returning to their village.

 Approaching Le Quon, the chopper eased onto a small landing pad located outside a perimeter consisting of a rough earthen berm, three to five feet high, about one hundred meters to a side. Near each corner was perched a machine gun bunker made of sandbags with a plastic sun cover. Along the perimeter were several dug-in firing positions. On the outside of the berm was an eight-foot deep moat. There was no water, just a lot of sharpened bamboo punji stakes, stuck in the ground to slow down a charging enemy, amidst thick green grass and growing bamboo shoots. Outside the moat were several rows of concertina razor wire. Surrounding the whole outpost was 150 meters of flat, cleared reddish Pleiku soil, ending at a tree line. The Highlands consisted of clayey subtropical soil, rich in iron and aluminum oxides, formed by weathering of igneous rocks in moist warm climates. The trees had been cleared out long before by Special Forces predecessors for a clean field of fire, using both Agent Orange and huge Rome bulldozers. There had been many half-joking thoughts of leveling the entire country with these behemoth plows, taking every tunnel and spider hole with them. As it was, thousands of acres of South Vietnam were changed in that exact way.

Inside the perimeter Wagner could see one-story wooden buildings topped with metal corrugated roofing. A five-foot high wall of green sandbags, stained a reddish tan from Pleiku dirt surrounded each structure. A twelve-foot wooden tower built of 8 x 8 timbers stood just outside a door. On top were two metal water tanks with a kerosene heater for showers underneath. Another small wooden building off to the side housed a three-holer latrine, with steel half-barrels placed under cutouts in a wooden bench. These barrels were pulled out to mix diesel fuel and gas with urine, feces and toilet paper to burn it away. Sandbags surrounded buildings just up to window level, windows protected by cyclone fence wire to fend off grenades. Other wooden buildings in the eastern end of the compound housed Vietnamese counterpart officers and soldiers.

"This is it, buddy," yelled the pilot over a *whirop-whirop-whirop* of rotary wings and whine of the turbines. Le Quon. "Good luck to you."

"Thanks for a great ride," he yelled back. Turning to Gordon Bailey, he waved and shouted an unheard goodbye over the noise. A red-brown dust cloud surrounded them, eddies swirling through adjacent concertina wire, drifting slowly toward the compound. The Huey immediately lifted off to take Bailey to his new home as well. Wagner turned to see a stocky, well-muscled black sergeant with a huge white grin walking toward him with a salute, then an outstretched hand. The grin showed large, white teeth, incorporating a gap in the front two. His jungle fatigues were faded and stained with the red laterite clay dirt that permeated teeth, hair, even underwear. The sergeant's bush hat was pushed up in front 'cavalry style'. A toothpick was clenched in his teeth. Wagner switched his duffle bag to his left hand to return the salute and shake the man's hand.

"Welcome to Le Quon, sir."

"Thanks. Glad to be here."

"You're Lt. Wagner, I believe?" he said, as he glanced at his nametag for verification.

"Yes, you expecting me?"

"Oh, yes sir, and we're happy to have all we can get here. My name is Sergeant Brandon Stewart, sir. I'm the heavy weapons adviser on the team."

Stewart immediately impressed Wagner as an outgoing, happy sort, with a southern accent, from Georgia he guessed. "Very pleased to meet you Sarge." Wagner scanned the compound while walking with the Sergeant around the west and south sides of the perimeter to the front entrance. Three helmeted Vietnamese RF soldiers stood in a six-foot high sandbagged guard tower outside the wire, under a wooden roof topped with three layers of more sandbags. Wagner's smile with a quick wave was met with only stares as the two Americans walked by. Proceeding through the entrance, they walked left into the American end of the compound. Two young girls were kneeling on a concrete shower floor, scrubbing fatigue uniforms. They looked up with bright smiles and chatted something in their native Montagnard tongue. A big hairy swayback pig sauntered in front of them, its stomach grazing the ground.

"Sir, I want you to meet the two most BEE-UT-EE-FUL

young ladies in all of VI-ET-NAM! This here is Manh and this one is Lenh!"

The two girls were giggling and grinning ear to ear. They were obviously not Vietnamese, but the first Montagnard people Wagner had seen up close. From a glance, Wagner guessed they were sixteen to eighteen years old. One was slightly heavy, with long black hair and features hinting of a woman from India. The other had streaks of red in otherwise light brown hair. Her face was a little wider, with a Polynesian or Malaysian look. They were dressed in traditional Montagnard loom-made black skirts with woven gold and red trim. Wagner saw they had no front teeth and were smoking short, cone-shaped green Montagnard cigars. Between giggles, the girls chattered in a guttural, one-syllable language filled with 'inhhh' and 'ooohh' noises, heavily accented. The last sound of each sentence drew out in a delayed pattern of decreasing decibels and frequencies, like a motor humming to a stop. Lenh paused in her giggling and chatter to turn slightly, removing her cigar to spit on the ground.

"Aren't they beautiful, sir?" Stewart said in his cheerful complimentary manner. "C'mon, I'll take you in the team house, so you can meet the rest of your team," he continued, never losing his broad, white smile. Grabbing Wagner's gear in one hand and adjusting his bush hat with the other, he led him into the screened door of the wooden team house. There were three men sitting at a kitchen table, all wearing jungle fatigue pants, green canvas-and-black leather polished jungle boots, and O.D. olive drab T-shirts. It was a little after noon. Two beers and a bottle of scotch were on the table. Stewart began his introductions. First was Lieutenant Jamus Robinson, the team leader, a first lieutenant with eleven months in country. His last two months were here at Le Quon, sent here from Nha Trang, and had been the team leader since replacing the last one, who DEROSed back to the states. He was a tall black man with a long, thin face and lanky build. His nose was narrow and long, but flared at the bottom abnormally wide. He presented himself with an attitude of defensive dignity yet authority. Next was

Sergeant First Class William Flanagan, the team medic. Flanagan was a big, overweight man, over six feet tall. At 39, he was the old man of the group. He could easily pass for fifty, with ruddy coarse-skinned cheeks, blemished and pitted, and a huge pocked nose from years of alcohol abuse. A bottle of Johnny Walker sat in front of him. His squinty eyes were topped with reddish-blonde eyebrows hanging on the edge of protruding bony eye sockets, reminiscent of a pair of caterpillars hanging on the edge of a leaf. Wagner sensed an attitude of defiance in Flanagan almost immediately. *"Could be a normal reaction to the new man here, especially a new lieutenant,"* he mused. Flanagan had stood up to shake his hand, greeted him, and immediately sat down and turned to talk to a Vietnamese woman, who was standing a few feet away by a stove, as if to send a message he wasn't impressed. The third man was Sergeant Manuel Blas, the light weapons advisor on the team. Blas was a staff sergeant with short dark curled hair, average height and a fit build, in his early thirties. He had a bronze-tan island look, serious eyes but kind smile. His father was an American, his mother Guamanian. The tiny island of Guam was his home until he joined the Army a dozen years before. He carried a professional soldier air, polite yet serious. Finally, Sergeant Stewart introduced him to the Vietnamese woman, Hoa Khe (Hwa-Kay), who had been a cook for the teams for several years. Hoa Khe was wearing traditional Vietnamese black pants and a silky purple blouse top. She was about 40 or 45, her long black hair was tied in a bun behind her head. She had a pleasant smile, and spoke English relatively well as she made her polite greeting.

Behind her, Wagner cast his eyes to a wall where several captured enemy weapons hung. There were a couple of AK-47 rifles, three RPG-7 rocket propelled grenade launchers, also called B-40s. They were made of wood tubes combined with steel parts. Two still had rockets stuck in the front end, ready to fire. Beside them hung four bamboo ladders. The ladder rails were made of 3" diameter bamboo, the rungs of smaller bamboo. They were tied with some woody strips, probably of bamboo as well. He was staring at them when Sergeant Flanagan grinned at Wagner and said, "Those are the little bastards' ladders, Lieutenant. They weren't long enough to make it across our moat." It wasn't a humorous grin, more leering, threatening, waiting for a nervous reaction from the new lieutenant.

Wagner smiled and said, "Okay. Real fine. Now that's the kind of confidence-building I like hearing on my first day."

Sergeant Stewart was laughing when he said, "Sir, I've been here for a couple of months, I was in Ban Me Thuot before they sent me up here on Team Seven Two. But Seven Two was dissolved, so now I've been transferred here to Five Seven, to replace Sergeant Lutz. He's in his hootch room in back. He's going home tomorrow."

"Going home? Finished his tour?" Wagner asked.

"In a manner of speakin', sir. He's pretty sick. He's had malaria, then hepatitis, and now he's got his *second* bout with malaria. He is go-i-i-n-g **HOME!**"

Sergeant Stewart led Wagner down the narrow hallway to the last room on the left. Stewart quietly knocked, and hearing a grunted "come in", slowly opened the door and peaked his smiling head in. "Well, hello, you big ugly kraut! How *are* you doing this fine morning?"

Wagner followed Stewart in and saw a large body lying in a disheveled camouflaged poncho liner, behind the veil of a mosquito bar, or net, hanging around his bunk. Lutz was an E-

7, Sergeant First Class, about 40 years old, looking more like 60. Like death warmed over. Wagner had decided many months before that he feared contracting malaria more than getting a bullet. With obvious exceptions, a bullet wound can heal; malaria keeps reoccurring, making its victim extremely weak. Pleiku was an area where the worst of the four types of malaria occurred---Falciparum. It was the deadly one. The symptoms typically occurred every 24 hours, with an aching back and seeing red in addition to severe weakness being typical symptoms.

"Hello, Brandon. It is nice to see your lovely old black face, too, yah?"

"I want you to meet our new lieutenant, Heinz. I am happy to introduce Lieutenant Wagner!" Stewart said, cheerily. "Sir, this is Sergeant First Class Heinz Lutz."

Wagner lifted the mosquito bar and shook his hand, saying, "How do you do, Sergeant Lutz. I'm sorry to hear about your malaria."

"Ah, Lieutenant Vahgner. Dat's a goot German name. Pleased to meet you, sir," he said in a strong accent.

"You're German?" Wagner asked.

"Yah, I am. I vas German soldier for many years before American Army. Long time soldier, I am." Lutz was a Hitler Youth back in 1945, a fourteen year old twenty five years earlier.

"So you're going home tomorrow, I hear. Sorry we couldn't know each other better, Sergeant Lutz."

"Yah. But I am okay, und now I go home. I coot be going home in verse vays, yah?"

"Yah. For sure. Yah."

From the narrow hallway behind them, a young Spec 4 squeezed his way past Stewart to introduce himself. "Hello, sir, I'm Spec-four Demers, your RTO."

"Hi, Specialist, pleased to meet you."

"I've only got a minute, can't leave the radio right now. I heard you coming in on the chopper on the network. Just came to welcome you." He turned his attention to Sergeant Lutz. "Hi

Sarge. Vie getz es einen?"

Lutz gingerly twisted his neck to see Demers. "I feel like dog shit, Timmy! Otherwise I am fine. I am zo tired, but fine."

Leaving Lutz to rest, Sergeant Stewart and Wagner left the team house to view the compound. There were additional one story wooden structures to the east of the MAT team house. These housed the Vietnamese and Montagnard soldiers that made up the local headquarters company of the RF units. There were perhaps fifty or sixty of them that shared the Le Quon compound with the MAT team. The surrounding area had been well cleared or defoliated, leaving open fields of fire in the event of attacks, save for the village on the south side. The enemy was known to often make their main assault on the village side of a compound like this, using the village for cover. They knew Americans normally wouldn't shoot into the village unless it was a last ditch effort. That wouldn't necessarily be a consideration for the Vietnamese unit in the compound, however.

IV OPENING

"The start of the game. Openings have names, and extensive theory has been worked out by masters. Traditionally, the opening ends when minor pieces have been developed."

From months of training in the states, Wagner had prepared a mental picture of how it might be as an adviser, working with just a few Americans, rarely seeing other U.S. personnel while training and advising indigenous troops. That image was wide of the mark, it was all so different; the weather, not so tropical here in the Highlands, the more than expected number of indigenous RF and PF troop units, and the people themselves---most were ethnic Montagnards, not Vietnamese.

Wagner spent the next several days in their compound, save for an accompanied stroll through Le Quon village now and then. He was receiving an education from the other team members on the people, the team's recent history of attacks on the compound, support weapons available, local food; but he wondered what they were supposed to be doing. So far, things appeared stagnant. There seemed to be no plan, no mission. No direction or leadership came from Robinson, and it appeared Robinson in turn received little to none. On the fifth day, Major Nichols, the MAT District Senior Adviser, showed up at the Le Quon compound in a Jeep. Le Quon was his home compound as well, but his quarters were a small metal travel trailer, separate from the wooden team house the MAT team called home when not in the field. With him was his Montagnard counterpart, Seht, who worked in some high-level civilian political capacity, but it was rarely discussed. Seht spoke fluent English as well as Vietnamese, and was involved with ferreting out the Viet Cong infrastructure, something the Major was so immersed in that he spent nearly all his time with it. So much so, he somewhat ignored the five MAT teams that reported to him. But he was a likable officer, a good leader who displayed courage and intelligence when he was sober. He wasn't a drunk, but he liked his scotch. Wagner learned the Major had an affection for straight scotch whiskey, and noticed the shared grins of awareness among the team members when Nichol's trademark fast speech began to blur and his eyes glazed over after a few belts. It didn't seem to affect his job, though, or his leadership ability.

Nichols was average height, in good shape, and a handsome man. His deep blue eyes and slightly curly hair endeared him to the local Vietnamese girls, though nobody knew him to cross the line as a married man. Wagner was to learn the Major nearly always travelled alone with Seht and a Montagnard bodyguard named Blote into some pretty hazardous surroundings, in an energetic quest for tracking the remaining V.C. infrastructure. The Major had majored in Criminal Justice with a minor in Psychology, which may have inspired his interests here in Vietnam. He was a West Pointer, now one of only two Wagner had ever met and knew that he was to respect. He did have an assignment for the team this day, and talking to Robinson and Wagner together, briefed them on it. "You'll be going into this village south of us on a pacification and MEDCAP operation," he said, pointing to the topographical map spread out on the kitchen table. MEDCAPs were Medical Civil Action Programs, consisting of American medical teams aiding the civilians in a pacification effort. He was smoking a half-smoked cigar, blowing smoke at the map, making it a bit difficult to see the tiny black squares that represented hootches, or houses, in the village on the green and white map. "Plei Ko Tu is a village that has been reconsolidated from several small ones not long ago. The purpose is to combine them into one large village complete with a PF platoon and an RF company. That way, they can defend it from attacks and tax collecting by the V.C. The result is a denial of food, supplies, and help from the V.C. infrastructure for the enemy." His eyes were already getting glassy, and his hand gestures while talking brought the lit cigar a little too close to Wagner's eyes more than once. "I want you to stay there four or five days and have the medics pull the MEDCAP. The Montagnards have been dying off like flies from an epidemic of diseases. Including plague. Bubonic plague."

No one said anything, they didn't seem surprised. Plague was never mentioned among a variety of diseases they would be exposed to. "Plague?" Wagner asked, incredulously.

Nichol's glassy eyes turned to Wagner. "Apparently. One of the villagers who was wounded in their last attack was brought in to the Pleiku field hospital by medevac chopper. He had plague boils all over him. I don't really know what the hell it looks like."

Wagner stood staring, absorbing.

Sgt. Flanagan, had entered the room. Hearing the last of the conversation, he sauntered to the table, and stood there with a toothpick clenched between his teeth. Looking at Wagner, he said with a leer, "Welcome to Vietnam, Lieutenant."

The Major continued, "It's not just plague. There's a lot of the other nasty stuff thrown together. Malaria, hepatitis, dysentery, encephalitis, and they have a small leper village."

Wagner, as much as they were trained to expect unsanitary conditions, was clearly not prepared for this. "Plague? Leprosy? What the hell is this, thirteenth century England?" he asked.

"That's nothin', Lieutenant," said Flanagan. "You'll get used to it. You'll wonder wh..."

The Major interrupted, as he had a habit of doing anyway, but it was becoming apparent he had little patience with Flanagan. "This is part of your function as a MAT team, but I believe any assistance to the villagers, especially medical, will help pacify an area quicker than anything else, and that's the name of this game."

Lt. Robinson inquired as to the RFs and PFs there, and what they could expect for defenses. "Is the location relatively secure, sir?"

"I believe so," he answered. "I want the perimeter checked out and I want to know the strengths of the RF and PF units and the number and type of weapons they're equipped with. And don't forget the PSDF."

"Yes, sir, and about th..."

"And I want you to make sure they have their Delta Tangos in order," he interrupted again.

It was difficult at times to converse with the Major, he interrupted so frequently, particularly with some Scotch in him.

"Uh, sir," Wagner said, quietly. "What's a Delta Tango?"

"Defensive targets," Flanagan intervened. "Artillery targets," as if to imply *everyone knows that, why not you*?

"Thank you," Wagner said. He had been taught 'Delta Foxtrots' in the phonetic alphabet for 'defensive fires'. Flanagan never missed a chance to leer, making it as obvious as possible, whenever the opportunity arose. It took little time to sense issues with this man.

The next morning, a green Army ambulance van arrived in the compound early to take Sergeant Lutz. With goodbyes, good lucks and well wishes, he was gone. The Major and his counterpart Seht left right behind them. After a ham, egg and rice breakfast from Hoa Khe, the team packed two Jeeps with gear. Bringing a young Montagnard interpreter with them, they rolled out of the compound for the fourteen-kilometer Jeep trek to Plei Ko Tu. With Lt. Robinson driving, they turned onto a narrow dirt Jeep trail that meandered through grassy, sparsely treed open terrain. The trail was crisscrossed with other dirt trails and paths over gently rolling land, with only an occasional shrub breaking the monotony of Brahma cattle-grazed bright green grass. A thick roiling eddy of red Pleiku dust followed behind, catching up to encircle them whenever they slowed, which was often. Ruts and humps in what was hardly a road at all sent the Jeeps twitching and bouncing, independent spring suspensions constantly storing and releasing energy. The thin Jeep seats afforded little comfort, everyone gripping to stay inside. Ahead was a tree line fronting the jungle behind it. The myriad of green shades was spectacular. It was the single most striking difference in the landscape from any place Wagner had ever seen. The lighter greens were brighter, the darker greens darker. Rice paddies glowed a brilliant chartreuse, bordered by darker grass pastures, against darker yet palms. Bamboo added a lighter shade to contrast with a darker green of taller trees and smaller bushes and shrubs. The smell was strange, but good, tropical and sweet. It seemed peaceful and natural.

Now the openness of the rolling grasslands gave way to thicker woodlands. Not quite jungle, but more foreboding than the open area behind them. Their little Montagnard interpreter, Kir, was pointing the way, first a left at a fork in the path, then two rights. Off to the left stood five rugged water buffalo, staring at the passing Jeeps. Two had horns six feet from tip to tip, curling behind broad sculls like giant handlebars. Their enormous, rectangular black hulks gave reason for Wagner to be wary. There were stories about water buffalo hating Americans, some having to blow charging buffalo away with full magazines of M-16s or an M-79 grenade launcher. One tale had it that it was the American's scent, a result of drinking milk. If true, it was a rarity, more likely a G.I.'s embellished story.

On ahead, a file of Montagnards trekked a well-worn footpath. A few older men, but mostly women and young children were walking parallel to the Jeep trail, woven bamboo back-packs heavily laden with wood, chickens, gourds, more baskets, and fresh jungle gleanings. They travelled in a perfect file, evenly spaced. Most returned their smiles and waves, with toothless grins and calloused hands. They wore no shoes or hats. The men wore dirty loincloths made of long narrow woven cloth, always the same color pattern of their village, black with red and gold patterns near the bottom, wrapped around the waist and through the crotch. Some of the men wore filthy U.S. Army fatigue shirts, always stained a brownish-red color of Pleiku dirt. The women wore larger pieces of cloth with the same pattern, but wrapped as a skirt to the ankles. Unlike the Vietnamese, most were bare breasted, and well endowed at that.

Sergeant Stewart sat in the back of Wagner's Jeep with Kir the interpreter. "Wow! Look at that honey," hissed Stewart. "What a set of kazooners.... Whoooo-eee!"

Kir couldn't have been more than 14 or 15. He was under five feet tall, a cute kid with short dark hair and big, dark, bright eyes. His happy innocent nature and constant infectious grin was a natural to win everybody's affection. He and Sgt. Stewart were inseparable when Kir was brought along, always joking and laughing together. Stewart practically adopted him, and vice-versa. Kir giggled and said, "She gah big tits, rah?"

"Right, Shorty. You ain't supposed to be lookin' at those, you know," replied the ever jolly Stewart, his perfect pearly white grin radiating out of a deep black face.

"Why nah?" Kir asked, still giggling.

"Why, you're too young for that stuff, Shorty!" What do you mean, "why not?" Why, I oughtta paddle your young ass."

Wagner was travelling in the 'shotgun' seat, his M-16 in his right hand, angled out at the dense vegetation that brushed the Jeep window, occasionally slapping his face and arm. His left hand was holding onto the windshield frame as the Jeep jostled and bounced. His first trip into the 'bush' was not at all what he'd imagined. Though the other members of the team were keeping their eyes open and guns at the ready, it seemed little more than a drive in the country to them. He couldn't believe they were driving down this Jeep trail in the jungle, with no point man, no flank security. Not once in all the months of training did they say it would be like this. What the other team members knew and he didn't was the area was relatively secure because of the crack local Montagnard Regional Force company that was assigned to it. The team had been down this road several times before, and knew the area was among the safest in the province.

Breaking into a more open terrain, before them lay Plei Ko Tu. They drove up a long sloping hill, then through a gate network of barbed wire entanglements that formed a large perimeter around the village. A nervous young Montagnard RF soldier stood guard at the gate, not sure what to do. A

Montagnard company commander, a second lieutenant, came to greet them. *"Chao, Thieu-uy."* "Hello, Second Lieutenant" Wagner said. Most Montagnard officers spoke Vietnamese, and some spoke English, he'd been told. *"Chao, Trung-uy."* "Hello, First Lieutenant," he replied. The commander, a thin Montagnard named Pom, was wearing a bush hat and camouflage tiger fatigues, tailored skin-tight. He was lean, bronze, rock-hard, near zero body fat. He yelled something to the gate guard, who quickly closed the barbed wire and snapped back to the position of attention. He spoke slowly, addressing the Americans in English to join him for an inspection of the compound.

Walking the perimeter, Pom stopping briefly to talk to a few soldiers who manned evenly spaced sandbagged foxholes located several meters inside the wire. Completing the perimeter walk, they passed between several grass roofed bamboo hootches, trying to avoid animal feces that fairly decorated the ground. By every small house, a variety of animals scavenged for food. Most noticeable were the water buffalo. They only turned their huge horned heads to look with curiosity at the

Americans. Wagner was wary, again from 'war stories', but they were unwarranted. They proved docile as cows, but much bigger. There were also huge, dark and hairy pot-bellied pigs, looking like wild boar. Their backs and bellies sagged, bulging hairy hammocks inches from earth, some actually rubbing the ground. Chickens, goats, and dogs made up the remainder. The entire village had a 'fecal floor', and every fly in the country must have heard about it. Huge green and black flies swarmed everywhere.

"Sir, I think Plei Ko Tu means 'fly heaven' in Montagnard," Stewart said.

More odors of Vietnam. Smells of excrement blended with pungent smoke of burning wet wood cooking fires. "Yeah. I thought the shithouse at Le Quon was bad."

"Yes-s-s, sir. Shooo-wee! THIS is what I joined this good Army for! You gotta love it. Ha-a Ha-a-a!" Stewart laughed, tip-toeing around large buffalo pies. Kir followed behind, giggling and laughing. They were led to a house with no walls. Vertical columns of bamboo supported a grass roof over a hard red dirt floor. This was the infirmary, they were told. The commander, Pom, ever smiling except when barking orders to his men, appeared to hinge on every word. He studied his American counterparts' expressions, eager for approval.

Sergeant Flanagan, not wishing to waste time with formalities, impatiently told Pom he was ready to begin the MEDCAP. He laid his medical gear out on a rough wooden workbench, telling Sergeant Blas where to line up the patients, while Robinson stood with his arms folded, scanning the nearby topless women, nearly oblivious to what the Montagnard commander was saying. Wagner tried to digest the entire scene, mentally piecing the events and surroundings together while politely listening to Pom.

Word of their MEDCAP was quickly spreading in the village. In minutes, villagers converged around their infirmary, politely keeping their distance. There was no crowding or maneuvering for position to be first in line. The majority were women, almost all topless, and nearly each was breast feeding or carrying a small child.

Wagner asked, "Sergeant Flanagan, these people are malnourished, even starving, so why do so many of the kids have protruding stomachs?"

"Worms," he replied. "Worms and malnutrition. They both cause it. Only difference is, with one the stomachs are hard. The other makes 'em soft."

"The women like those green cigars, don't they?"

"Yes, sir, Lieutenant," Sergeant Stewart said, rising from a kneeling position after talking to a little wide-eyed youngster. "They do lo-o-ve those cigars. And did you notice, sir, many of them don't have front teeth?"

"How could you not notice," Wagner replied, grinning.

"Well, you know, sir, they usually file those front teeth of the girls, when they're young. It's a sign of beauty."

Wagner pondered that. "You know, I'd read where some Indian tribes used to dangle shiny objects in front of their baby girl's eyes, to make them cross-eyed. Same reason. These people really are a lot like the Indians."

"You got that right, sir. Getting their damn land stolen the same way, too," Stewart said. "Just like them poor damn Indians. It ain't right."

Wagner added, "I was told in the advisor's school a little about them. They said that's been happening for centuries. People call them nomadic, but it isn't true. They've been pushed to move. Pushed here to the mountains. It's their last stronghold. There's no other place left."

"Yep, and they're even losing this now," Sergeant Flanagan said, getting ready to give a shot to his first patient, a small bronze two or three year-old naked girl. The little girl was crying, her tears leaving tracks down a dirty face. Her mother was smiling, comforting her.

"What's her problem, Billy?" Stewart asked Flanagan.

"She's got a cut on her leg that didn't heal right. Infected. Looks sore. Givin' her a little Wildroot," he said, poking his white-cream-filled syringe of penicillin into the girl's little fanny.

Sergeant Stewart, pulling up a small log bench, sat down

near Flanagan to help. He checked the little girl's head while Flanagan was finishing swabbing the needle mark with alcohol. "Woo-wee! Just look at these little monsters. She's just crawling with lice. You got some of that Kwell stuff, Billy?"

Flanagan slid his medical bag over, from which Stewart found a green tube. He squeezed a white cream onto the girl's head. Her mother turned to the others, laughing and talking in her Montagnard guttural tongue. "They teach you this in OCS, sir?" Stewart asked, never losing his smile.

"Not even close. But in those advisory classes, at Fort Bragg," Wagner said, "We had to learn to play Vietnamese Chess. It's called 'Co Tuong' chess…so we could play it with a village chief, the idea of gaining rapport…friendship and cooperation. Win their hearts and minds with chess, I suppose. It's like regular chess, but instead of a king, you've got a general. Vietnamese have been fighting wars for centuries, never seem to stop. So instead of queens, knights, and pawns, you've got general's aides, cannons, elephants, tanks, and privates. The cannons have to shoot over a man to take a piece. The tanks can shoot the hell out of anything…direct fire. And the privates---the 'pawns,' called binh shis---well, they're just expendable as hell. Once they cross the middle of the board--that's a river--they can't come back."

"Sounds like the 'Yards.....and us," Stewart said.

"Yep. Here we all are. Pawns. Pawns of Pleiku."

On the MEDCAP went, the whole team pitching in, learning from each other on the job what to give as a best guess for a variety of ailments. One woman, staggering to the table when her turn came, was so thin she could barely stand. She looked as if her leathery, bronze-brown skin had been draped over her skeleton. Still, she smiled. Wagner was reminded of magazine pictures of starving Biafrans, eyes sunken, bodies covered with flies. He had not expected it in Vietnam.

"Jamus, it looks like food is needed as bad as the medicine," Wagner said to Lt. Robinson. "What do you say tomorrow we head back and get some. A village cookout, so to speak."

"Good idea, sir," Stewart said, not waiting for Robinson to answer. "We can go down to Camp Holloway and scrounge up a bunch. While we're here, let's see about picking up some crossbows and helicopters for bargaining tools."

Robinson agreed, and asked Flanagan how his medical supplies looked.

"Not good, Lieutenant. I didn't figure on seein' the whole goddamn Montagnard population."

"This place has really expanded. I didn't know it had grown like this," Robinson said.

"What's this about crossbows and helicopters, Sarge," Wagner asked Stewart.

"Whoa, yes, sir, we have jus' got to show you some of the local art talent of Plei Ko Tu! Jus' lemme finish up on this big guy right here, and we will take a short station break to take in some of the artsy-craftsy stuff, and then we'll be right back." Talking to the next little boy in line, he added in his ever-jovial spirit, "Now don't you go away, you hear? Big daddy Brandon will be right back, okay?" at which Kir, by his side, giggled and translated.

Wagner noticed Kir's teeth were as white and his grin as wide as Stewart's. Stewart and Wagner picked up their M-16s and ammo bandoliers and with Kir walked further into the village of thatched roof houses. All the while, Stewart and Kir chattered away to each other. At one corner of the village, there were three men in loin cloths, maybe 40 to 50 years old, sitting on the ground carving wood. To one side were several models of Army Huey helicopters, eighteen to thirty inches long, complete with thin rotor blades and hollowed-out interiors. They even sported small antennas, landing skids and external miniguns. They were amazingly good replicas, nearly to scale. Along with helicopters were several crossbows, varying from sixteen inches wide to nearly three feet. All were made of a

tropical wood except for the strings of the crossbows, which were of vines. The top of each crossbow included a groove, on which a fourteen-inch long bamboo arrow rested. Two trailing 'feathers' on the arrows were formed into a thin bamboo fin. The tips were sharp and fire-hardened, with no stone or metal points.

"These are amazing," Wagner said. "All they're using is a sugar cane knife and a little sandpaper. How in the devil can they hollow these things out like that?"

"With patience, I would say, sir," Stewart replied. "Patience."

The men didn't try to push their wares as one might expect in some tourist area. Instead, they sat staring up with a serious, hopeful look, occasionally mumbling a few quiet words to each other.

Stewart told Kir to ask them how much for the whole bunch, and Kir asked, "all of this?" to be clear on what he said. Kir was the best Montagnard interpreter, in part because of his language skill, but also his untainted opinions in translating the words. Youth and corresponding innocence ensured a trusted, unbiased translation.

"That's right, Shorty. The whole shootin' match. The whole bunch!"

After a few minutes of Kir's interpreting, Wagner and Stewart split the meager cost and gathered up the array to take back to the Jeep.

"Tomorrow morning, sir, you will be amazed at the purchasing power of these little bits of art." Chortling with laughter, he said, "We will have more food and ammunition than we can carry, just for these little trinkets right here."

"Yeah? How do you do that?"

"Sir, those cats back in those places hardly get out of their secure little bases, except for maybe driving to Pleiku once in a while to contribute to the economy of the local female populace. They can take these here ar-tee-facts back home and tell they're mommas what heroes they were! And they have tons of food they don't need, or if they don't, all they have to do is requisition it, so to them, their stuff is free. And the ammunition…they're required to rotate their stock once in a while, and if they aren't getting' much Charlie action, which they ain't, they gotta blow it up when it's old. They don't like doin' that, so they give us all the ammo we want. Now, we're supposed to be getting all our ammo and food from the Vietnamese Army. That don't work much, and we prefer real food, so we just go down to a big post like Holloway and get what we need in a flash. No paperwork, no questions. Simple. That's why we call it a scrounge run. We also give a bunch of the ammo to the 'Yards. The Vietnamese don't give them what they need, so we try to take up the slack." All this was new to Wagner, but it made him respect these team sergeants more with every learning experience.

After treating several hundred village patients, the team retreated to an old Army mess tent that had been set up near the middle of the village previously. It was decorated with several shrapnel holes. They learned this is where they would be sleeping for the night. No bunkers, no foxholes. Just lay out a rain poncho and cover up with an insulated poncho liner. "Is this the normal way?" Wagner asked Robinson. "No bunkers or foxholes?"

Robinson just smiled and looked at Flanagan.

"What's the matter, Lieutenant?" Flanagan said. "Didn't they teach you this in OCS?" The condescending sneer again.

"Wouldn't it make sense, I mean, to have some ground cover? At least a foxhole to roll into? What happens if we get hit?" Wagner asked.

"Run like hell," Robinson chuckled.

"Yeah? Where?" Wagner said. "There's a concertina wire perimeter all around this village. The only sandbags or foxholes I saw were the perimeter guards' just inside the wire. We're sitting ducks here."

No one but Stewart seemed concerned, so Wagner let it rest. But again, not expected. It didn't seem like the time to make an issue of it, so he prepared his 'bed', smoothing the ground with his feet. Sleeping on hard ground was his first since training days many months before, and getting used to it didn't come easy. An insulated poncho liner yielded little comfort.

The Montagnards cooked inside their grass-roofed homes, all on four-foot stilts to keep their animals out. As the twilight glow dimmed, a strong odor of creosote from damp wood fires filtered through the roofs of houses. Amidst the bleating goats and lowing water buffalo came the sounds of gongs. Not terribly loud, but in six and seven note repertoires, over and over again, never ceasing, never changing. "What the hell is that?" Wagner asked.

"Funeral gongs," Flanagan said. "Get used to it, Lieutenant, you're gonna hear a lot more of 'em."

"Yeah, lovely little gongs," Stewart said. "And you know what scares me? I think I'm gettin' to like 'em! But they ain't exactly MO-town, you know what I mean? Hey, Shorty, you know MO-town?"

"MO-town? What MO-town?" Kir asked.

"Oh, Shorty, you just got so much to learn. Say RIGHTEOUS."

"Rawchous?"

"Yeah, that's right. Righteous."

"Rawchous. Rawchous."

"YEAH! You got it. Close enough. Now, that's all you have to know, Shorty. Good night."

Funeral gongs continued all night, waking Wagner up periodically. He regretted not having dug at least a rudimentary foxhole, while he imagined V.C. or NVA closing in on the village. It was all so strange.

At the first glow of morning sunlight, Wagner was the first to wake from sounds of villagers starting their day. Roosters a few hundred feet away crowed, unnerving several chickens outside the tent.

Slowly, the other team members roused, except for Flanagan, still snoring loudly. Wagner dressed and took a morning walk through the village by himself. The stilt bamboo houses were all in rows and columns, evenly spaced, he noticed. They hadn't looked that way at Le Quon, or flying over other villages on the mail run. Dodging excrement where he could, he wondered if all the villages were this filthy. Every villager met him with a smile, some with a few soft spoken words. Wagner tried to return their friendliness with a smile and a brief greeting, still trying to avoid endless animal waste. He studied their faces, which seemed to vary more than the Vietnamese. Some looked like a proud American Indian out of a 1950s movie, but with a concave, flat nose. Others looked more Polynesian. Under the dirt, their skin was a golden-light to dark reddish or bronze-brown, their hair black, unless reddish from malnutrition or lack of protein in their diets. The men's bodies were solid and muscular, from years of hard work. Most of the women were missing their front teeth. Their cheek bones were prominent and high, eyebrows and lashes dark and thicker than Vietnamese. Walking to the southwest corner of the village, another smaller group of homes stood on down-sloping terrain, separate from the main village. The houses were smaller, less sturdy. Few animals roamed near them. The first people Wagner saw sat in small circles. They looked emaciated, but still they smiled. Then he saw their hands and feet, and there were no fingers and toes. "My God, this is the leper colony." The more he walked, the more wretched were the sights. Still, they smiled. Some were very near death, just skin and bones, with varying degrees of flesh eaten away. Wagner turned and slowly returned to the team.

After a campfire breakfast, Wagner and Stewart climbed into their M-151 Jeep for the scrounge trip to Camp Holloway. With them was an RF soldier whom Pom had ordered to go with them as a 'gunner', who could also find the way back if they got lost. He never said a thing, but smiled whenever Wagner or Stewart glanced back at him. Other than that, he kept his eyes trained on the sides of the road ahead, his M-16 held firm and ready. Wagner did the same.

At Holloway, it was just as Stewart had said. Stewart knew the right men to work with. In addition to food, medical supplies and ammo, they were given an old Jeep trailer in return for Montagnard carvings. In it they heaped Claymore mines, concertina wire, boxes of M-16 and M-79 grenade launcher ammo, several boxes of 57 mm recoilless rifle and 81 mm mortar rounds. The 57 mm wasn't even officially in the Army inventory anymore, but somehow the rounds were here. For food, they stocked boxes of large Army olive drab cans of fruits and concentrated soups.

The return trip to Plei Ko Tu village at two o'clock was slowed by the jouncing trailer. "Can you imagine what would happen if this arsenal ran over a mine?" Wagner asked.

"HO-leee, sir, *Please* don't say that! They couldn't find enough of my black ass to mail me home on a post card."

Pom summoned the village chief and acted as interpreter, telling the chief to gather his people together and bring their largest pots. He told him the Americans were going to give the chief a feast in his honor.

"Kir, what are the gongs for? The funeral gongs I heard all night?"

"When someone die, and he still in house, you know? And people, they walk around the house, with gongs, you know? They keep the bad spirits away 'till they buried. The gongs…keep the spirits away."

Stewart was readying to resume his medical treatments with Flanagan and Blas, when he turned to Wagner, and in a serious tone said, "You know, sir, I wish all those damned reporters could see this, and tell some of all the good that we're doing here. All they want to talk about is My Lai, and soldiers burning villes, and….and how mean and nasty us GIs are. Man, most folks back home would never believe the conditions here."

"No shit. Sergeant Stewart, you sure as hell made a lot of new friends and believers. I think we've got some pretty appreciative people here."

"Looky this little beauty here," he said, with a beautiful little six or seven year old girl in front of him. "I'm gonna marry her someday." She was wrapped in a torn loom-woven sarong. Held to her back by another black, red, and gold woven cloth was a two year old brother, nearly half her own weight.

As Wagner looked around, nearly all the little girls were carrying a younger brother or sister, mostly babies, papoose style. Occasionally one bent forward to re-adjust the cloth around the baby's back and fanny, pulled it tight, and straightened again.

"No wonder they get so damn rugged," Wagner said.

"Yes, sir. These people will walk twenty miles a day carrying a full load of jungle food, or firewood, and return for more the next day. They're just amazing."

"You'd think, if they're starving to death, they'd eat a few of the animals, wouldn't you?"

Stewart pondered for a moment, then replied, "They don't have an awful lot of animals, for the amount of people that is, and I guess they know if they kill it, it's gone. Might also have to do with the religious thing. You know, ancestors in the buffalo kind of thing. All I know is, they normally don't kill a buffalo to eat until the owner dies."

Late that afternoon, several of the village men carried a three-foot diameter iron pot to an open area not far from the infirmary. Working rapidly with machetes and poles, they fashioned a tripod support and carved out a shallow fire pit underneath. Sergeant Blas and Kir directed the soup preparations, telling them to add water for dehydrated canned food. At a time decided on by the chief, villagers appeared for the feast. Again, there was no shoving or jockeying for position. They were patient and polite. Each had ample amounts of nutritious soup and other Camp Holloway rations, including potatoes and even potato chips, which the Montagnards ate with fascination. Their 'feast' was a far cry from four months of subsistence on roots, leaves, and some poorly-grown rice they had been accustomed to.

The meal finished, the team sat cleaning red sandy dirt from weapons and mess gear to look up and see three smiling Montagnard men walking toward them, each carrying a load of unopened soup cans.

"What's this, Kir?" Wagner asked. "Don't they like it?"

Kir turned and spoke to them, "*T'brai he huh-uh.*"
They answered in a similarly short sentence, as they always did. A few words seemed to say a lot in their language. Kir turned back and said, "They already cook. This lef' over."

"Don't they want the rest for later, or tomorrow?" Wagner asked.

"Raht. They wan'. You give them?"

"Hell, yes, we give them. That's theirs," Flanagan replied, incredulously. Kir turned and told them. Breaking into broad smiles, they nodded with guttural words of appreciation and returned in the direction they had come. "Unbelievable. Here they're starving, but they wouldn't keep that food, because they didn't feel it was theirs,"

"They just don't steal." Stewart said. "If their life depends on it. That's standard operating procedure. Too bad the rest of us didn't operate that way."

Later that evening, the team took a stroll through the village. The word of the medical work had spread to everyone in the village, and their appreciation was evident in each and every smile. Proud parents held up their children as the Americans walked by. And funeral gongs were bonging around several more houses.

"These people are dying like flies. The death rate must be incredible," Wagner said.

Stewart replied, "Sir, Kir told me that three hundred people have died this month. Just in this village. That's not from combat. Just disease and starvation."

"Are other villages as big as this? So far, I haven't seen any."

"No, sir. This is a reconsolidation village. Several villages from the area, kilometers away some of them, were moved here in this reconsolidation thing, you know, to 'pacify' the area, to prevent the V.C. from getting food and taxes from the locals. I don't know about the food and taxes part, but I don't see a lot of pacifyin' goin' on here."

Walking by one small home, an anxious older man wearing nothing but a filthy buttoned fatigue shirt and loin cloth approached them waving a cupped hand toward his chest, muttering something in a quiet voice. He wanted them to come into his hootch. It was dark inside, walls black and smelling of creosote. Eyes adjusting to dim light, they could see an older woman laying on a bamboo bed, staring at the ceiling. Her eyes barely moved, the rest of her lay still. She was starving, her arms no thicker than a thumb. She reminded Wagner of holocaust pictures. Whatever was wrong, malaria, dysentery, malnutrition, whatever, she was skin and bone. There was nothing the men could do, she wouldn't last another day. Sadly, they left the house, trying in Pigeon English to tell the man they could not help. Two more houses down, the same thing happened. In this hootch, a man lay on a similar bamboo bed. As their eyes got used to the dim light in this windowless, creosote blackened one room home, they saw his face gradually grow visible. It was covered in ugly blue-black boils. "Plague," Blas said. "Bubonic plague. I saw this as a kid."

Daylight was waning, the village was quiet except for the never ending seven note funeral gongs a few houses away. Wagner and Stewart walked past three young boys in filthy American T-shirts and loin cloths, sitting by a campfire. Beside them was a basket, and they were sharpening long bamboo sticks. They looked up, chattering and grinning. "Hi guys, what's happening?" Wagner asked, kneeling beside them. Laughing, they said something in Bahnaar, one grabbing his basket to show Wagner. In it were nine or ten young live rats, each about five inches long. "Oh, little pets, huh? They're nice."

One boy was holding the sharpened end of his bamboo stick above the flames, hardening the end. While they watched, the boy reached into the basket and grasped one of the rats. Holding the stick in the other hand, he ran the point into the rodent's mouth and out its rectum, while they watched in muted surprise.

"Oh, my God, what are..." Stewart gasped, as each boy picked another, and another rat until each had three squirming, furry living "hot dogs" on his stick. Still laughing, they each held the frantically wriggling animals over the fire, until the hair was burned off and the outer skin cooked to the point of being burned. Then they pulled one off at a time and proceeded to eat them as if they were marshmallows, all the while smiling, laughing, and chattering.

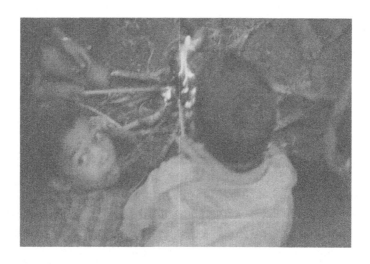

"Well, there's some protein for you," Wagner said, hearing small bones crunching.

Night was falling again and except for the gongs, everything was quiet, not even a breeze. It felt like the war must be over, it was too peaceful. After Wagner spoke with Pom, the team was offered some RF soldiers' underground bunkers to sleep in. They were four feet by six feet, and only three feet deep inside, with another foot of sandbag walls above the ground level. The roof had two layers of sandbags, supported by four-inch bamboo logs. The walls were simply dirt, but there were two bamboo mats laid on the floor, with a drain gutter running the inside perimeter to keep it dry. Entrances were small and difficult. Sergeant Flanagan and Wagner were to share one together. Flanagan's size presented a problem in these confined quarters. "Jesus Christ. Are we both supposed to fit in that little hole?" he said. "I don't see why we can't just sleep in the tent. Nothin' wrong with that."

"As for me, Sarge, I'll take the bunker. It was offered, and it just might be offensive if we don't use it. It's gonna be tight, any way you look at it." Flanagan resigned himself to it. He wanted the security the bunker provided, but had to go through machismo motions. They typically slept with clothes on and boots ready, but not before Flanagan had consumed four beers. "Better take it easy on the beer, Sarge, in case the bogeymen come," Wagner said, as Flanagan put down his last can before maneuvering under his poncho liner.

"Don't worry about me, Lieutenant, I can drink more than any six of you krauts. Hasn't killed me yet. Don't forget, this is my third tour of this friggin' jungle hole."

"When was your first tour?"

"Sixty-eight. When there was some real shit goin' on. You ain't seen no war till you been through that."

Wagner was sensing that Blas had a degree of respect for Flanagan, simply for his age and experience: Flanagan was a third-tour man. A Vietnam veteran, previous tours, that commanded a certain admiration with the men. "Where were you then?"

"Qui Nhon, mostly. Pleiku, too," Flanagan replied.

"Really! Pleiku?"

"Yeah, we flew in here a few times. Didn't stay too long."

"Was it much different then?"

"Well, I'll tell you what, Lieutenant. You wouldn't want to drive down to places like this. The Tet of sixty-eight broke Charlie's ass. We crushed him. He ain't been the same since. And the 'Yards keep places like Plei Ko Tu pretty safe. These RF troops are real soldiers. They keep Charlie away, and they sweep these dirt roads around here for mines. Generally, you won't find many mines or booby traps around here anyway. It's too country. And not a lot of V.C. Enemy's mostly NVA, and the 'Yards don't like their areas booby trapped.

"Qui Nhon. East of here, on the coast...were you a medic then?"

"Yeah."

After a night of funeral gongs, the men emerged to a bright morning Sun coming up over the Annamite mountains. A campfire breakfast found the men concurring how the war had changed. "The cities weren't safe, including the coast," Stewart said. "The jungle was owned by the V.C. and much of the cities, too." Blas nodded his head in agreement. "Then the coastal cities were cleaned up. Except for a major offensive, like a Tet, or occasional mortars or rockets, the coastal cities became as safe as New York. Then inland cities, like Pleiku. The countrysides along the coast were next. That's pretty safe now. The Highlands and inland countryside is last, but this has changed. Five years ago, we'd be in a world of hurt."

"I've heard the war in the Delta is essentially over," Wagner added.

Blas agreed and said, "The V.C. are pretty much dead or given up. And the NVA haven't been screwing around down that far. Pleiku Province is supposed to be the worst province in the country, if you can believe the reports."

Two hours later, Flanagan and Stewart continued with medical work. Wagner and Blas walked the perimeter with Pom and two of Pom's men, checking fields of fire, and mortar crews. Pom and Wagner discussed likely avenues of enemy approach and corresponding artillery pre-planned targets. All were impressive. The RFs were more than pleased to get the Claymore mines, recoilless rifle rounds, and mortar rounds the Jeep trailer carried. Supplies were immediately stored in a proper, safe, military manner, the results of Special Forces training from previous years. Pom, for the most part, interspersed his stern, serious look with occasional smiles for his American counterparts, proud of his men and defenses.

Villagers often tried to show their appreciation for medical help, but were too poor. After a patient was treated, a parent or spouse often offered their last chicken, or a trapped rabbit or serving of rice as a payment. Occasionally, a young daughter's services was offered. The gifts were nearly always offered to Robinson or Wagner, since protocol demanded that higher-ranking personnel should be the recipients. They had trouble understanding why their daughters would be refused, and careful wording through their interpreter was required to not offend.

On the third day, the team began receiving notes from local V.C., passed on by villagers. The notes were mostly directed to villagers, so poorly written they were hard to translate, but in a nutshell said, "Anyone who lets the American doctors treat them we will kill." Others said they would kill the Americans, and some even said specifically where. The water point was one. To the north side of the village, a natural spring flowed out of a horizontal four inch diameter bamboo pipe stuck into the side of a twenty foot deep ravine, the beginning of a creek. It was the reason the initially small village was located there. The entire village collected their water and bathed here, and now the team members individually took quick baths in the same spot, always with another standing guard at the top. Often they were joined by bathing Montagnard women who had an uncanny knack for not exposing body parts below the waste or above the calves, even while they alternately opened and closed parts of their sarong dresses.

The notes became common and the team, with trepidation, began to accept them as bluffs. In the late afternoon of the fourth day, however, Wagner was christened with his first enemy fire, as he stood naked in the stream of the water point. Three rounds hit mud several feet away with loud CRACK! CRACK! CRACK!s so close together the last mixed with the pops from a rifle travelling a hundred meters away down the ravine. As he leapt out of the stream bed, he nearly fell flat from spinning his feet in the mud, while Sergeant Blas, providing security from above, quickly sprayed a full magazine from his M-16 toward the source. Loading another magazine in lightning fashion, he unleashed another twenty rounds in three quick bursts, with Wagner sprinting naked to the top of the ravine, wearing only the rifle in his hand. Several Montagnard RF soldiers were already running their way as Wagner dove to the only cover, a tree Blas was sitting beside. Blas made a waving-pointing motion toward the source of fire, sending the RFs hustling to the edge of the ravine to fire several dozen more rounds into the greenery beyond. The whole thing happened in less than a minute. With the shooting over, Blas looked over and started laughing. Wagner, his mouth half open, broke into a grin, then laughed loudly. "Sarge, ya mind goin' down and getting my clothes?"

"Sir, thank you, no," he laughed.

That night, Wagner enjoyed his first taste of calling artillery he had learned so well, calling in Firebase Blackhawk's huge 175 mm rounds. The long barrels of the 175s were the only guns that could reach the distance to Plei Ko Tu. There was no enemy activity, it was to ensure coordinates were accurate if he needed to walk shells in. He picked likely avenues of enemy approach around the village for targets. An enormous *CR-U-N-N-C-C-H!* from the biggest guns the Army had were comforting, indeed. Vulnerability presented to MAT teams by diminishing American units made reliance on artillery their only hope in a major fight. Some locations would be out of any artillery range, the most unnerving situation of all. When the first rounds hit, the concussion could be felt as well as seen, even from hundreds of meters. Depending on the impact point, the explosions were either followed or preceded by an ominous rustling, crackling, air-ripping sound of the projectile, ending with a distant rumble of the gun as the sound of the round leaving the tube reached them from nearly twenty seven kilometers away. The speed of sound, slower than the rounds, was at first confusing. Artillery was, for all practical purposes, the only support they had. He felt a rush from it, obscuring vulnerability in an imposing and peculiar world. Robinson, enjoying the fireworks with the others, seemed happy that Wagner enjoyed artillery calls; he shunned it himself. The team at first watched apprehensively; a wrong coordinate or adjustment to a target could result in disaster. 175s had a casualty radius of a hundred meters, and here, at the far end of their range, inaccuracy due to "barrel whip" of long barrels called for a 'first-round' safety error of a thousand meters. There being no need for risk with these "harassment & interdiction" fires, he gave it a wide safety factor. The nervous NCOs soon gained confidence in his ability. Robinson asked him, "You like callin' artillery?"

"Yeah, I guess I do," he replied, waiting for the next round to hit.

"How'd you do in Benning? In the Artillery course."

Still waiting for the next round's 'splash' in order to adjust fire, he said, "Well, I think my Engineering background helped a bit. I did okay."

Sergeant Flanagan turned his head away with a "Ph-h-h-t-t-t-t" of sarcasm from his lips, raising his body up on straightened arms.

"Hey, I asked," Robinson told him.

Little Kir, sitting beside Wagner as he called the rounds in, said, "Those are the **BIG** guns, rah?"

"Rah." Wagner replied.

On their last day at Plei Ko Tu, the chief ordered the slaughter of a buffalo that belonged to a man who died that day from malaria.

"You see, sir," Stewart told Wagner, "when a Montagnard dies, it's a call for a celebration. They figure the man's going to a better place than this hell-hole. Now, most of these folks aren't rich enough to own a buffalo, but if he does, they usually kill the buffalo for a ceremony. But it's a happy ceremony."

The chief insisted the team stay for the celebration. Clearly, the medical work had won gratitude. With a brief ceremony, the tribesmen slashed the tied buffalo's throat. The team watched in fascination as the buffalo first sagged to his knees, then his hulking body crashed sideways to the ground. As well as possible, two men caught still pumping blood in a big wooden bowl. Nothing was wasted. Even before its last death heaves they began cutting the animal up. The same huge iron pot, half-filled with water, was heating from its tripod. Wagner watched in awe as body parts were thrown whole into the stew: liver, lungs, kidneys, and so on. Then he and Stewart turned to each other in a distorted grimace as they watched a woman strip the green contents of its large intestine into the stew. ***Nothing*** was wasted. As was the norm, the animal wasn't skinned or gutted. As chunks were cut off, skewer racks accepted the raw meat with the skin and hair still attached. Over the fire the hair burned away, and the meat cooked thoroughly, at least on the outside. Burnt, actually. Having been cooked, large chunks of meat were then stuck on bamboo stakes, six feet in the air to keep dogs from stealing it. The meat couldn't be recognized for the hordes of large green flies that enveloped it. When Wagner walked near the meat to inspect it, a cloud of green erupted in loud buzzing confusion. He recalled the flies covering the carpet of excrement on the ground, wondering if he would be capable of circumventing a revulsion to eat this repugnant 'gourmet'. To one side, the huge head stood high on a single bamboo pole, observing its abattoir and covered with flies. "*Lord of The Flies*, huh?" said Wagner, as the others stared.

"Lord of the what? What the hell is that?" Flanagan asked, toothpick twirling from clenched lips.

Ceremonial rice wine was brought forward, in five large urns, each standing two and a half feet high, with a six-inch opening at the top. Several bamboo quarter-inch straws, four feet long, arced out of the tops. Each urn had flat bamboo sticks, ten inches long, placed across the tops.

The team was invited to sit on log benches, in a line on one side of the urns. Robinson and Wagner sat on each side of the chief. Wooden bowls were handed to each man, half-filled with stew from the cast iron pot. Other bowls had rice. The bowl appeared to be filled with black and green beans, but a quick fan of a hand scattered the flies, revealing white rice. In front of them were three-foot high bamboo stakes, on which sections of large chunks of buffalo meat were skewered. Part of the chunks were red, while outer, hide-covered parts were burnt to a brown-black. As Wagner sampled the meat, he found the unburnt part was as tender and delicious as any steak, maybe better. The burnt part was not. The hide was tough, nearly too tough to chew. "Jamus, you could break your jaw on this hide," he said.

"You eatin' the hide? You are crazy, man!" he replied, laughing.

Wagner made some attempts at the stew, but opted for the meat and rice for the main course, trying his best to appear thoroughly enjoying it. The rice was pasty, hard, and bland, but less repulsive than what he knew was in the stew.

Rice wine was made from rice paddy water, fertilized with human waste. To this water was added rice stalks, chewed and spat into the urns to hasten fermentation. This contributed significantly to local diseases; tuberculosis and hepatitis were particularly common. The team was encouraged by the chief and several others to drink heavily. After the meal, the serious wine-drinking part of the ceremony commenced. As many as five people at once sucked from the array of bamboo straws. Two woman replenished water levels as the rice continually fermented. Now the purpose of the flat bamboo sticks laying across the top of the urns was discovered. The chief proclaimed something, at which he and the others laughed. He split a small sliver, about five-eighths of an inch long off one side of the stick, bending it down perpendicularly. He followed suit with each vase, the bent slivers pointing down into the wine. Kir told the team members, "This called a 'stick'. When your turn, you must drink until wine drops below end of stick. You not stop until it does."

"With the size of the opening, that's probably close to a pint," Robinson remarked.

"It's not so bad, you kinda grow a taste for it," Stewart replied.

Wagner sucked up his first full 'stick', relieved when done. It was a unique taste, not unlike fermented cider combined with a smoky wood tang. "Well, Sarge, if you start to like this shit too much, I should put you in for an early out." He watched Flanagan, sucking down stick after stick, boasting of his drinking prowess. Their hosts laughed in approval. He was getting very drunk.

The team rose the next morning to leave with hangovers and worse than normal diarrhea. Flanagan was in a particularly bad mood. At least once Wagner heard him mumbling derogatory comments about officers. He complained about MEDCAP operations, "that wasn't his job, etc.", while the rest grew more enthused as they learned the ropes of treating diseases, parasites and injuries.

After loading their Jeeps and trailer, they exchanged thanks and good-byes with Pom and the village chief. Barely had they begun to move when a father carrying his three year-old girl hustled toward the gate. Her foot was gashed wide open with the front half just hanging, bleeding profusely. Flanagan was still reeling from his hangover, but he quickly wrapped her in bandages. Kir was told to tell him to get in the back of the Jeep with his daughter, they would take them to the Pleiku Field Hospital. On the trip, Kir explained the girl had stepped on her father's cane knife, just outside the village. There were scores of seriously ill villagers in those few days that Wagner learned shouldn't be brought to the hospital. If they died away from their village, their souls would 'wander forever' and the Americans would be blamed. Besides, the facilities in Pleiku simply couldn't support the numbers dying from all their diseases and war wounds. But cases like this little girl were not only heart-wrenching and humanitarian, it made staunch allies, *"winning hearts and minds"*. Nothing meant as much as family to Vietnamese and Montagnards alike. After all, family was all they had. Medical aid was the greatest gift anyone could ever give.

After showers and sleep in Le Quon, the following days showed no apparent plans for any activity. The team did nothing but lie around, play a little volleyball with the Vietnamese, and drink. Especially Flanagan. He was drunk most of the time, and getting meaner, more testing, more insubordinate. He seemed to focus on Wagner, every chance he found. Wagner figured that being part of a team and not in a regular tactical operations unit, he should try to win Flanagan's respect, if not his friendship. He tried to avoid confrontations in these early days on the team and utilize his knowledge. Still, Flanagan grew increasingly annoying and even belligerent, especially when drunk. In addition, there was no discipline or direction from Robinson. Wagner spent his time asking questions, learning what he could from the team, from Kir, even from Lenh and Manh, the wash girls. Alone, he walked the perimeter several times, checking their defenses. Le Quon village was located across the road. It was a small Vietnamese village, while another small Montagnard village was only a few hundred meters west along the same road. The RF company that guarded Le Quon compound was mostly Vietnamese. Guards were seldom present in their small sandbagged positions during the day, as well as their spotting tower located in the center of the compound. In the evening, the foxhole positions were sometimes manned, sometimes not. The ones that were, Wagner found, had guards either reading, playing cards, or sleeping. They relied on trip flares and mines in the perimeter to warn of an attack, all but useless to prevent sappers from penetrating. Demonstrations in the three-day orientation training in Di An proved that, performed by a surrendered V.C. sapper with alarming ease. Wearing nothing but a tightly wrapped cloth around his waist and crotch, he alligator-crawled over and under concertina razor wire and trip wires in seconds, reversing Claymore mine directions, disarming flares and mines and cutting away wires meant to stop an attack. Incredible to watch and frightening to know.

His confidence was fading. The moat, just outside and below the earthen berm surrounding the compound still had old sharpened bamboo punji stakes sticking out of the sides and bottom, but tall green grass grew so thick they were difficult to inspect for effectiveness. Just outside the moat were three rows of concertina wire, each a few meters apart. Inside the wires were mines, placed there some time in the past, but no one knew where. Normally, mine cards map their locations, but through past Special Forces and MAT team changes of personnel, they were long lost. Only a few avenues could be accessed to reach their Claymore mines. No one he asked, American or Vietnamese, knew when the Claymores had been checked last. He was told several were inoperable during the last attack. Still, nobody replaced them. Inquiries to Robinson produced no results. Blas and Stewart shared his concerns, now that Wagner brought them up. Flanagan dismissed them as a 'cherry lieutenant's nervous jitters'. In his KIA *Know-It-All* attitude, he thought of himself as his personal hero, John Wayne. A little of this bled off onto Sergeant Blas. Newer in country, he respected his slightly older mentor with two previous tours under his belt. He trusted his apparent knowledge of the people, area, and experience. Flanagan had a burning chip on his shoulder, and when drunk he as much said he hated all officers, period. As Robinson never really gave any significant orders or direction and the living was easy, Flanagan pretty much ignored him, or at least co-existed. With Wagner, however, it was different. He constantly tested him, like a young child tests his parents, pushing to see how far he could go. Any reason at all brought a hint of a chiding, a snide remark, that didn't quite go over the line. Because this wasn't a normal combat unit, but rather a team, Wagner chose self-restraint before discipline, at least for the present. They would have to live together for a year. A poor relationship could lead to a lack of respect from the others as well. Better to keep a distance for now.

When Wagner questioned Robinson about the defenses, he could answer very little. He had been leaving it up to the Vietnamese RF Company to manage. During this discussion, Robinson told him where the team members each normally took a position during an attack on the compound. Those positions consisted entirely of sandbagged bunkers near the team house, well inside the perimeter of the compound.

"Who calls in the Artillery, you?" Wagner asked.

"Yeah, me, or Lutz. During the last attack, Lutz took the radio up on top of the water tower."

Wagner looked at the tower. It stood about twelve feet high. The bottom served as the team shower stall, enclosed with plywood for privacy. Two steel rectangular water tanks sat on top. Inside one tank was a mess-kit dishwater heater, the kind that used kerosene inside a metal pot. An older, toothless Montagnard handyman known as Friday was responsible for pumping water into the tanks and keeping the water hot. An integral, vertical wooden rung ladder was its access. There was no protection whatsoever around the top of the tanks. "He stood up there? Kind of a sittin' duck, wasn't he?" Wagner had been taught the enemy often shot high, and there were only two towers in the compound higher, the Vietnamese command tower and one other just behind their team house.

"It's the only thing in the whole friggin' compound that ain't never been hit!" Robinson said with a laugh. "But I'm glad you mentioned it, you like calling in Arty. Wanna do it?"

"Sure, Wagner replied. Actually, I do."

"Good. If we get hit, you take the PRC 25 radio up the tower. You get a good view there."

Wagner stood contemplating, checking out the tower. He walked to it and climbed the ladder. It was an excellent view, for sure. Both looking out and looking back in. "You do have it hangin' out up here, don't you?" Climbing back down, he asked Blas what the other tower behind the team house was for.

"It was going to be a bigger water tower, sir, for a bigger shower when they were planning to use this for a district headquarters. It never got finished," Blas answered.

"Couldn't we put some sandbags up there? It would make a hell of a lot better observation tower than this one. I could climb onto the roof, have a ladder up there to get on top of the tower, and pull the ladder up behind me, in case they get in."

"Nah, we still might use it for a water tower," Flanagan interjected.

"Well, I've heard cleanliness might be next to Godliness, but it might put me closer to Godliness sooner than I want. I'll be honest, I'm not real thrilled with that old water tower."

"Oh, Lieutenant, if we all worried the way you do, we might as well join the Girl Scouts," Flanagan said, with his usual sneer, prompting a grin from Blas.

"Thank you, Sarge, for sharing," Wagner replied facetiously.

When Major Nichols showed up at the compound at the end of the week, Wagner found time to speak with him alone about the defenses of the village. "Sir, I've been looking at the compound pretty close. It could use some heavy improvements."

The Major's main interest was his PSYOPS and pacification programs, and he apparently hadn't given it much thought. He should not necessarily have had to, if Robinson had been doing his homework. "Okay, Darryl, let's take a walk."

The Major led Wagner to the Vietnamese command post, where they met with their Vietnamese RF Commander. Together they toured the outer perimeter berm. Wagner knew as advisers they had no authority to order changes, only to suggest. He pointed out the rears of their firing positions were not sandbagged, exposing their men to shrapnel. In the Vietnamese belief in fate, the Vietnamese commander said, "That's okay. If he dies, he dies. It happen anyway," No amount of precautions would prevent what was already written down. Fate. Showing the Major various pitfalls, Wagner recommended getting an Army dozer in to refurbish the earthen berm around the perimeter. "I want the Claymore mines checked, I heard a bunch of them didn't fire in our last attack. I learned how to make Hirsh flares. They're made with empty artillery shell canisters, full of M4 thickened fuel. With an incendiary trip flare wired to the side and a pan of fuel below, they start cooking. Pretty soon it blows a stream of thickened fuel out through a small hole you drill in the top. It burns for hours, and Charlie can't put it out like he could a light. You put one on each corner of the compound to light up the perimeter if they get close. It lights up the perimeter and marks it for gunships."

The Major smiled, and nodded in agreement.

"Then, on each side, we can put a thickened fuel directional burster barrel in the berm."

Sergeant Stewart joined them, and hearing the last of the conversation, said, "Sir, we had one of those here before. The gooks were firing like hell at us, and our people were firing like hell. Even though the bad guys weren't even close to the wire yet, a perimeter guard popped the thing, and a huge mushroom ball of fire flew up in the air, lit the place up like day. Both sides stopped shootin'. It didn't hurt anyone, but I think it scared the hell out of everybody. Anyway, it was a full minute before anybody started shootin' again....from either side."

"Wow. Just how was this thing set up?"   "

"Oh, they just set this fifty-five gallon drum up in the wire, full of, you know, thickened fuel? It had one of them foxhole digger-bursters in it, and man, I'll tell you, it made one pretty sight! Hee-Heeeee!" Wagner and Nichols laughed.

"What I had in mind was along that idea, Wagner said, "but you lay it on its side at about a thirty degree angle. You fill it with thickened fuel and nails, glass, steel, anything nasty. You put a Claymore mine in the dug-out hole first, at the rear of the barrel. Then tie det cord from the blasting cap in the Claymore to a white phosphorus grenade in front of the barrel. The mine blows it out into the wire, and the willie-peter grenade ignites everything and adds to the fun and confusion."

"Ooo-wee, sir, you have some evil thoughts about you! And I love it!" chuckled Stewart.

"I can't take credit for it. They taught us that. And sir," continued Wagner, "I'm going to be the guy that's on the tower to call the Arty. I don't like that old open tower much. I'd like to put sandbags up on that one over there."

The Major looked back and forth at the towers in a pensive pose, trying to find the least offensive words in his leadership role. "Sorry. Sector has plans to improve the water tower. That's what it was built for a few months ago. The district headquarters is planning to eventually move here. But you're right about the security. I'll see about your dozer. Good job."

The Vietnamese counterpart was cooperative in checking their Claymores. Out of 440 Claymore mines around the perimeter they found 24 operable. The others were replaced or new blasting caps installed, with new hand-squeezed claquers added. Many of the old claquers could not generate the small voltage required to blow the blasting caps. Concertina wire, badly damaged in the last attack, was repaired wherever it was safe to avoid unknown mines. A dozer was requisitioned to rebuild the berm. In addition, Wagner supervised the placement of hidden white phosphorus grenades, effective in breaking up human wave assaults. Grass outside the berm in barbed wire entanglements was several feet high and needed burning. The ten foot moat that surrounded the berm was almost filled with grass and rapidly growing bamboo. Because of unmarked mines, they were unable to cut it. Burning didn't work, it was too green. They tried to mow it down with machine gun fire, the failure of which brought laughter from Vietnamese and Americans alike, providing more ammunition for Flanagan to add derogatory comments about wasting time over nothing. The answer came from a scrounging mission, finding some old flame throwers from Camp Holloway. It was effective and a lot of fun. After all, who doesn't like to dig in dirt and play with a flame thrower?

The Vietnamese PFs were growing gardens of corn and other vegetables inside the compound, which an enemy sapper would appreciate to move through undetected. Every machine gun was in an improper position, the mortars weren't sunk in pits, and ammunition was all stored in one place.

The team walked the inside perimeter that night with the Vietnamese District Chief, Thieu-ta Nguyen Van Kiet. They found they completely neglected to guard the east side, as there was a four-deuce (4.2" diameter) mortar section fifty meters away, figuring that would be enough. More likely they found it a poor place to sleep in those positions with loud 'harassment and interdiction' H & I mortar fires. Enemy sappers would make that their first priority.

Later, the Major convinced his counterpart to practice a few attack drills. At 2300 hours, a siren that had to be repaired to work cut loose and they fired some machine guns. The team was assigned positions around the inside perimeter to record the time it took for the PFs to man their positions. On the west end, where there wasn't even a guard on duty, it took seven minutes for a single man to appear. It took ten minutes on the north side, the side most prone to attack, all other things being equal. Nguyen Van Kiet then stopped at the living quarters for the PF soldiers, all Vietnamese, and woke up some of them by throwing heavy clods of dirt at them. After screaming at them and taking their weapons for later identification, he continued on around the berm. Many of the soldiers failed to bring any ammunition out with them, having only the one magazine in their M-16s. Still others neglected to even bring their weapons.

"Un-friggin'-believable," Wagner said to the Major, obviously embarrassed for failing to address the situation.

The chief proceeded to beat these soldiers about the head and shoulders, kicking them hard when they covered their heads with their arms. That was the Vietnamese method of leadership, all quite normal. He collected these soldiers' weapons as well, sending them to 'tiger cages'--- tiny 2' high barbed wire individual jails every Vietnamese compound included. They were full of prone PF soldiers the next morning.

Several more drills were held over the next few nights, each resulting in vast improvements.

The entire compound, Americans and counterparts, seemed to enjoy renewed vigor, simply from activity. The post began to lose its sloppy appearance. Debris and trash were picked up, things were more orderly. For sure, the team felt more confident. Even Sergeant Flanagan felt it, though he couldn't possibly admit to it.

V LUFT

"The German word for 'air', meaning a space made available by a pawn move"

Rainy season on the west side of the Mang Yang Pass was a little overdue, and several days of beautiful but hot weather found the team still stagnant. Robinson had absolutely no plans, no motivation. This was when Flanagan was happiest, at least when he was sober. Drinking usually slanted his personality toward the mean end, and a bordering on insubordination usually followed. Wagner grew restless from the lack of activity, as did Blas and Stewart. Flanagan's underlying insults and boisterous manner were wearing on him. Still, he tried to avoid an outright confrontation. This team-versus-a-unit situation would be better off without it if he could make it work. Only time would tell.

Eventually, Major Nichols returned, asking Robinson and Wagner to step into his trailer. This time he had an operation assignment. In two days, the team was to go with their 815 Montagnard Regional Force 'Mike-Strike' Company, considered the best around. The troops were all Montagnards, all previously Special Forces trained, and led by an outstanding commander. The mission was a normal 'search and destroy', an endeavor to dig out suspected NVA or V.C. gathering sites on one of many veins of the famous Ho Chi Minh Trail network that passed through the Pleiku area.

"You won't need to go to them," the Major said. "They're coming to you. They'll be here at O-seven hundred. You won't be going too far out." Pointing to a topo map, he continued, "The area you'll be going through will be just north of our compound. There have been some reports filtering through of activity in the area. Generally small groups scattered about, possibly getting ready to link up."

Returning to the team house, Wagner was told "When

we go with these guys, we won't be doing any advising, Lieutenant," instructed Flanagan. "We're only along to call in the artillery. You can't tell these guys *nothin'* they don't already know."

At O-seven hundred hours, the RF company seemed to appear out of nowhere out of the northwest horizon, right on time. Kir was the first to see them from the berm. "Here they come! They here! They here!" he yelled, in his excited exuberant manner.

Wagner shielded his eyes from the early light to distinguish their small heads that grew into shoulders, then bodies, spaced evenly across the horizon like Comanches in a cavalry movie, ready to ride down to blitz the wagon train. The team walked out of the perimeter to meet them and were quickly introduced to the company commander, Krue (pronounced Kroy). Wagner studied him carefully in those few minutes, for he was a striking character as an indigenous solder. He could easily have passed for a Yucatan Mexican with a bias of Central American Indian blood. He was, for a Montagnard, tall, at five-feet ten inches. His eyes were large and wide, dark eyebrows sloped down toward the bridge of his nose, riding a

pronounced brow, yielding an intense, fiery look. Still, Wagner could see an element of respectful submission when talking to Americans. He addressed the American sergeants as "Sir", though he outranked them. Prominent facial bones augmented bulges of jaw muscles as they moved, telegraphing his thoughts. Adding to the effect were his tailored tight jungle fatigues, as was the custom with the few Montagnards who were allowed officer rank. Krue's rocky-muscled frame fairly tortured his tight fatigues. Chiseled triceps rose in crescents from his arms, forming ledges for rolled up jungle fatigue sleeves. Krue introduced the Americans to an RTO who would carry the twenty four pound PRC-25 radio. He was a small, young rock-hard soldier named Blom. Montagnards had no family names or knew their own ages, but he was probably no more than sixteen. Lieutenant Robinson told Wagner, "I'll be doing the artillery if we need it. Blom will go with me."

"Sure," he answered.

The little Blom knew no English, only the adviser's call sign, which would be 'Dusty Arrow Five Seven'. Wagner would be 'Dusty Arrow Five Seven Alpha', the Alpha indicating Wagner's assistant team leader position on the team. If Blom heard Robinson's call sign, his job was to get the handset to his ear in a hurry.

Normally, the position of company commander called for the rank of captain, but the Vietnamese weren't eager to give rank to Montagnards, and Krue was only a second lieutenant. He would probably never obtain first. He spoke fair English, negating the need for an interpreter.

Wasting no time, Krue gave the order for his men to move out. It was immediately apparent Krue was *THE* commander. He spoke with authority and brevity, and his men reacted. They travelled in three files, with no confusion as to where every man was positioned. Their spacing was perfect, never bunched. Each file had a point man, roughly fifty meters ahead, and a rear security guard. The MAT team members were positioned in the center file, one-third the way back, in the vicinity of Krue. If fire support was needed close to Le Quon, the Americans could quickly call 4.2 inch 'four-deuce' mortars from the Vietnamese mortars inside their compound. Further away, it would have to come from American 155 mm howitzers from the FSB fire support base north of Pleiku, called Artillery Hill. The RFs knew it and loved the support it provided. They, in turn, would protect these Americans with their lives.

When they reached the tree line, their three point men made no hesitation, seeming to know exactly where they were going as if a line was painted on the jungle floor. The 'Yards travelled slightly hunched, low and fast, through vegetation dense enough to make Wagner wonder how the point men could break trail ahead this fast. He was in excellent condition, from years of weights, running and swimming, and hoped that he would have no problem keeping up and staying as quiet. The others also did well, except for Flanagan. His size and condition resulted in a puffing and stumbling that so violated noise discipline as to cause the wary Krue to turn often, nervously frowning at the cause. Wagner gave Flanagan credit, though, for doing his best, trying to hide his strain. Ducking under and around branches, carrying the extra weight....that had to be tough. The files stayed nearly parallel, even in the densest growth. The little Blom RTO stuck to Robinson like glue. If he stopped, Blom bumped into him. Krue kept his compass in hand, constantly checking his direction, while a soldier behind him kept a pace count for distance. Wagner did the same, watching Krue as much as the outer files of moving bushes. A pace count, map and compass, and if available, terrain features, were the only means to know where they were on the face of the Earth. That knowledge was critical to place artillery rounds when the fan got hit. The biggest problem, Wagner knew, was keeping track of the paces. One hundred and thirty eight of his paces in the jungle meant 100 meters, roughly. While this proved remarkably accurate on level, open ground, it was subject to the variables of hills and valleys, bushes and 'wait a minute' vines, the vines and bushes armed with nasty thorns up to 1" long. They grabbed, pierced and cut passersby, causing an inevitable 'wait a minute'. Some called them 'ooh-ahh' vines, triggering "Ooh!" and "Ahh!" sounds from passing soldiers. Sharp-edged tropical grasses and spiked leaves added to minor cuts and stabs, with a resulting myriad of small bleeding cuts and punctures. Then there was the job of keeping track of how many hundreds of meters covered. A radio call, a sudden stop by the point men from some hint of noise or movement, a painful bite from a fire ant, a zillion things that shifted his focus could turn into a *"where was I"* mental clot. Military topo maps were, at times, another problem. At 1:50,000 scale, their accuracy was dependent on the technology of the time over a foreign land never surveyed, at times extremely frustrating. Each map was 21 ¼" square, sectioned off in 1 kilometer grids, ¾" square. Twenty eight squares meant it covered 28,000 meters in both X and Y directions. Each sector had a two letter designation giving its north-south and east-west location to begin the one-klick grids. Finally, if travelling all day over relatively uniform land, with no streams, hills, or ravines to reference from, those many hundreds of paces turned into one big *Wherethefugawee*. Their initial entire MAT 57 Area of Operations (AO), was 45 kilometers, or 28 miles wide from an arbitrary grid line on the western edge a few kilometers east of Pleiku City, to Mang Yang Pass to the east. From the northern edge bordering Kontum Province, it was 35 kilometers, or 22 miles to an arbitrary line ten kilometers south of the city, totaling over 600 square miles. During the course of the entire year, reduction in strengths and operations outside of the initial AO would increase the range to the entire province of Pleiku. From the Cambodian border on the eastern edge to the western edge beyond Mang Yang Pass covered 85 kilometers, or 53 miles, and the northern edge bordering Kontum Province to the irregular southern tip of the province was 56 kilometers or 35 miles, totaling roughly 1500 square miles. Forty percent of the province was mountainous, and except for Pleiku City, it was very sparsely populated, primarily with Bahnaar and Jarai Montagnard tribesmen.

Shortly before the operation, Wagner remembered an

idea he'd heard about using Claymore mine bearing balls to keep track. Breaking into a Claymore, he stripped the little casualty-producing balls off the face of the C-4, taking twenty out. Putting them all into his right jungle fatigue pocket, he would transfer one to the left pocket every 138 paces. Ten balls was a 1000 meters, or one kilometer, or klick. "Like the need for a small map light, why couldn't this Army supply something as simple as a golf swing counter?"

Krue was amazing. Any modest variance from the planned course brought a quick "Hssss!" to veer to the left, or "Hsssss! Hsssss! to go right. Wagner was totally impressed with this commander, who walked tall when the foliage permitted, his eyes intent, serious. His head was erect, moving, watching, an occasional sound indicating a correction. His men always smiled.

Down, down, they marched, on a slope thick with bamboo trees, their thin, light-green leaves slapping their faces. These small, rocky Montagnard bodies were at home, sliding through vines and foliage like jungle cats, breathing easily, rhythmically, with every step. Their lack of noise, even with so many men, was incredible. Wagner's team tried to match them, a tall order for larger bodies, but they did well. Flanagan was another matter. His size made it difficult, but his weight and sorry condition made for wheezing and huffing sounds that were louder than the slapping and scraping noises from the bush. The Montagnards routinely glanced his way, silently wishing for a quieter approach. Then into a clear, fast little stream almost hidden by the brush. The vegetation was thicker here, but the water felt cool and fresh on Wagner's hot feet. Canteens were quickly topped off, an iodine pill added for purification. Then up the following side, through thicker vegetation than seemed penetrable. Frustrating wait-a-minute vines with their damnable thorns grabbed at arms, hats, web gear, bandoliers and pant legs, leaving small bleeding scratches on Wagner's exposed arms. He ducked as low as possible,

94

trying to go as fast and quiet through bushy tunnels as the RFs ahead that formed them, a tall order, indeed. The longer they travelled, the hotter, sweatier and dirtier they became. Now the water in Wagner's boots didn't feel so good. His feet were beginning to scrape and blister in his new jungle boots. He tried to watch the sides for undiscovered ambushes, but their pace nearly prohibited it. Suddenly, sounds of their bodies brushing through vegetation was shattered ahead with three quick *POP-POP-POPs* of semi-automatic M-16 fire, followed by distinctive echoing pops of AK-47s on full automatic. Then, fully automatic from one, then another, and another M-16. Here it was, that moment, the event nervously awaited since the draft greetings letter over two years ago, through all the months of training. ***The opening trial of combat.***

Wagner's mouth went dry, his stomach knotted. Instantly he flicked his M-16's safety selector to full auto and dropped prone, as training had taught. The Montagnards in the center column ran past him, toward the gunfire. This wasn't the way it was supposed to happen, was it? Regaining his feet he followed suit, but the shooting had already stopped. His heart was pounding, as every soldier's does in his first combat action. He quickly moved past Robinson by the right flank, who was kneeling on one knee while using the radio to call Le Quon for mortar support. Adrenalin flowing, he moved up the last twenty meters, noticing that the two outer flanks of the RFs had stayed positioned in a perfect radial array, keeping low and intensely alert. They reacted mechanically, orderly, from years of survival and working as a unit.

Already, Krue had barked out orders to deploy a small forward squad, fanning out in the jungle ahead, searching for more enemy. Reaching Krue, Wagner looked down to see three enemy soldiers before them, the first he'd seen. They lay twisted in their own awkward positions on the ground. Each had two or three pencil sized puncture wounds in their torsos that hardly bled. The other side had large gaping holes, internal parts and bone fragments visible through fluids and blood that collected below them. One had tubes of intestines falling from his blown away midsection, like giant larvae coiling around one another. Blood soaked their skin and the ground around them. Their uniforms were dirty, torn. Two NVA pith helmets lay on the ground. A third helmet was resting on the side of the owner's head. Each was armed with an AK-47 rifle, laying near where they lay. One of the wooden stocks was nearly severed, shattered from bullets. When Robinson reached the site, Krue turned to them and said, "Three V.C....Dead". They weren't Viet Cong, but NVA, North Vietnamese Army regular soldiers. They wore dark green uniforms, faded and stained in red Highlands dirt, as were their own. Krue knew they were NVA, but in his translation, 'V.C.' simply meant enemy. The RF point teams had surprised them where they had sat to eat. Wagner wondered how so many RFs could move through the jungle quickly and quietly enough that they could surprise three men at rest. If any noise of moving brush warned them, the dead men may have assumed the approaching troops were their own. Only a slight breeze, or the NVA soldiers' own conversation could have masked what little noise escaped from the RF's quick and quiet patrol in any case. Luckily, Flanagan was trailing the other four team members, a full third of the way back from the point.

As they stood there for a few brief moments before the bodies were searched, Wagner studied their lifeless forms. They were young. Perhaps eighteen, maybe less. His mind shifting from the precarious situation of seconds before, he considered the possibility of a reversal of roles. *"There, but for the grace of God,....."*

There were no useful papers, only some letters and pictures from people close to them, in another world. Their weapons and ammunition were gathered up and the bodies left for the animals and insects. There was neither time, resources or desire in this RF soldier's world to care for a dead enemy. A body count meant nothing to them, as it would have for highers in an American unit. For an RF private, there was no case of beer reward, rarely a medal. The only reward expected was very meager pay, the respect of friends they fought beside, and another day to live on this planet. Too much to hope for, probably, would be a piece of this Earth, some day, to hunt and farm on and raise a family in peace.

The noise discipline of this fleet patrol had served its purpose. The enemy had been found first, the element of surprise in a jungle war once again proving its precious worth. No enemy escaped to warn others, to allow for an ambush to be set up and the hunter to become the hunted. Now, however, the surprise element had vanished. It was time to move out again, and quickly, to vacate the area and renew the fleet, silent approach. Robinson had returned to his position at the flank. He was on the radio. He turned his head as Wagner approached, and told Wagner to tell Krue to stay put. "I've got mortar rounds coming. Tell them to stay down!" Wagner didn't question his experience or authority.

Krue, who had been wearing a new U.S. Army ruck sack, angrily tore out its new-design steel frame, and chucked it as hard as he could over the low lying trees. The poor design had been wearing into his back and sides, and he had had enough of it.

Soon the first rounds hit, sounding as big as a small artillery round, but several hundred meters away to their northeast. Wagner watched Robinson, then looked at Krue, who seemed confused. Robinson had not checked with Krue for the need for mortar support, let alone the location of the rest of the patrol. Krue quickly yelled to his men to pull in toward the center. Obviously, the mortar support was not part of Krue's game plan, but he did not question his American counterpart. Robinson adjusted his mortar fire, bringing the next trio of rounds in closer. Confused, Wagner wondered if he was somehow being given targets from the RFs. He looked at Krue, who was watching and wondering. Then he turned to see Sergeant Stewart trotting toward him, in a crouched posture. "Sarge, does he have bad guys out there?" Wagner asked.

Stewart shrugged his shoulders with a wondrous look. "Lieutenant, what have you got out there?" he yelled.

Robinson didn't hear; he was on the radio, talking with Tim Demers, the Le Quon RTO, who was busy shuttling translated information back and forth through the Vietnamese at his location, in order to direct the mortar fire.

This time, three more rounds came in just outside the right flank's position. Robinson let out a quick scream, and grabbed his thigh. He was yelling "Cease fire, cease fire!" in the handset when Wagner, Stewart, and Flanagan reached him. His leg was bleeding from a quarter-sized wound on his leg, hit by a hot piece of shrapnel from the last mortars he called in too close. Flanagan tended the wound, which did not appear serious. The shrapnel piece had expended most of its energy, barely visible poking out of his brown thigh. Flanagan was able to pull it out with a forceps. He wrapped a pressure bandage around it, stopping most of the bleeding. After several radio transmissions to Camp Holloway to ask for a helicopter to take Robinson back, Wagner was told they couldn't fly because of the low ceiling that had recently drifted in.

"A low ceiling?" Wagner asked, in wonderment. "They told us you're never more than fifteen minutes away from a dust-off, and they won't fly because of a low ceiling?"

"Welcome to the world of Camp Holloway, Lieutenant," Flanagan said dryly. "Worst bunch of pussies I ever seen. Never seen nothin' like it."

Turning and speaking softly to Flanagan, Stewart said, shaking his head, "I knew that man would do something like this one of these days."

Flanagan stood with the back of his wrists on his hips, stomach torturing his faded green shirt, and said, "Fuckin glad he did it to himself and not us."

As the patrol was only several hundred meters away from Le Quon, and Robinson was able to walk, it was decided that he would return to Le Quon along with several of the RFs and the patrol would continue on. Krue quickly directed his men to move out. Wagner now had Blom, the little RTO trailing close behind him, radio handset ready. Several hours of hard, fast bush-humping found even the RFs slowing a bit, but Flanagan looked like he was going to die. Still, he did his level best not to show it. He did well for a man of his size and condition, for this game of staying low and moving fast with the smaller tribesmen was not well suited for him at all. On and on they marched, reminding themselves to stay alert in spite of the heat and fatigue. Sweat streams ran down necks and backs, soaking their fatigues. Bits of matter from leaves and vines worked into sweaty pant waists, boots became soaked from sweat as well as from small streams. Tiny insects crawled across their dirty, exposed skin. Wagner alternated between searching the ever-malevolent bushes, watching his own footwork in the branches and ground cover, checking his compass, and studying the RFs. Even at the beginning of the operation, he noticed them quickly reaching for little white jungle peppers that grew interspersed with other jungle plants. Augmenting meager rice rations was a natural, normal, and necessary part of their soldiering existence. Young bamboo shoots were deftly cut away to slide into a rear pack without so much as a backward glance to ensure its placement. There was no telling how many insects lost their lives that day to these protein-hungry troops, who considered large beetles and five inch long chartreuse green grasshoppers a staple as normal as a pizza or hamburger to the foreigners with them. They did not eat them alive, but saved them en route to be cooked later.

The point men stopped ahead, and each soldier dropped into a crouch. Krue moved ahead, with Wagner and his RTO following. Ahead in a small clearing was a grave home, a fancy-roofed hootch, 12' by 8', with an ornate vertical sculpture running the length of its roof ridge line. Strange, out here in the middle of the jungle, with nothing else around. It was in good shape, partly because the outside walls were entirely sheathed with continuous sheet metal, all stamped with uncut Coors beer can labels. Its history would remain a mystery.

For a brief interval, Krue held his head high, searching from side to side in short jerky motions. Reaching a small opening in the heavy vegetation, he gave a hand signal to stop, and word passed to the point to follow suit. Quickly and quietly,

their flanks spread out and cleared individual fields of fire for their respective positions, whereupon most of the men prepared for lunch. A designated few guards maintained an outward watch, weapons ready. Krue, always expressing a tone of some underlying respectful submissiveness to his American counterparts whispered, "We eat now. T-T fire okay."

Sergeants Flanagan and Stewart joined Wagner. The sweat was fairly pouring off Flanagan's nose and eyebrows, and his fatigues were completely soaked. Even his bush hat was soaked. He looked miserable. Wagner whispered to him, "Are you okay, Sarge?"

"Yeah! Yeah, I'm fine." he replied, between puffings. His voice was raised. "You, Lieutenant?" He appeared insulted.

"Can I take some gear for you?" Wagner asked.

Still wheezing, he answered disgustedly, "Don't you worry about me, Lieutenant. I don't see you exactly rested and dry."

"You got that right, Sarge," he replied quietly.

Sergeant Stewart flashed Wagner an understanding grin as he hunched down behind Flanagan to join two young Montagnards for lunch. He readied his rations to eat with the RF sergeants, who were opening rice bags in the small clearing Krue had picked. Flanagan tried talking with them in Pigeon English, not even trying to whisper.

Krue turned to Flanagan, and said, sternly but politely, "No talk."

Flanagan nodded with a sneer, and removed his packs to eat. The American rations were LRRP, or Long Range Reconnaissance Patrol rations. Light, tasty dehydrated meals of rice and vegetables, with shrimp or beef, etc., sealed in a foil bag. A superb improvement in taste, weight, and nutrition over the Army's ancient C-rations, all they required was heated water. To the advisers' surprise, the Montagnard soldiers they sat with produced two cooking pots. Flanagan asked quietly in pigeon English and hand motions, succeeding quickly getting the point across, if they wanted to mix meals and eat together. Chuckling quietly, they readily agreed. Sergeant Stewart, watching one soldier preparing a fire, gently grabbed his arm and whispered, "Ah, wait, my man, I have a better way." Producing a stick of C-4 plastic explosive, he tore off two golf ball-sized chunks. Placing them under the canteen-filled pots of water, he lit them. The C-4 burned fiercely, producing a small bright-white light, quickly bringing the water to a boil. All the while, Montagnards worked deftly, quickly, cutting newly-procured bamboo shoots. Using razor-sharp bayonets to cut into the shoots, they threw away a part, kept another, threw away another, until the foot-long shoots were totally dismembered. The saved sections were then sliced into wafers, and dumped into one pot. The RFs poured in their rice, and the team added their LRRP contents, which always included dehydrated hot peppers. To this the RFs added their fiery hot white jungle peppers. In the other pot, the RFs dumped a small amount of their rice, and producing a small plastic U.S. Army bag, dumped about thirty fat black beetles in with it. They were like stateside May beetles, over an inch long, and squirming. As soon as they hit the hot water, the squirming stopped, and grinning RFs looked up at Stewart and said, "Numbah one!"

Brandon Stewart just smiled ear to ear and said quietly, "Yeah, Jack, that may be numbah one to you, but ol' Bran here will just stick to the rest of the vittles and grits we got, thank you please," pointing to the LRRP pot.

In a matter of minutes, chow was ready. As Wagner sampled his first taste, Flanagan and Stewart watched him with anxious anticipation. "Huhhh! Huhhh! Jeee-e-susss, that's hot!" Wagner whispered. "What in hell did you put in that, C-4?"

Flanagan and Stewart were convulsed. It was like an initiation ceremony. LRRP ration peppers were dynamite, but those little jungle peppers were *nuclear*! "You grow a taste for it, Lieutenant," Flanagan whispered. "*Nobody* makes hotter food than the 'Yards."

"Yeah, sir, you really do," Stewart said, alternating bites with swigs from his canteen.

With chow over, Wagner was proud he had suppressed his revulsion of consuming several beetles in the RFs' stew, hot jungle peppers helping to mask his distaste. The unit moved out, retaining the speed and quiet of the morning. Wagner's senses were peaked, now that his war had progressed one major step deeper into reality. From his earliest memories of Vietnam on the news in high school, home, and his college fraternity house; through concerns of the draft, recruitment, Basic Training, OCS, Adviser and Language Schools, it was all something far away, an unreal world, a movie, a surreal dream ahead. The sniper at Plei Ko Tu brought it closer, but it was still removed, distant. But now the three dead NVA changed it all, a major stepping stone in reality. That distance withered into the real world of death and removal of immortality, just as it has for millions of soldiers for centuries in Caesar's, Genghis Khan's, Washington's, Hitler's, and Eisenhower's armies. No doubt the sentiments are unchanged. On the latrine wall at Ton Son Nhut Airbase, Wagner remembered the words from an unknown writer:

God looked down from His clouds in the sky
He said I created man but I'm not sure why
Nothing but killing since creation day
Gonna flood this land and wash them away

The operation's events had answered a question Wagner had wondered for years---what was combat going to be like? He decided those few moments filled with anticipation, butterflies, noise and action had gelled into a familiar emotion; it was like a football game. The butterflies were there until the opening kickoff. Once the ball was in the air, the butterflies were gone. After that it was all business and decisions--even the fear was gone, at least until it was over. The only fear he felt during the action was making a bad decision that could get friendlies hurt or killed. And now he was thrown into command.

Wagner found that Flanagan had been right about one thing; the Montagnard Mike-Strike Force company really didn't need any advising. They were practically flawless. Special Forces training years before and all the years of fighting and surviving made them a well-oiled machine, reacting quickly and efficiently. No wonder Americans universally regarded them so highly. The remaining hours of their search-and-destroy operation produced no new results, and a tired company of RFs and Americans stopped to quietly set up a night perimeter. But for the sound of bayonets chopping stakes for rain poncho tents, little sound was made. Krue was already setting up his pre-planned artillery targets and listening posts around the perimeter when Wagner went to check.

Blom, the little RTO, who had been carrying the radio, was busy setting up a shelter that he and Wagner were to share. Wagner busied himself digging a shallow foxhole for the two of them. The speed with which Blom prepared the stakes and pegs from the material at hand was impressive. He finished the tent and went on to help dig the shallow foxhole. Then, the two of them mixed their rice and LRRPs, more bamboo shoots, peppers, and you-guess-its. Wagner decided it was a grand meal, with grand company. It was a beautiful starry night, in this end of the dry season. There was no light pollution to spoil the elegant brightness and serenity of a sky filled with the brightest stars he had ever seen.

After a quiet radio check with Le Quon, Wagner fell asleep quickly, only to be wakened minutes later by Blom's arms and legs wrapping around his body. "They didn't tell me about this in Adviser's school, either," he mumbled to himself, picking Blom's arms and legs off. A few minutes later, they were back, cuddling a back-to Wagner. "Hey, what the hell, Blom?" he whispered, again picking his arms off. He began to think this poor kid needed a leave badly. Blom got the message and kept to himself.

The night passed uneventfully, and with sunrise the team met with Krue to discuss the day's travels. Shortly afterward, as Wagner pulled a C-ration can of fruit cocktail from his pack for breakfast, Sergeant Stewart asked him how he slept. Stewart was squatting, running a razor over a canteen water-dampened face. Wagner replied, "Pretty good, considering I almost got married."

"Say what, Sir?"

"I think our little RTO needs a leave. We were getting pretty close for a while there."

"What do you mean?"

"Well, he kept wrapping his arms and legs around me. Wanted to cuddle," Wagner said.

"Oh, no, sir," Stewart laughed. "That's how the Montagnards keep warm. It was a bit chilly last night. The Montagnards just sleep that way. They don't have a linen closet with all the blankets and stuff." Stewart was cracking up. "Don't worry sir, it doesn't mean he loves you. I'll never forget the first time that happened to me. I was thinkin' the same thing!"

No time was wasted moving out again. Flanagan looked clearly pained, but he pressed on. Along the valley, following a small stream, the patrol discovered a series of well-built bunkers and trails. Several RF soldiers were assigned to check them out. The tension brought new life to the butterflies in Wagner's stomach, as he watched three teams of three men each checking individual bunkers. He imagined himself looking into those ominous dirt huts, anticipating the worst. It proved uneventful, and Krue declared the bunkers safe. No tunnels were found, just a bunker complex. He said they were old, unused for a while. They travelled on, never really slowing. By three o'clock, the heat was building, and even Krue was showing signs of stress. Angling west, they left the thick vegetation of the valley they had been following, eventually finding semi-open terrain on slightly higher ground where bright green two foot high grasses grew, interspersed by thick, leafy bushes. This was more open than Krue liked, preferring the element of surprise on his side. Moving into any open area left them exposed and invited an ambush. The files spread out accordingly, with only some hissing guidance sounds audible from Krue. Suddenly, a burst of activity took place to Wagner's left. All weapons swung toward the movements, eighty four safeties clicked off. Wagner, his mind once again racing to peak alert, crouched and flicked his M-16 on auto. He watched Montagnard soldiers diving, one after another, in the grasses 20 meters away. Then he saw it. A small reddish deer, bounding from side to side like a star halfback, was lunged at by every soldier in the column in sequence. Like outmaneuvered linebackers, one after another RF soldier dove to tackle this food on the hoof, all failing. They were all quietly smiling and laughing, as Blom said, "Numbah one chop-chop, Trung-uy."

Momentarily, at least, the noise discipline was tarnished, but it offered some relief. Sergeant Stewart said, "You know, if that was most Vietnamese units, they would have blown that deer away. Screw the noise. It's food!"

"Yeah, and if it was Americans, they would have blown it away, too. Just for the hell of it," said Flanagan, grinning.

On they pushed, moving shadows through dry, yellowing grasses that now grew over 6' high. A light wind kept eddies and gusts undulating the grass tops, hiding the snaking movement of three columns below. An enemy might notice the grass moving if he was on a high vantage point, but other than trees, none existed. Fifty meters ahead, a gradual rise marks the line where grasses end and short scrubby trees begin. The right point stops a meter short of breaking out of the grass, frozen in a crouch to scan the woods ahead, scarcely breathing. The next soldier instinctively freezes in a crouch as well, and so on down the column. Seconds later the center and left column points do the same. Ahead, in a small woods clearing past the first brushy growth, there is movement. Within seconds, the entire unit is crouched and frozen, as if they are rows of dominoes, each piece matching the one preceding it. Wagner watches as the two outside columns react in a pre-planned routine pattern, moving as two mirrored levers, the point man the fulcrum, the middle of the columns move up on line to form 'troops on line', ninety degrees to the direction of travel. The rear halves move up to form flank security. Both outside columns leave five men as rear security. The center column remains to counter flanking moves and to form a flexible reaction force. It all happened so quickly and mechanically. Wagner was in awe, the coordination and stealth of every soldier. This is how the indigenous people survived.

From the center file, Krue alone stands tall, sweeping his head to ensure the order. Wagner crouches with the rest, looking for what the point man saw. The dense grasses deny any chance of that, nothing can be seen a mere meter or two ahead. Then he hears it, almost imperceptible over the faint rustle of lightly dancing grass. A faint voice, slightly louder, then quiet, then a short laugh. The pitch is typically higher, a Vietnamese. The wind lulls for several seconds. Grasses stand still, the rustle of wind now silenced. Wagner hears the distinctive tonal sounds of Vietnamese. Another short chuckle. Krue moves up, noiselessly. Wagner moves slowly up two meters behind Krue, afraid to make the slightest sound. Sergeants Blas and Stewart watch to each side, knowing the front is covered. Flanagan crouches as much as his big frame allows, his eyes wide and terrified, his mouth hanging open. Krue turns, his right hand extended, his hand palm-down. Each soldier in turn lies noiselessly in a prone position, rifles pointed out, alternately half to the left, half to the right. Wagner's team follows suit. They lay absolutely quiet for eight, nine minutes. Hardly a breath. The wind still lightly gusts and stalls, grasses rustling with every puff. The smells are elephant grass, gentle woodsy pollens and their own sweat and body odor from sweaty marches. Wagner wonders if the NVA can smell them. How many are there? Are we in the middle of a Division, a Regiment? God help us. "Should I call for a fire mission?" he thinks. "If I do, they'll hear me. I can get everybody killed. How small a unit can we expect? How big?" As they lay perfectly still, Wagner's thoughts, only for seconds, drifted once again to his college coed, his lost love. "If I'm killed, will she know? What will she think? Will she care? Will she bother to come to my funeral?" Over the past five years, every single day brought hundreds of thoughts of her, fleeting or lasting, compiling hundreds of thousands of thoughts. He often wondered if it was possible to ever forget her, to fill that void with someone new. So far, every girl Wagner met, he compared to her, and they all came up lacking. He decided many months ago he would probably never marry. Staying single was better than settling. That was below him, not a chance.

Another barely perceptible "Hisss" from the commander instantly brought him back to reality. "My God, what am I doing? Get your friggin' head back in the game, Darryl." A pause of several seconds, then. . . . . ***POP POP BOOM BRRRRAAAAPPPPPPPP CRACKCRACKCRACK POPPOPPOP RATTTTTAARRRRAAATTTAP POP POP BOOM BOOM...*** The noise was an incredible din, louder than a training range at Dix. A cacophony of M-60s, M-16s, and M-79 'Thumper' rounds for a full seven or eight seconds, then.. nothing. Silence. It ended as quickly as it began. The pleasant smell of gunpowder wafted through the grass, masking all others. Wagner was already on the radio, moving up with Krue.

"Salty Bumper Niner Three, Salty Bumper Niner Three,

this is Dusty Arrow Five Seven Alpha, Dusty Arrow Five Seven Alpha, *Fire mission*, over!"

"Roger, Dusty Arrow Five Seven Alpha, this is Salty Bumper Niner Three, go ahead, over."

"Salty Bumper Niner Three, Five Seven Alpha, we have a contact, wait one."

"Roger, Five Seven Alpha, we're here for ya, over."

Wagner waited, thumbing the selector switch, every nerve on edge, wondering if he would need his M-16 or radio first. Several minutes elapsed. Finally, an RF soldier crawled back to Krue, talking rapidly, quietly to his commander. Krue turned to Wagner, and said, "V.C. Dead. We see if more. Think no."

"I have artillery ready. Let me know if your men need it," Wagner said, slowly articulating every word to ensure he understood.

Another five minutes., Krue discussed something with his sergeant, and turned to Wagner, "V.C. all dead. No more. No artillery. V.C. there," he pointed.

Wagner and the team quickly advanced to the firefight location. Nine NVA bodies lie in various positions, not one had the time or opportunity for cover. Each body was hit with multiple rounds. The RFs hadn't thrown a grenade. They saved their precious resources for when they absolutely needed them. After carefully, quietly assessing the enemy strength, they had let small arms fire do the work. Most of the bodies were shredded to some degree or another by their murderous enfilade. The 'Yards quickly stripped them, looking for weapons, documents, anything of use. Wagner saw the first body had defecated, squashed stool spread between the man's legs from a relaxed sphincter. A slight breeze in the small clearing stirred the smell of guts, blood and feces.

Krue wasted no time. He knew more of their enemy unit would likely be there soon, and in numbers. No longer having a surprise advantage, limited numbers of RFs demanded movement. Hit, move and hide, move and hide and wait. Stay alive. Again, the three columns were quickly in order and moving fast. Flanagan again tried to keep the pace, but he was holding Krue up. Krue kept turning his head, looking back at Flanagan, slowing his men to accommodate, clearly concerned. Always respectful of Americans, he showed no emotion, no disgust, no complaint. Only concern.

Just before dusk, the company once again found a modest clearing in which to set up a nightly perimeter. Another hot meal loaded with energy-providing carbohydrates from rice, and Wagner felt a second wind. From his pack, he pulled out a code book and KAK wheel, used to change numerical artillery coordinates to coded alphabetical letters, to prevent the enemy from knowing their location from monitored frequencies. After calling Salty Bumper again to plot defensive targets, he settled into the poncho tent again with Blom, lying on hard, uneven ground. It was almost dark, a faint azure glow providing scant light from the west, fading fast. There would be no moon. She came to his thoughts again, as she had every morning, noon, and night for five years. Vietnam exacerbated many a soldier's loneliness, nothing unusual there. He was under tall Maine pines, sunlight passing through branches and needles, reflecting a bronze-gold glow on a carpet of pine needles he was laying on. She was wearing a cobalt blue sleeveless shirt, tight white jeans cut off and frayed below the knees. Her thin arms folded around drawn up knees, bare feet half buried in pine needles. She was talking, smiling, cat-like eyes and deep dimples in a perfect image. The lake was only five feet away, clear, comfortably cool in July, small ripples from a gentle breeze lapping on the rocks along the sandy shoreline. So magical, perfect. Now so distant and lost forever. Would he ever kiss those lips again? No. She had a family now, it was over, gone forever. Wagner was ashamed of his self-pitying weakness. If someone else acted this way, he would see it as pathetic and weak. Wasn't he above all this? Would he ever get over her, or take his heartbreak to the grave? After five years and no change, he couldn't imagine... Exhausted leg and back muscles ignored the hard ground, and thoughts of her gradually turned to a revitalizing sleep.

Sleep was short-lived. At 2130 hours, Wagner found himself fairly leaping from under his poncho liner when the "**POP-POP   POP-POP-POP!s**" of M-16s, followed by a crescendo of small arms fire shattered the solitude. To one side of the clearing, a trip wire flare was burning its bright white incendiary glow, illuminating that side of the perimeter. Wagner grabbed the radio, turning the volume up as he nervously called Salty Bumper again to get the big guns ready. The thumping heart returned. Shooting quickly stopped, however, and as the artillery was readying their guns to fire Wagner's pre-planned targets, an RF soldier informed Wagner that a deer had tripped the trip flare, there was no enemy.

"Sorry, Salty Bumper Niner Three. I have no mission. It was a deer."

The soldier on the other end hesitated, then, laughing, said, "No problem. Understand it was just a deer?"

"Dusty Arrow Five Seven. Well, it was an NVA deer."

"Roger, Dusty Arrow, understand it was an NVA deer. We're here for you, Dusty Arrow. Over."

"Thanks much. Out."

Now the security of their quick, quiet approach was gone, causing the little RTO justified concern. Wagner could see it in his face, by what little light remained. The RTO was just a teenager, but his senses were honed as a soldier at his young age. Wagner felt it, too. Krue was a few meters away, talking quietly with his RF platoon sergeant. Wagner assembled his team to discuss their 'advisory position' on the matter, and once again, Flanagan said, "You don't need to get involved, Lieutenant, they'll do what they wanna do. I'm gonna go drain my lizard."

With Flanagan not interrupting, it was easier to confer with Blas and Stewart. "I want to know what you think. We can't command here, only advise. But we've blown our position. I'm thinking we should move out."

"Oh, yes, sir," they both said almost simultaneously. I have no problem with that. We needs to *di mau now-now*." Stewart said.

Krue was already approaching as Wagner turned to suggest they should move out. It was unnecessary, Krue had already instructed his sergeants to pass the word. The RFs packed up poncho tents and gear, and were ready to go within minutes, almost inaudibly. The loudest sounds came from Flanagan, huffing and puffing. "I told you they'd do what they wanna do, Lieutenant."

"And Sergeant Flanagan, you were correct." Wagner answered, patronizingly.

The three files formed up and the unit moved out as if they never stopped. In the moonless night, the files were closer now, only meters apart. Each man touched the man in front of him to stay connected. They marched for an hour, stopping to set up their NDP, a night defensive position. Repeating the earlier procedure, Wagner sent in new defensive fire targets and settled in, each team member pulling a two-hour guard. The team was on edge, the enemy knowing they were somewhere in the vicinity. Their own NDP could be not far away.

Sergeant Blas was pulling his guard, when first light saw the 'Yards moving. He woke Wagner, Flanagan, and Stewart. No time for breakfast, that can come later. Pack up and beat feet. They travelled 900 meters when the columns stopped. An RF soldier quickly moved back to Krue, telling him they had seen a V.C. running out of a night position ahead. No one had fired a shot. Krue barked some orders in his Bahnaar tongue, and his columns levered out, when a *whum-phat! s*ound came from two o'clock a few hundred meters ahead. *Mortar.* Everyone except Flanagan hit the ground, until seconds later, a nerve-shattering **CRUMP!** of an 82 mm enemy mortar round, landed a hundred meters left. Now Flanagan was on the ground as well, looking petrified. Krue sprang to his feet near the center of the perimeter, fully vulnerable, yelling at his soldiers. He looked at Wagner, who motioned his hand from his chest to a finger-point right. Krue barked to his men to run that way, pointing. It wasn't important which way, simply out of the kill zone of mortar impacts, in one direction as a unit. More *whum-phats.* Tents and gear abandoned, the men grabbed weapons, ammunition, and radios, running through the breaking light in a three o'clock direction, before the mortars could adjust to their position. A few more orders from Krue, and two groups split off, with little confusion. He already had them searching for the enemy mortar tube. By now the rounds were impacting, walking toward their NDP, but not close to the RFs. The NVA were guessing, hoping for tell-tale screams of wounded. Wagner kept near Krue, for he needed to know when and where his counterpart wanted the artillery, which he was already calling. Though he had considerable confidence in his ability to call it in, the greatest fear was hitting friendlies. He needed Krue.

Still moving through thick brush, Wagner keyed his handset and said, "Salty Bumper Niner Three, this is Dusty Arrow Five Seven Alpha, *Fire mission,* over!"

A benefit to working in this remote area, at this relatively late era of the war, was the priority through radio traffic. Calling artillery bases was almost never a problem. There simply were no other Americans in the area that needed artillery. All a forward observer needed to say following his call sign identification was, *"Fire mission, over!"* whereupon anyone else on the network would immediately relinquish it, for the F.O. in a firefight was the number one priority in the country. Literally e*veryone* else's job was in support of him.

Responding immediately, Artillery Hill replied in a calm, professional voice, "Roger, Dusty Arrow Five Seven Alpha, this is Salty Bumper Niner three, go ahead, over."

"Salty Bumper, this is Dusty Arrow Five Seven Alpha, we've got a contact, wait one, over." Wagner was preparing the artillery support for the worst case if required. Seconds were precious, and as firefight missions were rare these days, there was no problem in holding their attention. Indeed, the artillery gunners craved the action, now that troop withdrawals had diminished U.S. artillery calls. They wanted kills. Wagner laid his topo map out, and a green handkerchief covered his small penlight. With Krue pointing to the area his men should be, Wagner pointed to the pre-planned targets to the opposite end of the perimeter, and told him, "Krue, I will put *phao binh* --

artillery here, and here, okay?"

"Yah. Good. Good!" he said, with quick head nods. There was no need to discuss it, Krue knew the procedure. Subsequent rounds would be adjusted from the first.

Instead of the five minute wait they had enjoyed from Blackhawk, however, ten minutes went by with no artillery round. Wagner called to check.

CRUMP! CRUMP! CRUMP! CRUMP! Mortars were coming in again, near the area they had been sleeping. The enemy obviously didn't know where they were, so they were spreading the rounds out a bit.

"Roger," came the southern drawl from the artillery radio man. "We're still trying to get clearance, there's some Victor November helicopters somewhere in the area, we can't shoot yet, over."

"Well, c'mon, tell them to get the hell out of here, we've got bad guys, okay?"

"Roger, Five Seven Alpha, We're doing the best we can. I'll call you when I get some results." It was a full thirty minutes from the original call before Salty Bumper let Wagner know the first round would soon be on the way. The mortars were still landing behind and left of them. Finally, a "Shot out." came from the radio. The guns were One-Five-Fives, 155 mm howitzers, which had less power than a 175 mm, but had better accuracy, particularly at this range. They were capable of throwing six inch shells almost 15 kilometers, or 9 miles, and were accurate in spite of being near the end of their range. "*Shot out*" and "*Splash*" facilitated locating the impact in order to adjust for the next rounds and to identify which were friendly or enemy explosions.

"Splash," he called, just as the round hit with a deep, muffled *CCRRUUNCCH!* A bright glow and white smoke from burning phosphorus verified the coordinates. A 300 meter range to the target was long, but it was difficult in this terrain to know exactly where they were from the map and pace count of hiking all day without significant terrain features. Even 300 meters was risky. While white phosphorus, or 'Whiskey Papa' rounds are usually used for marking the target with a bright explosion of burning phosphorus and white smoke it produces, it is still casualty-producing, and in a horrific way. WP keeps burning completely through a body. He turned to tell Krue he would be adjusting closer with HE rounds, and needed input from the RFs. After the next three rounds, the mortars stopped.

Krue had been on the radio, speaking in Bahnaar with his men who were somehow dispersed in the thick trees and vines. They gave Krue the enemy locations, who relayed the input to Wagner. It was a careful, step-by-step process, necessary to keep friendlies from getting hurt, but at times painfully slow. Wagner changed his call to "HE Quick", high explosive-quick detonating shrapnel rounds and gave "Drop 100, left 100" orders. The friendly rounds came in with louder crunches from the HE, closer and to the left, stopping the enemy mortars entirely. The RFs stayed in their positions in silence, waiting for any forward or flanking movement, which never came. Krue sent a squad to the right flank to sweep through to determine if there was a larger unit left, or if they were planning to attack. After almost an hour, the squad came through the undergrowth from the direction of the artillery targets. Reporting "twelve V.C. dead and one mortar tube," the unit moved in a line sweep through the area. Nothing else was found. Ten were dead and two wounded when the first reaction team found them. The 'Yards wasted no time in quietly making it an even dozen. Wagner stared at a blood-painted boot on Trung-si Chot, one of the senior sergeants, then at one of the dead NVA soldier's beaten head. These men hated the NVA. No wonder the North Vietnamese feared these tough Montagnards so much. Years of atrocities from both the North and South Vietnamese burned a fierce reprisal attitude among many of them. Whole villages of their people had been murdered, lands stolen, persecutions of every kind. The Vietnamese derogatory term "*moi*", meaning savage was a misnomer. Americans found them fierce, friendly, loyal, happy, primitive. But savage was not in their description.

The mortar and rounds were quickly destroyed with C-4, and again the unit moved out. The bodies were left where they lay.

Krue set up his NDP early after an exhaustive march west, then south for several klicks. Flanagan was miserable, exhausted and sour. The unit stayed put for the remainder of the night, at fifty percent alert. The half not on alert slept however they could, but Wagner, at least, got not a wink, between the bugs, damp ground, and frayed nerves. When the first glimmer of dawn abated the nerve-wracking threat of a night attack, they quietly rose to move out. Returning to the original perimeter site to recover their equipment, they found it had not been discovered by the enemy. Krue first surrounded the area, ensuring its security, before allowing a few men to police up the gear. His every move was picture book leadership. Impressive. Regrouping, they swept the area, with Krue sending one platoon to the left flank first. Everything happened so smoothly and planned that Wagner could only wonder how the RFs communicated so well. He only wished he could be as fine a leader as Krue.

One of the artillery impact zones produced three enemy bodies, or what was left of them, and three NVA 82 mm mortar rounds. Following a drag trail, a bloody NVA boot lay at the edge of the trail, twenty meters away. Almost hidden from sight by a hasty attempt from the retreating soldiers to drag their comrades away were three AK-47 rifles. The bodies were torn almost beyond recognition, lying in awkward twisted positions, two with one leg folded impossibly below their torsos. The eyes of one were hanging from his sockets from close concussion. The ground was carpeted with small green leaves and splintered wood that ground bursts knocked from the trees. Blood soaked the ground in the immediate areas of the bodies, and one torso had entrails bulging out of it from a nearly severed midsection. The smell of death hung in the air, another memory of Vietnam. Wagner had lucked out with his adjusted artillery fire, it must have been dead on. Someone had to have drug others away, but from the tracks and the fact that three were left behind, Krue thought there were not many in this group. Krue looked at Wagner, and with a rare smile, said, "Artillery. You. Goot.. Goot." Rapport was developing quickly, both ways, and Wagner was getting into it. Fear and nerves were turning into a rush. He wanted more.

Two more days passed, with no more enemy contact. The RFs operated as fast and quiet as on the first day. Flanagan was visibly exhausted, huffing with every labored step. Krue noticed, too, but never said anything, just looked a little perplexed. The 'Yards never complained about an American. On the last night, Stewart, Blom, and Wagner shared a double-poncho tent. Stewart couldn't stand Flanagan's snoring. On one-third radio alert, Stewart took the first two-hour shift. Less than an hour into a light sleep, Wagner awoke to a commotion and suppressed laughter inside the tent. Blom, still asleep, had Sergeant Stewart's hands held together and he was kicking him in the stomach. Stewart whispered, laughing, "Sir, help me, help me!"

Wagner, half asleep, but his mind on edge, said, "Wh—what?"

At that moment, Blom nailed Stewart with a fist in the nose. With this, the little guy woke up, looking terrified for what he'd just done. *He slugged an American sergeant!* His embarrassment was evident, even in the dim moonlight. This little taciturn trooper said nary a word, he just pulled his poncho liner over his head and ceased all movement. He stayed there, motionless. Brandon Stewart, meanwhile, was splitting a gut, still holding his nose.

The return to Le Quon the following day found Wagner feeling refreshed and a little relieved to be on the last couple of kilometers return to the safety and rest waiting in their compound. Even so, words from training played back in his mind, *"Don't let your guard down, don't get lax on that trip back. And never follow the same route back. That's when Charlie's gonna do it."* Still, the day looked a little brighter, a little greener. The vegetation, the smells, it was all beautiful. The numbers and varieties of butterflies, in their iridescent blues, greens, reds, and yellows were remarkably beautiful, like none he had seen before. In a half hour, they were walking into the Le Quon compound.

Major Nichols told Wagner to come into the small metal trailer that served as his quarters. He wanted brief details of the RF operation, zeroing in on the Robinson-mortar incident. The Major's branch was Artillery, and he was particularly interested in the artillery calls during the mortar attack. He seemed pleased with the results, but also made several inquiries about Flanagan, obviously concerned. He cut the meeting short to meet some agenda back at Headquarters in Pleiku. Not much more happened in the ensuing days, and other than a quick Jeep trip to check out two PF units along Highway 19, not much direction was coming from Major Nichols. What limited activity they had seemed to come about only because Wagner had asked, and now he wondered what the next undertakings would be. This lack of interest and direction was disconcerting, but nobody else seemed concerned. Again, nothing in training prepared him for the situation he found himself in. It became more apparent that whatever work or war effort the team made would in large part be left to the team leader, but it wasn't clear. Days later, Robinson was still hobbling around the Le Quon team house and complaining about the Army in general and about not being awarded a purple heart for his 'self-inflicted' mistake. Without prior notice, Tim, the compound RTO, emerged from the TOC to tell him he was supposed to prepare to DEROS. Orders from Province Headquarters were to pack his take-home belongings and report the next day to Sector, then to the Pleiku Airbase to board a C-123 to Saigon, then home. It appeared his injury had prompted an 'early out', to curtail his tour of duty. This was common for serious injuries, though his was not. Unknown to Robinson or the rest of the team, Major Nichols and Colonel Bern had requested the DEROS, working the injury angle as the tool to terminate what was left of

Robinson's tour as soon as possible. By this time of the war, early-outs were common anyway, part of the American troop withdrawal. Robinson had no problem with it, in any case. In fact, he was euphoric, until Wagner saw him complaining to Sergeant Stewart in a corner of the common room of the team house. Then Robinson left the room to finish readying his belongings.

"Well, sir, it looks like you are the new boss," said a grinning Sergeant Blas.

"Congratulations, Five Seven!" yelled the smiling Stewart. "Say good-bye to Five Seven Alpha!" The Alpha designation pertained to the alphabetical sequence of the team, 'A' meaning #2, or Assistant Team Leader. 'Five Seven was the team leader designation for MAT team 57, a Captain's command position.

Flanagan, sitting at the team house supper table, just grunted, derisively rolling his eyes, while the toothpick clenched in his teeth danced.

"Thanks, Sarge," Wagner said to Stewart, "What's with Robinson? Looks like he's bitching about something."

"Yeah, sir, he's pissed off he's not gettin' a purple heart. Seems the Colonel doesn't like giving purple hearts when you screw up and wound yourself," he said, laughing.

"No shit," Blas said. "He expects a purple heart? For that? For chrissakes, he did it to himself. Hardly a cut."

"Figures," said Flanagan, his toothpick still dancing. "I ain't never seen nothin' like it."

Taking Wagner aside, Sergeant Stewart whispered to Wagner, "Sir, I love black folk. But that man is just a fuckin' nigger. And I can't stand a nigger. They give all us black folk a bad name."

VI COUNTER ATTACK

"When a player defends by attacking his chess opponent instead of making defensive moves."

It was early morning, the Sun was rising in a clear sky, and the air was still cool and comfortable. Wagner had been told to report to Major Nichols, who was at Sector headquarters. He guessed it involved his new command of the team, but he had been given no further information. Sergeant Blas offered to drive him in to Pleiku to find headquarters, though the building was easy to find. The route was directly out of the compound at Le Quon, down Highway 19 thirty kilometers or so, and the drive presented no significant danger in the daytime. After breakfast, he and Wagner gathered what they needed and were loading the M-151 Jeep when Sergeant Flanagan ran out, half-dressed, carrying his fatigue shirt, hat, and one boot. "Wait up, I'm coming, too!"

The road to Pleiku passed a few small roadside villages, all of them Vietnamese. One was particularly pretty. It had a small river running through it, complete with a five-foot waterfall near the center, fully visible from the road. It was surrounded by the dark green foliage of the banana trees, and those in turn surrounded by a bright chartreuse of rice paddies. A few villagers walked between the grass-roofed houses, and pigs and water buffalo walked lazily in the morning sun. Nowhere did it appear there was a war going on.

As they crossed a small bridge on the southeast outskirts of Pleiku, Flanagan told Wagner, "You better keep your hands in the Jeep, Lieutenant, the Vietnamese will steal your watch right off your wrist!"

Blas laughed, and said, "That can happen, sir. When I first came here, Lutz, Flanagan and I were driving through the center of town, Lutz was in the back. As we slowed down for a crowd of Vietnamese in the street, Lutz pointed at something out to one side, and this kid pulled his watch right off his arm.

The kid took off, ran like hell. Lutz was absolutely bullshit."

Pulling up to the side of the headquarters building, Wagner and Blas disembarked, while Flanagan climbed behind the wheel. "What time are you gonna need this Jeep back, Lieutenant?" he asked.

Surprised, Wagner turned and asked, "I have no idea. Where are you going?"

With a sinister grin and a wink to Blas, he replied, "Well, let's just say I've got a little R & R to take care of in Pleiku."

Wagner stared for a moment, his M-16 in one hand, a notebook in the other, while the meaning sunk in. "Alright. I guess there's no hurry. I expect we'll be done by, say, two. That okay with you, Sarge?" he asked Blas, wondering if he would instead be joining Flanagan.

Sergeant Blas, apparently a man of fidelity, showed no intention of going with him. "Sure. I don't get many chances to come in to Headquarters and see some of the guys. You may have to drive us home, though, sir," he said with a broad smile and a bending of the elbow.

Chuckling, Wagner said, "No problem. I would guess it would be best, though, if we leave before late afternoon, to avoid arguments with Ong Charles."

"Yes, sir, I roger that."

The headquarters sector building was a large white and pink concrete building located near a high point of Pleiku city. It was one of the nicest buildings in town, surrounded by a courtyard of tropical trees, vines, and other greenery. It was well protected by a contingent of military police and their V-100 armored vehicles. The V-100 was an imposing amphibious war car, nineteen feet long and seven and a half feet wide, weighing eleven tons. Four sizable tires and a powerful motor gave it a top speed of 62 mph. A variety of machine guns and heavy armor made it an excellent road security machine. It was used primarily by Military Police, both U.S. and ARVN. Each American V-100 had a G.I.-given name. The *Proud Mary*, aptly named with its big wheels, and the *Road Runner* were commonly seen in the area, occasionally visiting their friends at Le Quon.

The sector seemed over-staffed with NCOs and officers who had little to do. For the most part, it was a happy, office-type crew, with little to remind one of the presence of war. Groups of three or four people were sitting in various rooms, discussing lunch menus, Pleiku locations of interest, or most commonly, the recent political change in their command.

Wagner soon found Doug Hanson and Jerry Dulane in such a discussion, in Doug's quarters.

"Well, Darryl, glad you could make it," Doug said cheerfully. "We all heard about your excitement."

"Yeah, Darryl, heard you were in some serious shit out there. Can you fill us in?" Dulane asked.

"It wasn't that much," Wagner answered. "We almost got a deer, though."

"Yeah, we heard about that, too," Hanson said.

"Christ, doesn't anybody else have a war on around here? Sounds like it made the six o'clock news. It was over as quick as it started." Wagner was still under a mistaken impression that every day was going to be a combat experience. He related the gist of the experiences he had had thus far, while Doug and Jerry sat absorbing every detail. The prize for most interesting subject went to the toasted rats.

"So what's the story with Robinson?" Is it true he called the mortar in on himself?" Dulane asked.

"He did. I still don't know what the hell he was thinking. Our counterpart--that was Krue, the Montagnard RF company commander I told you about? He was as confused as I was. Poor guy, he didn't know what was going on when Jamus started calling in those rounds."

"Holy shit. So now you're the big Five Seven, huh? Not just the assistant team leader anymore. That's normally a captain's slot, Darryl...not bad."

"Luck of the draw, Jerry. Same thing at Aberdeen Proving Ground. I was a company commander as a second lieutenant. Nothing I did, just fell into it. All the other commanders were captain and above. Great for a career, I guess, if I stay in. I'll tell you one thing," Wagner continued, "That Plei Ko Tu village is a terrible place. This village reconsolidation thing, I don't know, man. The filth, the disease...these people aren't meant to live in large settlements. They're hunters, gatherers and farmers. They are starving to death. Red hair from lack of protein. Eating rats, insects, anything, malnourished as hell. I've never seen so much disease. People are dying every night and day like flies. Funeral gongs go on constantly. It's just filthy."

"Well, if that's what it takes to keep Charlie from getting it, that's the name of the game," replied Hanson.

"I suppose, but man, you've gotta see it. I can't believe this is the answer. You can't tell me we're helping our allies this way."

Jerry Dulane bent forward, his hands folded in an almost apologetic manner, and said, "Darryl, we used to argue about the pros and cons of this war. I was dead against it. You used to argue for a lot of the 'good' reasons for it. Now I see what you mean. They don't hate us. They really are scared shitless, scared when we leave, they're gonna die. They hate the damn communists."

It took Wagner by surprise. Jerry had never looked at the war from anything but an anti-war view, in spite of getting an officer's commission. "Well, Jerry, I have to say that I see some of your side now. It looks like we're really screwin' a lot of people here. At least the 'Yards. For why, I can't figure. But a lot of people are getting dealt a real bad hand in this war. Not just the soldiers. The civilians. Particularly these Montagnards. It's confusing."

"Darryl, you've gotta talk to Menh, this Montagnard maid who works here at Sector. She's really great. Nice lady. She'll open your eyes to what these friggin' commies are, I'm telling ya! She came all the way down here with her family, from North Vietnam, to get away from the bastards. On a bicycle! Can you imagine? Hundreds of miles, on shitty mud trails, all their belongings, on a bicycle! It's gotta be pretty friggin' bad, man."

Wagner was stunned. Two months earlier they had opposing views, for the most part. The communist domino threat was what he knew, and he had believed his government. Now Dulane was playing the hawk role, while he was showing skepticism. The only thing clear about this place was that nothing was black and white…only shades of gray. And now, to add to the mystery, he was seeing the other side of the Montagnards' plight. In spite of their treatment by the South Vietnamese, they traveled all the way here from the North for a better life away from communist dictators? Confusing.

"Getting back to the village, Darryl, what are your 'culinary delights' these days? Are you eating some of that shit? Did you have the rat? Or dog?"

"At the team house, it's good. The sergeants scrounge our chow from Camp Holloway or some other U.S. post. In the field it's C-rations or LRRPs. You know what the C's are like, but the LRRPs aren't bad. It's when you get invited to a village 'feast' that things get really bad." Wagner recounted the rat roast, buffalo stew, and rotten dog meat, anticipating the reactions from Doug and Jerry. He wasn't disappointed.

"Holy shit, I couldn't hack that," said a disgusted Dulane. "You better devour those iodine pills, man."

"At least the dog and rats, all they eat pretty much is rice. There's no garbage or anything else left to eat. I wonder how different they taste in the states."

"You are one sick puppy," Hanson said.

It was time for Wagner's appointment with Colonel Bern. "I'll take you up to his office," Hanson said. "He wants me there, too."

As Wagner and Hanson ascended the stairs, they met Master Sergeant Husky near the top. Husky was a big man, hair a flat top salt-and-pepper gray. His graying, thick eyebrows pressed down to his nose bridge, and contributed to an older presence than his forty-something age.

"Good morning, sirs, I believe you are here to see the Colonel?"

Hanson replied, "That's affirm, Sarge, is he ready for us?" The Master Sergeant was also new, arriving with the Colonel and displacing the First Sergeant who had served with Colonel Robichaud.

"He just informed me that he would meet you at the Quang Que Hotel. You familiar with that, Lieutenant Hanson?"

"Yes, I know where it is. Any reason why there?"

"I don't get paid to ask him personal questions, sir, he just said he would meet you there," the sergeant replied with a good-natured grin.

Hanson turned to Wagner with a puzzled look and a shrug. "Let's go. We'll go in my Jeep. It's a few blocks from here."

On the way over, he told Wagner, "This new Master Sergeant, he's a little different. Really nice guy, though. He seems in pretty tight with Colonel Bern. Don't know what to make of it yet."

They drove to the Quang Que, a two-story cement hotel, painted a light yellow. It was no palace, but about as good as they come in Pleiku. Outside, there were several Vietnamese V-

100 armored vehicles, and three 'deuce-and-a-half' truckloads of Vietnamese military police, or 'White Mice' as they were called, with their polished gear and white helmets.

"Holy shit, what's going down here?" Hanson asked. "Must be somebody special in town. Why the trucks?"

Hanson parked the Jeep across the street, and after being checked for identification, they were allowed through a front door. Entering the hotel, they were led through a narrow hallway to a private dining hall. They immediately met Major Nichols on his way out. "Good morning, sir," Wagner said.

"Good morning, Darryl. I didn't properly congratulate you on your operation. I didn't have much time, and I'm afraid I was a little too focused on the mortar incident. What did you think of the rest of the operation?"

"Well, sir, the RF Company was fantastic. Their commander Krue was incredible. Flanagan told me they didn't need any advising and...he was right. I learned a few things, though. Even the little RTO they gave me was incredible."

"Speaking of Sergeant Flanagan...how's he been?"

"Excuse me, sir? He *seems* healthy."

"Flanagan...he can be a bit of a handful. Everything okay?"

"Yes, sir, I believe so."

"Okay....if you run into problems, let me know."

"Yes, sir."

"Well, you did a good job. Twenty seven kills, no friendly casualties. I heard about the deer in the perimeter," the Major said, chuckling.

"I didn't do much. Didn't have to. Like I said, Krue and his men were incredible. The deer was a hoot. Did you hear about the RTO smacking Sergeant Stewart in the nose?"

"What?"

"Our little RTO...his name was Blom. We were asleep, Blas was on guard. Blom had a bad dream, and popped Stewart Right on the shnoz. Our only WIA."

Laughing, the Major said, "Well, glad everything turned out okay. Darryl, we'll be meeting with your PSA, the Province

Senior Adviser. His name's Colonel Bern."

"I met Colonel Bern, briefly, sir," said Wagner. Major Nichols, having mild Attention Deficit Disorder, didn't hear him.

Gordon Bailey just arrived for the same scheduled meeting. The major saw him outside and said to Wagner, "The team leader from MAT 46 is here. He, like you, was just moved into the team leader position. His name is Gordon Bailey."

"Yes, sir, Gordon Bailey is a good friend. We went through all of our training together."

The Major said, "Excellent, I guess that saves the introductions. Well, it's time, right through that door." He turned to lead them into the room, where they saw Bern and the civilian Friedman, who were standing at their grease penciled map, as though they hadn't left since Wagner was last in Bern's office. Another officer was standing back-to, still inspecting the map. They were also accompanied by an attractive Vietnamese woman in western dress, who had just entered through the door from the opposite side of the room. Wagner recognized the civilian Friedman, when Major Nichols said, "Colonel Bern, I'd like you to meet Lieutenant Wagner and Lieutenant Bailey. This is Colonel Bern,...."

"Uh, yes, sir, we've met, extending his hand. How are you, sir?" Wagner said.

"Fine, fine, Lieutenant. I trust you've both settled in?"

The Major, surprised, asked, "You've met?"

"Yes, sir. Briefly."

As the Colonel who was staring at the map turned, Colonel Bern continued, "And this is Colonel Hallard," Colonel Bern said, opening his arm toward the map-gazing Colonel with his back turned. "He's here from Nha Trang, S-2. Intel and Security." The blood fairly drained from Wagner's face as he instantly recognized Hallard, the Lieutenant Colonel he'd reproached in Nha Trang when his orders were switched.

"We've met," said Hallard, smiling. "How's it going, Lieutenant?"

"You've met?" Major Nichols asked.

"Yes, Major," Hallard replied.. "In Nha Trang." Looking sternly at Wagner, he said, "We discussed the Lieutenant's assignment. I'm sure the Lieutenant will find it very interesting." Eager to avoid further discussion regarding their brief discourse back at Nha Trang, he gave an almost imperceptible glare at Wagner.

"And this is David Friedman, our Officer Consulate here. Mr. Friedman's responsibilities are focused on efforts to prevent resources from falling into enemy hands."

Friedman smiled cordially and shook hands, still seeming out of place among the military.

"And the lady is Madam Phung, Mr. Friedman's assistant." Madam Phung was an attractive Vietnamese woman, wearing a white, silky tight western dress that clung to a slim curvaceous body looking all the part of a Tu Do street whore. A pattern of small black and silver crescents of varying sizes stretched and flexed with her hips and shoulders as she moved, seeking attention. Part of Madam Phung's duties, Wagner was told, was to act as an interpreter. She was holding Friedman's arm in one hand, a drink in the other, smiling flirtingly at the young lieutenant.

Wagner exchanged greetings, noting Madam Phung's moderately aging beauty, and the mismatch with the rather dumpy, older Friedman. Friedman noticed the woman's seductive stare and arrogantly glared at Wagner. Feeling awkward, Wagner turned his attention to Bern, and started to ask about the heavy Vietnamese security outside, when Bern interrupted with, "Major, that will be all, I'll brief the good lieutenants from here."

The Major seemed surprised, hesitated briefly, and said, "Yes, sir," and left the room. Friedman and the woman remained.

Bern turned to Wagner and Bailey, and said, "You men are part of a special team. A very special team. You are not alone. There are other teams, in other provinces, with people like yourselves, picked to do a tough job. You see, gentlemen, part of our job will be to deprive the enemy of his food, his weapons, his very existence. Beyond what you have learned through your infantry training, beyond what you've learned in your advisory schools, we are going to change the direction of this war by denying the V.C. and the North Vietnamese the provisions that have kept them sustained through this war. Through your efforts we will destroy Charlie's ability to survive in this region. You, with your exceptional physical, mental, and leadership skills, will be the spearhead of a movement that will help end this war. You were picked because of your scores in leadership ratings, your Physical Combat Proficiency Test, your AFQT tests, and even your language proficiency tests. I need your abilities to carry out what the Special Forces began. They lived in the villages you are living in and are responsible for many of our achievements today. They began the teaching and training of the indigenous forces to defend themselves." As he spoke, he emphasized by waiving at a six-foot topographical map with a long wooden pointer. "You will continue that tradition. I expect results and your cooperation."

The remainder of the week found no new direction from the Major. Wagner called for a meeting of the team to find what they knew about the numerous villages and RF/PF units in their AO. He was trying to form a plan, to advise and assist the various troops as he had been trained to do.

Every conceivable suggestion from each team member was met with some degree of criticism from Flanagan. As much as Sergeant Blas respected Flanagan for his age, rank, and experience, even he was not unscathed from Flanagan's comments, yet he accepted it with some underlying camaraderie. The team was slow to energize, but brainstorming sessions helped arouse interest from Blas and Stewart. Perhaps this would all have been easier had Wagner been the Assistant Team Leader for a while, in order to shed some of the new guy syndrome; to work into a deserved respect from these senior NCOs on the team. But this was the hand dealt, and Wagner had to deal with it.

Within a few days, all villages with RF, PF, and PSDF troops were listed and located on their map, and the current location and status of each PF and RF unit was logged. Unlike the map on Colonel Robichaud's wall, Wagner only put it up when discussing troop locations and strengths. Training had made it clear that the enemy could be anyone or everyone in the compound. The cook, the interpreters, the cleaning girls, even the Major's bodyguard could only be minimally trusted. Wagner didn't like the Colonel's seemingly careless attention to security at headquarters, but that wasn't in his hands.

He told the team the plan was to systematically visit each village if possible, when the team wasn't on an operation somewhere with the Ruff Puffs. Each man would be responsible to question and train troops as necessary. They needed to ensure the troops they were advising had adequate supplies. When it came to the Montagnards, often their allotted supplies would find their way to the Vietnamese black market instead of the soldiers. Though it wouldn't help much in the future after Americans were gone, the team could at least help in the present by delivering some of that themselves with nothing more than a Jeep and trailer. The RFs and PFs were extremely grateful.

Flanagan's derogatory comments grew worse. It was bordering on insubordination, but Wagner knew this was not a 'unit' per se, but a team. As a team, they would have to get along, and finding the right leadership tactic to change the direction wouldn't be easy. Mandating compliance is not good leadership. Discipline would only be a last resort. He wanted to talk with Flanagan, but it would have to be when the obnoxious sergeant was alone and sober, the latter becoming more infrequent. He was never completely drunk, just glassy-eyed and slurring, and more cynical.

On Sergeant Stewart's suggestion that their supplies were low, the team took the Jeep and trailer to Camp Holloway for another scrounging mission. This helicopter airbase was crawling with activity, all in support of Hueys, Chinooks,

Loachs, and Cobra gunships assigned or landing there. Individual aircraft parking areas defined by sandbagged revetments provided protection from explosions and shrapnel from occasional 82 mm NVA mortars and 122mm rockets. Camp Holloway had an exceptional history as a prime target for the VC and NVA alike. All of this dreadful firepower amassed in a relatively compact area presented a substantial magnet.

In addition to big CH-47 Chinook, or "*Shithook*" twin-engine, tandem rotor heavy lift helicopters, and even larger CH-54 Skycranes, the base had numerous smaller choppers that came to fame in 'the helicopter war'. Bell UH-1H Iroquois 'Huey' Gunships, equipped with heavy firepower from spinning multi-barreled mini guns, went under the call sign 'Avengers'. The same Hueys using M-60 machine guns but no external guns, were termed 'Slicks' and went under 'Ghost Riders'.

More firepower was wrought by 3-foot wide Bell AH-1G Cobras, which usually flew in "Hunter-Killer" teams, consisting of two small light observation Hughes OH-6 Cayuse helicopters, called 'Loaches' or 'Little Birds', used to blow the bushes apart at low altitude to draw fire as decoys. The Cobras would typically hang at 2,000 feet, ready to respond with two wing-mounted pods carrying eighteen 2.75" rockets, two more pods of 7.62 mm, 2,000 rounds per minute miniguns, and a chin mounted turret equipped with another mini gun and beside it, a 350 round per minute 40mm grenade launcher.

Stewart led the group to his favorite scrounging grounds, where a heavy first sergeant sat in a wooden orderly room. Several enemy weapons and Montagnard souvenirs adorned the walls, given in return for supplies on previous scrounging runs. When the team walked in carrying captured weapons and carved Montagnard helicopter models, the sergeant's eyes lit up. Stewart, who knew him well from a previous duty station, introduced the team.

While they discussed what they needed, a tall mustachioed W-4 Warrant Officer walked into the orderly room. His eyes had a narrow, grave look, but he smiled when he saw the team's offerings. He turned to Wagner to introduce himself. "Hi, I'm Jim Kalman. Where did all this come from?"

"Hi Jim, I'm Darryl Wagner. This is our team, we're a MAT team operating out of Le Quon. The captured weapons are from a recent small action east of here. The helicopter models are from Plei Prep Ge, a small Montagnard village back in the woods, about twenty klicks northeast. We're scrounging for food and ammunition." Wagner introduced Kalman to the rest of the team, as two more Camp Holloway sergeants stopped in to view the offerings.

"Twenty klicks? That's within my AO. What's your area of operations?"

Wagner replied, "Basically north to Kontum Province, west to Cambodia, east to Mang Yang Pass, and it varies a bit south, but down below Plei Do Rom."

"Pretty much the same AO as mine. I fly a Cobra, with a Hunter-Killer team. MAT teams…you live with the little people, right?"

Wagner knew about the Cobra Hunter-Killer teams. "Pretty much." Answered Wagner. "Man, you've got the job I want. If I could be a pilot, especially a Cobra pilot, I'd probably make a career of it. My eyes didn't pass."

Kalman's interest immediately grew. He, like most of the Hunter-Killer team pilots, was more than eager to use his awesome weaponry. In a way, pilots had their own Army, or at least had more 'flexibility'. "Look, we operate mostly from intel. We get word where the bad guys are, we scout it out. But it's almost always bad intelligence, or too late. It's usually from some Vietnamese group here, it goes to Saigon, gets changed or whatever, and after a few more channels, gets to me. I always wanted to set up a more direct line, and heard about the MAT teams. Who else would have the latest intel? Would you be able to let me know directly?"

"Sure, I think I can do that. The highers are telling me they don't want us to use air support, or even artillery for that matter, only as a last resort. We're supposed to encourage our counterparts to use Vietnamese support first, but you know how that goes," Wagner replied. "I've already begun a sort of intel net with the village chiefs of nearly every village we've visited. That hasn't actually produced yet, but I can suggest the area around the little village of Plei Trang Klah, east of here. We had some activity along the Dak Honol stream. The stream runs north-south, and our PFs were mortared along that area last night.

"Okay, my current call sign is Fancy Hobble Niner Two. If you call, I can be at your location fairly quick if I'm available. Would you care to go for a snake ride some time?"

"A what?"

"Snake ride. That's what we call an unauthorized ride in a Cobra," he said, as he ran his hands over a wood model of a Cobra.

"You're kidding! Oh, man, you don't have to ask twice. Talk about giving a left nut, I'd do it in a minute," Wagner exclaimed.

"It may be a little while, I just lost my Loach team, I've got four new Loach pilots we're breaking in."

"Lost?"

"A B-40 rocket took one out last week, flying debris got the second one, all four pilots were killed," Kalman said. "They were just above the trees up by Highway 14, just south of Kontum Province, the north end of my AO."

"My gosh, I'm sorry. I hadn't heard anything."

"You've been in other choppers?" he said.

"Yes, several Hueys, and briefly in a Chinook. A Huey pilot actually went over some of the controls with me when they dropped us in a village. I remember the cyclic and the collective, and the foot pedals." Wagner said. "But I couldn't touch them or try to fly it."

"This is great. We're heading out in a bit, but I'll be in touch. What's your call sign?" Kalman asked.

"Currently it's Burnt Cradle 57. It'll always be something 57. That's our team designation, MAT 57. The rest of the team is 57 Alpha, 57 Bravo, 57 Charlie, Delta, and Echo."

"Okay, really great to meet you. Stay tuned," Kalman

said, turning to leave with a quick wave.

It had been several weeks since the 815 RF Montagnard Company operation. With little guidance from Major Nichols, the team had begun their systematic visits to villages along paved east-west Highway QL 19, with intermittent trips to some that were located several klicks down old woods trails and foot paths, barely wide enough for the Jeep. Deep ruts and potholes made the travel slow here. The terrain would alternate between open grassy fields, a few rice paddies formed by long-ago dammed streams, dense woods, and worst of all, tall elephant grass, some nearly a dozen feet high. The grass was unnerving. There could be no warning whatsoever of a close ambush. There was barely room for the Jeeps to travel, and sometimes less. The men leaned away from the sides of the jeep as the sharp grass slapped at their exposed arms and grabbed at ready weapons. Visibility ended mere feet through thick, 6' high veils of waving light green. The M-151 Jeep lurched on the crude dirt path, independent suspension threatening to tilt and roll its short wheelbase with every rut and hump. The front wheels grabbed and jerked in short twitches, making for slow progress, adding to ambush fears.

As Wagner imagined himself as the ambusher, he thought, *"This is where I'd do it."* Other than depending on local Popular Forces to thwart the enemy, the only thing they could hope for was the enemy not knowing of their presence. A random enemy ambush was unlikely because friendlies didn't travel these trails. The same reason applied to mines and booby traps; there were not a lot of either in remote roads or jungles as there were in populated areas. If it was a more heavily travelled dirt road it was likely, or hopeful at least, that the PFs swept their road for mines.

The team had been visiting several Popular Force units in various villages with either Kloh or Trong as interpreters, depending if a unit was Montagnard or Vietnamese. Visits usually included inspecting their perimeters, helping to zero weapons, providing ammunition and Claymore mines, and whenever possible, providing medical help by setting up a small MEDCAP operation. Sergeants Flanagan and Stewart were usually the medical providers, while Wagner and Sergeant Blas leaned toward defense issues. They had begun a standard procedure of training PFs in Mechanical ambushes, or MAs, using Claymore mines. It was perfect for under-strength, under-equipped units in protecting their villages from the enemy without extensive risk. Through either Kloh or Trong, they carefully explained the procedure. The technique was intended for both patrol ambushes and to protect the village at night. It consisted of setting up two Claymore mines on a trail, one facing in one direction and one facing the other, about 30 meters apart. Between them was a trip wire and a hand grenade. The M18A1 Claymore is a horizontally convex curved rectangular mine, 1 ½" thick, 8 ½" wide, by almost 5" high, encased in a gray-green plastic. Two sets of small scissor legs hinge out from the bottom. It was designed in the mid-1950s, and still used extensively. Behind 700 ball bearings is a one-inch cake of C-4 explosive. An electrical blasting cap is inserted in the top, a battery is required to detonate it. Even a flashlight battery works. Without the blasting cap, the mines are safe to handle. The balls are propelled by the C-4 in a 60 degree fan, 6 ½ feet high and 165' wide at a distance of 165' at an initial velocity of 3,940 feet per second, more than double the speed of most bullets and 3 ½ times the speed of sound. Energy of a projectile increases with the square of its velocity, making the balls a formidable weapon.

It was early morning when the team began a Claymore class in the village of Plei Ro Krong, one of the more remote Popular Force platoon locations. They arrived by Huey helicopter, as no roads led to the village. The Huey crew wished them a safe stay and would return for an extraction at 1600 hours. This day was particularly worrisome, having immediately lost communication. The PRC-25 didn't have the range, leaving the team on its own with no chance of artillery.

To make it worse, the villagers didn't smile. The PF platoon protecting the village, however, was all Montagnard and provided a fairly reliable security. It was a pretty village, set at the base of one of the foothills that ran east from 'V.C. Valley'. It wasn't reconsolidated, and had been left untouched for most of the war. Large, palm-leafed trees grew close to the hootches, lending a tropical island air to the entire village. The PF platoon had been expecting them, and the outdoor 'classroom' was ready and waiting.

They began the class by running detonation, or 'det' cord, from the top of one mine, then to the grenade that had its own blasting cap and firing pin unscrewed and removed, then on to the other Claymore. PETN explosive in detonation cord burns at a rate of 21,000 feet per second, or 14,520 mph; thirteen times the speed of sound. Its purpose is to connect and blow all three devices at once. When an enemy trips the wire, the ambushing unit is poised a safe distance off the trail to spray the kill zone with small arms fire and grenades and then withdraw. If that unit were small, as in most cases with PF units, they would exit quickly on a pre-planned route, rather than engage a potentially large NVA unit. The kill area could be checked out at another time. These ambushes were a good and relatively safe way to deny the enemy movement at night as well as deny them food, weapons, and young men they were looking to recruit.

For the trigger, they taught the PFs how to form two 10" pieces of insulated electrical wire, stripping both ends off each, forming loops on both ends. The loop of one wire passed through the loop of the other to form two parallel wires, each held by the other's loops. The bare copper cannot touch. To the bare ends of the loops they attached nearly invisible trip wire. When the wire is tripped by an unwitting enemy, it would pull the two copper wires apart until the bare loops touched each other, completing the circuit, exploding the blasting cap in the Claymore. The det cord would, in turn, blow the grenade and the other Claymore.

It was important to emphasize the *last* step in setting it up and the *first* step in taking it down was to connect and disconnect the battery, without which it was safe. For a battery, a used PRC-25 radio battery sufficed well. For the purpose of training,

they tied a long cord to the middle of the trip wire, Tugging the rope to simulate the enemy. That blew the Claymores and the grenade. A chorus of approval from the Popular Force soldiers would ensue, shouting "Numbah one!" They hurried to inspect the results, careful to retrieve the bent insulated wire trigger. Their interest buoyed the team's confidence that they may actually use it. As usual, when Flanagan wasn't bitching about doing the medical work with villagers, he was denigrating the efforts of Wagner. Even Sergeant Blas was tiring of it, sometimes mocking Flanagan. "There's a law somewhere that says every flock of birds has one negative bitcher, and Billy's it," Blas said, half-jokingly. "Not a happy man."

Often their classes in the Montagnard villages were followed by invitations to the village chief's hootch for a rice wine party, including tribal delicacies. These were an unceasing dread to Wagner, probably more than to the others on the team, but all of them grimaced at the presentations. Sitting in half circles around vases of rice wine was a social event, however and important for villager rapport.

"Sir, you gotta wonder if any of this is worthwhile. Do you think any of these guys are going to make use of all this?" Blas said.

"Wondering the same thing, Sarge. I'm guessing most of the Vietnamese, no. Most of the 'Yards, yes. But that's just me guessing. I know that I would. I can't think of a safer way, and you know the Montagnards want and need to protect what little they have left. They know we're leaving. I'm not too sure what the Vietnamese PFs are thinking. But what do you think?" Wagner really did want to know what each team member thought, even Flanagan. All of them were in a learning situation, on-the-job training, so to speak. Nobody but Flanagan claimed to have all the answers.

"I think the 'Yards seem to love it. You can see the excitement in their eyes," Blas said, with a hint of futility in his grin. "And some of the Vietnamese, too. But we may never know."

Another upcoming two-day operation with a small PF Platoon resulted in a need for another resupply scrounge mission to Camp Holloway. Major Nichols informed Wagner,

"You'll go to Holloway in the morning, and meet with a pilot of an 0-1 Birddog. He'll take you up to look over your operation area. Ever been in one?"

"No, sir," Wagner answered. The O-1 Birddogs were L-19 Cessnas, a light observation aircraft. It was an all metal, over-powered and over-flapped Cessna high wing, used for observation and forward air control (FAC). They had been in service for decades, excellent for a job requiring good visuals, and slow moving. The pilot sat in front of its narrow fuselage, another seat was directly behind. The cabin sat high, with Plexiglas acrylic windows all around. They were equipped with rockets mounted under the wings. Though they were only permitted to carry white phosphorus marking rockets, they switched them out with HE and flechette "beehive" rounds whenever possible. The pilots all wanted to play fighter pilot, of course.

Major Nichols put some paper reports in his desk drawer. "Do you get air sick?" the Major asked.

"No, sir."

"That's good. These pilots are a little crazy. If he's anything like the ones I've gone up with, he'll scare the hell out of you."

Wagner returned to the teamhouse after Nichols gave him the details and call signs he'd need, and called the team together to go over the operation. Sergeants Stewart, Blas, and Flanagan sat with Wagner in the team house, a topo map before them. "This is ground unscouted for a long time, apparently," he began. "Some infrared intel says movement in the area, unknown size, and we'll be going with a Vietnamese unit of PFs from Phu Yen." Immediately the three sergeants looked at each other as if to say, 'Oh, shit.' "I haven't heard how many," Wagner continued, "but expect it to be well understrength. I'm guessing twenty to thirty. Have you been there before?"

Blas answered, "We visited. Just the village. The village chief, he's Vietnamese. Fat guy."

"Fat as hell," Flanagan added.

"Fat? Really?" Wagner asked. "I haven't seen a fat

Vietnamese since I've been here. What's with that?"

"Not your average rice paddy Daddy," Sergeant Stewart said. "I remember this guy. Weird. I don't trust him. He's gotta be some crooked SOB, pretty rich for a remote village honcho. He may be a V.C. sympathizer."

"Why do you think?" asked Wagner.

"Sir, there's just something fishy. Can't say 'zackly what," Sergeant Stewart said with a troubled scowl, his thick black fingers interlocked together in a meditative clump in front of his chin. They called him "Ong Mop."

"Ong Mop? 'Means Mr. Fat," Wagner replied.

"I remember him. Grinning little gook bastard," Sergeant Blas added, scowling. Blas, the Guamanian, had a contempt for most Vietnamese. Stewart didn't seem to mind them much, but all three sergeants were clearly concerned with operations working with Vietnamese. More so considering their recent contacts with NVA in the vicinity. The possibility of the village chief of Phu Yen being V.C. didn't help.

"The Major has a ride for me in the morning. An L-19, I'm supposed to go up and look over the area of our march. I don't know if it will help, but I like the idea. What I don't like, is a pre-planned route assigned. That's dumb."

"I hear ya, sir," Stewart said, "But you can have that Birddog, sir. I'm stayin' away from those crazy suckahs. Too many stories."

"Amen," is all Blas said.

The morning found Wagner meeting the L-19 pilot, a Warrant Officer W-3 named Lucien Oliver. Lucien was a thin, lanky man of twenty five, with sandy blonde hair and a moustache to match. A white Snoopy scarf wrapped around his neck. He met Wagner with a big grin and an extended hand. "Hello, Lt. Wagner. I'm Lucien Oliver. What's your first name?"

"Darryl. And you and Jim Kalman have my job."

"What? "

"If my eyes were good enough, I'd be in your shoes. Or

preferably, an F-4 pilot," Wagner said.

Lucien laughed. As they walked out of the Holloway HQ building to the runway, he asked, "You know Kalman?"

"Just met him a bit ago. Said he'd give me a snake ride. Hope he will."

Oliver was explaining the procedure as they reached the Cessna, a fragile looking giant green winged insect with "Headhunters" painted in white. He turned, holding onto a wing strut. "Darryl, the L-19 is a two seater. You'll have the back. Unless you want the front," he said, grinning. "I know where we're going, but you can tell me exactly where you want to fly and look. Do you get airsick?"

"Not yet. Never have."

"Good, because we have three options for you. One, keep this with you." Oliver handed him a brass artillery casing. "Throw up in that. Two, you can pay a Vietnamese mama-san to clean it up. Ten bucks."

"And the third?"

"Don't throw up."

They boarded the light 0-1, Wagner thinking how frail and fragile it looked. Easy target. He was thinking "every bad guy out there could be throwing AK rounds at it, and we won't know." Wagner picked up the round fiberglass and acrylic-shield helmet and put it on, nestling into the back seat, clicking the seat belt. A couple of radio transmissions from Oliver and they were taxiing down the Holloway air strip. Heading almost due east, the morning sun was in their eyes. It was a clear day, save for a few flat-bottomed Cumulus clouds scattered above the Annamites ahead. Phu Yen was 37 kilometers east. They flew directly over Le Quon, Wagner straining to see his team house and artillery tower below. The Montagnard wash girls and Friday were in the yard, working.

"What have you got for firepower?" Wagner asked over his commo helmet.

"Willie Pete," he said. Four 2.75" rockets. "Hard to get HE and flechette. See this grease pencil mark on my windshield?"

Wagner looked over his shoulder and saw a 3/8" black round dot about a foot up from the dash.

"That's my sight!"

"No shit?"

"That's it."

Reaching Phu Yen, Wagner told Oliver he wanted to head north, over a blue line—a stream, on a map--below. They banked left, 1,000 feet up.

"Can you drop down some?" Wagner asked.

"Affirmative. Going to 600'. Tell me if you like it."

They banked slightly left and right, traversing the stream bed and bushy banks that could be hiding the enemy. Wagner strained to see every detail, but quickly realized it would take a very dumb bad guy to be caught in the open. A reddish dirt trail roughly paralleled a north-south stream bed, two meters west, just south of a small Montagnard hamlet. Two trucks sat in the road, with several men nearby. "Check that out," Wagner said. Oliver banked and dropped low, only 200' over the trucks. Both trucks were laden with logs. Several more lay on the ground near them. Their flight continued, dipping down low over stream beds, up and over rises, but the terrain was relatively flat until the broad stream valley met the first Annamite mountains six kilometers east. The O-1 wasn't stealthy, fast, or quiet. No NVA in his right mind would be unconcealed and moving. The flight didn't produce a thing, other than giving Wagner a feel for the terrain he would be covering in their coming operation. That was something, anything. Before the return trip home,

Oliver said, "Darryl, you feel like playing stunt plane?"

"Sure. Go for it." Oliver put the little plane into a power dive, then pulled up quickly. The Cessna responded nicely, its prop and engine working hard. Now climbing, nearly vertical, slower, slower, slower.. the engine was struggling, then only propeller noise. They stopped moving, stalled out. It banked over, now falling and spinning, faster and faster. Wagner couldn't imagine knowing which way to turn to come out of it. Not far from the ground, Oliver pulled out and gunned the engine again.

"Hammerhead stall," he said. He took it up again, repeated the whole move. Then he performed a roll-loop maneuver that sent Wagner's stomach floating, a roller coaster effect. After a while, Oliver gave up trying to make him sick and headed for the mountains again, a few kilometers east. As they approached, Oliver said, "Darryl, you see that opening in the trees to your one o'clock? Looks like an opening in the rocks. Maybe a cave?"

"I see it. Gray, black opening. Big tree to the right?"

"Yep. Let's light it up. Watch." He banked slightly, tilted the nose down, and cut the engine. Now the only noise was the whirring of the prop and a rushing of air. Lining up his grease pencil sight, Oliver hit the red firing button. *BLAMMM!* A rocket from under the left wing, feet from the cabin, left its pod and reached the cave hundreds of meters away in seconds. No roar of a rocket, or whoosh. Just a jolting blast, a trail of white smoke, and the rocket was there. That fast. Immediately, Oliver started the engine and pulled up. His grease pencil and ability proved itself, the rocket found its mark precisely. A white burning flash hit the cave, white smoke now wafting away.

"Absolutely incredible. You lucky sonofagun, I'm envious as hell."

Oliver banked and headed home. Wagner's thoughts briefly turned to his coed again. "Lord, here I am, on the other side of the world from her, hundreds of feet above the Earth, and I'm thinking of her again. This is crazy.. ***Thwap! Thwap!*** Oliver lurched the plane hard left, revved higher, and dove slightly, gaining speed before banking right again.

"What's that?" he asked.

"Look at my wing," Oliver pointed at the left wing. Next to the inner rocket tube were two 3/8" holes, four feet apart. "We're taking fire!"

There was no way to know where it came from, or Oliver would have toasted their buns. Instead, he repeated some evasive moves for a minute, then climbed higher for the ride home.

"We can help you with your weapons," Wagner told him through the helmet commo. "Next time we're at Holloway, if you coordinate with your supply guys, we'll take some rockets home with us. You can land directly behind our compound. We'll switch you out."

"Out-fucking-standing," Oliver replied. "Wilco on that one."

Just before twenty-hundred hours, a noisy commotion was heard outside. Anticipating the worst, the men grabbed their weapons and ran out the door. A bright glow came from fifty meters off the end of the team house, where an 81 mm mortar pit was located. The pit had a tarp roof covering a ring of sand bags. Four Vietnamese RF soldiers were running towards them, their silhouettes crossing in front of the glow. The team jacked their M-16s in unison, and realized in the dim light the men were RF soldiers running away from their burning mortar pit. That soothed one fear but kindled another. It couldn't be doused, lives weren't worth the risk. RF soldiers evacuated to bunkers at the far end of the compound.

The pit stored scores of 81mm mortar rounds, most still in their boxes, others out and exposed. Each round consisted of a 3"+ diameter cylinder of high explosive and shrapnel, cone shaped front and rear, followed by a tubular tail section incorporating several holes. Around the rear of the tube were fins. Between those fins and the rear cone were bags of propellant, which burns like gunpowder when an igniter inside the tail hits the firing pin at the base of a mortar tube. Bags are left on or stripped away depending on the range desired. Obviously, the bags shouldn't be near a source of ignition. But the Vietnamese were cooking supper in their mortar pit, and it didn't go well.

The situation was rapidly worsening, with more and more bags catching fire in what was now a brilliant display. No shells exploded yet, however, and then.....the skies opened up with the start of the rainy season. It hadn't rained a drop for weeks, if not months. And now there was a deluge, as strong as any summer monsoon in Virginia. With the tarp roof burned away, and propellant on the remaining exposed rounds that weren't boxed up burned off, the rain killed the fire as quickly as it started.

The next morning, it was cloudy and still raining. Four Vietnamese RF soldiers were lying prone and wet in their respective disciplinary tiger cages on the grounds by the front entrance to the compound.

The team arrived in Phu Yen at 0900 hours, thirty minutes early. Wagner, Blas, Stewart, and Flanagan had their Vietnamese interpreter Trong with them. Trong had been the go-to guy for Five-Seven's previous team leader, Robinson, as well as for other province MAT teams when they worked with Vietnamese units. Robinson seldom had the team visit villages other than those along the main highway, and most of those were Vietnamese. The bulk of the Montagnard villages and hamlets were well into the rural woods and valleys, and Trong didn't speak Montagnard. Trong, a Vietnamese sergeant by rank, made it plain he hadn't cared for Robinson. Now he showed new enthusiasm working with MAT 57, and he particularly liked working with Stewart and Blas. Ineptness and languor of some of the Vietnamese units embarrassed Trong, though he and Wagner well understood how years of fighting with no end in sight, along with corruption and low pay impacted the ARVNs' attitudes. There were excellent Vietnamese units, in spite of a commonly held opinion by American soldiers, but the PF platoon at Phu Yen wasn't one of them.

Trong was the best Vietnamese interpreter in the Province. Happy, intelligent, and funny, he also had the best command of the English language. Even Blas liked him. He was known for his knowledge of G.I. slang as well. Flanagan treated Trong regularly with a dose of penicillin from days off spent at Pleiku whore houses. He was single and could afford it, being paid well above the average Vietnamese soldier.

The team stood by their Jeep, 20 meters from east-west Highway 19 that the village lived beside. The Vietnamese village was quiet, save for a few women outside working their rice. They wore traditional bamboo conical coolie hats, held down with chin strings. Black silken pajama pants and white tops shone brightly in a warm morning sun. They appeared to be dancing around an eight foot circle, eyes pointed at the ground, while crushing and separating areas of rice with bare feet. If they looked at the Americans, it wasn't noticeable.

Walking through the village, Vietnamese villagers of women, children, and a few old men hardly looked at them. Typically, no younger men were present. None smiled. "How different from people in Pleiku," Wagner thought. "not a good sign." A few sway-backed pigs and a water buffalo slowly shuffled around the grass-roofed hootches, redolent of a peaceful scene out of *National Geographic*. Chickens clucked and a Rooster crowed nearby, pecking at water buffalo pies. Sergeant Stewart said, "You notice, sir, the difference? This place is no reconsolidation. Banana trees growin' up between the houses, not much shit on the ground, hootches aren't all front-and-center. Pretty ville. They ain't makin' these Vietnamese reconsolidate."

"And I don't hear no funeral gongs," Flanagan added.

"There's your Awwnng Mop," Sergeant Blas said, sneering at a large round Vietnamese man stepping out of the adjacent hootch. He was round, even his face was round, strangely out of place in this land of small thin Vietnamese.

"*Chao ong,*" Wagner said, approaching the village chief. "*Manh goi, khong?*" Trong was beside him, waiting to translate if necessary.

"*Da Manh, Cam on ong,*" he said, with an expressive grin. "I speak Tee-Tee English," he said slowly. "How-are-you, Trung-uy?"

"*Vang, toi tot*, sir. *Toi* Trung-uy Wagner. Beautiful

village you have."

Mr. Fat called to someone walking past the adjacent hootch, who told him that Lieutenant Duc was in the PF perimeter.

Walking through the village, the team entered a barbed wire perimeter surrounding the PF platoon, bordering the west end of the village. Talking and smoking under a grass-roofed rectangular table twenty meters away were a few Vietnamese PF soldiers in U.S. jungle fatigues and combat boots. A minute later Thieu-uy 'Second Lieutenant' Le Duc walked out of a command bunker, its walls and roof made of green sand bags. "*Thieu-uy Le Duc o' day, khong?*" Wagner asked.

"*Da phai*, I am Thieu-uy Duc," he said, extending his hand.

"*Chao, Thieu-uy*," Wagner said.

In decent English, Le Duc smiled and asked if he would like to have a Tiger La Rue beer.

"Thanks, Duc, but I thought we were going on a *hainh quan* (operation)."

"Yah. We go. When you want?"

"Now would be good, Duc. I was told we'd be leaving when we got here."

"You wait. Have lunch. We go, maybe three hour."

As an adviser, Wagner couldn't command, only coax, whatever good that did. He turned, seeing disgust in his sergeants' faces. They were not surprised. By early afternoon it was hot and oppressively humid. The air was heavy, permeated with pungent cooking smells of *nuoc maam*, fermented fish oil, hanging in the still air. Another memorable smell of Vietnam. Afternoon came, and still no sign of operational readiness. Walking the PF's defensive perimeter next to the village, they noted deficiencies in firing positions and fields of fire, ammo and debris laying around, not so different from several other PF perimeters they had known. PF soldiers were taking afternoon naps. Flanagan couldn't stop bitching, and Blas simply muttered scornful comments about "the sorry-assed Vietnamese", fetching irritated glances from Trong. Walking back to the peaceful village, a small Vietnamese sergeant caught up to them to inform them they would go on their operation "*Ngai mai*" next day. It was a wasted day, and more time for an enemy to plan an ambush. Settling in, the team was shown an area to stay for the night inside the PF barbed wire perimeter. There were some old foxhole positions next to where they could erect poncho tents with cluttered bamboo, but no bunkers.

It was 0800 hours the next morning when the small PF platoon finally moved out, crossing Highway 19 that ran through the village. Wagner had some serious trepidations with this trip. Too many people knew they were going on this *hainh quan.* Leaving in the middle of daylight, across a main highway, from a village that may well be enemy sympathizers, it was all wrong. To top it off, their unit was a small contingent of unprofessional PF Vietnamese, poorly led and trained. On the plus side, they hadn't planned to go more than a few klicks north of Highway 19. It was fairly open and level ground, difficult to be ambushed, but easy to be spotted and followed. Wagner called in preplanned artillery targets along the approximate planned route. It was a cloudy day, wet and muddy from an overnight rain. They travelled in a single file, not particularly fast, to Flanagan's liking. Stewart and Blas shared Wagner's concerns, their eyes showed it. The two professional soldiers watched every bush, every tree, as three hundred meters north of the highway the terrain changed from short grassy open land to thicker vegetation and trees, 200 meters above a wide stream. Farmer-made foot-high radiused dams every 50 meters widened the stream below to form consecutive rice paddies, laced with rice stalks. Noise discipline improved, but not enough. A Vietnamese PF soldier walked point, followed by ten more soldiers. Following them was the Vietnamese lieutenant, Le Duc, carrying an M-16 and one bandolier of seven magazines. An RTO followed behind him, carrying the PRC-25 radio. Nothing else. Too heavy. Not even a side arm. Behind the RTO, another soldier carried food, canteens, and several M-33 frag grenades and four smoke grenades. No rifle or ammunition. Too heavy. Besides some food and water for himself, he carried food and ammo for Lt. Duc and the RTO. Behind him walked Wagner, Trong, and another PF soldier, then Blas with his M-79 grenade launcher. Another PF followed, then Stewart and Flanagan. The rest of the PFs followed behind. In all, there were twenty five men, twenty of them from the PF platoon. Not a lot of firepower.

A thousand meters into the march, they crossed a well-worn dirt road, three meters wide, with deep ruts. Duc angled north-northwest along the road, unconcerned of ambush potential. Ahead came a low rumble of a diesel engine idling, and occasional voices. Then chain saws. Duc seemed unconcerned. Another three hundred meters into some old-growth tropical trees brought them to the two logging trucks Wagner had seen from the air. A crew of Vietnamese civilian loggers were clear-cutting the trees, leaving a broad swath for 300 more meters all the way to a small isolated Montagnard hamlet of a dozen grass roofed hootches. The villagers were outside, old men and young women, yelling at the logging crew. The women had black tribal sarong skirts with red and gold trim, and most had babies clinging to their breasts or papoose-style on their backs. The old men, graying and toothless, wore only loin cloths. All had bare feet. "What's happening, Trong?" Sergeant Stewart asked, already guessing the answer.

"These lumber mans, you know, they cut. Trees not theirs. This belong to village. But they cut. *Nguoi Bahnaar*, they bullshit. Very mad.

The chainsaws stopped when they saw the soldiers, some looked frightened, others scowled. Wagner asked Duc what he knew about it. Flanagan yelled, "It's none of your business, Lieutenant, stay out of it." Wagner turned and cast a disgusted frown, quickly ignoring him.

Duc said, "Tree men not supposed to be here. Steal. Not from here... Pleiku."

Wagner knew what he wanted to do, but this was a new one. What authority did he have? He could suggest, coax, coerce, but ultimately it was in Duc's hands.

"Duc, this happen before?" Wagner asked.

"Yah. Many time."

"Do you want to get them out of here?"

"Yah. You wan'?

Trong quietly told Wagner that the lieutenant could be in trouble for intervening in the Vietnamese economy. Trong had been through this before. Wagner didn't care. "Yah. I want. If problem, my fault," he told Duc.

"I'm tellin' ya, Lieutenant, stay out of it," Flanagan said again. Wagner saw Stewart grab Flanagan's arm, telling him something. Sergeant Blas' scowl had turned to a grin. If it was up to Blas, he might have emptied a magazine on the logging crew.

Though Duc undoubtedly knew he didn't report to Americans, he wanted to cooperate, afraid to 'lose face' in front of his men. He turned to the loggers and barked orders that left no question what he was going to do if they didn't leave. Turning to his men, Duc shouted something in Vietnamese, and the soldiers leveled their weapons toward the men and their trucks. Several safeties clicked off. Abandoning their logs on the ground, they quickly boarded both trucks and drove out without a word.

Wagner returned the driver's scowl, and turning to Le Duc said, "Thanks, Thieu-uy, I will take blame. My fault. Okay?"

Duc stood proud and serious, the man in charge. "No problem!" he said.

Nothing of consequence happened during the slow march northeast of the logging site. Approaching 1800 hours, though plenty of daylight left, Duc picked a high lens of open ground for a night position. It wasn't a bad spot, surrounding bush allowed for decent cover for night listening posts. Duc set four LPs out of two men each, better than Wagner expected. Whether they would stay awake was a guess. He discussed with the team the option of checking on them, but it was decided the chance of being shot by the PFs mistaking them for enemy wasn't worth it. The PFs didn't dig in, they merely pitched poncho tents and went to sleep. No Claymores, no trip wires. Suggestions to Duc did no good. Nothing new. The team would rotate with two awake, only one awake for the first hour, with two hour overlapping shifts. They didn't share food with the Vietnamese as they did the Montagnards, the Vietnamese preferred their traditional rice and vegetable meals.

A small foldable P-38 can opener, supplied in monthly-issued SP packs of C-rations, cigarettes, toilet paper, insect repellent, etc. served to open C-ration cans. It also poked holes around an empty can to allow air in for makeshift stoves. C-4 plastic explosive fiercely burned inside, cooking food extremely fast with no smoke. Mostly, food was prepared from Long Range Reconnaissance Patrol (LRRP) rations, a major improvement over C's, but often mixed together. LRRP rations were dehydrated meal packages, a fraction of the weight, while much more palatable. Included was a small package of scorching hot dehydrated red peppers. The men were talking about the loggers' sudden departure, which Trong thought hilarious. Trong had no prejudice for the Montagnards, he felt the same way the Americans did regarding their reconsolidations. "I can't imagine the saws these guys go through, every frigging tree in the country must have shrapnel in it," Wagner said, well experienced in logging himself.

"They do," added Flanagan, always knowing everything about all. "Plays hell with 'em. Must go through ten chains a day."

"I was thinking more of the saw mills. Those big circular blades, carbide tips. Not cheap. Shrapnel is hardened steel, even a small chip would ruin a blade. I remember seeing a few hunting bullets in boards at the saw mill. Just lead and copper, that probably wasn't bad, just screwed up the board. Shrapnel's something else. Hardened steel, that's different. Occasionally a saw will hit an old round chain saw file someone stuck in a tree decades before. Very expensive."

Having more time to carefully pick coordinates for preplanned artillery fires was a plus, and Wagner sent them in. Carrying one folding entrenching tool among them, the team dug shallow foxhole trenches before a welcome early sleep. Wagner told Flanagan he would have the first watch. Less likelihood of falling asleep. It began raining again, and the day's heat and humidity turned into a cold, wet night. It was a three-quarter moon, affording scant light through the rain clouds above, a plus in Wagner's mind. He had come to loathe the moonlit nights, preferring to keep the darkness to their advantage, for they, for the most part, were the ambushers. Tonight was the exception.

At 0200, Sergeant Blas woke Wagner with a whisper. "Two AM, Sir, your guard. All quiet so far."

"Thanks, Sarge. Sleep well." As Blas quietly arranged his poncho liner under the poncho tent, Wagner shook the cobwebs from his mind and arranged the map, radio, and compass. He and Blas were at the easterly side of the small perimeter, surrounded by vegetation and thirty foot trees. It had stopped raining, but the trees dripped in a light breeze that sent chills down his spine. He sat crouched, knees up, arms holding them, M-16 propped vertically against his right leg. Quietly, he made a commo check with Blackhawk artillery. "Got you Lima-Chuck (loud and clear), out," he said under the poncho liner, double-pressing the squelch bar on the handset. Light noises from gust-driven leaves periodically heightened his senses, and twice he heard something more, probably a reptile or small animal. Several small beetles flew across with a low raspy buzz, others crawled under and over his boots. One huge *Coleoptera* with giant pincers slowly made its way across an 8" rotten log before him, barely discernible in the faint clouded moonlight, glistening like the wet log and bits of wet twigs and leaves below it. Wagner hoped it wasn't poisonous or painful. But it concerned him nowhere nearly as much as even the smallest spiders. Man, did he hate spiders. Mosquitos, tolerable until now, found them, communicated, probed them, and now were in a full *Dipterian wave* assault. With wet, muddy hands, he quietly slapped at them, transferring bits of mud and leaves from his hands to his face and neck. A cold shiver traveled from his traps to the base of his spine. He shrouded the poncho liner close around his face, leaving his nose and eyes exposed. His thoughts turned to his coed again. "It's daytime there now. Is she with her little boy? Maybe she's working? What is today there, I think it's Saturday. Is she with her husband, too? Maybe out on the lake. Maybe at her parent's farm. I wonder what the weather's like there right now. Is her hair the same? My God, she's so incredibly beau.... *Snapswwiisshh.* Something moved, he knew it moved. "I heard a snap," he thought. "Only ten meters ahead. Animal? Wagner lightly jostled Blas, who woke with a start.

"Huh?" he quietly said. Blas was too professional to make loud noise, even from a dead sleep.

Wagner bent over, inches from his ear. "I think something's out there, Sarge."

Another light swish of leafy branches had them both at peak alert. As Wagner reached for the radio handset, Blas definitely saw something move. Always a chance of a PF taking a leak, or coming in from an LP. Can't shoot. In another situation, he may have opted to wait, let the LPs and counterpart react, or expect a trip wire to set off a Claymore or incendiary grenade. But there weren't any employed.

Wagner called Fire Support Base Blackhawk. He was inside the range of Blackhawk's biggest guns. Located just east of Mang Yang Pass near Anh Khe, they had several artillery pieces, including big, highly accurate 8" guns and long range 175 MM cannons. The 8" guns fired huge shells up to 16.8 kilometers, or 10 miles away. The 175s fired 174 lb. shells 32 kilometers, or 19 miles, though at the extremities of their range they were inaccurate due to barrel whip of long tubes. They were just over 16 miles from their position. The best thing about Blackhawk, they usually sent rounds out within five minutes, a fifth of the time it took Artillery Hill. He made a last-minute decision to skip his preplanned fires, opting instead for a better-targeted call outside their tiny perimeter. In a hushed voice, Wagner called, "Sandy Panther Two Five, Sandy Panther Two Five, this is Murky Cinder Five Seven, Murky Cinder Five

Seven, *Fire Mission*, over."

Immediately, Blackhawk responded in a calm voice, "Roger, Murky Cinder Five Seven, this is Sandy Panther Two Five, go."

"Sandy Panther, Murky Cinder Five Seven, I need one round of Whisky Papa on coordinates Alpha Romeo one seven six, five seven niner. Range – four hundred meters, azimuth, fifteen hundred mils. Danger close. Will adjust. Give me shot and splash, over." Four hundred meters from their NDP to the target required a 'Danger close' for 175s, telling the artillerymen to check their fires to avoid friendly casualties. A white phosphorus round was safer, used to spot the impact for adjustment.

"Roger, understand Whiskey Papa, Alpha Romeo one seven six, five seven niner. Range, four hundred, azimuth fifteen hundred. Danger close. Wait one."

While waiting, Blas woke Trong, and crept to Duc's position to wake him. Five long minutes later, Wagner heard "*Shot out*" on his PRC 25, turned to a barely audible volume. Traveling at almost 1300 miles per hour, over a minute later the voice said "*Splash, over*," just as the 147 lb. white phosphorus projectile hit, lighting the sky with a bright white light. An immediate **CCRRUUMPP!**, then a crackling, rustling sound of the round breaking the sound barrier, and finally a muted rumbling *BOOOMMM* of the 175 MM cannon, sixteen miles away. The impact was to the left and closer then he liked for subsequent HE rounds, due to that 'barrel whip' and casualty radius. But 175s were the only guns that would reach.

Wagner still didn't know if an enemy was out there. The PFs were all awake and alert now. Duc had called his LPs to fall back to the perimeter, a scant twenty meters out. Three pairs of PFs on the four listening posts came in, one pair was still out on the eastern side, where Blas and Wagner found movement. Flanagan and Stewart had joined the group. Wagner called Blackhawk again. "Sandy Panther, Murky Cinder Five Seven, over."

"Roger, Murky Cinder, go." The net was clear, no radio

traffic at this hour.

"Sandy Panther, One round HE Quick, add one hundred, right 100, give me... .

Flanagan whisper-yelled at Wagner, "What the fuck are you doing, Lieutenant, you're gonna drop it right on top of us! Tell em' to put it farther away!".

Flanagan didn't know that the commands to add, drop, left, or right meant from the forward observer's location, not from the fire base. Because Blackhawk was on their side of the target, he intuitively thought 'add' meant adding to the projectile distance, putting the round closer to them. The firebase knows the location with respect to the forward observer, while the azimuth and range are taken into consideration with their equipment at the base. In the interest of safety, Wagner was telling Blackhawk to *add* one hundred, meaning 100 meters *farther* from their position, i.e., *closer* to the guns. Flanagan was furious, and out of control. Deciding that now wasn't the time to argue with his medic sergeant, he complied, continuing, "One round HE Quick, put it 100 *farther from me,* right 100. Give me shot and splash, wait one." He told Trong to let Duc know there would be a high explosive round coming to the east, get everybody down. Trong ran in a crouch to tell Duc and returned. Wagner continued with Blackhawk to fire. In three minutes, he heard *"Shot out."* Forty seconds in flight and the huge round landed safely ahead, on a perfect azimuth from their position, with an enormous **CRRUUUNCHH!**, followed again by a crackling and rustling sound of the round's path. Five seconds later, small arms fire opens up at the outside LP to the southeast. The perimeter opens up with M-60s and M-16s on full auto in a crescendo. White-blue muzzle flashes interrupt the black jungle walls to the east and south outside the perimeter. Wagner calls for more artillery. Sergeant Blas is firing his M-79 nearly vertically, landing rounds into the trees past the wood line. Firing directly may not allow the rounds to complete their necessary revolutions to arm the grenades before they hit the trees, rendering them useless. Duc, twenty meters away, is yelling at his men. A PF 60mm mortar tube, hand positioned without a bipod, is firing from inside their perimeter with muffled thumps, using only one propellant bag for close range. Lt. Duc is yelling at his mortar men to send out an illumination round. The mortar sends a bursting bright flare above, lazily swinging to and fro from its small parachute, trailing an eerie smoke in the bright incendiary light as it slowly falls to earth. In the light of the flare, two PF soldiers are screaming *"Dung ban! Dung ban!—*"Don't shoot," running full bore, Vietnamese-style: Flat-footed, knees pumping up and down, racing toward the perimeter. The LPs make it back, having been undetected by enemy soldiers surrounding them. The noise continues for over three minutes before more terrifying Blackhawk rounds land, walked in closer by Wagner. Each round sends a concussive wave through their heads and bodies, feeling the explosions through chests as much as ears. The last rounds are close enough to imperceptibly coincide sound with flashes. He doesn't dare bring them closer, with their 95 meter casualty radius. 105s or 155s would have been much more welcome, if within range.

Five Vietnamese privates 'Binh-sis' now lay close to the Americans, terrified by the massive artillery rounds. None of them had experienced the big guns, not up close and personal. Wagner, prone and hugging the earth in his small trench, is protected above the ground only by a rotting log, which offers little if any protection. A few intermittent shots from the black walls of jungle rekindle, followed by short volleys from the PFs. Then nothing, for over ten minutes. Wagner calls Blackhawk again, giving a quick sitrep and asking for illumination rounds. Thirty minutes later, with no more activity other than an occasional illumination round, he again finds himself thinking of her again. Laying here in the mud, amongst beetles, mosquitos and centipedes, and there's her face, eyes and dimples inviting, sitting by the lake.. *THWOP-CRACK!* A Vietnamese PF, not two meters away, blew backward several feet, an AK round hitting him dead center. The thirty caliber bullet had hit bone mass, sending his slight body flying backward, killing him instantly. *Inches and seconds. All the difference.* The perimeter opens up again, as Wagner calls Blackhawk and melts into the mud as low as every muscle and bone permits. Another minute finds silence. Wagner thought of Kalman and his Cobra. A call to Holloway brought a negative from Kalman's highers, they had a policy of not supporting Vietnamese units from edicts to 'Vietnamize the war'. Only Vietnamese pilots and helicopters could be called. Many calls from Vietnamese units, however, for non-emergency situations or conveniences created a 'Peter and the Wolf' situation, tying up choppers for ridiculous uses. Advisory efforts to change it did little good. Wagner called for several more rounds of HE and illumination, imagining the cost of each round to American taxpayers. "Good for them. Pay for it, you protesting bastards." He wanted to move out, terrified of an NVA assault on their tiny contingent, but Duc wanted to stay put.

No additional action occurred, and first light still saw no movement in the perimeter. Blackhawk waited eagerly to hear results, but Wagner and his team had no more intention of sweeping the area than Duc did. Wagner, anxiously waiting for Duc to get his men moving, asked for his plans. Duc and his platoon were clearly frightened and exhausted, wanting only to be out of there and home. They were not accustomed to battles outside of their village perimeter, with little support available. Typically, in their village perimeter they did not send out listening posts or observations posts at night, and did not patrol unless required to. Artillery or air support would be available only from Vietnamese ARVNs in late 1970, and their FSBs couldn't reach them. Though the team would love to report an enemy body count, it simply wasn't practical or worth it, even if they weren't low on ammunition. Friendly losses were limited to three PFs wounded from small arms fire, none critically, and the one KIA PF lying next to Wagner. It was incredibly lucky it wasn't worse. Wagner spent several minutes successfully convincing Duc not to take the easy trail back, where the enemy would likely be waiting. It meant tougher hiking, a longer route, but essential.

The operation was over by 1600 hours, the rain had come and gone, and they crossed Highway 19 to the village of Phu Yen. Ong Mop was still grinning from his hootch. "Ugly fat bastard," Blas growled as they walked by him.

There was no rice wine party, no village chief dinner to attend, and the team had no problem with that. Exhausted, they headed west on QL 19 in their Jeep, Trong laughing and exchanging insults with Stewart and Flanagan. Wagner was still incensed with Flanagan, his attitude and artillery comments. It wasn't the time to discuss it until after a meal and good night's sleep calmed his mood.

The team slept for ten hours. Done with breakfast, morning found Wagner, Stewart, and Flanagan alone in the team house. Wagner asked Stewart if he could have 'a few minutes alone'. Stewart knew what was coming, long overdue. Wagner asked Flanagan, "Sergeant Flanagan, can I have a word with you?" Flanagan stared at him with a surprised scowl. "We've got some problems. I can handle complaints, suggestions, whatever, as long as they're productive. But you clearly have a problem with my command." Unbeknownst to Wagner, Major Nichols was just outside the door, lighting a cigar before entering the team house for breakfast. He sat down on the porch bench outside and listened.

"You complain when we have operations to go on, you seem to think it's not in your job description. You don't like getting involved with what you see as Vietnamese decisions. I understand that. But if it's my decision, and you don't agree, talk to me later. Don't you *ever* even *think* of chastising me again as you've been doing, *do you understand me?*" Wagner was raising his voice now, clearly angry. It was uneasy, chastising a career senior NCO a dozen years older with much more time in service, but it wasn't the first time. A year earlier, as a new second lieutenant in a captain's position at Aberdeen Proving Ground, he found it necessary to reprimand senior sergeants several times before a new, professional first sergeant joined the company. That first sergeant, the finest he had known, quickly had the problem sergeants under him very much in line. "That artillery call.... you interfered. The last thing I needed when our shit was weak."

"But you.."

"Now I'm going to give you an artillery class. Right here, right now. And you're going to listen. Understand?"

Flanagan paused, his face red and contorted with anger. But he said nothing, just stared.

Wagner had a sheet of paper. On the right side, he drew on it a circle with a short line, indicating an artillery piece. On the left, a four inch circle. Then a small circle inside the right edge of it. Then an ellipse a few inches to the right of the large circle. "This is the artillery. This is our perimeter. This small circle, that's us. This ellipse, that's the bad guys. When I give the arty a target, I give them a coordinate. Here," he said, drawing an X to the right of the ellipse. "I give them the coordinate, than a distance, or 'range'. Then an azimuth, the direction from us to the target. Now when the arty gets all this, it's plotted out with a circular plotting board, computed out. They know their position, they know ours, they know the distance and direction from us to the target. When I adjust, they know 'add' to me means closer to them. Conversely, 'drop' to me means farther from them. 'Right' or 'Left' to me means the opposite to them. They know that. If the target's on the other side, over here," Wagner drew another X on the left edge... "then they know left is left, right is right, add is add, drop is drop to both of us. Do you understand?"

Flanagan just snorted, staring at the page.

"There is no 'bring it in closer to me'. But if you're in a situation that you need to call, and it's confusing, by all means tell 'em what's intuitive to you. Just don't correct me when I'm calling. Understand?"

"Just keeping us alive, Lieutenant," is all he could say. With a stern look, Wagner walked away. Major Nichols got up from his outside chair and entered for breakfast, as Flanagan wondered if he'd heard the conversation. Through thin team house walls, Blas and Stewart heard the entire discussion, chuckling to themselves.

Doug Hanson was sitting at his desk in Pleiku headquarters when he heard several vehicles and subsequent Vietnamese banter outside. He looked out to see several Vietnamese white-helmeted 'White Mice' MPs exiting their Jeeps, and an armored V-100 by the front curb. Behind the V-100 was a French Citroen. The older 'Cadillac of the French', it looked like a skinny 1949 Hudson, but uglier, painted a faded sky blue. Hanson got up for a better view, then walked across the laterite-cement floor toward the HQ entrance. Without warning, the door opened and two Vietnamese White Mice quickly entered, scanning the room with weapons ready. Just as quickly, they popped back outside the door at attention, weapons at a 'present arms' positon. Hanson worried for a moment if a daylight attack was pending, but seconds later a Vietnamese officer dressed in starched Army green fatigues came through the door. He looked sternly, almost reproachful at the First Lieutenant, as if offended being met by this low ranking officer. Recognizing the Vietnamese insignias, Hanson knew this was a two star, major general. Two Vietnamese aides, Colonels, stood behind him. Cocking his head slightly, he raised a cigarette to his mouth, holding it between three fingers and his thumb. His rather wide face and relatively rugged facial features added to an air of pompousness on a somewhat stocky frame, for a Vietnamese. Many days in the sun generated a deep brown tan on his arms below rolled up sleeves, matching his face. Looking down his nose with his head tilted back, he took a long, satisfying drag on an American cigarette.

Hanson was about to introduce himself when Colonel Bern stepped into the front room.

"Ah, General Ngo, I am pleased you are here."

"Ah, I am much pleased to see you, Colonel Bern," he replied, never losing his huge smile, smoke emanating between yellow teeth.

"I hope your trip was uneventful, General?" General Ngô was a Major General in the Army of the Republic of

Vietnam. A Catholic from Qui Nhơn and the son of a government official, he was educated at a French Catholic boys' school in Huế. More politician than soldier, he held few combat commands and had few connections with the South Vietnamese politically elite, yet attained the rank of a 2-star Major General. Assigning rank to educated elite and inexperienced was nothing new in South Vietnam, a major reason for the countless histories of poor leadership. But somehow Ngo was exceptionally successful. He lived in a beautiful French maison on the coast of Qui Nhon, north of his Nha Trang headquarters.

"Oh, yes, very good, thank you," He said, slowly, carefully choosing his English words. I am very pleased you are here now in Pleiku Province. We have much work to do. And is Colonel Robichaud here?"

"Yes, General, he is, you are early, we will let him know," gesturing to MSG Husky, who had just come in. Husky left to get the Colonel.

"Ah, and Mr. Friedman?"

"Certainly. He was expecting you." Colonel Bern said, cordially. "General, this is Lieutenant Hanson, our S-1 Personnel officer. Lieutenant, this is Major General Ngo."

The General shook his hand out of protocol and quickly turned away, not bothering to respond to Hanson's polite greeting.

"Come in to my office, won't you?" asked Bern. "That will be all, Lieutenant," he said, dismissing Hanson. The taciturn General's aides waited outside, looking all the part of a king's entourage in a fairy tale.

After some small talk with the Colonel, the General appeared impatient, ready to get down to business. "How is the pacification of the province coming, Colonel Bern? General Welling tells me we have made much progress."

"Yes, General, I believe we have. The action reports show a thirty percent increase in the numbers of pacified villages in our sector in the past three months. We now have advisory teams active in all districts of the Province. The Regional Force companies are at eighty four percent strength and the Popular Force Platoons are up from fifty four percent to seventy four percent as of the end of the month."

General Ngo nodded approvingly, but appeared impatient. With a smile and a twinkle of his eyes, he asked, "And, Colonel Bern, our reconsolidation efforts?" Before Bern could answer, Colonel Robichaud and the Civilian Friedman walked in. Ngo immediately resumed a pretentious air as the men exchanged pleasantries. The conversation continued until Colonel Bern was called to depart, with Robichaud, Friedman, and the General hashing over the details. General Ngo gave Colonel Bern a knowing smile, wishing him a safe trip. They planned to meet again in the morning.

Doug Hanson was at his desk in the adjoining office next to Colonel Bern's. A rocket attack from 1968 left a crack in the cement block-and-plaster wall, allowing only occasional audible words to pass through. There was talk of reconsolidation and body counts, and numbers of Americans killed. He heard Cambodia mentioned several times, as well as Bern's name, but it was garbled. The U.S. had several incursions into Cambodia and Laos during the past year, and small Special Operations Groups, 'SOG' units were still operating there.

The next morning, the White Mice were back, and Ngo and Bern were just beginning their meeting. It was the beginning of the rainy season on the west side of the Annamite mountain chain, ending the dry, windy season of red dust blowing everywhere on the many windy days, a constant annoyance to men and equipment. It turned hot, but not often oppressingly so, abetted by the wind that funneled down the Pleiku valley, making it more tolerable.

The team took a break for two days, interspersed with another scrounge mission and a trip for Flanagan to the brothels of Pleiku.

Outside by the shower tower the Montagnard handyman Friday was chasing something in the single small banana tree that grew in the dirty compound. The tree was sorry looking, for the Montagnard wash girls would strip off pieces of big leaves to roll as strong, foul cigars. Wagner always kiddingly gave them hell for smoking, but it was a Montagnard custom, more so among women. Scars of past shrapnel wounds did nothing to improve the banana tree's condition. Friday, a 50-ish Montagnard, front teeth gone, old Army fatigues almost completely reddish-brown from unwashed years of Pleiku dirt, carried a permanent smile. He was a few grains short of a full cup of rice, but did his job and was liked by all. He kept the shower tanks full, the kerosene water heater running, shoes shined, Jeeps arguably maintained, tires repaired, and anything else the wash girls and Vietnamese cook didn't do. Even after years of working with Americans, he spoke almost no English, but did well with Pigeon English, and was a part of the team community.

1Lt. Darryl Wagner stepped out of the wooden team house to hit the latrine. "Hi Friday, what you do?"

Friday turned with a huge toothless grin, gums protruding below his upper lip, and said, "Innh, ooh–ka Klah!" and laughed his loud staccato laugh. He was holding a 6" chartreuse grasshopper by the tips of its wings, showing it to Wagner. Grasshoppers 'back in the world' were a third this size.

"What you do?" asked Wagner again, grinning broadly.

"Numbah one chop-chop," Friday answered.

"Aaaagh! You gonna *eat* that thing?" Friday looked at Wagner in bewilderment, as if to say, "What are you, nuts, of course!" He began to play with the huge orthoptera, still holding the wings out and making airplane noises while he bombed and strafed the ground below. Then he wrapped it in a piece of paper, lit it, and singed the poor bug just enough to kill and crisp it. Then he ate it in four bites, never losing the grin. Friday always grinned.

Wagner and his friend Gordon had decided to take the opportunity to leave their respective compounds to meet at the Pleiku Air Force Base on the northeast end of Pleiku. It had a PX Post Exchange that sold a variety of iconic watches, cameras, electronic gear, stereos, radios, as well as various everyday wants and needs. Wagner especially needed a small flashlight to replace the small rechargeable light he bought in a Tan Son Nhut PX for the sole purpose of reading a map at night when in the field. He figured its compactness and light weight would be perfect for its essential purpose. Never having owned a rechargeable light before, he discovered its short battery life quickly died on the last operation. "Why in hell can't this damn Army supply you with something as basic as a map light?" he grumbled. It's one of those things they failed to teach in all the training, yet rudimentary. One of those simple things that can make the difference between success and failure, life and death. They give you weapons, radios, canteens, ammunition, food, maps, iodine pills--but no flashlight. Maybe in a regular Infantry unit? He didn't know. But it was an embarrassment at best, a disaster at worst, in a command position in the middle of the jungle at night, unprepared.

Gordon Bailey and Darryl Wagner pulled into the big Air Force Base at 1100 hours. They were in awe of the arsenal of aircraft. There were A-1E Skyraider propellered bombers, old C-47s, C-123s, Caribous, and C-130 Hercules. In the bright daylight, their sun-faded jungle fatigues showed the stained red Pleiku dirt. Even after the wash girls' coarse brush and harsh soap washings, the reddish stain endured. This, and the fact they carried their M-16 rifles with no secure place to leave them, differentiated them from the Air Force personnel manning the base. Their advisory rank insignias confused airmen, as advisers did not wear U.S. rank on their collars to avoid being a prime target as an American. Instead, a Vietnamese subdued black flower emblem was sewn next to their buttoned shirt opening on the chest, unfamiliar to most U.S. personnel. A single black subdued lieutenant bar pinned to their bush hats was the only indication of rank.

The PX brought an element of familiarity to Vietnam, and the bargains afforded by the Post Exchange were a welcome opportunity. Wagner found two 35 mm Konicas in a 'repaired electronics sale' in progress, one for himself, and one to send home to his Dad. Among other items, he found the small flashlight he needed, his main objective.

A commotion at the end of the electronics counter caught his attention. A black Army PFC private was yelling at a beautiful petite Vietnamese salesgirl. The girl was trying to tell him something, shaking her head slightly. The Private was swearing loudly, demanding something. Wagner walked toward the soldier and asked "Excuse me, what's the problem?"

The soldier turned his head and told Wagner "*to stay the fuck out of it*" and continued swearing at the girl. Wagner could ignore the insubordination, but when he tried to contain the issue and give him the benefit of the doubt, the Private grew wilder. Looking at his name tag, Wagner said, "Can you tell me what the problem is, Private Voss. Maybe I can help." He didn't answer the question, even as Wagner tried to mollify the screaming soldier. His insubordination had gone way past military limits, and finally Wagner said, "Come with me Private, you and I are going to the Provost Martial." At that, the Private ran out of the PX, a large portable 'Boom Box' radio tucked under his arm. Wagner ran after him, just as an MP drove his Jeep in front of the store. Seeing the commotion, the MP stopped abruptly. Wagner pointed to the private running across the adjacent field and told the Spec 5 MP, "Stop that man."

The MP said, "Let's go, sir." Wagner jumped in and the two headed across the large open grounds outside the PX. The driver carved a turn ahead of the running soldier, slammed on the brakes, and jumped out with a 12 gauge shotgun in the private's face, yelling "STOP"! The private complied.

Wagner briefly explained the situation to the MP, who was preparing his handcuffs, when another soldier reached the scene. He had witnessed the episode outside the PX and ran after the Jeep. He was a Major, also black. By now, there was an audience back at the PX.

"Lieutenant, you are way out of line here," he said in a loud voice.

"What? Sir, we have a situation here. You don't know….."

"Lieutenant," interrupted the Major, with a slight head nod to the private, "You have to understand there are a lot of racial problems, we've got to be cognizant of the way things are today, you are not here to make them worse, we…" They all turned their heads to watch the Private run off across the field.

"Sir, we…."

"What unit are you with, Lieutenant? Are you in regulation uniform?"

"What? Yes, I'm in MACV, I'm here…"

Again, the Major loudly interrupted, "I don't like what's going on here, you have to understand the problems in our present society. Lieutenant, you're aggravating the situation, *do you understand me?*" Racial tensions since the Martin Luther King murder in early 1968 were a constant tinder box in many rear areas, but Wagner had seen none of it in Vietnam.

The MP watched without saying a word, incredulous. Wagner knew he couldn't argue, but tilting his head to read the Major's name tag and shoulder patch, he made it obvious he was taking a mental note. His patch said RIGOR. The patch was MACV. Obviously the Major had recognized Wagner's proper Advisory jungle fatigue uniform, and it was just as obvious it was all part of a distraction show, allowing the private to escape.

"Yes, sir. I'll keep that in mind," said Wagner, glaring with a hint of 'this isn't over'. "Just so we're clear, sir, this is nothing about race." Without saluting the Major, he turned to the MP and said, "Thanks Specialist. Could you come with me back to the PX," and he and the MP walked away to hop into the Jeep. Accompanied by the MP, Wagner re-entered the PX to speak with the Vietnamese salesgirl. *"Chao Co, tenh toi Trung-Uy Wagner. Biet noi tieng My khong?"*

"Da Phai, I speak English." Her voice was typically soft and sweet. She was one of the prettiest Vietnamese girls he had seen. Her hair was coiffed into a below-the-jaw western style that went with her western clothing.

"What's your name?" he asked.

"My name is Co Dao," she answered slowly, obviously unnerved over the situation.

"Co Dao. *Miss Peach*. What was the problem with the soldier who was yelling at you?"

"He try to return radio. But he have no slip. No purchase slip. I am not allowed to take back."

"I understand. I'm sorry he treated you that way. He had no business doing so. Do you have his name… Information?"

"No, no know name, but he here before. Return things before."

The MP had his note pad out, and Wagner gave him the name Voss. It wouldn't be hard to find him, he was obviously stationed here at the Air Base. "I can't pursue this further here, in light of this Major Rigor. I'll talk to my highers to look into this. Thanks again for your help, you did great. I'll need your information as well."

"Yes, sir, I'll look into it from this end. I'm Specialist Cooper, here's my liaison info."

The excitement over, Wagner found Bailey in the music section of the PX. Gordon Bailey hadn't seen a bit of the conflict that just occurred, only heard somebody yelling. The two lieutenants picked up PX bathing suits and left for the swimming pool they knew existed at the 71st Medevac Hospital. The pool was like any outdoor hotel pool, albeit not fancy in surroundings. One-story wooden structures with sand bag revetments and corrugated metal roofs topped with more sand bags surrounded the 40' pool. The water was a welcome respite from weeks of only a few rice paddies and small streams in the Central Highlands. No one else was in the water, and other than a half dozen medical soldiers playing cards under a deck table umbrella, the pool was vacant. Enjoying the sun and water, only a few minutes passed when three nurses in swim suits walked out of the women's latrine to gather at one of the umbrella tables. One of the nurses was a striking blonde, immediately catching Wagner's stare. She was the first American girl he had seen since the flight to Tan San Nhut. "Wow, fox alert!" he said to Gordon. While her two friends sat down, she dove in and dolphin-kicked the length of the pool, mostly under water, emerging at the end of the pool just yards from Wagner at the shallow end. He could see she was pretty from the other end of the pool, with a great figure and a killer fanny. But now, eight feet apart, she was stunning, even with her wet shoulder-length blonde hair clinging to her neck. Five-foot three, soft Swedish features, large enchanting blue eyes, a slight tan. Wagner liked the 'cute' side of pretty, and she was. The kind of farm-grown, athletic, take-home-to-momma kind of cute.

Wagner said, "Beautiful kick. Do you swim the butterfly?"

"Yes, I did!" she exclaimed. "Four years in high school. Mostly I did the Individual Medley."

"Wow. So did I. Six years, including Junior High."

"That explains the pecs," she said, smiling. "Where was

that?" she asked.

"Maine."

"Where?"

In the Army, Wagner heard that same reply often, realizing early on that Maine is the only one-syllable state. People just expect a longer name. "Maine. Heard of it? You drive north through Canada, hit the Arctic Circle, turn right."

"Oh, Maine!" She laughed, perfect white teeth completing an entrancing smile. "I think I have water in my ears. I always wanted to go there. It's supposed to be beautiful."

"Depends. Like any place else, there's beautiful, and there's shades of ugly." Lots of water. And cold. They just got plumbing there last week. And where are you from?"

"Kansas. Western Kansas. Not so much water. But I think it has its own kind of beauty. Still, I'd love to have the water. Lakes, ocean, even rivers. Doesn't matter. I guess I'm sort of a water person at heart."

"Then I would guess Kansas may not be ideal for you. But I've been through it, and the wheat fields are amazing. Not so much the oil wells." He replied. "My name's Darryl Wagner," he said, extending his hand.

"Annelle Atchison." She said.

"Annelle. Pretty name. Are you a nurse?" He asked.

"Yes, I got here in April. Nothing about this has been what I expected. But what about you? I haven't seen you here before."

"No, you wouldn't. First time. I came over with a good friend, right over there," he said, pointing to Gordon. "So you must be a lieutenant?"

"Yes, she said. "I just turned First last week. So you're not medical? Not a patient?"

"Oh, no, just a grunt, so to speak. I'm part of a 5-man – uh, four right now…MAT Team. Like you said, nothing is what I expected."

"I've heard of them. But what *is* a MAT team, exactly?" she asked.

Wagner explained, and the conversation turned to the

amazing experiences with primitive Montagnard tribesmen and their village lives. Like Wagner, she said she had read many books about the early settlers in America and American Indians, both eastern and western plains. She was fascinated with Darryl's stories of recent experiences with the primitive Montagnard people. Unlike other girls, she was actually fascinated in combat recounts as well. Annelle felt the same with respect to Darryl Wagner's interest in her work. He listened intently to her personal horrors of war and what it did to her patients. He sensed she needed to talk to someone other than a doctor or nurse, someone not in her field yet wasn't sickened by her stories of horrible cases she encountered on a daily basis, and who understood her stress. The conversation lasted well over an hour, just standing in the water by the pool's edge. He suddenly realized he had been ignoring his good friend, who had likewise struck a conversation with one of Annelle's friends. The afternoon was moving along, they were already risking driving back in the dark, or dusky conditions at best. It was not advisable to drive unescorted without quad .50 caliber gun trucks or the like at night. That could easily go south, several incidents had resulted in ambushed vehicles and slit throats, all Vietnamese, just in the weeks Wagner had been in Pleiku.

Wagner hadn't been so struck by such a beauty since his romantic breakup, now several years in the past. Nobody had filled that void, and he thought they never would. Maybe it was the bleakness of war and the drought of romance following the now-distant break up that was enhancing her allure.

Annelle Atchison was likewise concerned about being late for her shift. When she told him that, he feared he was too presumptuous, this could be a blow-off. After all, wasn't this place full of successful doctors and a distinctly disparate supply of men, they must be all over her. What chance could he possibly have, a grunt from the sticks of Maine, no degree, no profession, no job at twenty five. She must be spoken for. Whatever techniques and confidence he carried in the past melted away in the last few years of not caring to get involved.

"If I could come back to the 71st some time, could I look you up? For the pool, I mean?" Wagner asked.

"Certainly," she said with a shake of her wet hair and a glowing parting smile. "I'd like that. I really do have to go. It's been nice. I hope you'll be safe out there."

The two MAT lieutenants decided to err on the side of safety, and head back to their respective compounds in the morning, staying the night in Pleiku instead. Back at Pleiku Headquarters, Doug Hanson had just entered the room when Gordon asked his friend, "Well, Darryl, you seemed pretty enthralled. She's a knockout. How'd that go?"

"Good. She's really neat. Name's Annelle.. Annelle." Wagner said, staring at a cloud out the sector window...... Hell, Grandma Moses looks pretty good by now."

Hanson interjected, "Yeah, I wouldn't mind taggin' Grandma Moses myself."

Laughing, Gordon leaned toward Doug and said, "As we say in the teaching profession, Doug, thank you for sharing."

Wagner, leaning back in his chair with his arms folded over his head, said, "Jee-zus, Hanson, I've just painted a mental picture of that. Not pretty."

Hanson was still laughing. "I'd like to have a few beers, but I'm due for a sitrep for Colonel Bern. See you guys later."

"So...Annelle." grinned Bailey. "You're saying she's just looking good because of the dearth of round eyed women?"

Wagner paused. "Nope. She really is an absolute doll... And nice. Man, nurses are great."

"So you've already scarfed your Combat Infantry Badge," Gordon said. The C.I.B.---a wreathed musket badge--- is earned when you've been under enemy fire at least six times.

"Yeah, but I'm surprised it hasn't been worse than this. I can't believe the places we've been, just driving to a village in a single damn Jeep, in the middle of the woods. That was never in the plan, but this has been a cake walk so far. The worst thing about Vietnam is the damn malaria pills. The only thing consistent in this friggin' country is diarrhea. And they're telling us the little daily white pill is because we're in the area of the country with Falciparum malaria, the one in four that kills you. The mosquitos are worse in Maine than here. Difference is, here they kill you. It's crazy, but the worse the weather, the worse the damn mosquitos. I heard they kill Caribou in Alaska, so thick they actually bleed them to death, "

Gordon laughed knowingly. "Cake walk? Doesn't sound like it so far for you. And I think it's the big orange pills that give you the shits."

"My rectum doesn't care. But Gordo, you've gotta fill me in on what you've found it like so far in your 'hood."

"Well, okay, Roger that. I've been wondering when we'd get together. Do you realize we're living about 20 klicks apart, and you're our closest American neighbors?"

"I guess that's right. Who'd a thunk it a few months ago. Speaking about who'd a thunk it, what about our chairborne ranger here? Hanson. The guy nobody thought would ever have to go to Nam. Got AG for a branch, and here he is. So tell me about it, Gordo. what's happened so far?"

"Not bad, not bad at all," he replied. He elaborated on his home compound of Plei Do Rom, another old Special Forces camp. As he described his compound's defenses, his eyes grew wider and his head projected forward, characteristic of whenever Gordon became excited. He grew more intense as he described three mini-guns, each firing 2,000 rounds a minute of 7.62 mm, and a 'four-deuce' mortar, two 81 mm mortars, a 57 mm recoilless rifle, several fifty caliber machineguns, some fifty thousand land mines planted around the compound by earlier Special Forces personnel, and the stockpile of Claymore mines, grenades, mortar rounds, M-79 grenade launcher rounds, and M-16 ammunition hidden underground.

Bailey wasn't a gung-ho, 'hunter-killer' type. He was certainly dedicated and professional, but his enthusiasm was more a reflection of his sense of security with the powerful arsenal at hand. After scores of stories of American-manned Special Forces base camps overrun, there was a heavy concern of the same thing happening to an under-strength outpost, practically void of Americans.

Wagner shared his fears and his excitement. "Sounds excellent. Tell me more, Gordon. Tell me what you've been through so far."

"Well, just before I got here, our compound got hit a lot, but since the end of May, we haven't been hit at all. They say it's due to the enemy's lack of supplies after the U.S. operations in Cambodia. Also the Nixon bombing campaign, B-52s and fighter bombers. The Ho Chi Minh Trail took some viscous shit, that did a number on them. The only thing is, almost all the Americans are gone, at least not in the field anymore. It's all part of the 'Vietnamization' of the war. Even the old Special Forces teams were taken out of the field. I've been working with this Montagnard Major, Thieu-ta Buhm. He's older, been around a long time. This guy *is the* commander. Really knows his stuff. When he talks, things happen. He's pretty revered by the RF companies under him. He controls everything in my area."

"What's he like?" Darryl asked. "I've only known a couple of Montagnard officers so far, both are only second lieutenants. But they've been super."

"One hell of a nice guy. A great counterpart. No formal education, but he speaks Vietnamese, French, German, and seven dialects of Montagnard."

"What? And German? How'd that get in there?"

Gordon leaned forward again, eyes wide open. "When the French—that was the French Foreign Legion-- were fighting the Viet Minh communists after World War II, the surviving Germans had no country left, everything was annihilated. They had no homes, often no families, and no jobs to come back to. So they joined the French Foreign Legion. A big portion of the Legion were Germans."

"Wow, I never knew that. Germans fighting for the French. A bit counterintuitive, but I guess it makes sense. Wonder how many people knew that. Those poor guys. So how old is this Major Buhm?"

"The Montagnards don't know their ages, I don't know.

I'd say at least late 40s, maybe 50s. Short, of course, a little paunchy, but a lot of energy."

"I have read that only two percent of the Americans are in the field now....us advisers and a few artillery outposts. That's it. The rest, what hasn't been sent home early, are in the REMF areas along the coast. So about 130,000 left, two percent.....that's about 2600 U.S. in the field."

"That's about right, said Bailey, swallowing the last of his '33' Vietnamese beer. I don't see any Americans at all, save for an occasional supply convoy on the main highway coming into Pleiku. These Montagnards are great, though. Super people. They're absolutely honest, brave, tough people. They really like Americans. There seems to be some rapport, something special. We just get along with them really easy."

Wagner mused again how Gordon had loved living the primitive lifestyle with the Eskimos, and now here he was, thrown right back to the French and Indian days of the 1700s. He loved that aspect of his job. Only the weapons were different. "Gordon, what do you think of this reconsolidation business?" Wagner asked. "I'm just learning about it. We weren't exactly prepared for this. We were never told anything about having to move villagers around."

"Not sure. I guess it's good to deprive the enemy, I can see that might help." Gordon replied, in his methodical way. "Maybe I'll figure it out in the morning," he said, standing up to stretch. The stay in Pleiku had been a welcome reprieve from the tensions of the job before returning to their teams the next day.

Returning to Le Quon early the next morning, Wagner prepared the team at the team house dining table for their next mission. It would be an outpost above famous Mang Yang Pass, located on the eastern extremity of the team's AO. The pass was a serpentine section of Highway QL 19, over the Annamite north-south mountain chain, a choke point along QL 19 between Pleiku and An Khe. Convoys had to negotiate this narrow and steep pass to supply large bases in Pleiku and

Kontum. Enemy VC and PAVN troops had often staged ambushes or at least placed snipers that would harass passing convoys. Previously, it was a never ending mission for U.S. forces to protect convoys from Qui Nhon to Pleiku. Countless operations, small and large, were launched including patrolling and clearing the mountain tops overlooking the passes. Its geography was perfect for enemy ambushes, as evidenced by the Viet Minh massacre of the French Legionnaires in June of 1954, only sixteen years prior.

Flanagan was bitching again. From his previous tour, he had known of Mang Yang's notoriety, and always balked at riskier missions. "Lieutenant, do you really think you're doing any good tryin' to convince these little bastards how to fight a war? They've got a basket more experience in this shit than you'll ever see." Sergeants Blas and Stewart still somehow held a level of respect for Flanagan. His age, rank, and previous tours all counted for something, even if his personality and physical shape did not. Wagner knew it, and used all his leadership training and skills to handle it without resorting to discipline. Inappropriate discipline, verbal or written, could damage the respect and rapport he had hoped was his with the rest of the team. But by now it almost seemed the other sergeants were expecting a reprimand of some kind. He didn't know. He reminded himself again that this wasn't a unit, it was a team. The hierarchy of a MAT command was fairly unique.

Major Nichols left his trailer and was about to open the screened kitchen door when he heard Wagner tell Flanagan, "You may be right, but I believe this location is militarily important, for sure, and why would we ignore this group over any other? You don't think we're accomplishing anything?"

"You gotta be shittin' me, Lieutenant!" Flanagan said.

From Flanagan's glassy look, Wagner was guessing he already had a drink before breakfast. Flanagan hid it well. "No, Sergeant Flanagan, I wouldn't shit you," he answered in a patronizing tone. "If I shit a turd like you, I'd have to push it back in and shit over again." A hardy laugh from the rest of the team broke the mounting tension, but not Flanagan's sneer. He just stared at Wagner with his two furry caterpillars forming a vee on his brow. "If you have a good reason we shouldn't go there, Sergeant Flanagan, by all means give me your thoughts. But it won't be because you believe it won't do any good." Other than a few previous private reproaches, this was the most confrontational Wagner had thus far presented. His turd response was perfect, it broke the tension and hit its mark, and didn't reflect badly with the other NCOs. If this had been a regular tactical unit, the lieutenant would see most insubordination issues handled by the senior NCO. But in this team, Flanagan *was* the senior NCO. The Major walked in, ending any possible retort from Flanagan.

The trip to Mang Yang Pass took less than an hour, heading east on the narrow highway. The Major's bodyguard-interpreter, Blote was with them, temporarily replacing Kloh or Trong. Most of the highway was relatively safe during the day, with perhaps 50 to 100 meters cleared of vegetation on both sides of the road by Agent Orange and huge Rome Plow bulldozers. A few intimidating exceptions, particularly near stream crossings and villages, always released adrenaline, automatically prompting a weapons-ready response. Nearly a mile from their destination, the Jeep had to maneuver around several American fuel tanker-trailer trucks stopped in the road. They had just come out of the pass, heading towards them for Pleiku, when a small mine had damaged the front end of one of the trucks. The GIs were working on it, waiting for an Army wrecker.

Reaching the outpost at the peak of the mountains overlooking the pass, they saw it was manned by a small contingent of twelve Vietnamese RF soldiers. They had expected over thirty. Having not been attacked for many months in this period of an attritioned enemy, the defenders had neglected its defenses to a sorry state. Laundry, radios and other personal effects were strewn around, indicating a lax situation with little leadership.

Wagner made an effort to avoid the unforgivable "loss of face" humiliation so essential to the Vietnamese. Speaking privately with the RF sergeant in charge, he carefully mentioned the lack of sandbags, shallow firing positions, mortar firing stakes, and tall grass limiting views in their fields of fire. "Trung-Si, could you consider please….clean out the firing positions and replace the sandbags? If you need sandbags to fill, I can help."

The Vietnamese sergeant smiled, and replied, "Da Phai, Trung-uy, chung-toi se duoc." *Yes, of course, we will do.*

Looking across to 1800 depressions in the ground on the adjacent mountain top, Sergeant Blas said, "Sir, see those dips in the ground over there? Those are French graves from the Viet Minh battle the last year the French were here."

"Really? How did you know that? I'd heard about it, but didn't know you could still see it." Wagner replied.

Blas said, "Major Buhm was with us, a Montagnard Major. He's been around a long time, told us all about it." Wagner was about to reply when a 6' black racer snake streaked across his boot, drawing a loud "Jeee-zus" out of him. Blote and one of the Vietnamese RF soldiers immediately unslung their

M-16s and began shooting on semi-automatic, inches from Wagner's and Blas's feet. "Hey! Stop! Khong, khong!" they yelled in unison. The lightning fast snake was gone through the tan grassy knoll in a flash, unscathed and scared out of its mind, like everyone else. Wagner remembered watching tracers ricocheting in crazy directions at the rifle ranges at Benning and Dix.

The visit and advising done, it was almost 1700 hours when they left to return to Le Quon. They had five miles behind them when they came upon the same American convoy, finally moving and on its way to Pleiku Air Base. It was travelling slowly, hindered by their damaged truck, its front end carried on a flatbed wrecker. Leading the convoy in typical fashion was a quad-fifty gun truck, a deuce and a half with a rotational gun platform housing a double .50 caliber Browning machine gun, two single .50s, and an M-60 machine gun mounted on the bed. A 60mm mortar completed the armament. Steel armor sides protected the gunners from small arms fire. Another gun truck completed the convoy, protecting the rear. A variety of Vietnamese vehicles were backed up behind the last gun truck when the team pulled up behind.

Training had taught Wagner the lead gun truck was the first target for the enemy, to block the path of the convoy as well as to take out their biggest threat. The second target was the trailing gun truck. With those gone, the rest of the convoy was easier pickings. He also knew the hours spent waiting for the wrecker allowed the V.C. or NVA plenty of time to set up an ambush at the tree line along the road clearings. It was getting late, with less light and more risk. More adrenaline. Wagner was driving, Sergeant Blas in the shotgun seat, with Stewart, Blote and Flanagan squeezed into the rear. This main highway was no wider than a backwoods country road in the states, and the convoy was taking up most of it, both lanes. The GI drivers had little respect for any Vietnamese vehicles coming the other way, their interest was in getting to Pleiku and out of a vulnerable position. Anyone coming the other way had to squeeze by or simply get run off the road.

Sergeant Blas's smile was replaced with a look of concern. "Sir, let's follow right behind that convoy. I like that gun truck!"

Wagner didn't like proximity to the "second target" gun truck, but it was late, they were tired and now stressed. In the interest of leadership, especially with a judgmental Flanagan on board, he complied. Blas was a great sergeant and an experienced soldier. Besides, adviser training said to use convoys for protection whenever possible. Rather than opt for what he thought best, he chose the leadership slant instead. He passed the smaller vehicles to catch up with the convoy, barely squeezing by. Just one large blue Vietnamese truck separated the gun truck from their Jeep. Travelling Vietnamese middle-of-the-road fashion, it prevented passing. At a slight hill and bend in the road, four explosions burst **CRUMP! CRUMP! CRUMP! CRUMP!** on both sides of the gun truck 40 meters ahead, all landing close in roadside ditches, none hitting the truck. SOP in a 'far ambush' requires speeding out of the kill zone, but the Vietnamese truck ahead stopped in the middle of the road, with more rounds exploding around it. Ahead, the convoy was moving on. He steered the Jeep to the left of the truck to squeeze beside it, just as two more explosions hit directly in front of the Jeep and to the right ahead of the truck. The truck driver instinctively steered to the left, blocking their path. A loud *'pang'* rang off the hood of the Jeep and the left windshield shattered. Wagner immediately assumed they were mortars, and now AK-47 rifle fire was cutting loose from the wood line 70 meters away, sending sound barrier *'CRACK's* over and around the Jeep. The gun trucks opened up with a crescendo of heavy machine gun fire and thumps of American 60 mm mortars leaving the tube. Every soldier in the convoy was firing small arms as well, while the team was stuck beside the stopped Vietnamese truck, fully exposed. Sergeant Blas was leaning around the front of the windshield from the shotgun seat, firing his single shot M-79 "Thumper" grenade launcher at the wood line with remarkable accuracy, swinging back under the canvas top to reload. Another explosion just to the left, and

Wagner realized these were B-40 rockets from the left wood line, not indirect fire from mortars. Unable to move the Jeep, he yelled, ***"Get in the ditch,"*** instinctively turning the dash ignition lever off. He and Blas were bailing out the open sides, their feet hitting the pavement when he heard Blote yell from the back seat, "No stop! No stop!," pointing to the Vietnamese truck ahead starting to move.

Jumping back in, Wagner cursed the foot starter button as the flooded motor chirred and failed to catch. Twice he tried. He had to feel, rather than hear, the motor start over the steady staccato of machine gun fire. More B-40s hit less than 20 meters ahead, shrapnel *'panging'* off the Jeep. On the third try the engine started and they were moving. Wagner arched forward as he felt a dozen hot M-16 shell casings slide down the back of his jungle fatigue shirt. Sergeant Stewart and Blote were firing on full auto from the rear seat behind him, their ejected hot casings funneling down Wagner's collar. The same happened to Blas as he sat back down to reload his M-79 grenade launcher, only the hot casings flying out of Blote's M-16 were falling into his crotch on the seat, sending Blas back up again, frantically batting them out of his seat, his balls cooking.

The Vietnamese truck ahead was painfully slow, only moving 20 meters from where it had stopped. Wagner was driving with his left hand while shooting aimed shots at the base of the tree line on semi-auto, all the time arched forward while they followed the bulky truck. Finally he found an opportunity to pass on the left, hitting the gas to catch up with the convoy. Sergeant Blas was still leaning around the windshield to fire his M-79, to the cheers from a G.I. on the gun truck. Blote had already expended all seven 20-round magazines from his M-16, while Wagner had just emptied his first on semi-auto.

Ahead on the left, two ARVN M-48 tanks providing road security at a stream crossing a kilometer west were barreling towards them across the cleared left side of the highway. They were firing as they moved with canister grapeshot rounds, giant shotguns blowing away ten meter swathes of trees from the area the B-40s had come from. The enemy fire stopped, the whole event taking less than three minutes but seeming like twenty.

The convoy continued ahead for a mile before stopping to repair some shrapnel damage in two of the tanker trucks. Jet fuel was copiously leaking out of several holes. A wet stream on the pavement and smell of gas trailed back to their Jeep, causing Wagner to increase the gap. Now that the convoy had stopped, he pulled beside to ask if anyone was hurt. Amazingly, no one was, and all the B-40s missed direct hits. As usual, enemy small arms fire had been mostly high, but a few rounds had pierced the trucks. American GIs scrambled to jam wooden pegs into leaking holes, sufficient until they could unload at Pleiku. The smell of jet fuel permeated the air, another unforgettable smell from the haunts of Vietnam. They all knew how this could have turned out with a direct hit. An after-rush of adrenalin left them spent but cheery, like the aftermath of a closely won football game, on steroids. Flanagan, who never fired his weapon, took the opportunity to throw in his contemptuous remarks. "Damn good thing we didn't jump in the fuckin' ditch. Could have had our asses blown away."

Wagner said nothing. He had to ponder this one. "What if they had? *What if they had?*" If someone had been killed, it was his decision. Such guilt issues have plagued leaders since men formed tribes. Long after the war, other leaders would wrestle with the same nightmares. But it was the right choice at the time, until the truck ahead moved. The ditch lent some protection from direct fire weapons. On the other hand, a direct hit with a B-40 would have killed them all. Did Flanagan have a point?

A mile down the road, Sergeant Stewart reached down to scratch his itching thigh. It was wet. He looked down to see his pant leg soaked and dark red, from just inside the thigh. "Oh my achin' Jesus, I've been hit."

Wagner pulled over. Sergeant Flanagan, the team Medic, cut the pant leg off, and saw a small entrance wound, bleeding. It wasn't pumping blood, so most likely it wasn't an artery. Wagner applied pressure to the wound while Flanagan prepared a pressure bandage. Sergeant Stewart was actually chuckling, normal for the upbeat, stocky black sergeant, saying, "You know, I never even felt it. Oh my Jesus, I never felt it."

They let Blote off at Le Quon, and drove on into Pleiku to the 71st Medevac to admit a now somewhat less jovial sergeant. Brandon Stewart's contentment with a lack of pain dissolved by the time they reached the hospital. Now his leg was burning and aching. The nurses immediately went to work, cleaning the wound and sticking needles and fluid IVs into him, assuring the team he would be fine. While waiting, Wagner wanted to look up Annelle again, but it really wasn't appropriate under the circumstances. They left Stewart in the 71st's good care, returning home in the dark. The team sat around the dining table, recounting the ambush, thinking about how it could have gone really sour. Flanagan didn't say much for a change, maybe because he was sober. Or possibly embarrassed over his inaction in the Jeep, or maybe just tired. They were all tired. Adrenalin does that. When Sergeant Blas went to the wooden latrine to relieve himself, in the light from the porch he noticed two bullet holes in the left side of the Jeep, one in the hood and one clean through the left side roof support tube. *Inches and seconds.*

The Major joined them for a few minutes to hear the day's events, and to report another ambush that happened that day, fifty kilometers south, near Phu Nhon. It was another MAT team. Major Nichols took a moment to choose his words. He looked down, his hands folded on the table. "A Captain Reese was driving, two NCOs were with him as well as a Vietnamese interpreter. It happened along a section of a remote dirt road that was flanked with six foot tall grasses on both sides. They were returning from a village later than they should have been, around 1900 hours. They were hit by small arms fire through the windshield, Captain Reese took two rounds in the head. He died instantly. Both sergeants with him jumped out and returned fire, but they were both killed. The interpreter made it back. They suspect he may have been involved."

The news hit hard, they didn't know the men of the other MAT team, but they were all putting themselves in that Jeep, imagining the entire sequence of events as though it was them. The threat of a Jeep ambush en route to a village was always a possibility. Of particular concern was the part about the interpreter. What if......

Major Nichols hesitated for a moment, and put his cigar to his lips, blowing the smoke quickly to his left, and said, "Another thing. I don't want anyone jumping to conclusions about this, but I do want you to know something that just happened today. A couple of V.C. suspects were picked up in Plei Ko Tu, and they put the finger on Blote as an informer and supplier to the V.C."

The words hit like a sledge hammer. Blote was everybody's friend, the Major's smiling Montagnard bodyguard, trusted and respected. No way he could be the enemy. He did, however, have easy access to information, as he cleaned the Major's trailer every day, as well as travelling with him most of the time in the Major's daily pursuit of the V.C. infrastructure.

"Apparently the times the suspects gave as to when Blote was at Plei Ko Tu," the Major continued, "correspond to when we know he was actually there visiting his family, so there may be some truth to it. However, it's common to make enemies in this area, and the suspects could be just trying to put the finger on Blote for personal reasons. It happens. Blote's being interrogated in the city now." After the men opted for their bunks, he asked Wagner to come with him to the trailer. "Can you go over this again with me, Headquarters will want a report. I'll be going in tomorrow morning. Sounds like overall, you were all lucky it wasn't worse. You're sure Sergeant Stewart's okay?" he asked, a short cigar in hand. Other than an occasional cigar with his scotch, the Major didn't smoke, and neither did Wagner. Flanagan smoked the free SP pack cigarettes non-stop. Blas and Stewart, not so much. If the enemy doesn't kill you, the Army will.

"Yes, sir. He's in good spirits. The man always is. The pain started kicking in when we were almost to the 71st, but they were working on it. It doesn't appear too serious, the hole was small, but there was no exit wound, so they'll have to remove it. They said the prognosis was good. He should be coming back."

"That's good. I'll stop by in the morning before I meet with Colonel Bern. What about Mang Yang?"

Wagner was rubbing his tender neck, still stinging from the hot cartridges. "For starters," Wagner said, leaning forward on the Major's table, "there were just a dozen Vietnamese RFs at the outpost. We were told thirty. The place was pretty decrepit, junk everywhere, grass was high all around, shallow firing positions, bunkers falling in, rather shabby overall. A Vietnamese Sergeant was in charge, he promised to fix things up, but you know how that goes. We couldn't do much more than try. I'd like to go back and check sometime."

The Major nodded, knowingly. "What about Flanagan?"

"Sir?"

"Is he giving you trouble?"

"He's a handful, sir," answered Wagner. "Constant complainer, and I think he drinks a lot, but I can't say for sure." Wagner hesitated to seek assistance from the Major, it would reflect poorly on his own ability to lead, almost an admission of failure. Getting rid of Flanagan would only send him to another MAT team somewhere, giving them his problems. Regarding the drinking, the Major usually had drinks with the men in the team house after suppers, making it more difficult to curb Flanagan, though it really was a safety issue. The Major looked him firmly in the eye and said, "The Captain you replaced, Gerson, was a good officer. He had problems with Flanagan, too. Sergeant Flanagan fell asleep on his guard watch on a bridge ambush position. Nearly got everyone killed. A month later, he took it upon himself to drop a brick of C-4 in Plei Djering's village well to 'help out' the village to get more water out of their well. Then he told the village chief to go down and check it out. The blast ate up the oxygen. He suffocated. So he sent another villager down to get the chief. Same thing. He died, too. Before it was over, three villagers died, including the village chief."

"Holy. Nobody told me that. Problem is, the other NCOs still look up to him, but I can't for the life of me figure why. I just figure there's something I don't see that they do. I'm trying to keep cohesion in the team. But if he gets sent somewhere else, he's now their problem instead of mine."

"If this were a TO&E unit," the Major said, "a problem with a sergeant would normally be addressed by the senior sergeant. In this case, the problem *is* the senior sergeant. Sergeant Flanagan feels threatened by you." Nichols was using his psychology background now. "He's insecure, out of shape, his manhood is threatened. Inside, he's got an inferiority complex. He uses machismo to hide it. It's not you, he was the same way with Lt. Gerson. He hates officers, period. But if it gets too deep, let me know."

"Yes, sir." Replied Wagner, a little relieved to have the support, and it helped remove some self-doubts he had with his own leadership. The Major seemed eager to get rid of Flanagan.

"I'm concerned about Kir, continued the Major. He's probably no more than fifteen years old. He's a great little kid, and an orphan. One of our best English speaking interpreters. But I don't think we should be using him on dangerous missions, it's just not ethical. This thing that happened today with the MAT team,...."

"I agree, sir. Our team has already discussed exactly that. Sergeant Stewart brought it up. Stewart's like a father to Kir. We try to take Kloh or Trong whenever they're available, depending on who we're training. We save Kir for the safer stuff along the highway, unless we have no choice."

"Thank you, Darryl. I'd rather not see him going any place off the main highway, or overnight." Getting up to grab an ice cube, he inquired, "How did your trip to Pleiku go?"

"Great, sir. Bailey and I hit the PX, we took in the hospital's pool at the 71st, saw a lot of great aircraft at the Air Force Base. Also met a really nice nurse. At the pool. She's a fox."

The Major gave a laudatory grin.

"One more thing. I had a little dispute at the PX..." Wagner related the story to the Major about the Private and interference from Major Rigor.

Before they were through, Wagner reminded the Major about the need for a better forward observer tower. Their meeting done, he walked back across the small court yard to his room in the team house. H & I -- Harassment and Interdiction Fires -- from their 4.2" Vietnamese mortars were booming from the RF end of the compound, quick flashes visible on a moonless night. They periodically fired nearly every night to keep the enemy from freely travelling outside the perimeter. He was amazed at himself that he could soon sleep through it, though they fired several times a night, yet an incoming round had him flying out of bed. During the day he had trouble distinguishing a difference between outgoing and incoming crunching BOOMs they both made, but at night, asleep, the mind instantly discerned the two. Perhaps it was the pinging and pattering of shrapnel...

The news about Blote superseded the day's action. Wagner had been in a small hostile action alongside Blote before, but who knows where he was really shooting, he could have fired over the tree tops for all anyone knew. Could they trust him along with them again? The Major had also said he was reported to have given food and clothing to the V.C. Before Sergeant Lutz left, he had given Blote all his jungle fatigues and other equipment he no longer needed before being lugged out with malaria. It didn't look good.

At 0700, the team members straggled in to be met with the smells of Hoa Khe's cooking and coffee. The team mascot, a big sway-back pig named 'Mat' was begging at her feet. He normally stayed outside, but Hoa Khe truly loved this pig, as inconsistent as it was with what Wagner knew of this society. Every bird, animal, fish, or insect was food, period. Dog, cat, water buffalo, pig, duck, whatever --- it was food. He saw very few, if any pets since he'd arrived. A sliced monkey's head was dished out for the brains, raw. An unlucky duck would be held by its neck, upside down, while the tip of a bayonet dug into and opened up the bloody vein at the tip of its beak, draining the blood into a bowl for curdled 'duck blood soup'. Every time it coagulated, the bayonet once again dug it out to resume the bleeding. So it went, the poor duck, head down, flapping its wings the entire time in pain and fear, until it succumbed and there was no more blood. Small pigs found their throats being slit for the same purpose. The clots coming out were a delicacy. Con Ga, or duck egg, was another delicacy. Not an egg, per se, but an almost emerged duckling, broken out of its shell to be eaten raw. Yet, Hoa Khe found her mothering instinct to love and protect this pig with all her being. "I'm thinking, with all her family dead, this is all the family she has left," presumed Wagner. At any rate, teasing comments from the team about Mat being the next main course was met with angry reproaches from Hoa Khe, swinging her broom.

Timmy, their Spec 4 radio telephone operator walked in to make an announcement. Timmy was only 18, their youngest G.I., but already a crackerjack at his job and keeping the generator running, among other duties. The team and the Major had just sat down for breakfast when he came running. Looking at Wagner, he said, "Sir, guess what!"

"We just surrendered," said Wagner.

"No, better than that. We just got a call from the PFs at Plei Kran. They got a kill with your Claymore ambush."

"Fantastic, Sergeant Blas said, excited to hear results. "What did they get?"

"They got a deer. They want to know if you can come to Plei Kran for supper."

The table erupted with laughter. "Did they really get it with the trip wire ambush?" Wagner asked.

"Yes sir," he laughed. "How many is that now for your mechanical ambushes?"

"Uh, let me see now... That would be one." Wagner answered.

"Fantastic, sir," said Blas, grinning ear to ear. Like Wagner, he was elated their time hadn't been a waste. It proved that it had, at least, been employed and working. Even Flanagan was grinning, and for once, had no derisive comment. The Major was clearly impressed. The team had become an effective, active group, replacing a dismal performance since Gerson had left. Even Flanagan was performing, if not under protest. Blas and Stewart were good, dedicated soldiers, and the recent activity and successes had invigorated them.

Accepting the invitation would be important. It was a 'showing of the flag', that their advisers were proud and impressed that the PFs employed their ambush techniques. That afternoon they arranged with the PF platoon at Plei Kran to be expecting Team 57 for supper. The village was five miles east on QL 19, about half way to Mang Yang, then four kilometers south on another Jeep-width path through the Highlands jungle, paralleling the mountain chain. Arriving at the village, Flanagan, Blas, Wagner, and Kloh saw the gutted small red deer hanging from a tripod near the village chief's hootch. A Montagnard Private PF was working on the last of the innards removal, carefully saving each and every part. Literally every part. The deer was torn to shreds from an onslaught of 700 bearing balls, which would probably be considered a 'spoiling of the meat' if it was shot in the states. It didn't matter much to the 'Yards, nothing was wasted anyway. Roasting over a fire, its hair would be burned away, and hide and all would be cut into small pieces. Even the hooves were chewed. The entrails were cut up into what Sergeant Stewart had taught were '*chitlins*', or chitterlings in his Georgia accent.

The team was met with always happy, smiling faces of soldiers and villagers alike. These villagers were a marked improvement over the first time Team 57 arrived here, only a short while before, due in no small part to the MEDCAP mission to help their village with medical issues. Nothing won their 'hearts and minds' more. The village chief and the Montagnard PF lieutenant, Thieu-uy Nhan, led Wagner to his seat near the chief's.

On the long table were various wooden bowls of rice, bamboo shoots, and a variety of deer parts. This time, the meat wasn't rotten, albeit coated with a never ending swarm of large black and green flies. And of course, the ground everywhere in the village was a carpet of animal feces.

After clumsy attempts with chop sticks, the ever present rice wine in 30" high vases filled to the rim were ready for an inevitable rice wine party. Each adviser was presented a Montagnard bracelet made of brass, probably beat into its 1/8" wire frame from bullet or artillery casings. No one seemed to know for sure, it was just conjecture. All the team had two or three each from previous villages. They spent the night in two PF bunkers with old cots inside, and barely room to squeeze between. Always on edge, Wagner considered the effects the

mandatory rice wine would have on the men, though Flanagan was the only one who drank a significant amount. Regardless, artillery was the main hope, the saving grace they depended on.

VII   MIDDLE GAME

"The part of the chess game which follows the opening.   Plans are formed, based on the position and put into action."

The team had just arrived for a two night stay at a Vietnamese village, protected by another understrength platoon of Vietnamese PFs. It wasn't far from the main highway, which ordinarily lessened some of the 'hanging out there' concerns, but the PFs' lackadaisical attitude and the condition of the defenses made the stay more unnerving.

The first thing they noticed in this relatively pretty village was its somewhat cleaner appearance, similar to Phu Yen. Much more so than reconsolidated Montagnard villages they had stayed in. Grass roofed hootches were more random, not in perfect rows and columns as were reconsolidated villages. Much smaller and older, it had banana trees and palms next to houses. An old well provided ready water, and every day conveniences of rice grinding and chaff separating areas were well established. There was no apparent death and disease, from what they could see.

Wagner's first order of business was to plan and call in artillery defensive targets, trying to guess the enemy's likely avenues of attack. It was SOP, time saved to bring the big guns in when needed.

Customarily, the team commander was invited to the village chief's hootch for supper, something Wagner had begun to consider the worst part about his war. The food was less repulsive here, but not necessarily more hygienic. Nuoc maam was one of those 'acquired tastes' that he was slowly coming to accept, requiring a staged pleased look so as not to offend the chief's wife. *Nuoc maam,* a traditional fermented fish oil sauce was used liberally on every meal other than soup. Soups were often quite good, usually consisting of chicken, bamboo shoots, various vegetables, and jungle peppers. This was an exception: Duck blood soup. Coagulated clots of blood were mixed with veins, gristle, and bits of organs. Getting it down may have been easy for some, but it was a big hurdle for Wagner. Even C-rations were preferable, a matter of health versus taste, let alone the repulsion angle. But then came the dreaded event learned in advisory schools tutelage: A head of a small monkey, the top of its head sliced away, was presented by the chief's wife. A spoon was beside the head, ready for the hosts and guest to scoop uncooked spoonfuls of brains as an appetizer, the guest being first, of course. This wasn't a common meal, monkeys weren't that easy to find to kill, but the chief was trying to impress. How could he refuse? Wagner hesitated, scooped a tiny portion, closed his eyes, and pretended hard it was a scallop, to everyone's delight. Trying hard not to grimace or vomit, Wagner eked out a tortured smile, "It's great!" The social supper and customs over, another Thieu-uy, or second lieutenant assigned with their platoon was offering to trade a Vietnamese combat medal for a pen flare gun from Wagner. The little pen flare guns, hung from a white nylon cord with six metallic red cartridges was considered a status symbol. It was common to hear their Vietnamese counterpart officers pestering the team with "give me, give me", the two most heard words in Vietnam. Greed and disrespect for a medal's purpose was nothing unusual, and many American heroes wore them home.

Wagner rejoined the team, met with grins and jokes about culinary delights, and they were hardly upset about being excluded. On the return trip, they discussed differences they found in Vietnamese villages, none of which had been reconsolidated, and Montagnard villages, many of which had. "You don't see the filth, all the diseases, do you?" asked Blas.

"I didn't see a single dying villager," said Stewart.

"The whole damn village didn't have that starkness, that lack of vegetation. It just looked more comfortable, missing the bareness of Plei Ko Tu and the rest." Added Wagner.

"All Montagnard villages don't look like that," Flanagan said. "What the hell is the sense in all this reconsolidation shit, anyway. Seems like one more way the friggin' Vietnamese can steal their goddam land."

"I'm thinking you nailed it," Wagner said, "I've been guessing the same thing. We've all been told it's to 'deprive the enemy', but this is looking like chicken-shit instead of chicken salad to me. Where do you think this scheme came from, anyway. Washington or Saigon?"

"Westmoreland", said Flanagan. "Gotta be."

"I wonder if people in the states have any idea how bad this is. I think we're killing our best allies, certainly not winning hearts and minds. What if it was us getting told we had to move our home, maybe generations old, into some city…by some foreigner?" said Wagner.

"This Army is some good shit, ain't it sir?" asked Stewart, the usual smile gone. "This isn't exactly savin' the world."

"*Men who die, for those oppressed,*" sang Blas, from '*The Ballad of the Green Berets'*".

It was August, 1970, and the rainy season was well underway. Wagner was now a veteran of two and a half months in country. The rainy season differed, depending on which side of the Annamite mountains you were on, among other things. Again, it wasn't what Wagner expected Vietnam to be like. *Every location in Vietnam, every year, every job, every unit, was a different war than the next guy saw.* The Delta had almost no enemy activity by the middle of 1970. The war there was almost non-existent, where friends in the same MAT Team assignment never heard a shot fired all year in anger. They could travel safely at night on 50cc motorcycles to various rice wine parties in the villages. Yet the press still said we were losing.

The rains in the Central Highlands were nothing compared to the Delta, or along the coast. There were heavy monsoons at times, to be sure, but not as bad, and certainly not as often or long lasting. Here in Pleiku Province, there were few streams to swell into dangerous rivers or rapids. There was mud, but not the kind that mired vehicles and sucked jungle boots with every step. And it was often cold. Yes, *cold*, here in Vietnam. At night, laying awake on an ambush position, not moving a muscle and soaked, it could be miserable. The Army supplied only a water proof poncho, which doubled as a pup tent or a litter, among other things, and a quilted camo 'poncho liner' blanket for warmth. Someone figured nothing else was needed in Vietnam. They were wrong. In the winter dry months, it reached 40 degrees Fahrenheit at night. Dry, to be sure, but the day's sweat from 'humping the boonies' negated some of that advantage. And laying awake on an ambush, not moving a muscle---that's cold. Wagner thanked his stars they weren't those poor bastards in the Battle of the Bulge in December of 1944 to January, 1945. The unbelievable torture of those poor soldiers, with inadequate military clothing, living with frostbite day and night for weeks in foxholes, the elements a worse enemy than the Germans, was unimaginable. Wagner himself had nearly died of hypothermia in OCS while on a Field Exercise in the woods of eastern Georgia. He had run off the side of a small wooden bridge on a moonless night during a simulated 'aggressor attack', into a fast-moving icy stream in January. It was a snow-rain mixture that night. Everything he wore and carried in his pack was soaked. He stood the entire night holding an O.D. Army blanket over his head and away from his naked body to protect him from 29 degree freezing rain. Shivering uncontrollably, he spent the night repeating to himself, "this too, shall pass."

Night time fell on the Le Quon compound, the team having returned hours before from a 3-day RF operation in the mountainous northeastern side of Pleiku Province. The team was tired, especially Flanagan, who barely survived a hard hike up and down hills and valleys. These operations were probably the best thing for his overweight body, he was losing weight and went without alcohol for the duration. One of his problems was pretending he didn't need water like the 'other pussies'. Dehydration was one of the worst enemies of soldiers in Vietnam. It robs strength first, then the ability to think right. Heat exhaustion and heat stroke may follow, leading to death. There was enough water, one simply had to fill his canteen at every stream, though in the dry season sometimes streams were scarce. Stream waters were safer here than near polluted rice paddies, where human waste was dumped to fertilize the rice, iodine tablets required to keep it safe.

The team was asleep in their team house, with night security provided by PFs and one or more of the interpreters or bodyguards, whoever hadn't been on a given village visit or 'search and destroy' RF operation. At 2300 hours, Wagner fairly flew out of his bunk at the first "*CRUMP-P!* sound of 82mm mortars. That ability while asleep to distinguish between incoming and outgoing rounds worked again. Not bothering to dress, he ran outside wearing nothing but a steel 'pot' helmet, untied boots, O.D. boxer shorts, and a cloth bandolier of seven M-16 magazines. He carried a PRC-25 radio on his back and slung his M-16 on his right shoulder. Sprinting the 40' to the west end of the team house, he turned right across the kitchen front, and another 20' to the water/shower tower. He bolted up the dozen feet of wooden 2 X 3 rungs and onto the water tanks. Naked to incoming rounds, he turned the radio on and called Artillery Hill, the nearest of their two artillery fire bases.

"Rubber Badger Niner Three, Rubber Badger Niner Three, this is Murky Cinder Five Seven, Murky Cinder Five Seven, *Fire mission*, over."

Several rounds went off to the right about 50 meters, near the mortar pit. Some yells and screams reached him, but he couldn't tell where they came from as he saw his team members sprinting to their positions below. By now the perimeter guards had opened up with machine guns and M-16s. Red tracers were spewing out toward the east, north, and west. The village of Plei Piom was across the QL 19 highway, and hopefully the enemy wasn't using that as an attack route. They often would choose that option during the course of the war, hoping Americans wouldn't shoot toward the village, but this was a Vietnamese compound, and that same regard would not apply. Another mortar landed almost at the perimeter, 20 meters to his left. Instantaneous flashes disappeared as fast as they came, no Hollywood balls of fire.

"Roger, Murky Cinder Five Seven, go." Came the reply from the fire base at Artillery Hill.

"Rubber Badger Niner Three, this is Murky Cinder Five Seven, we are under fire, wait one."

Wagner decided not to use his pre-planned fires, he had thought he saw a semblance of a flash from enemy mortars inside the distant tree line. A wait of a dozen seconds and he thought he saw another brief flash from the same spot. Pointing his lensatic compass to get an azimuth from his tower, he guessed the range to be about 200 meters.

"Rubber Badger Niner Three, this is Murky Cinder Five Seven, I want one round Whiskey Papa on coordinates Alpha Romeo eight niner six, five one four. Range 200 meters, Azimuth 5800 hundred mils. Give me shot and splash, will adjust, over." He had to shout over the clamor around him. Waiting for clearances a painfully long twenty five minutes, he was standing on the tower, alone and fully exposed, with tracers going both ways. He wished he had brought up hand grenades in case they were penetrated.

Amidst the cacophony of incoming, outgoing, and machine guns, he heard closer *POP* sounds just in front of the team house. In the light of a parachute flare, he saw Sergeant Flanagan, drunk, firing a pistol in the air. "What in hell is that crazy sonofabitch doing?" he wondered. Did he see enemy coming over the berm?

Finally, Artillery Hill called back. "Murky Cinder Five Seven, this is Rubber Badger Niner Three, over."

"Roger, Rubber Badger Niner Three, this is Murky Cinder Five Seven, over."

"Murky Cinder, we have clearance. Are you ready for fire?"

"Affirmative, Rubber Badger, we are waiting."

Several seconds went by, then the call, *"Shot out!"* . . . .
. .. .. a half minute later, *"Splash!"* as a bright white shower of
burning white phosphorus hit just short and to the left of the
target.

"Rubber Badger Niner Three, This is Murky Cinder
Five Seven, I want one round of HE Quick, right one hundred,
add five zero." Now a fury of enemy mortars were leaving their
tube, falling in an array around the compound, mostly on the
Vietnamese PF end. In less than a minute, Wagner's round hit
with a resounding **CRUNNCHH!** just into the wood line, the
abrupt flash barely visible through the growth. "Rubber Badger,
this is Murky Cinder Five Seven, Left five-zero. Three rounds
HE Quick, along an azimuth of sixteen hundred mils, spaced
five zero apart. Fire for effect," he shouted. In minutes, his
rounds came in, hitting perfectly. The enemy mortars stopped.

"Rubber Badger, this is Murky Cinder Five Seven, give
me three more rounds, space them one hundred apart, add one-
fifty," he said, hoping to catch them moving out. In the sporadic
light of parachute flares fired from their compound mortars, he
searched for and hoped not to see enemy sappers snaking
through the concertina wire. None of the corner trip wire Hirsch
flares had been tripped, and no perimeter claymores were yet

popped, but he felt relief in knowing the mines had been replaced and in working order.

After several more artillery rounds, the action was over. They would search the area the next day for results. Wagner climbed down from the tower and went back to his room to get into jungle fatigues. When he came back out, the generator was running again and some of the compound lights were on. There were five RFs wounded by shrapnel, one seriously, and one shot in the jaw, but otherwise the damage to both men and equipment was minimal. The jaw injury belonged to a Montagnard PF, at his firing position at the north berm behind the team house. It was a pistol bullet. The bullet had passed through a steel culvert connector, taking the brunt of the energy before it hit him. It wasn't life-threatening.

The next morning, the compound was a bee hive of activity, assessing damage and cleaning up. The PF commander was readying his men for a sweep of the area for enemy dead and mortar locations. The team was doing the same, as a serious looking Sergeant Blas said to Wagner, "Sir, there we were, surrounded. No chance to get out alive. Then I looked up, and by the light of the flares, I saw my commander up on that tower, in a steel pot and undershorts... and I was no longer afraid..."

"Ha, funny," Wagner said, grinning.

"Did you know about the guard that got shot last night, the perimeter guard who got shot in the jaw?" Blas asked.

"I just heard. What do you know about it?"
"The shot came from behind, in the compound. It went through a steel culvert behind him before it hit him in the jaw."

"What the hell? Friendly fire?" Wagner asked, his expression turning serious. "I was on the tower. Hard to say for sure, but I'm pretty sure I saw Sergeant Flanagan shooting his pistol. What shape was he in when you went to bed?"

"Drunk. He was making up for lost time in the bush," answered Blas.

"I'm going to have to talk with the Major. We shouldn't jump to conclusions, but I don't like it. Bad enough these poor guys are getting shot at by the NVA, now they've got us to worry about."

"You know, sir, Billy wasn't a medic his prior tour here."

"No?"

"He was an ambulance platoon sergeant in Qui Nhon. Never went in the field."

"What? You mean all the Flanagan war stories are bullshit?" Wagner asked.

"I can't say for sure, sir. But he was reduced in rank back in '66," Blas said. "Took four years to get it back."

"How'd you know this?"

"Sergeant Allistair, old friend from Fort Ord. He's stationed at Artillery Hill now. He was in Billy's unit in Qhi Nhon. They never left the city."

Wagner just stared at the ground, disgusted. "I'll have to talk with the Major."

The team didn't accompany the RFs on the sweep. The Major apparently had other unfinalized plans handed down, but had not divulged them, and for whatever reason kept them in the compound. With plenty to do with repairs, the team kept busy. The RF company commander had not accompanied the sweep around the compound, but gave the results to his counterpart, Major Nichols. Nichols called the men together for the findings. "They found the mortar firing site, in the area you put the first rounds, Lieutenant. There were no indications there of casualties, but a hundred meters out, they found blood, drag marks, and 'small body parts'. Apparently, one or more were vaporized with a direct hit. Good job on the artillery calls," he said, looking at Wagner. "There were twenty seven NVA bodies a few hundred meters to the east of that, mostly killed by small arms fire. They swept the woods beyond another five hundred meters, but found nothing more."

When he was finished, he told Wagner to come back to his office. His expression turned serious, as he asked, "What do you know about this guard being shot in our sector?"

Wagner thought for a moment, and said, "I found out

about that this morning, sir. Last night, I was pretty sure I saw Flanagan early in the attack, shooting his pistol in the air... I can't be positive, it was dark, but it looked like Sergeant Flanagan, just from his size. There was a lot of confusion, I was thinking there may be some bad guys in the compound. But Sergeant Blas told me this morning the shot came from behind, from inside. And I guess Flanagan got pretty drunk last night."

"It was a pistol bullet," Nichols said.

"Blas also informed me that Flanagan wasn't a medic on his previous tour. He was an ambulance platoon sergeant, in Qhi Nhon."

"Okay. About the guard, keep this low key. I'll look into it," the Major said.

It was scarcely three days after the compound attack when the Major told Wagner his request to take the second, taller wooden tower for his artillery calls was a go. The prior conditions of the compound and the attack provided the impetus for the decision. The Major also said there would be a Rome plow coming in the next week to revamp the perimeter. Wagner would be responsible to coordinate with the RF counterparts in the compound to make whatever revisions he and the counterparts could agree on.

With the help of the RTO Tim and the interpreters, the sandbagging job on the tower was finished in four hours. Wagner confiscated one of the NVA moat ladders that hung on the wall to leave up on the roof. He told Tim, "During an attack, I'll climb the sandbag revetment next to the team house, climb onto the roof, and then lean the bamboo straight ladder against the tower. When I get inside the sandbagged top, I'll pull the ladder up to keep the bad guys out if they get into the compound." Inside the 5' X 5' sandbagged top, Wagner left a large, heavy weapons crew-served starlight scope for calling in artillery at night. It had been scrounged months or years before, and never used. His armament included an ammo box filled with M-16 magazines, another ammo box full of M-79 grenade launcher ammo, and a box of hand grenades. "When we're attacked, I'll throw on my radio, carry my M-16 and a grenade launcher up with me. I'm putting a stretcher up there to sleep on if I have to, stretched across the sandbag walls."

"And Lieutenant Wagner looked upon all that he had made, and indeed it was very good. And there was evening and there was morning............"

"Cat's ass. This is Cat's ass good," he said to Trong, looking very pleased.

"What Catsass?" asked Trong.

Later that afternoon, a Jeep from HQ pulled into the compound. Two American officers and a small thin, nervous Vietnamese stepped out in GI fatigues. One of the officers asked where the Major was. Handyman Friday showed them to the Major's trailer, where Tung was introduced. Tung was a Kit Carson Scout, an ex-North Vietnamese soldier, or NVA. He was a *Hoi Chan,* an enemy who surrendered under the *Chieu Hoi* "Open Arms" program. A B-52 raid on the Ho Chi Minh Trail along the Pleiku/Cambodia border had wiped out his entire battalion, including the battalion commander, prompting his surrender. "Arc Light" B-52 raids were incredible, unleashing the "Terrible Swift Sword" of thousands of tons of bombs with incredible accuracy from 28,000 to 50,000 feet. Pilots flying over the areas afterward looking for results would find enemy survivors stumbling around in a concussed daze, easy targets for their guns. Explosions from hundreds of bombs were felt 60 miles away in Le Quon as a constant trembling of the ground and strange muffled steady thunder that went on for a period of time, causing mirrors and wall hangings to vibrate. The first time it happened, Wagner thought it was an earthquake. 'Close up and personal' would be something horrifying to experience.

In his home town in the North, Tung's father had been killed years before by the new regime of Nguyen Sinh Cung, later known as Nguyen Al Quoc, and finally Ho Chi Minh, or "Uncle Ho". Typically, communist take-overs result in brutality and murder to end all resistance. Tung's three brothers, all opposed to the regime as well, had all been killed in the South within the last three years. Tung was the youngest, and he blamed the deaths on his own government, surprising Wagner to no end. But Tung was well educated, and seemed to know more of American history than most Americans. He was interested in knowing more.

The reports on these scouts were typically outstanding. In most cases they were, or at least appeared to be, loyal, trustworthy, and courageous. With some understandable trepidation, the team accepted Tung into the fold as their scout and often the interpreter. He spoke surprisingly good English, having learned it in school in the North prior to his draft. His Vietnamese had a distinct dialect. A 'G' is a "Yah" sound in the South and a "Zuh" in the North, among others. Like Boston and Dallas, exacerbated by centuries of limited mobility.

Tung was to be the nicest, most congenial of all the Vietnamese anyone on the team had met. Ever polite, soft spoken and always anxious to perform and please, Wagner would come to believe the man would risk his life for him. Another bit of incongruity in this war. Would he be the same if the situation was reversed? Tung already impressed him with his polite nature and positive attitude, though the question of trust was difficult to guarantee.

Wagner was still conversing with the Kit Carson when the Major asked him if he could have a word when he was through. Sergeant Flanagan helped Tung get situated, and Wagner walked with the Major to his trailer.

"Darryl, I want to discuss your incident at the PX."

"Yes, sir." Wagner wondered how this was going to go. Strange consequences were never unexpected in this good Army.

"I spoke to Colonel Robichaud. He'd like to discuss this with you, particularly regarding this Major Rigor."

"Yes, sir. Sorry if I opened a bee hive."

"Not at all. You did the right thing. I think he just wants to hear it from you, details and all. He'd like to see you tomorrow morning. I doubt there will be any problem. Have

202

you discussed this with anyone else?"

"No, sir, not yet. Well, Yeah, with Lt. Bailey. We were at the PX together. I shouldn't have?"

"Robichaud says Colonel Bern would like to keep it quiet, due to a perceived race issue. I'll talk to Bailey. I wouldn't be too worried about it. He'll see you at his office at 0900 tomorrow."

"Yes, sir," Wagner said, aware that the Major never brought up the Flanagan-shooting incident.

In the morning, Wagner drove to Pleiku MACV Headquarters at 0900 hours, still a little apprehensive. It started raining again just before he arrived. Road spray in the open sided Jeep soaked his entire side.

The first person he saw was Doug Hanson. "Hey, Darryl, how's it going? What brings you here on this rainy vacation mecca morning?"

"I've got to report to Colonel Bern on some recent thing," Wagner replied. "Catch you later?"

"Yeah, I'd like to talk," Hanson said, with a concerned look, Wagner thought.

MSG Husky was smiling knowingly when he found Wagner as Hanson was leaving. "Good morning, sir. The Colonel's expecting you, go right in."

"Thanks, Sergeant Husky. You look bright and cheery today!"

"Always a thrill to be here in the gracious vacation paradise we all share, sir."

Wagner walked in and saluted Colonel Bern. "Good morning, sir."

"Have a seat, Lieutenant. Things going pretty well back in Indian country?" Bern asked. His thin, dark eyes were peering down, his head tilted back slightly.

"It's been pretty interesting, sir. Something new all the time, and not much in the ordinary."

"Well, I'm hearing good things. Major Nichols is very

pleased with you and your team. Sounds like you did a commendable job in your compound attack."

"Thank you, sir."

"Now this PX thing. I've gotten the gist of it from your Major, but I'd like a run down. Don't leave anything out, if you will." Colonel Bern was now up and slowly pacing, hands behind his back.

Wagner recounted the story, all the while watching to see body language that might reveal disapproval. To his relief, he saw none.

"Seems the MP involved..." the Colonel said, looking down through his bifocals at the report from the Provost Marshall... "Spec 5 Cooper? Apparently he did his job after you left. He questioned the sales girl some more, then went through the trash in the basement, looking for recent receipts. This Private Voss, he's been stealing items from other men in his unit--radios, cameras, whatever--and returning them to the PX for cash. They already had suspected him. According to the report, this time he didn't have a receipt. The Vietnamese girl did the right thing. And so did you."

Wagner, relieved, said "Thank you, sir."

"As far as I'm concerned, this is the last straw for Major Rigor. I had moved him out of his last assignment to get his lazy ass in gear. Didn't work. Thought it might. He's been the District Senior Advisor in Phu Nhot, and hasn't accomplished a god damn thing. Thinks he's here for some kind of goddamned free ride vacation. Your action gave me the straw I needed. He's being relieved of duty, end of career. And Voss... Court martial. Dishonorable.

"Wow," was all Wagner could say.

"Lieutenant Wagner, we can use a lot more young officers like you. Not many would have taken the initiative or handled this very well. Looks like we made the right decision. You're a leader."

"Thank you sir. Spec 5 Cooper. Maybe a little recognition for him? He was outstanding."

"Already done. Keep this incident under wraps, I don't

want any goddamn race riots coming into play, this has nothing to do with race. Just two personnel problems, period."

"No problem, sir."

As Wagner left the HQ building, a Vietnamese V-100 armored vehicle and a Jeep with Vietnamese MP 'White Mice' were pulling in. In the shotgun seat of the Jeep was a Vietnamese lieutenant colonel.

Inside, Colonel Bern and the civilian, David Friedman were behind closed doors. Hanson knocked, and the talking stopped momentarily, then Bern opened the door. "You have company, sir, General Ngo's aide, Colonel Duong just arrived," said Hanson.

"Thank you, Lieutenant," Bern said. "Show him in."

The White Mice entourage waited outside on each side of the door at 'parade rest', while Colonel Duong strode into Bern's office. Unknown to the participants, Doug had taken the trouble to snake a tiny Sony cassette microphone, courtesy of the PX, through the damaged wall crack in a space where the wall met the floor. A small wooden wire-way running along the base of the other side of the wall concealed it. Normally, this would be unthinkable for the inherently professional Hanson, but too many private meetings and so many phone conversations behind closed doors peaked his interest. General Ngo had made the news as a suspected ring leader in an illegal drug operation, operating out of Cambodia. Boredom on the job and occasional gleanings about drugs and body counts added to a decision to spy on Bern. Again, the *what are they gonna do, send me to Vietnam'* line came to mind. Doug Hanson had a high-level position back home, he never planned on making a career of the Army. He'd be home in eight months. They weren't about to catch him anyway.

It was morning in late August when Wagner pulled the Jeep into the compound at Le Quon, Tim Demers emerged from the radio TOC to meet him. "Sir, I've got a call from Plei Deng, they think they've got some movement of troops."

"Thanks. Did they give any details?"

"No, sir. The PF there sounded pretty distressed. I got the message to Captain Nguyen here at Le Quon, but I was hoping you'd get back."

"Tell you what....Plei Deng. The Montagnard PF lieutenant there - - That's B'dai Klot. He speaks fair English. We're not in the best shape to saddle up, and that's back in there. Perfect chance to call my Cobra friend. Name's Jim Kalman. Give me a second, I'll get my map. Tell them to get Victor November artillery ready, I'll fill in with U.S. Arty if that doesn't work, but don't tell them that part. We're supposed to be turning this over to them, they can't keep counting on U.S. support."

Wagner came out of his room, map in hand, and quickly ran the 20 meters to the TOC. "Timmy, let me use your radio," giving him the frequency at Holloway.

"Fancy Hobble Niner Two, Fancy Hobble Niner Two, this is Murky Cinder Five Seven, over," called Wagner. "Fancy Hobble Niner Two, Fancy Hobble Niner Two, this is Murky Cinder Five Seven, Murky Cinder Five Seven, over."
In a few seconds, the voice of a radio transmission broken statically by the chopping blades of a helicopter came back, "Murky Cinder Five Seven, this is Fancy Hobble Niner Two, over."

"Fancy Hobble Niner Two, this is Murky Cinder Five Seven, I'm the MAT Five Seven Leader you met at your base, with the carved helicopters. I have possible targets for you, are you available, over?"

"That's affirm," came the broken reply. "I was wondering when I'd hear from you. Where can I find you, Five Seven?"

"Fancy Hobble Niner Two, this is Murky Cinder Five Seven, drop down a dime and we'll talk, over," said Wagner, indicating a change to a 10 Hz lower frequency, providing their own 'personal' channel, thereby avoiding interference for easier communications. "Be advised, I am not at that location," said Wagner. "I have some little people possibly in need of help ASAP. Village of Plei Deng, about twenty klicks east of your base, nine north of the highway. I can give you coordinates, wait one."

"I know the village," he replied. "Do you have people on the ground that can pop smoke?"

"I believe so, I will give you his call sign, you can talk directly to him. He's Montagnard, speaks some English, may be hard to understand. Also, be advised I have Vietnamese artillery on notice, but it will take them a while, guaranteed. Can you coordinate, and what would be your ETA, over?" Wagner was hand signaling to Tim Demers to write the PF's call sign down.

"Roger, Five Seven, I can and I estimate I'm four mikes out, over."

Demers wrote down the Vietnamese PF's call sign and Wagner read it to Jim Kalman in his Cobra. "Niner Two, I'm going to switch to the PF's freq at this time, I will stay out of this unless required, over."

"Roger that, Five Seven, thanks for thinking of us."

Wagner and Demers listened to Kalman's 'Hunter-Killer' team of two Loaches and his Cobra the entire four minutes it took to reach Plei Ko Tu, only a minute after the suspected enemy tripped the first trip wire and shooting commenced. Wagner could only hope the smoke grenades and the PF platoon leader's English could be understood well enough to coordinate.

It was over in thirty minutes. The three Cobra and two 'Little Birds' expended their ammo, and whatever enemy was involved checked out instantly, either from a murderous spray of 7.62 mm rounds, 40mm grenades and rockets, or by foot if they were lucky.

Wagner called Kalman to inform that Vietnamese artillery was ready and he should *di mau.* Leave fast. The PF platoon leader was ecstatic over the overwhelming support offered by the deadly *mai bai truc than* helicopters.

It ended well. Well for Wagner, who was happy to help

his Cobra pilot friend. Well for the ever blood thirsty pilots, and especially well for the PFs on the ground. Not so much for the bad guys.

With a well-needed break, Wagner radioed Gordon Bailey at Plei Do Rom to see if he could meet for another PX run and a visit to the pool at the 71st Medevac Hospital. Toothless Montagnard women, for the most part, were the only ones to look at, and if they were over sixteen, guaranteed they had a baby clutching a bare boob. The team members needed a break from each other, and a trip into the safety of Pleiku without constant tensions of leadership and war would be a welcome respite. And there was Annelle. The lack of female companionship did nothing to lessen the attraction he felt from their one meeting.

Wagner and Bailey drove to Pleiku, stopping for what appeared to be two Vietnamese attacking someone on the ground. Instead, they had come across another 50 cc Honda road casualty, nothing at all rare. They had come to believe the war wasn't necessary for the North, attrition from motorcycle accidents would do the job sooner. It would be cheaper to send a few hundred thousand Hondas down the Ho Chi Minh Trail. The two Vietnamese owned the old Renault that hit the motorcycle. The motorcyclist was unconscious and bleeding from the head and waist, and one leg clearly had a compound fracture. Vietnamese first aid consisted of yanking, dragging, and kicking a casualty to wake him up. It wasn't intentional, just ignorance in basics of medical aid.

The two lieutenants stopped them, Wagner yelling, *"Khong! Chung toi muon giup ong-ai,"* the quickest instructions he could come up with. They formed a makeshift litter with a poncho and rifles, which proved agonizingly short even for the small Vietnamese motorcyclist, but it was better than nothing. They placed him on the back seat with Bailey, Wagner driving the Jeep. Maneuvering through Pleiku traffic was a scene out of the Keystone Cops, but when other drivers, angry at the 'belligerent Americans' honking and cutting them

208

off saw the now copious blood of the Vietnamese man in the back, they quickly veered away. Wagner sped into the 71st Medevac, honking the horn for help. In an instant, the capable staff had the man off the Jeep and on a stretcher, headed for the emergency room.

The situation out of their hands, they hosed off the bloody Jeep and drove to the pool area. Bailey went to what would roughly be described as the Men's locker room, while Wagner, blood still on his hands, arms, and shirt, asked one of the Army nurses, dressed in green fatigues, if she knew an Annelle Atchison.

"Yes, of course," she said, looking at his name tag. "I'm Kelly, Lieutenant Wagner...Kelly Foster. I work with Annelle."

"Hi, Kelly, nice to meet you ma'am. I'm Darryl Wagner. I'm not sure Annelle remembers me, I was wondering if she would be free today. For the pool, I mean."

"Oh, yes. I mean, Yes, let me check for you. Can you wait here?

"Sure, thanks very much," he said, still nervous that he was one more GI infatuated with this beauty, one more pain in the ass suitor.

Kelly disappeared around the pool entrance at the far end. Annelle was in scrubs, bloodier than Wagner's shirt. She stood over a patient with two other nurses, just coming out of emergency surgery. Her hair was in a sanitary cap, she had bloody rubber gloves on. "Annelle!" Kelly said, "Your Montagnard is here."

"My what?"

"The cute soldier, the Montagnard," she laughed.

"*KELLY!* You mean Wagner? Darryl Wagner?"

"Yes. You didn't tell me he was a lieutenant."

"Oh. I didn't know. He was in a bathing suit."

"Well, he's not now. He's standing out there in bloody jungle fatigues. I don't *think* it's his blood, he seems okay. He seems *more* than okay. *Oh yeah!*"

"Kelly, can you cover for me? We just cleared our last casualty."

"No problem, Annie, go get your Montagnard. I'll let him know, maybe fifteen minutes?"

"*Kelly!*" she yelled, "Yeah, fifteen," untying her scrubs as she headed for the door.

Outside, Wagner waited uneasily as Kelly returned. He fully expected to hear "Annelle couldn't make it, thanks anyway for asking, maybe another time, whatever..."

"Hello, sir. Annelle's just coming off her shift. She can be here in about fifteen minutes?" Kelly said, smiling.

"Oh. Sure. Yeah, that'd be great. I'm heading into the locker room. Gotta change. Thanks a lot, Kelly." He wanted to know more, was he being a pain in the ass? Did she feel a need to not 'brush off' this poor grunt in the field? After all, she saw nothing but sad cases all day, every day, of guys like him that she could only wish had never found themselves horribly burned or mutilated.

Wagner was entering the locker room as Gordon was coming out. Bailey asked, "Did you find Annelle?"

"Yeah. She'll be out in a bit. I'll be right out."

The pool felt great. As much as Wagner loved water, a pool never felt so good. The skies had cleared and the Sun was out. Dank smells of Pleiku and the rainy season were the norm here at the hospital, but they were sweet compared to Montagnard creosote-saturated grass roofs, animal feces and Montagnard cigars. The chlorine smell of the pool had its own pleasant familiarity in this foreign place where nothing else was.

When Annelle walked out, she was transformed. Her sweat and blood soaked scrubs became a bathing suit, white with a black and magenta diagonal swath, and her pulled-into-a-bun hair was now lightly blowing in the warm light breeze. Her skin was still only lightly tanned, long hours of work prohibited more. She had washed her hair, applied makeup, and restored herself in minutes, all unknown, of course, to Wagner, who pictured her looking the same while working on a patient. "Hi Darryl, nice to see you again."

"Wow, you look really beautiful, Annelle. Beautiful suit."

"Thank you. I don't get to wear it often. This place is crazy. I was worried you might have been hurt. It's been a while."

"I hoped you'd remember me. My only trips in to Pleiku have been for some request by Headquarters. Back in the woods, it's been pretty crazy. Unbelievable what's been going on."

"Really? I hope I don't see you come through here. Some of the guys lately, it's….just hard. We're all pretty well burned out, I think. The doctors, they're great. They're all great. But some days, it just doesn't stop. With the other field units being pulled out, more guys are being sent here, from all over. And there's even talk of the 71st being taken out," she said. "These poor guys. There are some days I just cry. It's so sad."

Wagner heard her, but he was staring at her eyes, her lips….and her suit, trying not to stare. Annelle tried not to show she noticed. He glanced over to see Gordon, chatting with two nurses, the only other people at the pool. He intended to introduce Annelle, but their conversation went on. He told her about the operations, the Cobra, the attack at the compound, about Sergeant Flanagan, but mostly the Montagnards. She was as fascinated by the primitive tribesmen as he was. Annelle couldn't hear enough about them.

"So you're a lieutenant." She said.

"Yes, turned First a week before I got here."

"And your team, what's your position?"

"I'm the team leader. Nothing I did, I just fell into it. It's a captain's slot, a command position, just like a company commander, but with only three or four men. Nothing I did, just a luck of the draw thing. Apparently, no other officers to fill it. I'm guessing that's a result of our 'reductions in force'."

Wagner looked at her for a second, then broke into a broad grin.

"What?" she said.

"Nothing."

"No, what? I saw that."

"What?" Wagner was grinning.

"There, that. What's that?"

"Well, I just imagined for a minute."

"Really? What?" Annelle asked, also imagining …"

"You. With filed off front teeth and a Montagnard cigar."

"AAAHH!" She screamed.

"Spitting on the ground."

"Oh my God! Really? What is *wrong* with you? And a topless sarong I suppose?"

"I didn't *say* that."

"Definitely something wrong," she said, smiling.

"It's inherited. Not my fault."

Forty five minutes passed and one of the nurses talking with Gordon left. Gordon and the remaining nurse, Corrine, jumped into the pool. Wagner and Annelle did the same, and introductions were made.

This time, the visit was ended due to both nurses' work requirements. The Sun had gone in, the skies were turning a slate dark gray as Gordon and Darryl left the Medevac Hospital to stop at Headquarters in Pleiku. On the way to the Jeep, they stopped briefly to inquire about the Vietnamese motorcyclist. He had died.

Arriving at HQ to turn in paperwork and reports to Colonel Bern's office, they both stopped in Doug Hanson's office for a visit. He was filing through reams of paperwork, deep in his work when they came through the old wooden office door. "Doug, you big ol' Chairborne Ranger, you. We showered for you," Wagner said.

"Oh, excellent!" he said, adjusting his military plastic framed glasses as he stood to shake hands. "I was hoping you would. Good to see you guys. I didn't know you were in the 'hood, haven't seen you for a while."

"Yeah, Doug, we've meant to do lunch, but it's rainy season in the jungle," Bailey said, with his usual low-key smile.

"Everything okay out there? No poison crossbow arrows or hungry tigers?"

"Nope. Just V.C. rats and throngs of horny, toothless, topless women. It's been tough, beatin' em away," replied Wagner. "But y'know, war's hell."

"Yeah, well, somebody's gotta do it. Have a seat. What brings you in?" Hanson asked, sitting back down with his usual smile.

"We're just bringing in the action reports. We write' em, Major Nichols piles' em, then we bring 'em here. Probably nobody ever reads them," said Wagner, chuckling.

Gordon leaned toward Doug and said, "So who does read this stuff? Does anyone really know, or care what we're doing out there?"

Wagner added, looking at Bailey, "Yeah, the Major's a great guy, good officer. But honestly, I don't think he much cares what we do or where we go. We're kind of on our own, like, our own bosses out there."

Doug Hanson's smile dissolved, and he turned serious. Putting a silencing finger to his lips, he got up to close the door behind his guests. He returned to his desk and leaned forward. He spoke in a hushed voice, Wagner and Bailey likewise leaning forward to hear. "Listen, guys. Something's going on that I don't understand, nor am I privy to. But there's a visit on a weekly basis from General Ngo, or at least one of his Colonel aides. They show up, behind a closed door with either Colonel Robichaud or Bern, and later they leave."

"So what?" Bailey asked. "I don't imagine they make their plans public knowledge."

"Right," replied Hanson. "But I've overheard some of it. Besides the usual talk about village reconsolidations, they talk about drugs and body counts. Not enemy, it's American bodies. And it's not just occasional; it's most of their meetings. I can't make out all of it, but...and guys, we've got to keep this absolutely confidential...this is serious shit. I honestly think

General Ngo and Colonel Bern may be involved in some drug business."

"Oh my friggin' word," Wagner said, dumbstruck.

"Are you sure about this, Doug?" asked Bailey.

"No, I'm not. But you two, and possibly Jerry Dulane, are the only people I can confide in this. We've been through a lot, I know you guys, but *anyone* else, Vietnamese or American, I wouldn't trust.

"I've read about Ngo, when we were at Fort Bliss. He's been suspect in drugs before, and he's made the news. But Colonel Bern?," Bailey said.

"You know, I've never even seen a marijuana joint, nor a plant, let alone drugs." Wagner said. "Not just here. Not in my life. I don't need that shit. We've all heard about drugs over here, maybe in the rear areas, but I haven't seen it here. I doubt like hell my sergeants use drugs, and the Montagnards don't. The Vietnamese chew some Beetlenut, but that's about it for what I've seen."

"Well, I've seen plenty of it in Los Angeles, but like you, Darryl, I haven't seen anything here," added Bailey. "I doubt my sergeants are using any either. How would I know, they're drunk half the time,"

"Darryl, what do you know about Colonel Hallard?" Hanson asked.

"He was the Colonel in Nha Trang I told you about. The one that got my orders for Cam Ranh Bay switched to here. He actually seems like a sharp cat, decent, my little confrontation with him aside," Wagner said. "Why?"

"I don't know. He calls here a lot, talks to Bern first, then to Robichaud. I think he's working with Robichaud and Friedman in some kind of investigation." Hanson answered.

"That might make sense," Wagner added. "Hallard's an MP Colonel. Friedman is a Criminal Investigation Division special agent, CID. A civilian. From my company commander stint in Aberdeen—I read the Miranda rights to men in my company a hundred times- I know that a CID special agent does not charge, but he turns his findings over to the cops and courts.

I remember talking about this with an MP friend from the Advisory schools, Ron Hewitt. He's in Saigon. The CID agent can exercise jurisdiction over military personnel who are suspected of offenses under the Uniform Code of Military Justice. The special agent is not typically in a combat position. Officers *cannot* be a special agent. So Friedman would fill that slot as the civilian special agent."

"And Hallard?" Hanson asked.

"Hallard would be the MP to work with him. He would be the guy to charge the suspect."

"Jeezus, what next in this friggin' war?" asked Bailey, disgustedly. "Is there no end to the bullshit we're in?"

"Let's not jump to any conclusions," Hanson said, his hand hovering in a level position a few inches off the desk. Hanson was staring intently at his friends' eyes, accentuating his point. "I wanted to give you guys a heads-up. Keep your eyes and ears open. If something gets nasty here, I don't want to bring it home with me, and neither do you."

"Understood."

"And please, guys, remember this is confidential. Now listen to this," Hanson said, pulling out his cassette recorder.

What they heard was beyond comprehension. Whatever else revealed the most disgusting side of man about Vietnam, this topped it all. The conversation on the tape described gutting dead American soldiers, killed in Cambodia, and stuffing their remains with 22 kilograms--fifty pounds each--of heroin for shipment back to the states. Once there, officers and NCOs at Norton Air Force Base in California would receive their bodies, allowing them to remove the smuggled heroin. A mortuary in Danang was involved before the flight to Travis Air Force Base. A 'Chang Mai' factory was discussed on the tape. At this factory, the dead soldiers' bodies were labeled with a code to enable the receiving end to determine which bodies held the heroin.

Finally, it became apparent that Major Rigor--the Major in the PX incident--was involved for some time in the drug trade. It seemed he had been working with Colonel Bern, the

Senior Province Adviser, the highest ranking officer in their province. But now Bern said he's getting rid of Major Rigor, ending his military career. Wagner didn't know what to believe. He and Bailey left for their compounds, swearing their silence and cooperation to their friend. A lot to think about on the Jeep drive home.

VIII   DOUBLED PAWNS

"Two pawns of the same side on the same file."

The team was preparing for an operation coming up soon that Major Nichols had discussed with Wagner the day before. The idea had come up - - who knew where - - of combining a unit from the 54th Security Attachment group from the helicopter base at Camp Holloway with MAT 57 and the 818 Montagnard Regional Force Mike Strike Company. This was the first time Wagner would be able to work with Americans other than his team. The security guards were almost entirely 'green', however, with little to none experience in the field for all but a few men. Most of that limited experience was in staying outside their perimeter overnight in a group of from two to four men as a listening post. An LP's purpose was to give early warning of an attack on the base. Those LPs were typically no more than one to three hundred meters outside the wire.

The team was amenable to this, it should be considerably safer and comforting to have American firepower and numbers with them. If they ran into a large enemy force, Camp Holloway would surely send the cavalry with the helicopter armada based there. Nice to know when it took up to thirty minutes to get artillery fire after all the clearances were made to avoid friendly units or aircraft....assuming the artillery could reach their location.

It was 1300 hours when Tim Demers emerged from the TOC radio bunker to find Lt. Wagner. Wagner was loading the new PRC-25 radio that Sergeant Stewart had traded for some enemy weapons at the Blackhawk artillery fire base a week before. For some reason it delivered a better range than the old one. Without commo to the artillery, their 'shit was weak'.

"Sir, I've got a call from a "Fancy Hobble" for you. Sounds like he's in a chopper."

"Ahh, I know who that guy is," said Wagner, smiling.

"He said he's en route to our location, sir. Coming in to our chopper pad," the RTO said.

Wagner ran past the team house, where Sergeants Stewart and Blas were working out with weights. "That Cobra pilot is coming in, he's picking me up. Gotta get a smoke grenade," he yelled, turning the corner to the outside door to his room. Grabbing one from his gear, he strapped on the .38 Smith & Wesson revolver he carried wherever he didn't carry his M-16. He ran down into the TOC, where Tim handed him the handset. "Fancy Hobble Niner Two, this is Murky Cinder Five Seven, over."

"Roger, Murky Cinder. This is Fancy Hobble Niner Two, do you have time for me?" Jim Kalman asked.

"Fancy Hobble Niner Two, Five Seven here. That's a big affirmative, over."

"Roger that, Five Seven, I'll be at your location in five mikes, over"

"Fancy Hobble, do you want me to pop smoke?" Wagner asked.

"Cinder Five Seven, Niner Two. You can do that, I know your location, but it would help, over."

"Roger that, Hobble, I'm on my way to the pad now. I won't have a radio, just look for Goofy Grape smoke, out." He ran out the front gate to circumvent the perimeter berm, throwing his purple smoke grenade on the downwind side of the scrubby helicopter landing pad. By the time he popped smoke, he could see small silhouettes of three helicopters to the east.

The Cobra looks mean just to look at, a predatory raptor searching for a kill. The aircraft weighs 14,750 lbs., stands over 14' high, 58' long. Top speed is 175 miles per hour, though higher in 'unauthorized dives', and pretty much everything in Vietnam was unauthorized. Kalman landed the Cobra with precision and speed. He was in the pilot's back seat of the three-foot wide warbird, a foot higher than the gunner's seat in front. He had the encompassing Plexiglas acrylic canopy opened and ready for Wagner to climb in. The blades were still spinning while Kalman briefed him on controls, commo, and guns before taking off. Closing the canopy, he gave Wagner a helmet, turning the intercom switch on. Now they could talk easily without the roar of the turbine and rotary wings drowning them out.

"Where're we going?" Kalman asked.

Wagner was going on his joint operation the next day, and this was a good opportunity to look it over before the march.

"I'll show you," he said, pointing to his map.

The Cobra had dual controls, either the pilot or the front gunner could control it. "Okay, Darryl. In your hands..." He went over the cyclic and collective, one hand controlling throttle, the other blade pitch for steering, diving, and climbing. On the right hand control was a red button that fired their rockets.

"Don't touch that now, we're hot," he warned.

Two foot-pedals on the floor operated the rear rotor, just as in a plane's rudder. Then he went over the guns. Jim would operate the two pods hanging on the three-foot wings, which held Gatling miniguns of 7.62mm bullets. Wagner would be responsible for the two pods of thirty nine rockets, each 2.75" in diameter. The chin mounted turret underneath Wagner's feet would also be his responsibility, operated by a box-like sight that hung on the left side of the cockpit. It was held by its two handles on the sides to point at the target. Wherever the sight was aimed, the guns in the chin pod turret pointed. It could be moved from side to side in the cockpit to shoot to either side or anywhere in between. The turret held a side by side mounting of another minigun and a 350 round per minute grenade launcher, fired by red buttons on the handle.

"The red button on the left handle is the grenade launcher. The one on the right is the minigun. Those are hot, too," Kalman said over the intercom.

All the while, the two Loaches were flying circles around the compound, bringing the RFs as well as the team out to watch.

"If we see bad guys, do you want me to shoot?" Wagner asked.

"You're the gunner," was the reply. He lifted the Cobra up and dipped forward, heading toward the East and "V.C.

Valley" as they called it. On the way, he went over the controls again, in case he was injured and unable to fly. Kalman reminded Wagner of the loss of the two Loaches and four pilots shortly before. He let Wagner take the controls for a couple of minutes to get the feel, which came surprisingly easy. "If you can ride a motorcycle, you can fly a helicopter," he said. Wagner owned a 650cc motorcycle before coming to Vietnam. He also had experience operating a skidder on the logging job, which may have helped in coordinating the controls on this beast.

When they reached the intended area, the two 'Little Bird' Loaches were working out down below, their four-bladed rotors blowing trees and bushes apart, while their Cobra climbed to 2,000 feet. The small and agile "Olive With a Toothpick" loaches, as they were called from their appearance, flitted around trees, first one scooting over the branches, then the other buzzing around in front, taking its turn, like bees flirting with flowers in a field. Forward, side to side, and backwards, fast and maneuverable. Each carried a minigun on its side. They hovered for a moment, separating the green cover below them with their rotor wash, then they flew sideways, skidding around in short turns, first right, then left. All the while, the Cobra waited above, the Falcon ready to dive on a hapless sparrow.

"Those guys live a hairy life," Kalman said. "We lost a lot of Loach pilots. We're all a little crazy, they say, but those guys are certifiably nuts. They'll do anything, including in the O-club."

Wagner kept concentrating on what he'd do if the gunner's job came to fruition. A solid two hours later, there was less light and shadows made it difficult to see. Kalman sent the two Loaches home and said, "Now we can play. You want to fly her?"

Kalman went over their dual controls again, with Wagner taking partial control. He found the Cobra responded quickly but smoothly. He tried to coordinate the foot controls, which swung the tail left or right for direction. The steering stick was a little difficult at first. Coordinating the blade pitch and the RPM took a bit of getting used to. Too much pitch and not enough power could cause a stall, akin to a plane climbing too fast without enough power and propeller to keep flying. Kalman didn't want him to try to hover, the most difficult part of learning to fly. When Wagner pushed forward on the stick, he thought it was a steep dive, and he instinctively pulled back. The Cobra quickly responded and they were pointing up, the two big blades digging hard at the air, shaking the entire ship. Gradually, he learned to ease into the motions, and it was actually getting easy. He remembered the Cobras he'd seen when he first arrived in country, in Di An. English Spitfire pilots in WW II had a routine of doing barrel rolls over the runway when they returned from a kill. The Cobra pilots did it by diving from 2,000 feet, pulling up just above the runway to complete a 360 loop, upside down. Feeling more confident and knowing Kalman had the dual controls, Wagner took it up, heeled over, and put it in a dive. In what he thought was a nearly vertical dive, he expected in any second to hear Kalman yell at him over the helmet commo. It never came. He was several hundred feet up when he pulled the nose up, and though banking slightly to the right, he completed his upside down loop.

Kalman finally spoke. "Okay, I'll take over now. 'You ready?"

"Sure."

Kalman took the Cobra back up to 4,000 feet, banked hard to the right, and put it in a vertical power dive. It only took a dozen seconds to go from 4,000 feet to what looked like it would be minus 10. In that big surrounding bubble of plastic, feet from the nose, it felt like a screaming roller coaster with no rails. The ground came up so fast it seemed impossible to make it out of the dive as Jim pulled up on the stick to swing up hard, at max speed. The G-forces plastered Wagner to his seat, the skids barely missing the tree tops, nose suddenly pointing up. Continuing through the loop, he was now upside down, thankful to still be on this side of dirt. The G-forces turned into brief weightlessness at the apex before the agile Cobra was back to a right side up position, sling-shotted out at high speed, a perfect loop.

"How's that?" Kalman asked.

"Wow!" was all Wagner could say. It was the high point of his tour.

Late the next day, the team was joined by some visiting friends of two of the NCOs. Along with their RTO Tim, the Major, and interpreters, they gathered for a customary volleyball game. A court by the team house helped to relieve tension and stress of many men before and after, whenever time not in 'the field' and weather permitted. They often included Vietnamese soldiers assigned in the compound. It was the only game that could be held in the constrained space on rough, sloping ground. "Jungle rules volleyball" prevailed, translating to 'there are no rules', including pulling up or down on the net, all parts of the body over the net, etc. If the sides weren't 'evened out' by mixing teams, the Americans always clobbered the small Vietnamese, particularly with the aforementioned guidelines.

After the games, they reminisced about a trip a few months before, up QL 14 to a larger Vietnamese village. The small Vietnamese challenged the team to a volleyball game. "No problem," said the team, might be a good rapport thing.

"We bet you four case Budweiser," the counterparts said.

"No problem," came the American team's reply.

The Vietnamese told them they would be back in ten minutes. Problem: The Vietnamese trotted out in pretty little green and white numbered uniforms. They would not agree to 'jungle rules'. They served backhand over-the-head Olympic style, the team was structured and orderly, and they wiped the taller American's asses. In a fifteen point game, they spotted the team twelve points and they still won. But four cases of beer was a small price to pay for rapport, better than Co Tuong

Chess.

Following the games, Sergeant Flanagan was razzing his visiting friend, Sergeant Perez. Perez, like Flanagan, was an old NCO, at the ripe old age of 43. Thin and grizzled, he looked 53. Perez, of Hispanic descent, was bragging of his tolerance for hot food. Flanagan said, "You ain't seen nothin yet. You ain't had hot food until you had Montagnard food." Perez worked in Supply in the city, and had no contacts with Montagnards, including his first tour in Cam Ranh. The argument rose and fell with each slug of scotch, and Wagner watched in awe as Perez swallowed a packet of LRRP dehydrated peppers, washing it down with Tabasco sauce. Tears came to his eyes, but he was successful, showing little other discomfort. Flanagan swung in his seat to tell the young interpreter, Kir, to run to the adjacent small village of Plei Piom, and bring back some Montagnard stew. Forty five minutes later, Kir returned with a small pot. Perez had to swallow his pride, because the stew soon won, dwarfing their dehydrated peppers.

Wagner, Blas, and Major Nichols had returned to their rooms. Someone was yelling outside. Flanagan and Stewart went outside to find a man being carried in on a stretcher. He had been brought in by a Lambretta from the Chieu Hoi village, two klicks away. Drunk on rice wine, he shot his two kids, killing them. Then he went after his wife with a white phosphorus grenade, tripped and fell, and the grenade went off several feet from him. His wife was burned, but not badly. He was not so lucky.

"Where did it get him?" Wagner asked.

"Face, shoulders, one hand," Flanagan answered.

One of the visiting NCOs, Sergeant Hort, was another older medic. "Oh, God, that has to be bad," he said. "Willie Peter just keeps burning--right into the body."

"Have you called for a dust-off?" asked Wagner.

"Chopper's already on the way," Flanagan said, still with his derisive tone, but clearly shaken by the man's condition.

The man was carried into the team house's makeshift

medical room on a stretcher. It was dim in the room, with one small light hanging by an electrical wire from the ceiling. A barely visible blue glow emanated from one eye socket, a piece of phosphorus still burning, producing a thin veil of smoke slowly wafting up in the little light afforded. His left hand was gone, either amputated by the grenade or burned off. His head and shoulders were black and blistered, his features undistinguishable. The dust-off was called off, the man was dead within five minutes.

Sergeant Stewart asked, "Where the hell did he get the white phosphorus grenade, anyway?"

"He's from the Chieu Hoi village. Ex-V.C. We *think.*" added Blas.

"It does beg the question, doesn't it?" Wagner said, pondering the body as it was being lugged out.

The American 54th Security Attachment Platoon arrived in deuce-and-a-half trucks the next morning. MAT 57 was ready, with some rough guidelines handed to Wagner of the coordinates to where they were headed. The designated area was east and slightly north of Camp Holloway. Obviously, the helicopter base would like to cover an area more likely to be a threat to them, and that in itself was not a problem with Wagner. But he disliked any 'preplanned' routes or locations from the highers. The enemy often had an effective intelligence network set up, from things as simple as a map on MACV Headquarters' wall. A quick discussion with Major Nichols lead to an agreement with the 54th to coordinate a more sensible operation into areas that, in his experience thus far, could be more productive. He was eager to make use of the firepower luxury offered in this joint operation.

The Americans got off the trucks in front of the main compound and stood in a rough formation in an early morning sun to organize their squads. The team introduced themselves to the platoon leader and sergeants. The 54th ground commander was a Captain Knowles. Knowles said he wanted it to be a fifty-fifty operation, with the RF commander, a Montagnard 3rd lieutenant, or 'Chuan-uy' Glah in charge of his RFs. Wagner's team, as per normal, could not command, only advise and coordinate the Montagnard counterparts. Knowles added that he wanted the men who were walking the point to be both Montagnard and American, something Wagner worried might cause safety and confusion in the event of a firefight.

Wagner informed Captain Knowles of the 'Yards' impressive capabilities and three-file tactics, but that got lost along the way somewhere. He also informed Knowles a company in the world of Montagnard RF units might mean roughly eighty five men if they were lucky, give or take a dozen, half of an American company.

Right away, the team saw a problem as they watched the men climb out of the trucks. They were loaded for bear, grossly overloaded with ammunition and gear. Experienced units would travel lean unless they had no confidence in a resupply. This unit would have no problem with resupply, being attached to a nearby base loaded with helicopters.

The American squads now organized, Wagner and the team joined Knowles and his sergeant, Buck Sergeant Charles Shields. Wagner would stay near them, a third of the way back in the two-file column that Knowles wanted. Sergeants Blas, Stewart, and Flanagan would follow behind, each with one or two American soldiers between them. An American RTO stayed behind the Captain, as per the norm. An RTO usually had some of the radio's weight reduced by other soldiers helping with some of his gear. Wagner learned early on to always carry his own twenty four pound radio, along with all his other gear; food, flashlight, seven-magazine bandolier, two hand grenades, two smoke grenades, map, compass, Claymore ball bearings, canteen, poncho and poncho liner. The only exceptions were when working with one of the two Mike Strike Montagnard companies, whereupon an RTO would be assigned and trusted to stay with him. Today, he wanted the radio on his own back not only to call in support, but to coordinate between the two units.

They filed around the compound to the north side, just as a line of Montagnard RF soldiers appeared rising over the hill at the tree line a couple hundred meters away. They were spaced well, small, and moving quickly. Their smaller stature and lighter loads made a discernible difference, the closer they came to the U.S. soldiers. When they reached the American group, Wagner introduced the leaders. Chuan-uy Glah, clearly in charge of his men, appeared to await orders from the Americans. Wagner was quick to explain the plan and the desire of the Americans to travel in two files, and they wanted to share the point man's responsibility. Glah would not argue if he was asked to carry the G.I.s on their backs.

Knowles was making a macho effort to show his men he was the commander. Tying a camo bandana around his head, no hat, he did his best to look the part. Wagner understood that, and had no problem with it, though it did come across as a bit of a stretch. The rest of the Captain's men were wearing steel pots. Wagner and his team typically only wore steel helmets when under attack in their home compound or occasionally in the Jeep. Helmets were never a bad idea, but the name of the game was to look as much like their indigenous counterparts as possible, opting for the standard bush hat. To do otherwise made them target number one. Wagner often checked to see if a given unit they would be operating with wore standard jungle fatigues or striped camo 'Tiger Fatigues", and would follow suit, for the same reason.

Pulling the map from his thigh pocket, Wagner unfolded it and briefly explained the destination and azimuth, slightly east of due north, to some stream connections where the enemy was more likely to be congregating. All troops need water and food. There were many secure mountain tops in Vietnam, but the enemy was living in thickly vegetated valleys.

The formalities done, the group headed toward the tree line, crossing open and level areas to the north of the compound. The two files kept even intervals, nobody was bunching up, and nobody was breathing hard except Sergeant

Flanagan. When they hit the tree line, that all changed. The Montagnards, small and moving low and fast, were used to crouching and moving quickly around and through vines, branches and fallen logs. The taller Americans would be disadvantaged enough without their excessive combat loads, and after a few hundred meters they were suffering. In addition, they were unnervingly noisy plowing through the bush. Much of whatever they may or may not have learned in Basic Training and AIT was long forgotten, failing to maintain noise discipline and now bunching up. *"One Round Will Get Us All"* and *'Maintain Your Interval',* were the two most common lines in stateside training, but somehow it just didn't stick. Bulky backpacks and gear got hopelessly snarled in vines and bushes, further inhibiting progress. When they stopped three hours later for lunch, the Americans didn't set up security, another basic for a unit in the bush. The men from Holloway were eager and willing soldiers, they simply needed more men with experience. This all had a bad advisory effect on the Montagnard RFs. These fine, experienced Montagnard troops carried a false sense of security with their all-powerful Americans. Wagner could, from the onset, see they were figuring anything the GIs did was okay, and they were beginning to follow suit. Years of Special Forces and Advisory Team training was falling by the wayside within hours.

The 'Yards couldn't get accustomed to the way their American friends travelled in two files. When the vegetation became too thick, the files morphed into one. That often resulted in staying in that one file, with no flank security. The 'little people' became apprehensive.

When the unit finally stopped for a break and to allow the rear to catch up, Wagner spoke with his team about the observations. "I'm going to see if the Captain will agree to giving the RFs some responsibility, maybe we'll all learn something," he said.

Immediately Sergeant Flanagan said, "Stay out of it, Lieutenant, we're doin' just fine. The RFs got this under control." Sergeant Blas and Sergeant Stewart looked at each other as if to say, "not too sure about that,"

"You don't see any problems here, Sergeant?" asked Wagner, questioningly. Sergeant Flanagan just stared with a scowl. Wagner supposed there was nothing the man *could* agree with. "I'd prefer to err on the side of safety, Sergeant, let alone not screw up our RFs," he countered. Flanagan didn't notice, but both Blas and Stewart gave a slight nod of agreement behind him.

Packing his mess gear and picking up his rifle, Wagner made his way to Captain Knowles. Talking low to keep it private, he said, "Sir, could I suggest the Montagnards take the lead here, I think it might be in all of our interests. These guys know the land, they're out here all the time, and trust me, they're really good at it. I know I could never lead men in the bush the way they can."

Knowles wouldn't hear of it, possibly afraid to appear lacking, and Wagner understood.

"I'd like to tell Glah to form his three files, and to have his men take the points on the two outside files. We can put an American right behind each point man, to take their lead, and keep your man on the center file point."

This, Captain Knowles accepted. "We can keep the Americans interspaced with them, of course," Wagner added.

When the Montagnards moved out on an assigned azimuth, they pretty well stuck to it with only minor variations around difficult obstacles. Partly due to his size, the American center file point man was meandering through the bushes, trying to find the easiest path, often no better off for it. This confused the Montagnard point men, but as per the norm, they wouldn't consider taking the initiative away from an American. Instead, they did their best to stay parallel with him. Following behind, the rest of the column became confused, and things wound up from time to time with one, two, or three files. Wagner never knew if someone was on his flank or not. Not good in an ambush situation. There would always be a fear to shoot, not knowing if they had friendlies between them and the enemy. And if the command element got cleaned out, the ability to call artillery or air support would be lost as well as command and control.

Due to the pace and confusion, when it came time to set up a night defensive position, they had not reached the planned location. There was nothing tactical requiring it anyway, and they may as well have given the enemy their coordinates with flares. It wasn't enough some of the men were yelling to each other and making little bonfires for their C-rations, Knowles had a helicopter come in fifty meters from their night location to drop in food and sleeping gear a few had neglected to bring.

"What do you suppose, sir, "Sergeant Blas whispered, "Those people had in those big-assed rucksacks if they didn't carry any food or sleeping gear?"

"Not a clue, Sarge," Wagner replied. "Maybe Coleman lanterns and Sony radios. If it was raining, they may not have gotten their resupply, the choppers wouldn't be flying." The problem wasn't with the pilots, Wagner knew they would go through hell and back. It was their commanders' decision. It was into October, and the rainy season wasn't yet willing to give up its grip.

"Well, it's going to rain like hell in a while. Dumb-assed Americans, we are," he said, still carrying a bit of his Guamanian accent after decades.

When dusk came, Wagner had called in his coded defensive targets, circled in thin grease pencil on his map. Early on, he had laminated a clear, self-adhesive film on his topo maps, something he asked his father to find and send him from the states. *One more thing the Army should supply, but didn't.* It kept the maps dry, and accepted erasable grease pencil targets for artillery targets. Then there was that damned radio. At 24 lbs., the PRC "Prick" 25 was a rugged but big and heavy relic issued long after World War II, but not looking all that different. It was labelled as "state of the art", but there was plenty of technology to make something a fraction of the size and weight, with better range. But somehow, it never got through as a priority in this system they call the military. If those responsible had to carry them in Vietnam, the outcome would be different. They should have contracted Japan to do it.

Captain Knowles wanted to set up two ambushes, each involving a third of the unit. They would consist of a mix of Americans and Montagnards. Sergeant Blas and Wagner would go with one, Sergeants Flanagan and Stewart would go with the other. Wagner's experience prepared him to expect some Vietnamese units to smoke, talk, play radios, and fall asleep. Conversely, the Montagnards would stay quiet, hidden, and one man would stay awake out of three to six, depending on the level of alert. The Montagnard tribesmen had fought too long with too much to fight for to be lax. The word from Captain Knowles, however, was fifty percent alert. Of course, that would only have to apply to his American personnel.

Two Claymore mines were set up along the trail, plus another two behind them for rear security. Sergeant Blas and Lieutenant Wagner decided their hours for guard. Blas pulled the first watch, waking Wagner at midnight. A check on the Montagnard guards would be unnecessary, but not so with the Americans. It wasn't raining yet, but there were no stars and not much light from the moon through the cloud cover. The ambush position was along the trail, which had a twenty five foot wide opening in the trees, filled in with two foot high grasses, thick and green from the long rainy season. The jungle smelled good, sweet, and gentle, belying the menace it hid.

Wagner decided to check the guards. There were a dozen Americans and two Montagnards in the position. One Montagnard was awake, the other taking his turn asleep. Not one American was awake. Wagner quietly woke the squad leader, Towney, who had made no attempt to stay awake, snuggled into a mummy bag. He told Wagner he thought fifty percent meant one Montagnard and Sergeant Blas.

"Bullshit your mother, not me, Towney," Wagner whispered, angrily. "You get your lazy ass and somebody else up, NOW! And you had better check your men, because if I see this shit again you'll wish you'd chieu hoi'd to the other side. Now move!"

Wagner wasn't the squad leader's commander, and of

course it didn't matter, Wagner had the rank. There was a reported seventy NVA unit somewhere in the AO, and if it came upon this unit, it wouldn't go well. Apparently his reprimand wasn't strong enough, for when he checked again in the pouring rain, just before waking Blas for his turn at 2:00 am, they were all asleep. Wagner grabbed Towney by the throat out of his sound sleep, and said, "If I find you asleep again and two of your men aren't awake, I'll either court martial you or shoot you myself you sonofabitch!"

"I was awake," he said.

"I say again, bullshit your mother, not me. I don't want to see a lot of good men die because some douchebag fell asleep. People down this trail are counting on *you*."

Wagner returned to Blas and explained the situation. When Blas later checked, he found them awake and alert. It was a miserable night, pouring rain and getting cold. To make it worse, Wagner brought with him one of the new Army issue lightweight nylon quilted poncho liners, which soaked water like a sponge if not covered. If it touched the body, one might as well wrap up in a cotton sheet. He was soaked and shivering all night, curled up in a ball inside his poncho, waiting for morning. It didn't seem to rain much when he tried sleeping, but it opened up every time he took watch from Blas. The activity of checking the guards let in more water with each move.

Early morning brought a faint light to the east, and the Montagnards were getting up. Wagner was awake anyway, having had very little sleep and happy it was over. It was still cool and pouring.

Breakfast would be cold C-s and some canned fruit cocktail his father had sent him from home. He always craved *Del Monte's* canned fruit cocktail when on operations, and they couldn't get them here, save for one small can in every sixth box of C-rations. His body probably liked the energy and hydration. It was heavy to carry, but worth it.

The night position, short of their intended coordinates, was for some reason a problem with Major Nichols. Wagner, hearing his call sign on the radio, wasn't prepared to hear the

Major shouting at him, "You aren't at the designated location, Five Seven. We discussed this!"

Wagner tried to briefly explain that he wasn't in command of either the Americans or his Montagnard counterparts, all he could do was *advise,* and this is where they wound up. The Major, whose branch was Artillery and had never been on an Infantry operation in his life, wasn't listening, only chewing the lieutenant's ass over the now-busy radio traffic.

Wagner sat after the conversation, wet, shivering from cold, hungry, tired, radio handset in hand, staring out at the still darkened jungle. Sergeant Blas was sitting beside him, having heard the conversation. He simply said, "You know, sir, this Army is alright. This Army is some *goo-od shit.*" They both just looked at each other and laughed.

At the end of the second day, the operation set up for another night ambush. The men from the 54th were improving, and the operation along with it, and it stopped raining. The Americans were quickly growing attached to their Montagnard friends, a new experience for them. It was amazing how well and how consistently their two cultures melded. It was an education for the men of the 54th, observing these indigenous Montagnards, who were stooping as they marched to cut bamboo shoots or grab jungle peppers and insects. The Montagnards and GIs were sharing meals, more or less, depending on the individual American's *ICK* level. The noise discipline was improved, but not great. Another night of checking the guards happily went with nobody asleep. The word had gotten out about the sleeping guard's experience with Wagner, and, of course, it wasn't raining.

In the morning, a Huey arrived from Holloway, and an Infantry first lieutenant jumped off. Unbeknownst to Wagner, Captain Knowles was returning to Holloway and had a lieutenant replacing him. Knowles didn't say a word, he didn't have the courtesy to even inform Wagner, he just left. Wagner, Stewart, Flanagan and Blas stood there, looking at the departing

Huey, than at each other, as if to say "What the...."

Flanagan spit and said, "Fuckin' pussy."

The soldiers took a solid hour mulling about, talking, relieving themselves and chatting pigeon talk with their Montagnard friends. The team met the new 54th commander, Lieutenant Fornwalt. Fornwalt was wide eyed and about as happy to be there as a chipmunk in a weasel's den. Wagner tried to quickly explain the situation regarding the methods and tactics of the Montagnards, and what he might expect, including the potential of men sleeping on guard, noise discipline, etc.

It was Fornwalt's first time in the field, and he seemed overwhelmed from the get-go. He agreed to continue Wagner's wishes to let the Montagnards create the point, with an American in the center of three files. They headed out, now on a slightly different azimuth, 20 degrees west of the initial direction. Wagner had chosen another stream intersection on the map and was still hoping to hit some terrain features possibly desirable to an NVA unit, always trying to put himself in their position.

The movement was much improved, the files moved much straighter, and they stayed spaced in three files. The points, including the American who volunteered the point, operated together better.

Sergeant Shields and Wagner stayed close, both observing the new lieutenant. Wagner checked his compass constantly, along with the pace count. Lieutenant Fornwalt had his compass out, but more for show. He was hopelessly incapable of travelling more than a kilometer before becoming completely lost. Wagner felt sorry for him. The job's responsibilities were greater than that of a CEO of the largest company in the world. Arguably it was the most dangerous job in the world, prepared for by only months of training schools, all the while being paid peanuts. Men's lives depended on his ability and leadership. No experience, early twenties, and thrown into a position of leading men who, for the most part, hated being here, hated the Army, and probably hated their leaders without even knowing them. Though most of them couldn't do any better, they expected no less, and with reason. If there was nothing else the men deserved, it was good leadership. As they continued, Wagner found himself increasingly taking command of the 54th, out of necessity. Sergeant Shields was more than happy with that, having no respect or confidence in Fornwalt. At one point, during a rest stop, Wagner quietly told Shields, "Look, I don't mean to take over command of your guys, I know you don't report to me, but it might help us all out here."

"Oh, no sir, *please*, no problem. So glad to have you here. Whatever it takes," he replied.

Shields, a truly capable soldier with a prior half-year tour in Vietnam, was a buck sergeant from the woods and mountains of Idaho. At twenty three, he was the oldest man in the company, and a two digit midget, meaning he had only fourteen days left to his tour, but he was considering extending. In spite of limited experience, he was an impressive leader in giving his men instructions and discipline. He had his work cut out on the latter, it wasn't a simple matter to keep an entire inexperienced company in line here in the woods. He didn't have much to work with in delegating, as his four squad leaders, though eager and compliant, were nearly as green as most of the rest.

After four hours of humping on fairly uniform terrain, Wagner, too, was very unsure of their position. There were no significant streams or prominent hills to identify on his inaccurate map or to take azimuths to triangulate by.

Wagner told Shields to hold up and set out a quick perimeter. He, Fornwalt, Sergeant Stewart, and Chuan-uy Glah kneeled together to try to figure it out. He briefly explained the problem of lacking terrain features and unknown location. No one person, including Glah, could honestly give an accurate answer where they were, only best guesses. Wagner told Shields to pick a capable volunteer who could use a lensatic compass, to climb a lone tree on the incline where they had stopped. Fornwalt just watched quietly, happy to be left out of the picture. While Shields chose his man, Wagner laid the map on a level spot amid the grasses and vines to orient it to magnetic north. The clearing in the trees was small, but enough to view the skies from several feet up a tree. He picked up the radio handset and called, "Rubber Badger Niner Three, Rubber Badger Niner Three, This is Murky Cinder Five Seven, Murky Cinder Five Seven, *Fire mission*, over,"

Immediately, Artillery Hill replied, "Murky Cinder Five Seven, this is Rubber Badger Niner Three, Go."

"Roger, Rubber Badger Niner Three, this is Murky Cinder Five Seven, I want two illumination rounds, the first on coordinates Alpha Romeo Niner Five Zero, Six Eight Zero. The second will be on Niner Niner Zero, Six Three Zero. Give me a shot and splash on the first target, wait for my call on each target, over."

Wagner explained to the tree volunteer that he would get the two parachute illumination rounds, several hundred meters north and another east. "I need an accurate reading on the first one. After that, another round will be roughly ninety degrees east. See that light tree over there?" he said, pointing to a tall, thin trunk 20 meters away.

"Yes, sir."

"What's your compass reading on that?"

The Corporal gave it Wagner, and Wagner confirmed with his own, making sure the Corporal was familiar with his compass. Satisfied, he said, "Okay, that tree is yours. Can you climb okay?"

"Yes, sir. No problem."

With the Corporal looking like a bear cub up a tree, Wagner called the firebase to fire the first target.

A minute passed, Rubber Badger called Wagner with a *"Shot out!"*. . A half minute later, the radio voice said, *"Splash!"* Wagner looked up and said, "Now!"

The Corporal easily saw the flare, roughly due north of their position and gave the direction to Wagner below. The Americans and RFs waited quietly, facing outward in their narrow perimeter positions. Wagner wondered what the men could be thinking, were they being led by two incapable

236

Lieutenants, the blind and the stupid?

"Rubber Badger Niner Three, this is Murky Cinder Five Seven, give me target number two, with shot and splash, over," he called.

Again, the call came from Artillery Hill with the shot and splash, Wagner repeating "Now!" to the Corporal, who gave the second azimuth to him.

"Corporal, can you make out anything like a hill or stream, anything to take a reading on?" Wagner asked.

"Yes, sir, I've got what looks like a notch in the hills that way," he said, pointing.

"How far?"

"Maybe five hundred meters…maybe?"

Checking the map, Wagner said, "Okay, we're good. Give me an azimuth to it. And nice job, thanks. Come on down."

"Monty Hall. Come on down," whispered Shields.

Wagner opened his lensatic compass flat on the oriented map, drawing the two azimuths through the target locations. He marked the intersection on the map. The notch the Corporal saw looked like it belonged, confirming their location. "Here we are. We're good."

Fornwalt quietly asked if he wanted another illume round above them, to check.

"No, that might tell Chuck where to kill us, I think we're good. Can you tell Shields we can move out now?" Wagner replied.

Later in the day, they had found no signs of enemy activity, and finding an excellent spot of higher ground with an open clearing, they chose to set up for the night. By now, Wagner had taken complete control of the U.S. unit, and Fornwalt was only too happy to have it that way. Wagner told Shields to have his men quietly dig foxholes. The higher ground helped to lessen pooling up if it rained. The Montagnards rarely, in Wagner's experience, dug foxholes, they didn't even carry entrenching tools. Instead, they relied on light loads, quiet and quick movement beforehand, and alertness and speed if an enemy contact was made. The element of surprise was nearly always in their favor, not the NVA's. They did the ambushing, not the other way around. That was something the U.S. was painfully slow in learning in guerilla warfare. Small, fast, and quiet was good. Large, slow, and noisy, not so much. Wagner often wondered how the war would have differed had the entire effort been slanted this way. The colossal advantage of artillery and air superiority lent itself well. Small units could hit with surprise and impairment, letting the big guns do the real damage with far fewer casualties; *Bombs, not Bullets*. This is exactly how the advisers found themselves fighting this war, and it was effective, particularly with Montagnard units, but with well-led Vietnamese units as well. Bravery and abandon while charging a dug in machine gun nest Audie Murphy style may be heroic, but not desirable, given the choice.

The Americans began digging foxholes when the 'Yards allowed them, but for the most part, the smiling Montagnard soldiers did it for them, as well as quickly cutting forked saplings for poncho tent supports. Wagner, checking the perimeter, told several of the men "Let the "Yard dig it, it's a matter of pride. He'll feel hurt if you don't let him." The rapport just kept growing between these soldiers from two different worlds.

When Captain Knowles left on the Huey, a few of his men left also, with no communication to the team. As their numbers diminished, so did their ambush parties. On this night, Wagner sent two four-man ambushes a hundred meters down the trail with Claymores, and a three-man listening post up the hill behind them, in thick brush of the jungle. He and Chuan-uy Glah assigned two RF soldiers along with two Americans in each four man party. The listening post would have two RFs and one American, keeping with the intended 'joint' operation, while preserving some safety regarding the experience level and possibility of a man asleep on guard. The one American was a nineteen year old Specialist Fourth Class named Kellogg. Kellogg was a typical young soldier; thin, eager, excited, but uncertain of the prospects of spending the night alone with two tribesmen. Wagner recognized his expression and approached him. "You aren't too sure about this, are you Specialist?" Wagner asked.

"Well, I didn't exactly picture this," Kellogg said.

Wagner leaned close to keep the conversation quiet, and said, "Look, I was the one who chose this arrangement because we shouldn't have more than three men on an LP. You want to keep it small and quiet. When I came into this job, a Colonel told me the Montagnards will take care of me. He was right. Trust me, you will be safer with these two Montagnard RFs than your buddies, they will take care of you and greatly enhance your ability to survive. You'll see. Follow their lead, stay quiet and still. They won't like you making noise. You'll have a radio with you, you'll know what to do."

The Specialist managed a smile, stood up straight, and with a hint of confidence said, "Yes, sir. I will, sir."

At 2300 hours, it started raining again. The perimeter was surrounded by tall, straight bamboo trees, a grenade's throw away. Very little light was afforded by the Moon behind the rain clouds, a good thing, as Wagner had come to believe. While the green troops around him probably hated it, Wagner had learned to prefer the dark and hate the bright moonlit nights, the opposite of what he felt early on. It made him feel vulnerable, losing that edge of surprise. The enemy was more at home in these bushes than he was and he knew it, but he tried not to believe it. It was all a competition, a big game, and as such he reassured himself within that he was better, and if not more cunning, he was smarter, and the winner. He would not lose to these little bastards that he was coming to hate. That emotion in eons of wars would not change in this one.

The darkness and rain all but eliminated the possibility of hearing an enemy approach. He hoped the rain would limit the enemy's activity as well, though this is what he was here for, to find the enemy and kill him. His recent experiences with the American unit reduced that commitment considerably, even with the advantage of the cavalry coming to the rescue. Most firefights were over within a minute, the damage already done. Waiting thirty or forty minutes for chopper support probably wouldn't help in most cases. Wagner was awake on his guard shift, Sergeant Stewart trying unsuccessfully to sleep beside him. Rain and imagination spawned unnerving sounds, his mind beginning to see movement behind the black wet leaves, twitching with every drop, adding to rivulets pouring off them. Specialist Kellogg double clicked his handset, then whispered into it. "Murky Cinder Five Seven, Shallow Bubbles Two Seven, over."

Wagner responded, "Shallow Bubbles Two Seven, Five Seven, go."

"Uh….Murky Cinder Five Seven, I think I hear something."

"Roger, Two Seven. Stay quiet, tell me if you're sure. Keep your volume turned down. I'll send up an illumination round, it may be a while, stay alert." Wagner changed his frequency and called Artillery Hill. "Rubber Badger Niner Three, Rubber Badger Niner Three, Murky Cinder Five Seven, Murky Cinder Five Seven, *Fire mission*, over."

The handset crackled and the soldier on the other end replied, "Roger, Murky Cinder Five Seven, Rubber Badger Niner Three, go."

"Rubber Badger Niner Three, I want one illume round, coordinates Alpha Romeo Niner Eight Zero, Seven Niner Zero, over." Wagner was putting the parachute illumination round behind them, to illuminate the direction Kellogg was looking at from his rear. Stewart was awake and up, intent on what was in store. Wagner appreciated the professionalism and knowledge that Stewart and Blas had. They were excellent Infantrymen, experienced, dedicated and knowledgeable. No small factor were their amiable and understanding personalities. He was lucky to be on their team.

After a long thirty five agonizing minutes, crazy for something as safe as an illumination round, the flare popped in front of them, not behind. It was fired on the wrong coordinate. Doing so lit up Kellogg and the patrol to the enemy instead of the other way around. Wagner was beside himself. It couldn't be his error, the round was put far enough away that it was in no way a mistaken position of where they were. The wrong delivery gave him a grave concern that they could make the same mistake on an HE round on another call, killing friendlies. This was something new, and it didn't sit well. But for the moment, the fear was the bad guys taking advantage of the light for their benefit.

"Rubber Badger Niner Three, Murky Cinder Five Seven, over.

"Roger, Five Seven, this is Rubber Badger Niner Three, over."

"Rubber Badger Niner Three, what the hell? Check your fires, that couldn't be my coordinates I gave you, over."

"Murky Cinder Five Seven, Rubber Badger Niner Three, be advised we had a possible friendly in the air, we had the guns already set up for that target, so we put it in to your Sierra, over."

"You what?" Wagner asked, trying to keep his voice low, "Who the hell are you to put a round where I don't want it. I've got possible bad guys out here, you just lit us up. Now get another round where I told you… Now!"

While they waited, Kellogg radioed back to Wagner that he still thought he had movement. Wagner hoped it was an animal, maybe a deer, a pig, snake, or even a tiger. He had seen 6" tiger tracks on previous trips into the boonies, but never saw one. Finally, the 155mm illumination round popped in the sky in the appropriate area behind them, and the jungle transformed from a wet, black curtain to a green-gray glow of visible bamboo, shrubs, and vines. A relieved Kellogg radioed back that he saw nothing.

"Good job," said Wagner, "Stay alert."

The radio crackled lightly again. It was Captain Knowles, calling Wagner. He had been monitoring the conversations. "This is Shallow Bubbles One Three, Shallow Bubbles One Three," over.

Wagner answered, and Captain Knowles said, "I want to

speak to Shallow Bubbles One Seven," over.

Wagner handed the handset to Lt. Fornwalt, who responded with, "Oh, Christ, here we go.." The voice of Captain Knowles fairly boomed over the radio. "Shallow Bubbles One Seven, you're in command there, I want you to remember that! You have lost the respect and confidence of every man in that unit..." The rest of the conversation Wagner did not hear, but it must have been ripe. After he was through, Wagner called the Captain back and told him he had the first watch, and Fornwalt had been asleep on his turn off. He hoped it might be easier on Fornwalt, the poor man was beyond saving at this point, but honestly, he only wanted out of there.

Wagner was asleep later in the night when the loud 'Boom!-Whoosh' of enemy 122mm rockets broke the stillness only two klicks away. The squad leader in the ambush position to the southwest reported they thought they saw flashes. Wagner told him to take an azimuth from his position. Wagner, covering his map and small flashlight with a poncho, did his best to approximate the position on the map. That position was precisely on one of the preplanned defensive targets he had chosen to call in several hours earlier, a small clearing above a stream where a foot trail passed, shown on the topo map. He immediately called Artillery Hill again for another fire mission for three rounds of HE Quick. Their 105mm guns wouldn't reach this far, they would have to use their 155s, which were three times as powerful, with a range of almost fifteen kilometers, nearly nine miles. Sounds of crackling, rustling projectiles through the air was quickly followed by loud **CRUNNCHHs!** of exploding shells. Twenty seconds later, the faint sound of the guns reached them, chasing faster-than-sound rounds through the sky, boom-rumblings sounding like distant thunder in the rainy darkness. He called nine more rounds spaced around the first target before calling a cease fire.

The next morning the unit moved out again, heading toward the area of the rocket launches. They followed a stream for two klicks, then angled right to the coordinates of the artillery rounds. Along the stream were remnants of rice paddies

242

from an abandoned Montagnard village. Where the jungle was too thick, they walked a vague trail that led to bamboo clusters which had served as shelters at one time, if not recently. All of this was far from active villages, and Wagner assumed they were V.C. or NVA trails, though not well used. Beside a slightly open stretch of the stream, they discovered bunkers. There were signs of recent use. If there were tunnels here, they hid them well, and none were found. Sergeant Blas said, "I wonder if we're over an ant farm of tunnels right now. They could be right below our feet."

Leaving the denser vegetation of the stream, they headed toward the launch site. On a rise in the land, they found a clearing, pocked with artillery craters of the night before. In the middle of the clearing was a fan-shaped burnt area in the grass, four meters wide at one end and six meters long, funneling to a spot from east to west. Looking ahead in the direction given by the funnel, there was a notch in the trees, yielding a view of Camp Holloway in the distance. A huge red and white bullseye was prominently in view on the roof of one of the largest hangars, painted in the past by the GIs at Holloway. No doubt the rocketeers of last night's event couldn't resist the temptation. Flanagan chuckled, "GIs are the same everywhere." This was the launch site, the grasses burned by 4.8 inch diameter silver 122 mm rockets, the biggest weapon they had, definitely a headache-maker. They had been firing at Holloway until the artillery ended their fun. In large part luck, the artillery grids Wagner picked were right on once again. A search of the area turned up absolutely nothing, not even blood or body parts. There wasn't even a scrap of trash or litter, the enemy was disciplined in that respect, not that they had a lot to throw away anyway. Wagner called in to Captain Knowles to give him coordinates of the launch site, valuable information in their next attack.

Another day of humping the boonies revealed no results. Reaching the planned night location that Glah and Wagner had agreed upon, Wagner took Glah aside and said, "Chuan-uy, tell your men not to do what the Americans do, they number 10 here. They are new, they don't know." Glah only smiled, and Wagner couldn't know if the translation was understood, or if Glah already knew.

With some of the usual noise, they began setting up the perimeter. Typically, the Montagnard RFs would travel until later in the day, setting up well after dusk, when it was more difficult to be located or observed by the enemy, but the 'Yards took it all in stride. Kellogg, the previous night's nervous LP, approached Wagner and said, "Sir, are you going to put out an LP tonight?"

"Affirmative. You want to go again?" asked Wagner, half-jokingly.

"Yes, sir, would that be okay?"

"They must have taken care of you."

"Yes sir, L-T. You were right. Any time."

"Ask Sergeant Shields, but fine with me. Stay alert."

"Thank you sir."

All around the perimeter the Montagnard RFs were paired off with their American counterparts, whom they had begun to know well in their short time together. Still digging foxholes and making shelters, more and more they shared food. Some of the GIs were getting over some of the *ICK* factor, trying various foods from Montagnard gleanings. Nearly every Montagnard cooking pot had a different stew of C-rations meat, bamboo shoots, some kind of leaves, and always hot, white jungle peppers. Occasionally an American would ask Five Seven's interpreter or one of the team members to ask his counterpart some question, but they did well conversing on their own.

The night went well, and it didn't rain once. When the unit was ready to move out, Lt. Fornwalt was called by Knowles.

When Fornwalt finished, Wagner asked, "What's happening, Lieutenant?"

Fornwalt had a deer-in-the-headlights look. "That was Captain Knowles. He's coming out. He's taking me out. Wants us to stay put until he gets here."

"Oh," Wagner said, surprised. "That's too bad. I thought you were getting into this okay." It was not a lie, just an exaggeration. Fornwalt actually did look more comfortable now that his feet were wet, though clearly happy to get out of the field. Wagner, given the choice, would have preferred that he stayed, things were going smoother with the comingling of the units and understanding of responsibilities. That would now revert back to the original, which was not ideal. Still, they had the cavalry…

The rest of the day was spent on another azimuth, which had been taken out of Wagner's and Glah's hands. Not really a problem, one shitty tree looks like another in the jungle, and they might find the bad guys anywhere. They were headed back in the general direction of Le Quon. Captain Knowles was wearing his O.D. bandana again, and walking directly behind his point man, ignoring the rules of Infantry. Without knowledge of it, Wagner again was surprised when, at 1530 hours, he was told Hueys were on their way to meet them at the chopper pad outside Le Quon's perimeter. The joint operation was over.

Major Nichols wasn't in Le Quon that night, but in the morning he arrived in his Jeep with Seht, his PSYOPS counterpart. He asked Wagner to come in for a debriefing.

"Well, sir, I'm afraid I'm going to appear a tad negative, but what I was pretty excited about turned into a bit of a fiasco. It all started with. . ." Wagner recounted some of the problems and dangers encountered with the inexperienced unit and leaders, but then he zeroed in on the illumination round put in the wrong place, his main bitch.

Major Nichols told him, "Give me a complete, detailed report on the artillery call, I'll carry it myself to the highers at Artillery Hill." Major Nichols was good that way, reliable and supportive for his men if the situation called for it.

The debriefing over, the Major said, "Some bad news. The Mang Yang outpost…it was overrun. Completely wiped out. You were right, and they didn't listen."

Wagner called the team together to tell them. It came as a shock, if not a surprise. While Blas and Stewart stood staring and pondering, Sergeant Flanagan glared at Wagner and said, "You should've insisted, Lieutenant, now they're all dead. A lot of good that did."

Tired from the operation and sorry for the Vietnamese at Mang Yang, he quietly wondered if he should have done more. He held his contempt for Flanagan, letting the other team members judge for themselves.

Wagner wrote his weekly report covering the joint operation. More concerned about the Montagnards picking up bad habits from the Americans than of safety concerns, he recommended that the joint operations be discontinued.

That night, Hoa Khe was preparing supper, with steak on the menu compliments of the scrounge team. Major Nichols had more information for the men. "The malaria pills. . . the big, once per week orange quinine pills. . . you should keep taking those. But the little daily white pills, don't take them anymore. Word is, they turn your bone marrow to mush."

"Bone marrow to mush?" Sergeant Blas said, his eyebrows furrowed with ire. "One more thing this godamned Army does screwed all to hell. What the hell are we, lab mice?"

Sergeant Stewart added, "Like the G.I.s they had watching atomic bombs, ya know? They died of cancers. This good Army is killing us. Now, my Momma didn't raise no fool, sir, but just what the hell are we supposed to believe any more?"

"I hear you," Nichols said. "Also, the monthly drop came in, it's piled behind the gear closet."

The Major was referring to the once-a-month delivery via Huey of a net bag of various books and 16mm movies, the latter for a movie projector occasionally used when the team was back in the team house.

Along with the delivery came the mail. Wagner's father had sent a letter along with some more cans of Del Monte fruit cocktail, and 25 packets of various flavors of Kool-Aid, a request Wagner had made from his Dad to mask the purifying iodine pills' bad taste in canteen water. His father didn't have much to say, not that he didn't want to, it was just hard for him to converse. He hadn't been particularly close with his father. A workaholic, different interests, whatever. But he was trying, it was simply difficult for him. He had a tough life, dealing with an alcoholic wife. People in the mid-20th century didn't understand alcoholism, how some were prone to addiction and some were not, not so different from being susceptible to cancer or other diseases. Drug and alcohol addictions make liars and horrible people out of wonderful people. A 'Doctor Jeckle and Mr. Hyde' syndrome. The grip that endorphins and addictions have, trumping all else no matter how deep the love, is difficult to understand for those who don't have it. Years of stress and embarrassment to everyone close can't help but have their effect. Overcoming that takes discipline, conviction, and character.

Quickly looking over the books, Darryl Wagner picked up a paperback that caught his eye. The cover said in bold letters "How to Study Guide".

Sergeant Blas was the team's Light Weapons Advisor. He had been wanting to try some old weapons that had been handed down from previous Special Forces teams, one being a 9mm Swedish K machinegun, another a .45 caliber M3 submachine, or 'grease' gun, and finally a .45 caliber Thompson submachine gun. The Swedish K was a green, stamped-sheet metal design. The grease gun was a heavy, 12 lb. auto submachine gun, designed by a German, George Hyde, in 1941 in World War II. It had a 2" round cylinder body that really looked like a grease gun. The firing mechanism relied on a sliding 2" diameter rod of heavy steel. The recoil of the .45 caliber pistol round sent the rod back to eject and insert shells, spring loaded to bounce forward to chamber and fire the next. It was designed for simplicity and reliability, with a slow rate of fire. Like the other two guns, it fired a slow, heavy bullet that was good for busting through brush and knocking down an enemy rather than passing 'through and through'. A thick wire frame unfolded to form a short stock, the entire length only 23". The Thompson, another WW II weapon, had to be held solidly from a faster firing heavy recoil.

1400 hours found Blas, Wagner, and Flanagan on the top of the perimeter berm, weapons and shells in hand. Sergeant Blas fired a full magazine from his Swedish K into the berm before Wagner stood ready to try the grease gun.

Sergeant Flanagan stood with his hands on his hips, ready to criticize with a sneer and derisive tone. "You better hold onto that tight, Lieutenant, that grease gun will set you right on your ass!"

Wagner took the advice, he was familiar with the kick from a single shot .45 pistol. Bracing, he aimed into the dirt 10' below his perch on the berm and squeezed the trigger. *BANG-BANG-BANG-BANG-BANG-BANG*. Surprised, Wagner said, "This thing is great! You can hold it in one spot all day. There's no kick at all!" That big, heavy bolt absorbed almost all of the recoil. Flanagan just uttered a "Hmmpphh," and turned to walk away.

After a full day of catching up on reports and equipment maintenance, Wagner ended it with final touches to the new tower. That night, he had the opportunity to break it in. At 0100 hours in the morning, the compound came under attack. Incoming rounds and patter of shrapnel once again had him leaping out of the rack, into boots, grabbing radio, M-16, M-79 grenade launcher, flak jacket and helmet. Throwing open the outside door to his team house room, five strides alongside the sandbagged wall, up onto the sandbags, throwing the weapons onto the roof, climbing onto the roof, all in less than a minute. Then the straight ladder up the tower, and over the new sandbagged wall. After calling a fire mission from Artillery Hill on probable locations beyond the tree line, the incoming stopped. The RFs on the perimeter, meanwhile, had opened up with small arms into the darkness. Wagner didn't know if this was just a mortar attack or full scale assault. The fifty caliber and M-60 machineguns were shooting too high, the tracers burning out in the black night at nine hundred meters out. Making radio contact with the TOC, he talked to the Major who in turn got the counterpart commander to tell their men to lower their fire. Soon the tracers dropped to a proper grazing fire, red phosphorus flying in crazy directions upon impact. He listened to the Major calling headquarters, reporting that some mortars and B-40s hit, and the attack was over. No sooner than he said it, something exploded 20 meters to his left rear. A shower of orange-white sparks rained down, looking like a transformer exploding on a telephone pole while shrapnel slapped into the latrine and team house. "It seemed too low for a B-40 rocket to make it over the wall, yet too high off the ground for a mortar," he thought. "But the sparks? Mortars don't make sparks." He called the Major in the TOC. "We just had another explosion inside the compound. I guess a mortar... didn't sound like it."

He looked through the big fifty caliber crew-served Starlight scope to search for enemy sappers, seeing none. The outgoing tracers were still firing away, blinding much of the field of view. Everything in the eyepiece glowed a ghostly green-gray, except the red tracers, glowing brightly in a bright white spray of bullets. Every blast caused the starlight to shut down momentarily from over-exposure, rendering it momentarily useless.

The attack dwindled quickly, and an hour later it was over, Wagner climbing down. In the morning, damage assessment had begun. Again, minimal damage was discovered. The sparks were still a mystery. Wagner and Stewart searched for the impact point of the explosion he witnessed, but found none. Suddenly, Sergeant Stewart looked straight in front of him at the cyclone fence four feet away that formed part of the inner perimeter. He pointed at it and said, "Sir, do you see what I see? Was that hole there before?"

In the cyclone fence was a 30" diameter hole, the wire blackened and twisted in contorted directions. They both looked toward the north, where the attack probably came from, and stared at the team Jeep 20 meters away. The recently replaced front windshield had a 6" hole through it. Walking toward the Jeep, they saw the back window in the canvas top also had a hole. Another ten meters from that was their wooden 3-holer latrine, with its waste barrels underneath. A splintered streak ran across the side of the weathered boards. It didn't take long to figure it was from a 75 mm recoilless rifle round, fired far enough off to allow the round to make it over the berm on a downward path. It glanced off the shithouse wall, went through both rear and front windows of the Jeep, exploding in the cyclone fence. Burning steel wire produced the sparks. "OOOHWEE," Stewart said. "That's something I ain't seen before."

Nobody could figure out how crumpled hand-written notes,

found near craters, could be carried in with a projectile and not destroyed, but they all had various threats written on them. Most of the notes didn't make sense, possibly written by drugged up attackers.

After morning chow, the team was preparing for another village and PF unit visit, when the Major announced they would be going on a second joint operation in two days, with the 54th again. Surprised, Wagner requested some changes from the Major if possible. The word must have been passed on, because when the 54th showed up, the new lieutenant assigned to lead the platoon was amenable to Wagner's wish to work with three files, a Montagnard taking point in each file. The same RF group arrived, this time in deuce and a half Army trucks. The same Chuan-uy Glah was in command of his RFs, and immediately things were, indeed, improved. Wagner had told Flanagan he could stay at the compound for this operation, as the 54th would have a medic with them. Flanagan didn't argue. The bad side: most of the men were new and as inexperienced as in the first operation. On the good side, Sergeant Shields was back, by his own request, as was Specialist Kellogg. The team was glad to see them. Also, the new Kit Carson Scout, Tung, would join them, a good chance to alleviate some of the 'concerns of intent' of their former NVA soldier. Wagner would keep him close, in part to protect Tung from possible reprisals from the RFs. He really didn't know how they would respond to a Vietnamese, a former NVA soldier.

They moved out in an organized fashion, on a pre-determined azimuth. With the Montagnard RFs in the lead, they were *really* moving out. Once again, the Americans were loaded for bear, carrying three times the ammunition needed. Wagner had to ask Glah to take a break by ten o'clock, the Americans were struggling and straggling. Carrying far less and accustomed to the treks, MAT 57 kept up with few problems.

Lieutenant Dowery was the new 54th platoon leader. He was a slightly heavy six foot Irishman, sporting a red haired flattop that earned him the name "Redbird". Dowery was as green as Fornwalt before him, but not afraid of leadership. Like Captain Knowles, he pushed it a little to play the role.

Within an hour, the Americans were already soaked in sweat, in not yet the hottest part of the day. It was hot and humid, however, with sparse clouds and a bright tropical sun. "Lean and mean" were words often taught in training. They were right. At 2:00 p.m., a Huey came in to extract much of their extra load, but still not enough, in the team's opinion. Several well-used trails were found, plus three bunkers near a stream. Wagner noted the coordinates in grease pencil on the topo map for future fire missions from his tower. Further up a path from the bunkers, they found a well-used recoilless rifle position. The recoilless could have been carried out, but it was a heavy weapon that he considered might be stored here. Lt. Dowery agreed to search the area, but without results.

Three days of working with their Mike Strike Montagnards resulted in the same great rapport. No enemy contacts, only locations were produced, but on the bright side, no casualties. The 54th sent Hueys in for extraction, a welcome change for the RFs. Back in the compound hours later, the team

ate and showered, relieved it was over. All agreed they would prefer to be with a small RF unit, overall. When the team finished recounting the various problems and concerns, the Major agreed it wasn't the great idea they all thought it would be at the onset, ending their joint operations.

While the team was gone, the Rome plow was delivered by a Corps of Engineers group, making quick work of revamping the perimeter berm. It vastly improved their defenses and confidence as well. Their cleanly formed berm became a deep reddish brown of moist earth instead of grass covered mounds and notches, altered from years of rains. Unfortunately, the Vietnamese commander had never come through with pulling in the many trip wires and Claymore detonation wires. Torn up by the plow, they needed to be replaced. In addition, he was no help in directing his men to create new fighting positions on the berm, nor in changing positions of .50 caliber and M-60 7.62mm machine guns to the corners for interlacing grazing fires. No amount of advising helped, leaving the compound less than desired. Their Vietnamese counterpart simply told them, "Oh no, the V.C. attack this way." That belief in only one possible offense was one more glaring example why the Vietnamese officer selection method contributed greatly to the South's inferiority in combat.

Wagner had the opportunity to visit the 71st Medevac Hospital only three times since he first met Annelle, and in the last visit she hadn't been available. The staff was often over worked. Annelle Atchison was "in the middle of her shift," and "she can't break away," he was told. He hoped that was the real reason, not an excuse. He found himself picturing her more in his mind and less of the love that still haunted him from years before, the only girl he had ever truly loved. Now, in this incredibly foreign land where everything was alien to everything American soldiers ever knew, he was drawn to this sweet, smiling nurse. Was it the loneliness of the war? Like the guy on the tiny desert island, marooned with only a toothless hag that kept looking better every day. Or was he finally on the mend? And Annelle was anything but a hag. He yearned for the confidence he once possessed, but the abundance and constant presence of men, many successful medical doctors... He saw himself appearing desperate and lonely. Why not, *he was*. He couldn't even be alone with her, always in daylight, never at night. Where could he take her, to a movie in a rice paddy? He never touched or kissed her, nothing more than a handshake. Crazy. He couldn't smell her hair, her skin, or perfume over the smell of chlorinated pool water and an occasional waft of jet fuel and burning shit barrels. Romantic.

IX LIVING CHESS

"Chess played with human beings as pieces on a giant board. A spectacle which has been performed since the 15th century. Masters decide the moves, and a steward instructs the 'pieces' where to move."

Rainy season was over. On November 17, 1970, the dry season was beginning, a little late, as did the rainy season months before. Stunning tropical foliage grew less colorful, turning paler, thinner, drier. Red clayish soil was drying out, winds were picking up. It would continue to intensify until well into January and February, when every weapon, article of clothing, and every bite of food would be besieged by red dirt. Millions of spider webs were intensifying from colorful, merciless killers, patiently lying in wait for many more millions of flying and crawling tropical insects. The end of the rainy season meant fewer prey for the eight legged arachnids, meaning more webs needed to fill their dietary needs. Innumerable orders of *Arachnida* existed in the tropical and sub-tropical vegetation of Pleiku. If poisonous snakes weren't enough to further malign a U.S. soldiers' opinions of this land, the spiders and leeches surely would. Many spiders were poisonous, varying from painful to cell death, though rarely fatal. Interesting and colorful, if not repulsive. Red-headed Centipedes, with a hundred exceptionally long disgusting legs and long bite parts, killed everything from bats to Wolf Spiders, also causing cell death. Even the little "Fuck you Lizards" seemed to hate the foreign invaders, causing many a Marine or Soldier to swear a V.C. was taunting him from behind a log, with a series of sharp and clear *"Fuck You"* calls. Village MEDCAP services provided by the team included treating two snake bites and several spider bites, assuming the uneducated guesses from both Americans and Montagnards were correct. The Montagnards had their own herbal remedies and tribal witch doctors, and it was a toss-up who was more effective in those cases. As with their religions, often the populace considered more is better. Use them all. One lovely Vietnamese girl, a singer who came to entertain the Vietnamese RFs in the Le Quon compound, very nearly died from an allergic reaction to penicillin. She had taken it for a sore throat.

Those spider webs were among the annoyances and fears that troops encountered in Vietnam, and there was nothing Wagner hated or feared more than spiders. Snakes were a serious threat, but spiders more terrifying. Everyone has a phobia of some kind; snakes, rats, heights--- spiders were his. Many trips through the jungle resulted in a variety of bites, ranging from the constant mosquitos to brutal fire ant attacks, but a few severe reactions, he assumed, were from spiders. One entire week was spent in Le Quon waiting for deep purple, swollen toes to return to somewhat normal just to fit in a boot again. There were no neighborhood doctors or drug stores available.

In the early morning, Team 57 travelled to another Montagnard location, a place called Plei J'Rok, one more growing reconsolidation village, assigned to the team to help in moving inhabitants from surrounding hamlets. The new village wasn't far from the highway, and their young Montagnard interpreter, Kir, accompanied them, due to the village's relative safety. Again, Wagner was invited to the village chief's hootch for supper, as was the custom. Squatting on an eight inch high log seat by a foot-high wooden table made of machete-hewn logs, Wagner was trying his best to politely converse with the chief and his wife while being served. The insides of the grass roofed hootch were entirely black, coated with creosote from hundreds of wood fires. Wet creosote smell permeated every house, never to be forgotten. Outside grounds of this reconsolidated village were carpeted with animal feces, far worse than in small unconsolidated hamlets. The people here, like many others had reddish hair due to protein deficiency, and large stomachs from both worms and malnutrition. But because they had a guest, what little meat they had was served. It could have been dog, pig, rabbit, rat, or any other creature that walked, swam, or flew. In the corner, a dog's head and leg lay, answering that question. Still wearing its brown and black hair, its eyes were staring at the ceiling, half hidden with a squadron of flies. The chief's wife, always smiling, brought a wooden bowl with the same appearance as seen before, black and green beans. The beans moved. When she waved her hand over it, the flies left and white rice appeared. Then she brought the meat, proud that they could offer it in spite of their shortage. Typically, the meat was cut into small ¾" pieces, burned to death with the hide still attached, hair burnt away. Burned would have been okay, but rotten was not. Wagner had sensed the onset of the flu for the last two days, with aches and a slight fever, hoping it would pass. That didn't make the putrefied chunks, already emitting a repulsive smell when it was placed in front of him any more appetizing. It was his most nauseating meal yet. Trying his best to get it down without chewing, without vomiting, he had to give up on the fifth piece. It was literally all he could do to keep from retching in front of his hosts. Finally, he asked Kir to come into the chief's hootch for a moment.

"Kir, tell the chief that my father doesn't eat meat, it's a religious thing, so I shouldn't," Wagner said.

The teenager looked at the lieutenant with his big brown obliging eyes to see if he understood him, wondering why. He repeated it to make sure.

"Right. Kir, I can't eat this meat, it's bad, very bad. But please don't let him think I don't like it."

After Kir relayed the interpreted message, Wagner tried to concentrate on rice while batting away large black and green persistent hungry flies, pretending he loved it. Abiding with common customs, he left a few grains of rice in the bowl, signifying he had been fully satisfied by his host. The meal done, these grains were fed to a waiting living dog, which lapped them eagerly from the bowl. Canine-tongue cleaning done, the chief's wife reached for a filthy, red-dirt stained towel hanging from a wooden peg, and quickly swiped the bowl, returning the "clean" bowl to its spot on a wooden shelf. A rice wine party ensued, the entire team involved as usual, even young Kir.

Nighttime found Wagner in more than the usual alimentary distress. Diarrhea was normal from food, wine, and malaria pills, but this was unusually anguishing. By ten at night, Wagner was outside his poncho tent, looking for the so-called latrine, a nearby hole dug by the villagers. It was coming out both ends, violently. His night was interspersed with sessions of vomiting and diarrhea. Finally, at four in the morning, Sergeant Stewart told Blas and Flanagan they had to leave, the Lieutenant was 'shitting himself to death'.

Three stops on the way home for more bowel activity and they were back at Le Quon by six a.m. Wagner hit the wooden latrine again before crawling into bed. There he stayed for two entire days and nights, getting up only to run the thirty meters to the latrine. The rank outhouse, everyone else's routine diarrhea mixing with his own plus vomit, didn't help relieve the uncontrollable need to vomit more, far into the merciless 'dry heaves', with not an ounce of spit to show for it. That's when the abdominals feel they are rolling over each other in a vice grip. Faint memories of hallucinations from soaring temperatures had him wondering about his own mental state.

On the third day, Wagner lay semi-awake under multiple covers, trying to bake the illness that he assumed was a simple flu out of his system. He didn't know that he had infectious hepatitis A, the virus found in diseased food, water, or wine. His eyes were becoming tinged with yellow, but he didn't know that either. All he knew was his muscles ached over his entire body, he had no strength, his stomach muscles were in spasm from vomiting. He became dehydrated, dangerously so. But there were no doctors, only the team medic. Flanagan by now was well-versed on battle first aid, and could identify a myriad of MEDCAP symptoms and treatments of malnutrition, worms, dysentery, malaria, TB, leprosy, even plague. He could treat the worms, give penicillin for infections and gonorrhea, etc., but treating hepatitis and the rest was out of his league. He was

258

unable or unwilling to recognize it in any case. Wagner still assumed he had a simple flu. Sergeants Blas and Stewart had checked in on him periodically, but he always reassured them "it was just the flu, he was fine."

Emerging from his room on the fourth day, with only water and some broth having replenished his famished body, Sergeant Stewart told him, "Sir, we were getting pretty worried about you. You sounded like you were having a war in there at times."

Flanagan quipped "Lieutenant, sounded like you were partying it up in there. You always talk to yourself?"

"What? What'd I say?" Wagner asked, looking like he'd spent a month in a P.O.W. camp.

"What the hell *didn't* you say?" Flanagan remarked, with a sneering smile. "We know things now you didn't even know about yourself."

The team stood down for several days, catching up on miscellaneous chores and repairs to the compound, the generator receiving attention from Sergeant Blas and the RTO Tim. The Major, typically busy with Seht and the Psyops business, came and went without a great deal of interaction or interest in the team. Fully one week after the team's trip to Plei J'Rok, he asked his nearly recovered lieutenant, "Were you sick, Darryl?"

In the late Fall of 1970, more Americans had been systematically pulled out. The rainy season was coming to an end. Heavy rains that had replenished thick and beautiful sub-tropical vegetation in the highlands for several months were faltering. Iridescent butterflies of blues, yellows, and oranges still visited random trees and flowers, some of the most beautiful and plentiful Lepidoptera in the world. Birds of various colors and sizes flitted about in the bushes and trees, though unlike butterflies, their numbers were drastically reduced by the presence of so many rifles and hungry soldiers, with no laws to protect them. The tiniest colorful finches were still considered food. Birds were not the only denizens to suffer, everything from monkeys to tigers and elephants had been blown away by every uncaring and angry soldier with a weapon simply for a lark, it didn't matter what his country or political beliefs were. Such are the cruel natures of men. But for wars, most of these species may not exist. Wars and disease had sustained them and their habitat by limiting the numbers and labors of the greatest pestilence and predators in the world: *man*. What man doesn't kill, he eliminates by the economics of theft. Theft of entire ecosystems. War had prevented most of Vietnam from becoming agricultural land. Commonly called "progress", economics trumps all else. Economics determines everything, it changes everything.

Before recorded history, inhabitants of Vietnam were dark skinned pygmies. Much later, peoples from China migrated to the area, drawn by a lure of tropical coastlines and fertile rice valleys further south. The Vietnamese have been fighting for centuries, well before the birth of Christ. Chinese were primarily the enemy, including Kublai Khan. Persistence paid off, for time and time again the indigenous Vietnamese drove out the Chinese. In 197 A.D., the Kingdom of Champa settled peoples from the area of India into the coastal areas of what was to be defined as military II Corps by 1962, running roughly from Cam Ranh Bay on the coast, north to Da Nang. The settlers from India, often referred to as "Jews of the Orient" were traders. In the latter 1400s, the Vietnamese destruction of the kingdom of Champa in 'The Golden Age of Vietnam' drove these people, ancestors of today's Montagnards, from the coastal lands into the Annamite mountains. Though many argue they were descended from Polynesia or Malaysia, it is unlikely. In appearance, they could be either. Decades later, they would collectively be called 'Degar', for *mountain people*.

The blowing red dirt had been a memory, but now it was gradually becoming dry long enough to remind them of the previous Spring's dusty filth. The Summer's varied shades of green were remarkably beautiful, one of the brighter sides of this alien world, but the subsequent thicker growth and reduction of visibility into the 'bush' did nothing to lessen constant tension to a bush soldier. A drier, thinner vegetation, however, worked both ways, for the ambusher and ambushee.

The Major's initial lack of guidance had changed into assigning several two to four day missions of village reconsolidations, orders from his highers. The team joined with Vietnamese and Montagnard counterparts, directing and coordinating consolidations of small surrounding hamlets into single, large villages. Each one seemed more pathetic than the last. The team members never stopped grumbling about it, including Wagner. He was torn between the duties of following orders as an Army officer and what they were doing to these primitive hunter-gatherers, forcing them into a Vietnamese version of Indian reservations. The United States insisted that the reconsolidation plans were entirely Vietnamese, but in reality, Americans and their equipment were a major part of the effort. Pleiku wasn't the only place; the entire country supposedly had a reconsolidation effort, but not in the same manner or extent as this. The Montagnards were victims of a corrupt and evil system that was killing them--no, *murdering them*--through disease and starvation. Their ancestral lands were literally being stolen from under their feet. It was nothing new. For hundreds of years, scores of tribes of these indigenous peoples had been the outcasts of Vietnam, not nomadic as often described, but *driven* to the mountainous regions. These were the least desirable domains of the country; mountains with poor laterite soil and hilly terrain unsuitable for growing most crops. They lacked large areas of water for rice, the staple of the orient. Centuries of intrusions have ripped apart their tribal communities, and would not end after the war. As early as 1945, American and allied 'Deer Teams' began the Vietnam anti-communist war, after the universally despised Japanese were driven out of Vietnam and every other country they ravaged, primarily by Americans. Later, Kennedy's 1960s Special Forces teams continued to train and recruit the tough and skillful Montagnards. By 1970, U.S. Army advisers, the MAT teams, had replaced those predecessors. The war had swung full circle from Deer Teams to Mobile Advisory Teams. The Special Forces had embraced the Montagnards, recognizing their abilities and loyalties that the Vietnamese would not admit to. That relationship taught the South Vietnamese to recognize their inability to fight the North and the Viet Cong in the Highlands without the alliance of these tough Montagnard soldiers. The U.S. withdrawals, along with the chaos in a U.S. political system now entwined with anti-war sentiments were allowing corrupt Vietnamese to continue to ravage the primitive indigenous tribes. Years of productive efforts by Special Forces teams, many giving their lives in the process, were being reversed with the aid of their sequels, the MAT teams. Though advisers were intended to 'Vietnamize' the war through training and advising akin to their predecessors, their role was suddenly changing to help force the consolidations of the indigenous tribesmen. At first, the team believed its purpose was for the good, that being to deny food, support, and men to the enemy. How could the U.S. government and its military be wrong?

It was mid-December, 1970. Major Nichols sat with Wagner at the kitchen table in the team house. A Fuck You lizard was castigating them from a dank wall under the kitchen sink. Outside, the constant wind was blowing red dust in little dervishes, while Hoa Khe's pig, Mat was furrowing his nose through loose soil blown off the volleyball court. Friday, the team handyman, was polishing boots by the water tower. Beside him were Lenh and Manh, happily chattering away while on their hands and knees aggressively scrubbing team fatigues with stiff bristle brushes and harsh liquid soap. Ten meters away, two shit barrels were burning furiously, thick black smoke racing sideways toward Pleiku and luckily away from the team house.

"Your team will be temporarily replacing Team 46 in Plei Do Rom," the Major told him. "You'll be working with

Major Buhm, the Montagnard commander down there.

Wagner winced at the news. Plei Do Rom was the home compound of his friend, Gordon Bailey. "We're replacing Bailey's team?" he asked.

"That's correct..... you'll be working with Major Buhm on some security sweeps. We're seeing a possible buildup of NVA activity from the immediate north and east from there all the way down to Phu Nhon in the south. Major Buhm has a good RF Mike Strike Force company, 813."

Wagner was immediately thinking there may not be an opportunity to discuss the reconsolidation problems once they were relocated to Plei Do Rom. "Sir, I've been meaning to discuss this village moving business with you. My men and I got the word a long time ago about this being a good thing, depriving the enemy and all that, but I've got to tell you, we're making enemies here. Talk about winning the hearts and minds, shit, we're killing these people. Our best friggin' allies. And we're killin' em. They're dying like flies, they're starving, is all this worth it?" Wagner asked.

The Major stared, trying to think of the appropriate response. He knew the problems, he was in and out of villages as often as Wagner was, practically on a daily basis. Not staying overnight in them, he may not have seen the extent of the dead and dying that Wagner's team had, but he was certainly cognizant of the deplorable conditions. And he was, realistically, a lifer. His career depended on every order, every decision, to one extent or another. "I know, there is a down side, but we have our orders. The statistics tell us it's raising hell with the Viet Cong infrastructure. One prisoner said, 'because we've moved twenty four hamlets near the Cambodian border, an entire Viet Cong battalion has had to split up because of their inability to be resupplied by the villagers.'"

Wagner didn't, *couldn't* argue. It was a done deal, he was getting his orders, what could he do? Refusing was an option again, but that was a major step. Would he be willing to lose the respect of his team, the Major, everyone around him? As an extreme, maybe a dishonorable discharge? And did he know that it *wasn't* in the best interest of the war effort, with the lives of all those men who died in the process? It wasn't a new conundrum, he'd been struggling with it for months now, it was simply getting worse. "I just feel, sir, the outcome of this war isn't as important to me as it was. My whole war here is becoming one of how the Montagnards fare when it's done. What if, when we leave, the other side's better for them? Will we be glad we lost?"

"I won't say it hasn't crossed my mind," said the Major.

"I've heard both sides on that, regarding the North. Have you met Menh, a Montagnard maid, she works at Sector headquarters?" he asked the Major.

"Menh? No, I don't think I have. But I think I know who she is. Older, maybe fifty?"

"Yes, sir. Jerry Dulane at HQ told me months ago that she travelled all the way down here to get away from Uncle Ho's bullshit. All by bicycle, probably walking it most of the way, with everything she owned. That's one side. Then in the same breath she tells me, '*It different here. They don't hate us in the North*'. So what the hell? They don't hate her there, but it's gotta be pretty damn bad to hoof it all the way here to get away from it. Crazy. But you know, that was before village reconsolidations. Maybe '*it different now*'."

The Major contemplated this for a moment, looking slightly away. Then he looked back at Wagner and said, "In any case, Colonel Bern would like to see you and Lieutenant Bailey tomorrow at Headquarters, ten hundred hours. It's primarily about the reconsolidations you're concerned with."

In the morning, Wagner rose to the sound of *Buc-Bawk-Buc-BAAAAWWK!* on the AFRN, Armed Forces Radio Network, playing "*Chickenman*", a radio comedy series about a winged warrior super hero wannabe in a chicken suit. It opened the station at the same time every morning. If he was back in the home compound team house at Le Quon, he sometimes recorded it upon wakening on a Sony cassette recorder. After Chickenman's opening chicken call, Wagner was getting into clean jungle fatigues and handyman-shined jungle boots, while Miss Hellfinger was patronizingly deriding her boss, the *Winged Warrior* Chickenman to get down off her desk. Sergeants Blas and Stewart were on the same schedule for breakfast, for which Flanagan usually showed up late, almost never in a sociable mood. Sergeant Stewart was his usual cheery self, jostling Kir, who stuck with him like glue most of the time. "Whachu do today, Shorty?"

"Whuuhh? Kir replied, laughing."

"I said, whachu do today? What kinda trouble you gettin' into today? You is just no good, are you?"

"Yeah? Same-same you, you no good."

"WHAT? You don't talk to me that way, Shorty! What kind of talk is that for a five year old? You need to show me more respect!"

So it went every morning with Kir around, the fourteen-ish Bahnaar Montagnard kid who didn't know how to stop smiling and laughing at anything said to him by any of the team, but particularly Stewart.

After breakfast, Wagner radiocd Bailey again to check on his expected presence at the meeting and for plans after. They arrived at headquarters at nearly the same time, thirty minutes prior to their meeting with Colonel Bern. Wagner had left early to stop in at the 71st to try to plan a 'date', if it could be called that, with Annelle and Corrine later. He left word with a nurse that they would try to be at the pool at 1300 hours, if it were convenient.

Gordon Bailey asked Darryl, "What do you know about the Major's plans for us? Nichols radioed me something about getting replaced by your team, and a reconsolidation mission.

"You probably know as much as I do. I sat down with him yesterday to get the word. I'm coming to Plei Do Rom. You're the postman delivering hamlets and hootches, and I'm the post office box receiving them," Wagner replied.

"The village moves we've done," Bailey said, "they've all been close enough to pick up the hootches and carry them to the new spots. The hamlets around Plei Do Rom are klicks away, through jungle. How do they expect us to move those?"

"Haven't a friggin' clue. On another note… I stopped at the 71st to let Annelle and Corrine know…. you gonna be able to stop at the pool?" Wagner asked.

"Sure. When?"

"I said 1300. That okay?"

"Yeah, sure, I guess so." Gordon had about as much confidence from many dry months in the dating field as Wagner did, having been bounced from one duty station to another, in nothing but military towns. Darryl hadn't met an exciting female since before his enlistment in January of '68. As he told Gordon, "Every girl in every Army town, you say 'Hello' and they're so numb they're stuck for an answer."

"Sure, yeah, that'd be great. 1300 hours."

Both lieutenants reported to Headquarters, and the White Mice entourage was back, but this time no Citroen car. General Ngo had come in by helicopter to Holloway, and had been driven in from there. Ngo was meeting with Bern, while the CIDG civilian Friedman and Colonel Robichaud were behind their closed doors. Doug Hanson already had his microphone in place and Sony cassette recording. Seeing Bailey and Wagner outside, Bern motioned for them to come in.

"I want to introduce you to some of my officers who are guiding our efforts, General," Colonel Bern said, smiling, but with dark eyebrows looking serious. This is Lieutenant Wagner."

"*Chou, Thieu Tuong Ngo,*" Wagner said, leaning forward to shake the General's hand. Major General Ngo was typically short, with a forced smile that Wagner met with an almost imperceptible scorn. He knew about Ngo and Bern, did they know he knew? Unlikely.

Ngo replied cordially, "*Chou, Trung-uy Wagg-nehr, Manh goi?*"

Bailey followed suit, and Ngo again smiled his forced smile, *"Chao Trung-uy Bae-lee. Manh goi?"*

"Gia manh, cam on ong, Thieu Tuong," Bailey answered.

Colonel Bern briefly told the General about the 'successes' his lieutenants had with the ongoing reconsolidation efforts over the last few months, and was now focusing on upcoming reconsolidations. Now he was directing his comments to Bailey and Wagner, obviously a show for the general. "By your work in the reconsolidation of these villages, you will *deny* the enemy his ability to carry on. We are helping the villagers by giving them metal roofing material, to replace their grass roofs. We'll give them all they need, as a token of our desire to win their friendship. Their hearts and minds, if you will."

Darryl Wagner pondered the starving people of Plei Ko Tu, and the deaths and disease in that village, and all the villages that followed. *"Hearts and minds"*? He wanted to say-- no-- *scream* BULLSHIT! Still, a first lieutenant does not argue with a colonel. Wagner's eyes shifted to Bailey, who, for the moment, seemed to be swallowing this bovine effluent. Gordon appeared intent and proud, if only for the moment. *Star struck*, if you will. It was rare for any lieutenant to be in a room with any general, let alone in a conversation with him. Most junior officers would only see two or three American generals up close in their entire two or three years. And this general was even known in *'The world'*, back in the United States. Wagner actually shared a little pride for the moment, proud to be a part in possibly shortening the war and demolishing the enemy's ability to endure. But only for a moment. He stared at Bern, wondering if, or how, any man could be as contemptible as this, in any way involved with stuffing dead soldiers with drugs for personal profit. He hardly heard Bern's spiel for the next few minutes as his mind imagined the corpse factory at work.

The Colonel proceeded to describe which small hamlets would be moved to several proposed or already begun new reconsolidation areas. "Your teams will be working with Hueys and Chinooks from the One Eighty Ninth Ghostriders Helicopter Assault Company, moving people, homes, their food and animals. And you, Lieutenant Wagner, have already been involved with the movement of these villages to Plei Ko Tu, one of the most successful moves to date. And there are more villages to come."

"Successful," Wagner almost said out loud. "Does he have a friggin' clue? Is anybody listening? Probably. But does he give a shit? Probably not."

The Colonel proceeded to indicate key resettlement areas over the entire province, accenting the importance of the timetable he expected. As he spoke, Wagner wondered if Gordon was sharing his concerns. Was this the answer to the war? Would it deny the enemy his food and supplies, his so-called 'taxes'? From what he'd learned so far, would the Montagnards have supplied the North Vietnamese anything, regardless? It seemed unlikely these tough, independent people would be an ally to the North Vietnamese, willing or not. They only wanted to be left alone, without the slightest knowledge or care about politics. And so far, from what he already knew, it seemed the North Vietnamese were, for the most part, the only enemy left to fight. Most of the V.C. appeared to be either dead or surrendered, wiped out or exposed from the 1968 Tet. The few V.C. remaining in this area were Montagnards *and I probably would be, too, if I was a Montagnard getting screwed by this government,"* thought Wagner. The Colonel had not once asked about his recent operations, or about enemy activity. He evidently wasn't concerned with battles, only reconsolidations. The only input he asked for was what they knew about some remote, small hamlets several klicks from Plei Do Rom.

Wagner waited for an opportune moment to mention his observations. It was after the discussion of one of those small hamlets that Wagner had actually stayed overnight in when finally, he said, "Sir, I understand the purpose of the reconsolidation effort, but these big villages are pretty pathetic." That brought a head-snap from the Colonel, a half-foot taller than Wagner. He stood a little straighter and tilted his head back slightly, peering down his nose as if he was going to hang him for insubordination. Wagner continued, "The filth, disease, starvation…they're dying like flies, it's pretty brutal. I don't think these people are meant to live in big populations. It's creating enemies for us."

Colonel Bern, his dark eyebrows furrowing tighter, looked like he was going to ream Wagner's asshole. In Ngo's Army, this insolence would never be dreamed of, the Lieutenant would be shot, most likely, and not after a trial, but right then and there. One of the worst things in a Vietnamese's mind is "losing face", or being embarrassed, and here was a young lieutenant doing just that to a Full Colonel. Ngo's head was turned toward Bern as if to say, "Are you going to shoot him or should I?"

Bern tried to maintain self-control. With a stern voice, he said, "Lieutenant, there are people starving all over this country. You aren't seeing anything new. If you haven't learned it already, you will learn war does that to civilians. I saw it in Okinawa, right after World War II. Saw it again in Korea. Same story. Their men are gone, fighting on one side or the other, and the civilians don't have the manpower and resources. That's not the fault of the reconsolidations. In fact, it's saving their goddam rice from the enemy. Without your work helping them, they'd be a hell of a lot worse off. It's not open for discussion, Lieutenant Wagner."

"Yes, sir."

When it was over, Wagner and Bailey got the "Thank you for coming, gentlemen" kiss-off, followed by plastic smiling formalities of "Nice to meet you."

"Bullshit," Wagner whispered to Bailey on their way out the door.

Walking to Doug Hanson's office, they met the Montagnard maid, Menh. Jerry Dulane had told him about her months before, the Montagnard woman who walked her bicycle hundreds of miles from North Vietnam. She was a woman of slight build, probably around 45, hips widened with age and child bearing. She wore a white *ao dai*, or 'long dress', the traditional Vietnamese woman's apparel made of flowing silk. He had never seen a Montagnard woman wearing one before. She spoke Vietnamese well, but with a strong Northern dialect. She spoke relatively clear English as well. Her voice was soft and gentle, so much so that Wagner had to strain to hear her words. He listened with fascination to her story of fleeing the North.

"It was several years ago," she said. "The communists were taking over. We knew it was not like that in the South. We brought what we could, and came here. To live."

"How did you get here? There weren't roads, were there?"

"No, no roads. Trails. We used bicycles to carry."

"Bicycles. You travelled hundreds of miles, hundreds of kilometers. On bicycles."

"Yes, that right. Long way, long time."

"Well, Menh, it must have been bad up north to make that decision. A lot of people in America should hear your side of things. You might change a lot of people's way of thinking back there. The North Vietnamese must have been horrible."

"Yes, maybe," she smiled.

"What about the Montagnards in the North? Did the Vietnamese treat the Montagnards badly there, too? Is that part of the reason you left?"

"No, it different there. They no hate us there."

"Can this get any more confusing?" he wondered. The Vietnamese didn't hate them there, they were thought of differently, yet they came here, where they are treated like dog meat. To get away from communism? Could it be that bad, even for a primitive society? On the other hand, nearly every communist takeover results in a genocide," he thought. But more shades of gray. Nothing was black and white. "So what was so bad that you come here?" Wagner asked her.

"My father, they kill. Because his father, he kill leader in new government. They kill my father. They say he the same, so kill. Then my brother. They kill my cousin, village chief, others."

"I'm sorry, Menh. I'm sorry. I hope it gets better for you and your family," Wagner said, still a little confused.

After meeting Menh, Wagner asked Bailey, "You get the feeling Bern didn't finish the details?"

"Yeah," Gordon replied, chuckling. "I think we sort of 'took a back seat'. We were there for the show."

"Dog-and-pony show," Wagner added.

"Dog and pig," answered Bailey, just as Doug Hanson returned to his office to join them. "I don't know. What if they're right? I know the Montagnards aren't too pleased with it," he said in his slow, methodical way.

"What's that?" Hanson interjected. "The resettlements?"

"Yeah," Wagner said. "Hi Doug. I don't know either, maybe it's good. Maybe it's the answer to win this fiasco sooner. But hell, it isn't right. I think we're destroying our best allies. And we're part of it. I don't like it," Wagner said.

"Yeah, I think you may be right," Hanson replied.

Wagner looked at Hanson with a long concerned-sad look. "I don't believe these people can survive for long, living in big villages. And in return we give them metal roofing."

"Well," Hanson said, "The word from Saigon is this is what's going to choke the enemy. There's a lot of pressure to take away Charlie's supplies. If it works..."

"Take away Charlie's supplies, or take away the Montagnards' land?" Wagner interrupted. "Seems like we've seen this movie before. Something about the settlers and the Indians? How'd that work out?"

"I don't think we want to settle here," Doug said with a grin.

"No, but I think the Vietnamese figure it's theirs," Bailey added. "The 'Yards don't fit in their picture."

"This metal roofing crap," Wagner said. "You know, these people have used grass roofs for centuries. It works. It lets smoke out when they're cooking inside their hootches.

American Santa Clauses don't know that. They don't deafen you like jackhammers when it rains. They're replaceable. They insulate. From cold *and* heat. Santa Clauses don't know that, either."

"Doug, any more clandestine info regarding things we discussed before?" Gordon asked.

"Not much new," Hanson replied, getting up to close his office door. Talking quieter, he told them, "As you know, Ngo was here today. I haven't dared play it back yet, but I recorded him and Bern. Remember, guys, this has to stay just between us. But I did hear Friedman and Colonel Robichaud last week. I didn't hear much, the tape was hard to understand, but I know I heard drugs and reconsolidation in their conversation. When I came in, they stopped. I think they could be ready to make a move on this."

"Hope they get him. I can't believe this shit," Gordon said, disgustedly.

"I don't trust this Ngo cat whatsoever," Wagner replied. "Maybe my opinion's been tainted a tad, but he just seems like a weasel. What a world. I think I'm getting a bad attitude, ya think?"

The M-151 Jeep passed through white, pink, and pastel blue buildings along narrow streets of Pleiku, stopping in front of a small restaurant recommended to them. After a quick lunch of a chicken, rice, bamboo shoots and vegetable stew, washed down with a bottle of Tiger La Rue beer, they headed up to the 71st Medevac.

"Gordon, I'm not even sure she even wants to see me again."

"She wants to see you."

"I'm not so sure. I mean, she never asked when I'd be back to the 71st. She never even asked *IF* I'd be back," Wagner said. "The damn place is crawling with horny GIs. She's got the pick of the litter, so to speak."

"What makes you think they're all after her?" Hanson asked.

"Yeah, what," Gordon added.

"C'mon, Gordo, you've seen her. Who wouldn't be all over her?"

"Oh, c'mon, she's not *that* gorgeous. I've seen better," Bailey said, with a shit eating grin.

"Hell-lloooo," Wagner retorted, "You lived next door to Barbara Eden, for Chrissakes."

Hanson departed for HQ official business, while Bailey and Wagner continued to the pool. Checking M-16s and Wagner's Smith and Wesson .38 holstered revolver at the entrance, they walked into the pool facility. The pool wasn't fancy, by any means, but the most inviting thing around. A Spec 4 in fatigue pants, O.D. Tee shirt and jungle boots was cleaning the pool bottom with a long handled brush. He made a quick salute, and yelled, "How ya doin', sirs?"

"Great, Specialist, thanks for asking. How's everything going in the land of blood and bandages?" Wagner asked with a returned smile.

"Not bad," he said, eyes lowered to their buttoned shirts. "I've got to ask. What's the emblem on your chest?"

"We have to wear Vietnamese rank. I still haven't figured it out," Bailey said, chuckling.

"Advisers? I can tell by the faded threads."

"Ha, yes. Would you by any chance know Annelle and Corrine...they're nurses? We're just here for a couple of hours." Wagner still worried about assuming too much. Were they really welcome, or an annoyance?

"Sure do, sir. I'll see if..." He stopped as Annelle and Corrine were just coming out of the women's locker room, in bathing suits and short terry cloth beach robes. It was 12:45 on a welcome warm and dry sunny day.

"Hi Darryl. Hi Gordon," they called, walking along the concrete pool border toward them. Wagner's eyes focused on hers, feeling an attraction lacking so long. Annelle looked radiant, hair and face prepped as if for a prom. Blonde hair swept across her forehead and her pale skin had more color now that dry season had begun, ending incessant clouds and rain of the last several months. Darryl was still cautiously optimistic, still not certain if he was an imposition. She could still be acting out of kindness and guilt, as in *what if he became one of my patients who didn't make it?* A single kiss might let him know, if opportunity allowed, but demands of the job and travel at night made that unrealistic. Still, those pouty cheeks and soft lips were so inviting..

Gordon and Corrine were joined by two other 71st nurses while conversing under an overhanging pool house roof. Darryl and Annelle, having taken the time to be the 'water people' they were, were oblivious to them now. They lazily dolphined and breast stroked the length of the pool together. Darryl wished he had a swim mask, to better see her undulating dolphin kick. Her derriere was perfect, and she knew he was watching. Out of the water and sitting on the pool side, they talked for what seemed days. She was normally quiet, but talk came easy for her with Darryl. They were both surprised many times when each was thinking the same thing before it was said. ESP. Extra Sensory Perception. Was there really such a thing? He asked her scores of questions. What Kansas town was she from, how big, what was high school like, what about her family, her childhood, nursing school, and particularly, "Why did you choose the Army?"

"Oh, you know, opportunity, travel, all the usual clichés. But I really did think this is where I could do the most good. All those poor guys. My Dad was in the Army, in Germany in 1944 to 1945. He was an artillery captain. Ever hear of the Bridge at Remagen?"

"Yes! The bridge was called.. uh, I think it was the Ludendorff. The 9th Armored Division captured it to get across the Rhine, if I remember right."

"Wow, you're good! My Dad was there, right after, I think. He was in the 28th Division, 112th Infantry Regiment."

"Cut it out. One of my best friend's Dad was also

there... he was a captain in the same outfit, I think. An Artillery captain. Stellar man. One of those people who influences your life. I want to talk to him more about it when I get home. Is your Dad still alive?"

"Yes. He likes to talk about it, but only if he's asked."

"I was just going to ask you that.. will you get out of my mind? I'd love to talk to him about it. I wonder if he knew my friend's Dad...Charles Goodspeed. You should ask him. I've watched just about every World War II documentary and movie made, and I read a lot. I'm fascinated with what those poor guys went through, especially in Germany. I'd hate to fight a war in winter."

"Was your father in the war?"

"No. He was in the Civilian Construction Corps, and had two children by then, but I don't know the details. I was born in December of '44. Never asked. I did have two uncles, though. My Father's brother Walter was in the Navy, he had four and a half ships sunk under him. My Mom's brother was a Marine lieutenant, named Vernon Fisher. He fought at Okinawa and Iwo Jima, got a battlefield commission when most of his company was killed, and a Silver Star. Some amazing stories about that guy."

"How does one get a half of a ship sunk under him?"

"He was on a cruiser. A torpedo hit it, the front half sunk. He was on the back half. They backed it all the way from the Marianas to Australia, using the screws to steer."

"Oh my God. What a story."

"He made it all the way up through the ranks from an enlisted swabby to Commander before the war was over. We moved from Iowa to Maine when I was young, so I never got to talk to either of them about it."

"Maybe they didn't want to talk about it."

"Possibly. But in my experience, a lot of the guys who say they don't want to talk about it....they hardly saw combat. The guys in the field, all of them talk about it, at least all the ones that I've known. I think that a lot of guys don't talk about it because anybody who hasn't experienced it really doesn't want to hear it. After awhile you tune out."

"I think you're right. Are you staying in? Career, I mean?"

"Not sure. I don't believe so. I have a year left on my degree. I've got to finish that. But I am considering it." Darryl Wagner was embarrassed to tell her about his dismal scholastic failure of the last two college years and fears that he would never improve it to graduate. This weighed heavily on his upcoming decision to risk going back to school and failing or making a career out of proven success. A great career track was underway in light of command time almost since his commission as an officer. Particularly so in a war. And he enjoyed most of his service time ever since that congressman helped him out of the Army Fire Department. The social life, however, or lack thereof, was not so enticing. "Also, I'm afraid of a RIF," he said.

"What's a RIF?"

"Reduction in Force. I knew a girl at Bliss. Her father had been a Colonel. He was Riffed down to a first sergeant. After wars, they RIF a lot of people. I just don't trust this Army," he said, with a slight frown.

"Wow. I had no idea. What will your degree be in?"

"Engineering."

"What kind of engineer will you be?"

"A great one," Wagner answered, smiling.

Her glistening white teeth were smiling back, between soft alluring lips. "No, I mean, Electrical, mechanical, what?"

"I started out in Engineering Physics. Physics is my favorite course. But in college it was different, all theoretical and electrical, not what I had in mind at all. My brother and my Dad were engineers, but they never really told me what an engineer does….and the professors, I asked them. They couldn't tell me because they didn't know. They never worked for a living….in engineering, I mean."

"That's too bad," she said, leaning forward and pulling her knees under her chin.

"Criminal is more like it. There should be a law.

Nobody gets to teach college until they've worked in their field for at least five years."

"I agree. You learn most of what you know on the job, not in school. What I've learned here can't be duplicated anywhere."

"Wow. Annelle, you took that right out of my play book. Anyway, I've switched into Mechanical Engineering. What about you, are you staying in?"

"No, I'm getting out in April. DEROSing and out. Going back home. I feel guilty about leaving, but this is hard here. I don't think I can take any more," she said, her gaze falling to watch a small butterfly flitting above the concrete deck. "In a hospital, back home...everything is under control, so to speak. It's a controlled situation. There are enough doctors and nurses, plenty of rooms, sanitation, equipment.. and nobody is left to die because they aren't going to make it. There have been days... we've been so swamped with incoming patients, they have to be triaged, and you sort out who's worth saving, who isn't, and all the horribly... I'm sorry. Do you worry about..you know, getting hurt?

"Sure, who doesn't?" Wagner said. He didn't want to tell her he had decided if he was permanently disabled, lost an appendage, blinded, whatever, he'd be a one-man suicide squad. He didn't want to go home that way. The war produced scores of 'close calls' for Wagner. *Inches and seconds* make all the difference between unscathed or mutilated. Wagner had come to believe God doesn't protect you in some plan; hopefully He picks up the pieces after. People die because they were in a wrong spot only seconds or hours after they were in the very same right spot. *Inches and seconds.*

"Tell me more about your language school. I imagine Vietnamese is very difficult," she said.

"Yes and no. It has no verb conjugations, and no male-female adjectives like French. And it's a very literal language. A military tank is a 'war car'. A helicopter is a *mai bai truc tanh*, a 'flying machine go straight up'," he said, twirling his fingers upward.

She laughed. Those radiant blue eyes sparkled in the afternoon sunlight, made all the more lovely from a reflection of pool water. "That's funny," she said.

"Your eyes are incredibly blue in this light." He told her.

"Now you're in my mind. I was just thinking how blue your eyes are. Now get out of *my* mind!" she said, laughing.

"The 'no' part," he continued, "that's the tonal sing-song effect you hear, same as in Chinese. The up-and-down inflections. Each word can mean as many as seven entirely different things. The word 'ly' can mean a cup, or glass, and six other things, depending on how you say it." He said it the seven different ways, conducting with an index finger to draw out each tonal mark, written over or under words. "That's what makes it hard. If they're talking fast, I'm lost in a minute."

"Oh, I can't imagine. That's impossible."

"A church and a whorehouse…very similar. You have to be careful. Another easy part, though.. grammatically, it's simple. 'I go store'. There is no 'I am going to the store'. And to make it future tense, you just add an *"ess-ee"* before the verb, or a *"da"* to make it past tense.

"See?" she asked.

"It's spelled s-e, but it's pronounced shay. The s is a shh sound. Saigon is really *Shai-gon*."

"How long did this take you?"

"We had four weeks in Fort Bragg, eight more at Bliss."

"And you learned all that in twelve weeks?"

"Yes, but it was Vietnamese language all day, five days a week, seven hours a day plus homework. Nothing but Vietnamese. The teachers were young Vietnamese girls. Some were prostitutes, some just educated here in Saigon schools. The hookers were the best. At English, I mean."

"Glad you made that clear," she said. "You must have an aptitude for language. Did you do well in it?"

"I surprised myself, Annelle. Placed third in a class of one hundred and forty. I had no idea.. But the aptitude thing.. probably not. I failed French II in high school. Useless language. Never used it once. But there was no goal, no incentive. I knew it then, and know it better now. Vietnamese was different, there was an actual purpose, a goal. That makes all the difference. It may have even saved my tail on an artillery call one night."

"How did that happen?"

"My counterpart gave me coordinates that should have been the bad guys. He actually had given me *our* coordinates. I could have called it in on us. If I hadn't clarified it in Vietnamese, it could have been embarrassing. I probably would have checked anyway, but still... what about you?"

"I had Spanish. I've used it a little. It's come in handy on the job, back home. A few patients didn't speak any English at all, only Spanish."

"I think that was a good choice. My Dad always thought there was use in it. Up in Maine, though, everyone is French and Irish. Italians in Portland. Not many Mexican guys."

"I can understand that. You're above the Arctic circle, right?"

Wagner was happy to hear she remembered their earlier conversation, it bolstered his growing confidence he wasn't her pity patient. "Right. I've discovered that the Vietnamese here have a different accent then the Saigon teachers we had. Imagine Texas and Boston, on steroids. These guys aren't mobile, their language has drifted apart. And I'm working with three tribes of Montagnards, who don't even speak each other's languages. You have to rely on your interpreters. I'm learning a lot of things get lost in the translations." Wagner felt more comfortable with her now. ESP thoughts kept occurring, affecting a harmony of sorts. It was growing magical for Darryl. He found himself less plagued by visions of his college sweetheart.

It was getting late, thoughts of the ambushed MAT team was on their minds, and while there were still several hours of daylight, Wagner and Bailey once again headed out of the 71st in their Jeeps. Navigating through a stench of poorly tuned diesel engines on the busy streets of Pleiku, Gordon said with his dry humor, "So, Darryl old buddy, when do you think you'll start taggin' that?"

"You think so little of me, you filthy man. You seem to be grooving pretty good with Corrine, whatdaya think?"

"Well," Gordon mused with a grin, "She's no Barbara Eden."

"You've been staring at Eden with binoculars too long, you sack of shit."

"I never did that."

"C'mon, shitheels, you can tell me. It'll never leave Pleiku. I promise," Darryl said, narrowly missing an interweaving Lambretta with three Vietnamese men hanging on in alternating leans to see.

"Never did."

"Right. Anyway, Annelle is DEROSing in April. Going home to Kansas."

Two sergeants from Gordon's MAT Team returned to the headquarters building, one of them loud and obnoxiously drunk. Their laid back lieutenant ignored and endured their loud banter on the long trip back to their home compound of Plei Do Rom. Darryl worried privately for their safety, much of the trip was on remote dirt roads, far from QL 14.

Well into the dry season, wind and red sandy dirt were even more the norm. Nothing was free of it, radios, clothing, food, teeth, the team Jeeps; everything wore a dull red coat. Any food outside the confines of the team house was permeated with abrasive red grit. It ground between molars, audible as much as felt. Untold kilos of digested tooth enamel remained in the highlands long after this war would be over. Giant red ghosts of eddying dust threatened to devour their souls. It haunted the Jeeps relentlessly, intermittently falling just out of reach, then catching and enveloping them when the rough Jeep trail demanded it, falling inches behind again when the road improved.

Sergeant Flanagan had left for R & R, and Wagner was frankly happy to see him go. Royal pain in the ass. For most battlefield injuries, Blas and Stewart were adept at first aid. Anything worse would depend on a Huey medevac. Flanagan's derisive nature had gnawed on the team for months, contributing little. The trip to Plei Do Rom was long. Six miles west on Highway 19, another five south down Highway 14, then eight more through moderately undulating high ground on a narrow Jeep trail. Trees and light jungle straddled this trail in places, but it was mostly open, grassy land, including ominous twelve foot high elephant grass areas that invited an ambush. It also passed through two remote rice paddy areas, formed from Montagnard-made foot high dams, some as wide as a kilometer. The paved highway segments totaled just over twenty minutes and were reasonably safe; not so the latter eight miles on the Jeep trail, on similar terrain to where the massacred MAT team had been ambushed. The slow going was a forty minute trip at best, thirty percent faster now that the rainy season was over. It seemed much longer.

The Plei Do Rom compound was large and well defended, but not much changed since Barry Sadler's Special Forces team operated here several years before. Row upon row of barbed and concertina wire extended from the berm, often protected by a full Bahnaar Montagnard company. Over fifty thousand mines were planted inside the wire rows a few years before by the Special Forces team and their counterparts. Nobody knew where the mines were. Gordon still kept their miniguns, but he instructed Darryl not to tell anyone, as they were 'unauthorized'. "Who in hell comes up with these rules, anyway," Wagner wondered. They also had an arsenal of 2.75" rockets on hand, both HE and flechette rounds. As in Le Quon, they re-supplied their Headhunter 0-1 Birddog friends from their own tiny airstrip as well. Many 0-1s had been shot down as a result of playing fighter pilot instead of using WP marking rounds, causing the use of casualty-producing armaments to be 'unauthorized'.

The MAT team house in Plei Do Rom was more like a clubhouse. It was clean and roomy for the four Americans who were living there. Bailey and his team had been informed by the Major that they were being switched with MAT 57 and temporarily moving to Le Quon. They drove to headquarters to complain to Colonel Bern, but Bern and Nichols were already in agreement. It was a done deal. They returned to Plei Do Rom late that afternoon, all but Bailey convinced that Wagner had somehow been responsible, and they were pissed. In reality, Wagner would have preferred to stay in his own A.O., now the largest MAT A.O. in the country. He knew the area, and there were many RF, PF, and PSDF units that needed attention, often simply with resupply problems.

Because MACV headquarters had sent a notice about ambush failures the RF/PFs had had, Wagner decided they would emphasize their training in mechanical Claymore ambushes. He firmly believed MAs were an outstanding means for the understrength RFs and PFs to defend their villages in relative safety. Without strong leadership, there would be very few men willing to set ambushes out at night against potentially overwhelming odds, with little chance of reinforcements. The mechanical ambush, or MA solved much of the problem.

In two days, Team 46 had vacated and moved to Le Quon. Wagner imagined the friction between the Team 46 NCOs and the Major.

Every day, Team 57 went to a different PF village, all Montagnards, to go over their defenses, ensure resupply, and to teach their MA. Sometimes, Thieu-Ta, or *Major* Buhm, the Montagnard commander of the three RF companies in the area, accompanied them with a small escort contingent to give a propaganda rally. Major Buhm was the finest and most influential Regional Force officer in the province. As the cliché goes, "Small in stature, a giant of a man." Team 57 had met him on Wagner's first job, in Plei Ko Tu, when they pulled that first five-day MEDCAP. Bailey had told him all about Buhm, and it was all true. He had perhaps, the most 'pacified' area, for lack of a better term, in all the land that bordered the eastern rugged mountain-valley terrain, including well known "V.C. Valley", as it was called. He liked to have Americans join him in these remote villages, as they were a big part of his spiel. In each village, his procedures were much the same. First, the PF platoon, all Montagnards, would assemble in a platoon formation. Next, the villagers were called by the village chief. They formed a large horseshoe, women and children on one side, men on the other. The Major told them to be seated, whereupon they all squatted in a 'knees up-fanny down' position that no American could hold for more than a few minutes.

On this day, the Major, his aide, Lt. Wagner, Sergeant Blas, and interpreter Kloh stood before the horseshoe of villagers. Major Buhm stood in clean fatigues, stiff Army baseball cap, a pearl handled .45 pistol holstered at his hip. As the Major spoke, Kloh interpreted. Wagner had no idea what the speech would entail, he was hearing it through Kloh.

It seemed one of the hamlets that had been moved into a nearby reconsolidation area wanted to move back to their old village site, as most did. A hamlet chief represented this hamlet.

"If you go back to your hamlet, I'll have the Americans blow your village apart with artillery," Major Buhm said.

Wagner looked back at Sergeant Blas, stunned. Then back at Kloh. "Are you sure that's what he said?"

"Yes, sir," Kloh answered. "That what he tell them."

Buhm continued, "The Americans will come in with planes and spray and kill all of your crops." A muffled murmur rose across the kneeling audience, their heads pivoting back and forth as they looked at their families and neighbors in dread. Years of Agent Orange defoliant left no doubt what it did to vegetation. "Then the planes will drop napalm on your homes and everything will burn." The villagers were extremely nervous now. Wagner watched desperate, frightened villagers in the horseshoe, afraid to talk. Each time Buhm spoke, he turned and waited for Kloh to interpret, appearing to look for Wagner's approval. He never stopped smiling. "Then the Americans will come with big helicopters and bring you all to Cambodia." Finally, they talked rapidly among themselves, as this last threat was the worst fate of all. After a moment the chief, standing now in front of the deck said, "We no go, we want to stay here. We no want help V.C."

Wagner was in shock. From the first threat, he didn't know what to say. What could he say? His counterpart, Buhn, was the most respected man in the southern half, probably all of, Pleiku Province. He had more authority and control than anyone. He was revered. After all, didn't he have the most secure area in Pleiku Province? This man had been fighting in this same area for twenty seven years, since 1943. "He must know what he's doing, right?" Wagner said, turning to Sergeant Blas. Both men wondered what the villagers must think of these powerful, evil Americans. "What happened to 'winning hearts and minds'? Are we going to make it out of this ville alive?" he asked.

"Sure brought smoke on that poor chief," Blas replied.

When this particular speech was over, Wagner privately asked Major Buhm if he could refrain from making the Americans out to be such bad guys. "You know we aren't going to do all that, don't you?" he asked Buhm. Buhm just smiled, his eyes glistening. He knew they wouldn't, of course.

The whole show confused Wagner. Why is Buhm helping these brutal reconsolidations? Doesn't he see the harm they're creating for his people? This was comparable to the Indian scouts helping the cavalry slaughter Indians, though they were usually from another reviled Indian tribe. Realistically, the Major was caught up in this mess, this system, just as they were... .another helpless pawn. It was his job, his duty, and maybe he believed it was necessary to win the war. Major Buhm had many times looked Wagner sadly in the eyes to say, "I think when the Americans leave.. we all die." Wagner had heard the same lament on many occasions throughout the tour, from leaders and soldiers, both Vietnamese and Montagnard. But Buhm was smarter, more knowledgeable, and certainly more experienced. He knew.

The village and hamlet trips often ended with rice wine parties. They didn't get any easier, particularly with memories of hepatitis. He was immune to hepatitis A now, but he did not know that. Thieu-Ta Buhm knew Wagner wasn't a fan of rice wine, but he enjoyed putting him through it in a teasing way, always including the village chief and elders. Sergeants Blas and Stewart usually found an excuse to work on the Jeep or sauntered off to help with villager medical problems.

Plei Do Rom was off the path, an 'island fortress' with no American bases or sizable hamlets for miles around. Many miles north in Kontum Province, west of the Annamite mountain chain, centuries of erosion formed hundreds of tiny creek troughs. The troughs run into scores of small streams, each snaking around eroded contours until they bleed into the Dak Ayun River, flowing north to south. The river grows larger from each vein adding to this Dak Ayun artery, until it reaches the lowlands directly east of Plei Do Rom, where it now earns the name Ia Ayun. Still more tiny capillaries become veins from the watershed west of Plei Do Rom to continue feeding the slow snaking monster. Three kilometers south of the beginning of the Ia Ayun a large and beautiful rapids flows over and around one of the rare geological features of Pleiku Province: rocks. Left from prehistoric volcanic activity, they remain unburied, kept bare by the forces of the mighty snake flowing over them. The area earned the name "V.C. Valley" from several years of serving as a haven for the enemy. Thick vegetation, rugged terrain, and adequate water provided a home relatively safe from superior artillery and air power. The river meanders and flows one hundred and twenty miles away to just above Nha Trang on the coast, where its waters reacquaint with the sea. The journey is much longer for the river, which loops and twists from every damming deposit, created by washouts from thousands of rainy seasons.

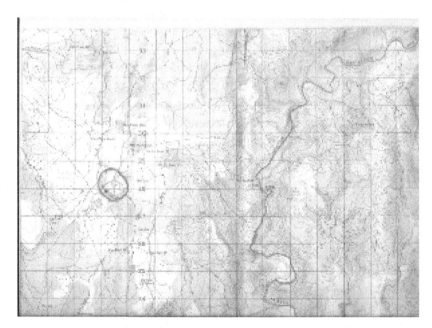

Sergeant Blas had taken a Jeep back to Le Quon with their Kit Carson Scout Tung and another Vietnamese RF for resupplies as well as a break to recover from some sort of malaise and excessive diarrhea. That wasn't uncommon. The rest of the team left Plei Do Rom with the other Jeep with Sergeant Stewart at the wheel. Wagner was riding shotgun, Flanagan and Kloh were in the rear. They weren't driving alone, they accompanied Major Buhm and two platoons of Montagnard RF soldiers in two deuce-and-a-half Army trucks. Their Jeep was oreo cookied between the two trucks.

A village named De Poui was several kilometers south, in an extremely remote area with no other hamlets within kilometers. Situated near the Ia Dron stream, it was the furthest south the team had ventured yet. It was only fifteen kilometers, or 9 miles east of the Ia Drang three-day battle that occurred in 1965, the 'start of the helicopter war' that Colonel Hal Moore led. Being further south, towards Ban Me Thuot, the jungle grew taller, thicker, almost into triple canopy, where no light penetrated to the forest floor. The first few klicks passed through risky low lying elephant grasslands, raising their pucker factor. Dust broiled up from the truck ahead, weapons flicked off safety and pointed out. Exiting the grasses was a relief, but now a thick jungle growth sandwiched them, closer and darker than any the team had yet experienced. The truck ahead was fairly plowing through branches that had grown in from the sides, lacking traffic to shunt their growth. RF soldiers ducked forward in their side benches, escaping slapping branches that bent and released like bowstrings against steel frames supporting a tarp covering the top.

The village consisted of four small hamlets, fifty meters of grass and trees between each. Passing out of the narrow road, the lead truck stopped abruptly before entering the first hamlet. Stewart hit the brakes hard, thirty meters behind. Some orders were barked ahead, and small Montagnard soldiers quickly dismounted the truck, fanning out in a perimeter.

"Oh, shit, what have we here?" said Stewart, M-16 in hand and one leg out. A canvas Jeep top with steel tubes for support prevented a quick exit from the back seat, especially for Flanagan, who was busily bitching again. Wagner jumped out, turning to walk quickly to Major Buhm's truck, his M-16 off safety. Looking ahead, nothing was moving. Not even chickens or animals. Something was wrong, and Buhm had instantly sensed it, stopping the truck and deploying his men.

The RFs were moving now, slowly, a third of them prone, weapons pointed out. Wagner quickened his pace to join the Major, Stewart quickly following, surveying the flanks. Montagnard sergeants yelled at their men, who reacted in quick sprints and crouches. Ahead lay a dead water buffalo, lying on its side. Rotting and bloated, it was half again its normal massive size, attracting a thousand flies buzzing crazily in a dense dark cloud. Black rigored legs extended out, held at an upward angle by the swollen carcass. A brief eddy filled the warm air with an intense nauseating odor, causing involuntary gag reflexes among the soldiers, who turned their heads and grimaced, each one well versed with the smell of death. Moving ahead, they saw goats and pigs, also dead and bloated, crawling with flies. They had been dead for several hours. Moving faster now, a third of the men alternating in prone covering positions, they moved between the Montagnard grass roofed hootches. More dead animals, including two skinny speckled brown dogs, but no people. The stench was incredible, stifling, eerie. Past the fourth hootch was an open area, the center of the village. A sixty foot square formed by interlaced tree branches formed a stockade fence in the open area. The leading RFs stopped, staring. Others caught up. Buhm shouted something to the men, and a small sergeant shouted something back. A worried, dismayed look from Major Buhm's face gave Wagner pause. The old Major was running now, rounding the hootch, pulling up short. Then he walked slowly, head turning side to side. The RFs said nothing, just stared. Wagner and Stewart hurriedly caught up, followed by Flanagan and Kloh. There, before them, lay a ghastly sight. The entire village, five hundred strong, old men, women, children, and babies. All piled on top one another, in contorted positions, pools of dark dried blood everywhere. It reminded Wagner of pictures of the Holocaust. Skin and dried blood was mixed with traditional black dresses and loin cloths, trimmed in red and gold of their native ancestry. Bodies were sliced and shot, some mutilated. And now swarming with flies. Wagner looked at Buhm, who was crying, as were several soldiers. The NVA had massacred this village, people who had no other weapons than sugar cane knives and crossbows. Slaughtered for psychological effect, intensified by ethnocentrism. Whatever the RF soldiers had felt for their ruthless enemy before, it just tripled.

Returning to Plei Do Rom, the team discovered the village of De Poui had been the temporary base of an American Civil Action Team over a year earlier. That small compound had been overrun, the Americans killed. If they had lasted until last week, they would have only extended their lives another year.

Sergeant Blas had returned, and the team was finishing up coordination efforts regarding the clean-up of De Poui. The sights and smells of that day would not be forgotten, not in a lifetime. Wagner could only imagine the nightmares the RFs with them had experienced in their short lives. How many other De Pouis had they been through? And Major Buhm, what about him? Who were the people, the systems, that put people through this?

Most of the detail work and reports complete, the team spent the morning reviewing the Plei Do Rom team house and perimeter defenses, which thankfully proved impressive. Shortly after a lunch provided by the excellent Vietnamese cook who worked for Bailey's team, the men joined Thieu-Ta Buhm and a few of his officers in the center of the village for a pep rally of sorts with the villagers. Major Buhm, standing on the short log platform to deliver his speech, asked Wagner to join them. Kloh, of course came up as well to interpret. Buhm began with threats to the villagers not to return to their pre-reconsolidation village sites, then shifted to the central topic: He wanted to display a young Montagnard PF soldier-prisoner who stood on the log platform with them. A bit of 'psychological operations' of his own. The Major had already questioned the prisoner at length, who had reportedly been meeting Viet Cong in the jungle. He stood with hands tied behind his back, an RF sergeant holding one arm, Buhm holding the other. Buhm was smiling. Almost always smiling.

"Kloh, what are they saying?" Wagner asked.

"He say, they kill a pig or goat. Eat blood and bullet," he said.

Wagner looked at Blas, Stewart, and Flanagan below. They heard it too. "Say again, over?"

"They gonna kill pig or goat, you know?" he said, pulling a finger across his throat. "Pour blood into bowl, put bullet in. They eat." Buhm had been holding a gourd, and Kloh didn't know the word, calling it a bowl.

"What's this about a bullet?" Wagner asked.

"I don't know. Something they put in bowl with blood. If he lie again, or meet V.C., he drink blood, bullet will kill him."

"If you say so, Kloh."

"It okay. He believe."

The Montagnards, like the Vietnamese, are very superstitious. This commander, the voice and soul of their world, could tell them it would snow tomorrow and not be questioned. Major Buhm turned to fill Wagner and Kloh in. "I no believe in soopstition. Me Catholic. But maybe he no lie again. If he lie, we kill him," he said, laughing. Wagner had heard stories of the Major blowing men's' brains out with his .45, and he knew he would. In front of the entire village, Buhm's sergeant produced a small black and white pig. Another soldier held a 10" wide wooden bowl. With a bayonet, he dug into the squirming pig's throat with a "Pop" sound. He didn't bother to slit its throat, the

pig's suffering meant nothing. The pig was screaming and kicking, as they held it up to let it bleed into the waiting bowl. Blood was pumping out in fast little squirts. The pig was making gasping noises mixed with squeals and the sound of frothing blood. The bleeding gradually slowed, and the pig slowly died. While Buhm poured blood carefully into the waiting gourd, Wagner noticed him picking small clots that stuck to the bowl, dropping them into the gourd as well. Wagner, on the spot in front of the village and the Major, had almost talked himself into drinking a little of it for show if he had to. The clots were too much. "No way, not here, not now, not ever."

Now the Major turned to Wagner, and in broad view of all, he asked Wagner for a bullet from his M-16. Wagner complied, jacking a round to allow the Major to take both the bullet and his M-16 while his sergeant held the gourd. Using the hole in the rear sight handle, he inserted the lead through it to twist and pry the bullet from its brass. He held the bullet up with one hand, Wagner's arm up with the other, for all to see. With a few words in guttural Bahnaar Montagnard, he dropped the small .223 bullet into the gourd of blood, shaking it for all to see. He took a drink, wiping a bright red rivulet from his chin, still smiling. Then he handed it to Wagner, who made a poor pretense of a swig, with a resounding "*Aaah*", as in 'good'.

The last part of this display was the little PF soldier-suspect. He was clearly terrified, and would not drink. The Major, still smiling, unholstered his pearl handled .45, thumb-clicked the safety off, and pushed the barrel hard to the PF's temple. "You drink," he said...Still smiling. And the little PF drank.

The speech concluded with the Major chastising the RFs and PFs for shooting all the birds in the area. It was mostly a show for the villagers, for Wagner had seen Buhm himself shoot the head off a dove. "Numbah-one chop-chop," he grinned.

Back in the team house, the Major laughed about it, insisting it always worked.

Another dry, cool windy morning found the team travelling alone without their RF escort to an isolated Montagnard village to the west, not far from north-south highway QL 14. Tung was accompanying the team, nervous and saying little in his new position as their Kit Carson. The village was quite small, only accessible by foot from the highway, but a Jeep trail connected it via a torturous path from Plei Do Rom. A small PF platoon held a small perimeter there, consisting of thirty three Montagnard PF soldiers and one Vietnamese platoon leader *Thieu-uy*, or second lieutenant. "Can you imagine, sir, how that Vietnamese lieutenant must feel, surrounded by nothing but Montagnards?" asked Sergeant Stewart.

"Probably something like the segregated units of World War II, I'd imagine," answered Wagner, bringing a grin to Stewart and a head-snap from Flanagan, who was hoping for an angry response. But Stewart was cool, he could talk sensibly about racial problems with any of the men when no offense was intended.

Entering the perimeter, they found nobody assembled or

ready for their arrival, as most units had been. Taking a tour through the village, they noted again how the hootches weren't lined up in rows and columns, but randomly arranged to create an attractive neighborhood. It was suspiciously vacant, with only a few women and young children in sight. Not even older men. Beside the first hootch, a bamboo mat covered a hole two feet in diameter, ending in darkness. Suspecting an enemy tunnel or cache, Wagner asked Tung what he thought. He answered something that sounded like "Horseshit."

"What? Horseshit?"

A slight delay, then, "Hoe-shit."

"Hoe-shit. What is hoe-shit?"

Tung tried again. "Hole-shit. *Di Cau*. People shit."

"You mean shithole?" asked Wagner.

"Yeah. Yeah. Shithole!" He answered. "*Di cau* (Go shit.)"

Wondering if it was an arms cache or tunnel, he tried to look down, but couldn't tell. It was at least six feet deep. It didn't smell. But he wasn't going down there to find out. An American patrol would most likely drop a grenade in to be sure, but he decided to let it be handled by the RFs. They would know a lot more about it, without creating more enemy in the process.

An hour later, the PFs were finally organized and ready for a class on mechanical ambushes. Halfway through the class, the Vietnamese lieutenant told Wagner he had to go to a platoon leader's meeting in the city. There were no such meetings, and they knew he was lying.

"You can't go now, you're the platoon leader. You're paid to do the job here, now stay and do it," Wagner said, disgusted. The lieutenant turned to go. "You go, Thieu-uy, you get reported. The Major won't be very happy with you." With that, he stopped and turned, deciding to stay. But five minutes into the class, he hopped on his 50cc Honda and left for Pleiku, the noisy bike leaving a blue trail of oil smoke trailing behind. Their Trung-si platoon sergeant said 'the lieutenant left for the city nearly every day'. On this day he 'needed to be at a lottery in Pleiku'. His platoon's morale was nil, the defenses were a disaster, and all semblance of discipline was gone.

With the Vietnamese platoon leader gone, in charge was Sergeant Krok, an older Montagnard soldier whose face reflected years of war and poverty. Typically, that worn face also wore a smile. Part of the advisory routine included questions of supply and support, and just as routine, the answers were discouraging. The Montagnard PFs had no supply system or artillery of their own, and depended on the Vietnamese. In truth, part of the problem was a lack of knowledge in making proper requests from Vietnamese S-4 supply, which advisers were trained to teach. Often, however, the Vietnamese were reluctant to deliver ammunition, food, etc., unless an adviser was present. Artillery was a far bigger problem. Wagner asked Sergeant Krok, "Do you know how to call artillery?"

"No, we no call artillery," he answered. "Last time, they put one land outside, there," he said, pointing outside the perimeter. "Put one land inside. Here," he said, pointing again a few meters away. "Kill one, wound others. Vietnamese no care. We no call again." Wagner heard the story several times before. The Montagnards, were, at times, fighting both the North and the South Vietnamese.

Before the team left, they watched a crew of five Montagnard PFs chopping at one lone tree, blocking their field of fire to the south of their perimeter. The tree was a foot thick, a four-inch notch hacked out of the side with a machete. Blas stopped the Jeep, staring at the work. "You know, sir, we used to blow landing zones with Det Cord and C-4. Do you suppose we could help them out?" Blas and Wagner had become somewhat demolitions experts. What guy doesn't like blowing the shit out of something? Fireworks on steroids. And all the C-4, det cord, and blasting caps you want for free.

"Sounds like a plan to me. What do we have left?" Looking into their trailer, they had only one Claymore mine, two blasting caps, twenty five feet of det cord and some grenades. Approaching the RFs, they asked if they could help.

The Montagnards, as always, were smiling and chattering. Wagner wrapped eight trips of det cord around the notched bole of the tree, taped on a blasting cap, and ran a claquer wire back to the Jeep. A deafening *SNAPP!* blew bark and ants in all directions, but the tree stood proudly. A one-and-a-half inch deep gap encircled the tree, and hundreds of large black ants lay dead at the base. The RFs, all sitting on a nearby bunker, were laughing and chatting. "Let's try again sir," said Blas. "No NVA tree is gonna laugh at us."

Blas wrapped the remainder of the det cord around the tree, attached the last blasting cap and again, a resounding *SNAPP!* The tree stood its ground, the gap deepened another inch. The RFs sat chatting and laughing.

"What have we got left?" Wagner asked.

"Just this Claymore, sir. No more det cord, no more caps.

"We've got grenades. Let's use the Claymore." Wagner stripped the Claymore from its gray-green plastic skin, removing its inch thick cake of C-4 and packed it into the chopped notch. He unscrewed the fuse and cap from an M-33 grenade. After penciling a hole in the C-4, he pulled the grenade pin and inserted the shiny blasting cap into the hole. Letting go, he sprinted to dive behind the Jeep when it blew six seconds later.

The tree still stood proud, laughing at them. The RFs were laughing, too. With a 'sorry, we tried' look, Wagner turned to board the Jeep with the rest of the team. "Sorry assed Americans," Blas said, laughing. "We can't even kill a damn NVA tree."

"Well, they've got less to chop," said Wagner. He started the Jeep and drove a dozen feet when they heard the crash behind them. The tree was KIA. The RFs cheered.

A quick discussion with Major Buhm about the Vietnamese PF platoon leader and he was relieved the next day, demoted to a private in the ARVN.

Sergeant Stewart, with his big benevolent smile, said,

"The man does not fool around, you mess with Thieu-ta Buhm, you get the horn."

Later that afternoon in Plei Do Rom, Wagner's 0-1 Birddog friend called, having heard '*Murky Cinder 57*' calling on the radio. Flying over the compound, Lucien Oliver performed a hammerhead stall, falling overhead like a Maple seed before pulling up a few hundred feet above, just to say "Hi". Oliver's acrobatics brought smiles to the men, in part just knowing they weren't completely stranded and alone out here. Wagner continued his radio call, returning a call from Major Nichols. The Major wanted the team back in Le Quon for a personal report on their previous events, as well as for new directives. The return on the Jeep trail was uneventful, only passing a long column of bare breasted and barefooted Montagnard women who barely looked up as they passed along the trail. The women travelled single file in even, two meter intervals, carrying woven back-baskets filled with meter-long branches of firewood, bamboo shoots and jungle-gathered foodstuffs. Many had babies slung under their bare breasts. Most had green cone-shaped leaf cigars between their lips.

After arriving at Le Quon, the men showered and ate before Major Nichols called them into the team house. Bailey's Team 46, now working out of 57's compound, was joining them. "We have a new reconsolidation move," the Major began, fetching a collective moan through both teams. "A number of small hamlets three to five kilometers northeast of Plei Do Rom will be moved to add to the reconsolidation village on the east side of Plei Ko Tu." More hushed moans. "They're mostly small hamlets, only a few houses each, but spread out. About thirty homes total. Team 46 will be on the gathering and sending end, Team 57 on the receiving end, at Plei Ko Tu. We'll have Chinooks out of Holloway to move them," he said, looking side to side as if to quell any objections. "Lieutenant Bailey, 46's call sign has been changed. It will now be Stolen Slipper. Lieutenant Wagner, your team will be Gray Phantom. Major Buhm will be coordinating the move, you'll have RF

Company 879 working with you. They're about 70% strength, Mike-Strike Force Montagnards. I don't have to tell you, the NVA don't like these reconsolidations, and we've had reports of activity moving west from the mountains, here," the Major said, circling his index finger on the topo map laying on the dining table before them. The area he indicated was around the steep, dense beginnings of mountains rising sharply up from the Ia Ayun River, only six kilometers east of Plei Do Rom.

It was one week before Christmas, 1970. The early dry season only became drier, lacking even a brief rain shower in three weeks. MAT 57 had settled into Plei Ko Tu, living atop a slightly convexed lens of high ground inside a perimeter of Mike Strike Montagnards, 879 Company. Bailey's team helicoptered in to their location for the sending end of the operation, setting up a perimeter between two of the Hamlets to be moved. Half the company, about 60 men, were with Bailey's team, the other half with Wagner's Team 57. The men felt more secure here than normal, happy to be living and operating with a crack unit of Mike Strike Montagnards. Unfortunately, the mostly Vietnamese PF platoon that had been here had left a deplorable perimeter. Major Buhm's leaders were already beginning to dress up the perimeter defenses, negating advising needs from MAT 57. Sergeants Stewart and Flanagan had employed four villagers to dig a sizable bunker, complete with sandbags and a bamboo/sandbagged roof, enough to protect them from 82 mm mortars. 6" firing windows on all four sides completed the bunker, three and a half feet deep with two feet of walls above ground. Another foot and a half of roof thickness rose above the walls. A few meters away, they erected a 292 antenna from a military kit package containing twelve sections, 33" each, to total 33' in height. It increased the range of their PRC 25 radios to any artillery or support base in the Province. Five meters from the bunker they erected an Army mess tent, roughly sixteen feet square, to house a variety of supplies, tables, and chairs. The site provided visibility and open terrain three hundred meters out on three sides, with little vegetation. The fourth side bordered the village eighty meters away. The openness was a safety plus, but it exacerbated the annoyance of blowing dust, now that the middle of dry season was approaching.

A Big Chinook CH-47 helicopter arrived early the next morning, landing just outside the perimeter. It was one of two that were assigned to the move. At a combined cost of $59.6 million dollars and $1800 per hour to operate, they added to ginormous resources at their disposal that most men would never match in a lifetime. It looked like a giant insect, 52' long and 16' wide, or 99' long including the swing of the twin 3-bladed rotors. This initial landing resulted in a temporary 'brown-out' of red Pleiku dust. One hundred-plus mph winds turned up a dustbowl that was, for a minute, impenetrable, all but the windward front end hidden. After the cloud slowly

drifted away, skirting part of the village in the process, most of the surface dust was gone, providing cleaner ensuing landings. After the blades slowed to steady *Ssshhwopp – Ssshhwopp - Ssshhwopps* overhead, the tailgate lowered, exposing the giant insect's rectum, straining to evacuate its bowels. Wagner and the team joined the RFs in conducting an exodus of villagers, pigs, ducks, chickens, vases, baskets, bowls, crossbows, basically everything these displaced Montagnards owned, which wasn't much. A CH-47 had a max gross weight of 33,000 lbs., leaving 10,000 lbs. carrying capacity, more with a slung load.

Crouching in a trot to the tail, a hot blast of turbine exhausts met the men, intensifying the misery of a sweltering day. Animal feces left inside the craft, deposited by terrified farm creatures intermingled with jet fuel fumes and rank Montagnard cigars. The Montagnards, old and young alike, were experiencing yet one more violation in their lives, which had been many. It showed in their faces as they filed out of the monster tailgate. Fear, wonderment, anger. The powerful Chinook immediately lifted off, not wishing to remain a target. A pile of corrugated metal roof panels, destined for reconsolidated hootches yet to be built, lay stacked sixty meters away, two sandbags laying on top ensured they wouldn't blow away. Hurricane winds of an approaching Chinook weren't accounted for, sending several panels into cartwheeling and bouncing paths toward the village, along with a myriad of baskets that escaped with the initial exit. Before it was over, several people had been badly cut, two seriously. Flanagan ran toward them, medical case in hand, swearing and screaming at the departing Chinook pilot, who wasn't aware and not his fault in any case. The pilot had been complaining of being on the ground too long, an inviting target, but after seeing the problems the American advisers faced, they learned to live with it.

Trip after trip followed, each filled with cavalcades of Montagnard pawns. Coordination problems mounted as some Vietnamese R.D. Cadre, assigned to help load and unload, sat and observed the Americans doing most of the work. There weren't enough rice bags. Tons of rice were dumped on the ground from the bags they had, so they could be reused for the next trip. The villagers would have to somehow sort it out later how much each had. Each trip was met by a crew of twenty or so villagers, mostly kids, as they were the only ones not scared of the jet exhaust and whirling blades. Bailey called Wagner before the last flight, warning "We're sending a water buffalo. He's in a sling." Sure enough, as the distant Chinook rose across the valley, a dark speck could be seen hanging from its belly. Approaching the landing zone, a huge water buffalo hung underneath, laying on its back, hooves up, horns protruding through the net. Thoughts reemerged of Americans being charged and trampled by these mountains of muscle and horns. The team decided wisely to let the Montagnards, all accustomed to handling *nhieu Con Trau,* unwrap this bovine monster. Vietnam's national animal stands seven feet high and weighs over a ton. Capable of 30 mph, and just having been slung upside down a thousand feet in the air, the team expected it to be extremely frightened and dangerous. Carefully peeling away cargo net from horns and legs, the RFs showed caution, but not

exceedingly so. Mr. *Con trau* slowly staggered to his feet and was led slowly away. No problem.

At 1330 hours, Major Nichols drove in, accompanied by his Montagnard bodyguard Blote, per the norm. The Major had balls, he usually travelled alone with Blote, even after being shot at a few times. On one occasion, an AK-47 round passed through the rear panel. On another, a round passed through the steel side of the Jeep and struck Blote in the knee. Luckily, the round was spent from distance and steel, and Blote was uninjured, save for a very sore knee. Major Nichols had needed a count of all the material being carried to the new village. "Sir," Wagner said, trying to keep composed, "There's people running in and out of the Chinook as soon as it sets down. The rice is coming out in two different sized bags, carried by people running everywhere. I got a good count on the first load and that's it. The slings aren't emptied in time for the next load coming in, and I've got to get the people working on them. The damn district chief says a few words to get them going, but the people don't understand Vietnamese, so he gives up. The hook pilots are pissed from sitting on the ground too long. The friggin' Vietnamese R.D. Cadre are useless as teats on a bull, and I even got involved with a damn water buffalo they slung in." This wasn't enough to satisfy the Major, so he told Wagner to try to estimate the rice load as close as possible.

By 1500 hours, the last flight landed, deposited, and left. New villagers were being led to their new homes, each with a bright shiny metal roof. Wagner threw out an estimate to the Major of thirty tons of rice with a giant SWAG, a Scientific Wild-Assed Guess. That seemed to work.

The reconsolidation move went on for five more days. Nearing completion, it was Christmas Eve, and so far no enemy actions had occurred, other than a few threatening notes. As happened many months before, notes were passed by villagers from the V.C. that the team members would be killed at the water point. A bamboo pipe stuck into the side of a stream bed one hundred and fifty meters to the west, still served as a bathing facility. Water flowed freely as a natural spring, in spite of the dryness. As they did early in the year, the men took turns at guard atop the stream bank while another quickly washed off sweat and red dirt. Two Montagnard girls bathed on each side of them, proficient at covering their privates while they bathed. Several other Montagnards, amused at having the Americans join them, laughed and joked at the crowded wash site. Unlike before, no shots had been fired, due in large part to the presence of the Mike Strike Force of RFs.

After a supper of dehydrated LRRP rations mixed with real food brought from Le Quon and local items purchased from villagers, the team readied for the night. Every year, the war had a Christmas Eve truce. Every year, the enemy broke the truce. Nobody expected differently tonight. It began at dusk, when Wagner and Tung entered the bunker, where cots were set up to enhance their comforts in the tight quarters. Carrying a flashlight and his M-16, Wagner immediately saw movement across from the steps leading down into the bunker. Nothing new, he knew it was a rat. As he shined the light on the rat, it momentarily froze. A deafening staccato, a rate of 720 rounds per minute, exploded directly behind his ear. In one quick 'dip-and-turn' reflex, Wagner looked up to see Tung, his M-16's barrel emitting light wisps of white smoke, staring at the wall. For a fraction of a second, Wagner thought of the possibility this NVA...

"Jesus Christ, Tung, what in hell are you doing?" Wagner yelled. The entire perimeter heard the gunfire, weapons pointed their way.

"Con chuot, Trung-uy!" (*Rat*)

"What the hell? You scared the living shit out of me!"

Trung looked scared to death. He hated rats, they were his personal phobia. But now he was scared of Wagner. He didn't really know Wagner yet, and still wasn't convinced the Americans weren't going to kill him.

"Okay, take it easy now. You wanna kill that commie rat? I'll hold the light, you shoot. But not auto. One shot, okay?"

"Okay. Sorry. Sorry." They searched, but the rat was gone.

Flanagan, Blas, and Stewart had run to the bunker by then. "Even the fucking rats don't observe the truce," Flanagan quipped.

The team limited themselves to one beer each for a Christmas cheer. Even Flanagan knew it wasn't a time for drinking. Sergeant Stewart looked across the small bunker to Blas, who hadn't had the opportunity to wash the caked red dirt off his face, and said, "Manuel, this Army is alright, huh? It just don' get any better than this, do it?"

"Right," Blas answered. "Just think. A lot of people are paying big bucks for doing what we're doin' right now. We can do it for free. We've got some of the best hunting in the world, free guns and ammunition included. Year-'round open season, even. We don't even need to buy a license."

"Right," continued Stewart. "It's alright. They give us a fine ride for free, your sport version of the M-151 convertible. Camping gear, free LRRP rations, even free gas!"

"Don't forget free housing," Wagner added. "But you're wrong about free food. We're supposed to buy our C's and LRRPs." Wagner wasn't wrong, they actually had been given a directive that MAT advisers were supposed to buy C-Rations and LRRPs.

"Right, sir, replied Stewart. And plenty of exercise. I like the hiking best, if I had to choose... Yep. This Army is some good shee-it."

The conversation changed to the horrors of De Poui massacre, which nobody really wanted to talk about, but Stewart said, "You know, all we hear about is My Lai and Lieutenant Calley, Captain Medina, American atrocities. I bet you, mister, we never ever again hear about what we just saw at De Poui. Damn the press."

Flanagan more than added his two cents. He hated the Jane Fondas, Tom Haydens, the press, the freaks and hippies, and a growing drug culture. His feelings weren't unlike those of the rest of the team. Wagner shared a revulsion for protesters and freaks, but above all, draft dodgers.

Brandon Stewart continued, "We are alive today from the blood of those before us."

"And the thousands of tons of Nixon's B-52 bombs, thank you, Dick," Wagner said. "I do appreciate that."

Flanagan was expounding on the great merits of his hero, John Wayne, while Sergeant Stewart's new PX Sony radio was playing Christmas carols. Wagner was briefly thinking of his coed again. The string of carols coming from the Armed Forces Radio Network was broken with the next song by Joan Baez singing *The Green, Green Grass of Home.* Suddenly, unexpectedly, he was struck with a wave of home sickness and thoughts of her by the lake. He never experienced anything like it before. Scant light offered by a small battery lantern hanging from the bunker roof wasn't enough to expose watery eyes. Embarrassed at his weakness, he squelched it quickly.

After a round of *"Merry Christmas"* beer toasts, the team retired to their cots. One man would stay awake on two hour shifts, expecting a short night. They wouldn't be disappointed. Wagner wanted Flanagan to take first watch, in light of his history of falling asleep on guard. For a few minutes, Wagner laid in his cot, listening to a rat scurrying along the ledge that circumvented the bunker walls. Lonely thoughts returned to his coed and the sunny Maine lake. He figured it was twelve hours later there, about 9:30 in the morning. The other side of the Earth. "Must be just about done opening presents, little ones running around. Wonder where she's living now..." Then his thoughts drifted to Annelle. Those eyes, lips. Is she alone? Working? Maybe getting sleep, ready for a broken Christmas truce, no sleep for the next eighteen hours... Does she still want to see him?

A wind chill dropped the dry bulb temperature of forty degrees to freezing. Wind was screaming across their crest of land, whistling through bunker firing ports and giving no respite from blowing red dirt. An air mattress helped to insulate the canvas cot below him. He slept with fatigues and boots on for readiness and an insulated poncho liner and two O.D. wool blankets, but Wagner was shivering with cold. Still, it was better than laying unmoving in an ambush position with only a poncho liner for warmth. He pitied the many Montagnards who had been uprooted and moved that day. Many had no shelter and only thin Montagnard blankets woven on wooden looms. They slept huddled together for warmth. Every night, a steady seven-note chant of funeral gongs permeated the air, as many as four funerals in a single night. Brass gongs, from mere inches in diameter to three feet, played dusk to dawn. The latest was for a baby that died the first day of the move. The infant would be buried the next day, but until then the evil spirits had to be warded off at night by the gongs. Wagner had finally dozed off, but only briefly. He awoke to another sound--scores of people chopping wood for fires, and for the warmth of physical effort in the middle of the night.

0130 hours, Blas was awake for his shift when the first incoming mortars hit. The first two fell well outside the perimeter, but they are adjusting in. ***CRRUMMP! CRRUMMP! CRUMMP!*** Only seconds apart. Wagner instantly grabs the radio handset beside his bed, calling Blackhawk before he finishes swinging legs to the dirt floor. Preplanned fires were chosen with an experienced confidence gained by many 'lucky' selections before. He calls for three rounds spread on each target. Two dozen enemy mortars had exploded by the time Blackhawk gives him the first *"Shot out"*. The enormous ***CCRRUUNNCH!*** of big One Seven Fives send a wave of adrenalin through his veins. God, he loves this job! The power, the ability to bring a whole world of shit down on some asshole who's trying to ruin your day, just by a simple radio call, who wouldn't love it? The mortars instantly stop with the first round, but the RFs are firing all around the perimeter, slowing now, then sporadic, then stopping. A last call to Blackhawk and Wagner thanks his saviors, telling them he'd give them a report on body parts in the morning, always greatly appreciated by the gunners.

Wagner walked to Buhm's command bunker to see if the Major wanted any more artillery. Major Buhm did not, and told Wagner only one RF had been wounded, but *"T-T, no problem. Only bandage."*

By 0245 hours, Tung was on guard atop the bunker. The others regained sleep in their bunker, except for Wagner. He could hear their raspy breaths and Flanagan's perpetual snore. A rat ran over his poncho liner, calling for another flashlight chase around the upper ledge until it escaped through a firing port. He envied the others, somehow able to sleep. Adrenalin and images of massacred villagers at De Poui precluded it until he finally drifted into a state of half-awake, half-asleep, when day dreams morph into dreams that seem real…but make no sense upon wakening….. ***CRRUMMP! CRRUMMP! CRRUMMP! CRRUUNNCH!*** Had them all swinging out of cots. The last explosion was much louder than the first bursting mortars, a close hit from an RPG, rocket propelled grenade. Firing erupts all over, red tracers radiating out from the perimeter, blue-green tracers coming in from the north and east. Claymores are exploding in the perimeter, one on the western perimeter. Wagner is screaming over the noise, "Sandy Panther, Sandy Panther, this is Gray Phantom Five Seven, *Fire mission*, over!"

"Roger, Gray Phantom Five Seven, Sandy Panther Two Five, go."

Wagner calls for his preplanned defensive fire targets for the north and east sides of the perimeter, adding "Danger Close" due to a short range to the target, inaccuracy at their distance, and the village next to them. Radio traffic erupts from Gordon Bailey's position kilometers away as well. They are both under attack from respective ends of the moving operation. Blackhawk is the only fire support base that can reach either of them, requiring their guns to be shared. Mortars sporadically hit, raining in at times. A few more B-40 RPG rockets slam in, one passing through the compound and hitting an ill-fated Montagnard home behind them to the south. A .51 caliber machinegun sends tracers looking as big as footballs tearing over their heads, disappearing into grass-roofed hootches behind the perimeter. Untold numbers of other aimless bullets find their way into the village as well. An RPG rocket explodes close, peppering the bunker with shrapnel from its impact only ten meters away. The team sergeants, along with Tung and Kloh are peaking from the firing ports every few seconds, watching for enemy sappers. They can't shoot, as RFs are in firing positions on the perimeter around them. Wagner, carrying his 24 lb. radio to the bunker roof to observe and adjust fire, is trying to communicate with Blackhawk, but radio traffic interferes. It's coming from Bailey, a helicopter pilot somewhere, Major Nichols, and others more distant, adding to the confusion and tying up the net. Suddenly Wagner hears "Gray Phantom Five Seven, Gray Phantom Five Seven, this is Solid Demon Seven Niner, Solid Demon Seven Niner, over".

Wagner is prone on the bunker roof now, mating with the contour of sandbags as close as he possibly can. Even his shirt buttons are too thick. "Solid Demon, this is Gray Phantom Five Seven, over."

"Roger, Gray Phantom Five Seven, I am en route to your Lima to support you, sir, we are here with a Stinger, ETA three-two mikes, over."

Wagner yells down to the team, "Holy shit, we've got a Stinger coming! Thirty two minutes." Stingers were much larger sequels to 'Puff The Magic Dragon' AC-47s, but in the form of an AC-119 'Flying Boxcar' cargo plane. A large, elongated box fuselage with twin tail booms, it carried a crew of six. 86 feet in length, it had a wingspan of 109 feet. Empty, it weighed twenty tons, with a maximum cargo of eleven more tons, nearly all in guns and ammunition. Two 3,500 HP radial engines powered it. It was one big terrible swift sword, carrying four 7.62 mm Gatling miniguns at 1,500 rounds per minute each, and two Vulcan 20 mm 6-barreled Gatling cannons, firing 6,000 three-quarter inch diameter incendiary rounds per minute each, all totaling 300 rounds every second, all fired out the side of the aircraft. Evidently, the highers had contacted somebody important, and before long Wagner and Bailey had artillery, gunships, a searchlight "Firefly" Huey, and now a Stinger supporting them. Very little was happening across the country, affording the luxury of their attention. The Stinger is piloted by an Air Force major, who would call Wagner and Bailey "Sir" the entire time of the mission, the only time either lieutenant heard it from a senior officer.

"Roger that, Solid Demon, be advised we have artillery coming in at this time, and enemy activity to the north and east of our location, over."

"Yes sir, understand you have arty coming in, we will coordinate with them, I would appreciate it if you could mark your perimeter for us, I will report in periodically with our ETA to your position, over," the pilot said with a calm, professional voice.

Intelligence had said that Wagner's end of the operation would be hit, or hit the hardest of the two ends of the operation. Nearly every intel received during the year was wrong, often initiated by the enemy as a decoy to hit somewhere else. By the time it made the rounds from Saigon and who knows where, it was always wrong. This time they got it right. Wagner's team was getting hit hard by a sizable force. Another call comes in, choppy sentences broken by the static from helicopter blades. "Gray Phantom Five Seven, Gray Phantom Five Seven, this is Shaggy Candle One Seven, Shaggy Candle One Seven, over."

"Shaggy Candle One Seven, this is Gray Phantom Five Seven, go."

"Uh-h, roger Five Seven, I'm en route to your location with a Firefly searchlight Huey, you sound like you need help?" over.

"Shaggy Candle One Seven, Gray Phantom Five Seven. Help would be good. We're taking heavy fire from the east and north of our position. Do you have guns?"

"Uhh, not at this time, Gray Phantom. Just M-60s and a big flashlight," comes the choppy static voice, broken by rotary wings of his Huey.

"Be advised we have arty coming in. You'll have to coordinate, I'm a little busy." The noise was intense, the pilot could hear it over Wagner's voice. Full automatic M-60s, scores of M-16s, and incoming cracks of AK-47 rounds overhead and

around the compound are deafening, mixed with mortars leaving their tubes from Buhm's RFs and occasional explosions from incoming RPGs adding to the din.

"Gray Phantom Five Seven, this is Solid Demon Seven Niner, be advised I am now Two Four mikes from your location, over," from the Stinger pilot.

"Roger, Solid Demon, I have perimeter corner Hirsh flares ready to pop, holding off until you're a couple of mikes away, over," Wagner said, scanning for sappers who might be breaching the perimeter. RFs are running across the compound, resupplying perimeter positions with ammunition and bolstering the attacking sides. Running men at night could be infiltrators, and now Sergeant Blas posts himself just outside the entrance, facing south, in case a breach is made on the village side. RF positions are kept there, but not firing. That's a good sign. Blas is a smart Infantryman, as is Stewart, always dependable on anticipating the worst, hoping for the best.

Another voice comes over the radio, it's from someone at Holloway yelling at the Firefly pilot to "RTB"--- return to base. It is the pilot's immediate commander, probably worried about his OER 'Officer's Efficiency Report'.

"What?" the pilot says. "What in hell for, these guys need us!" He now has two gunships from Holloway coming in with him, armed with miniguns.

"You are outside your A.O., you'll have to return to base."

"Outside my A.O.? You gotta be shitting me!"

"I said RTB now."

"I'm having trouble reading you," comes the reply.

"I say again, RTB Asap!"

"You're coming in extremely weak and broken. Please say again, over."

"I said return to base, over!" The commander is shouting now.

"You're coming in extremely weak and broken, I can't hear you at all," the pilot answers.

"Don't give me that crap, I said *return to base, now!*" shouts his commander.

"Go to hell," the pilot replies. Wagner calls a cease-fire to Blackhawk, allowing the Hueys to come in. They arrive only a minute after. The end of concussive explosions from 175 mm shells is welcome in terms of hearing and nerves, in light of their casualty radii and distance inaccuracy. Now the Huey's searchlights light up the north side of the perimeter, exposing hapless NVA just behind the stream bank running parallel to the perimeter, a hundred meters out. The gunships open up, churning minigun 7.62 mm rounds into dirt, trees, and bodies. Two passes are made, then they work the east side. Wagner can't see what is happening past the edge of the eastern perimeter, but within a minute most of the firing stops, from both sides. Wagner relaxes a little, and stands to observe atop the bunker. The gunships and Firefly leave for Bailey's position across the valley... With a grin, Wagner wonders how the war between the Firefly pilot and his commander will go when they return to Holloway.

Now Bailey is getting hit hard. They lack the fortified positions at their location that Plei Ko Tu enjoyed, as they are on the new, temporary end of the operation. Gordon doesn't have Hirsh flares, or any other means ready to mark their perimeter as Wagner had done, and for good reason considering the chaos and available time. The reconsolidation had taken a priority over defenses, not the fault of Bailey or his team.

"Yes, sir, I am now zero eight mikes from your location, Gray Phantom Five Seven. Do you have your perimeter marked yet," the Air Force major asked.

"Negative, Solid Demon," Wagner tells him. "We're ready to light up, but our situation has improved with gunnies. Stolen Slipper is taking heavy fire, suggest you help him first, he's east of my location a few klicks,"

Flanagan glares at him, shocked that he would reject the help. "What in hell are you doin', Lieutenant?"

"Billy, shut the fuck up," yells Sergeant Blas from his position outside. Wagner felt like saying the same, but now wasn't the time. He was happy to have Blas intercede. "Leave the L-T alone, he's got enough to worry about without your sorry ass." It was the first time Wagner heard his men chastise the senior NCO, at least in front of him. Flanagan turns back to his port, peering just over the edge. Sergeant Stewart leaves the bunker to better observe the north side defenses. Parachute flares from Buhm's mortars keep the perimeter reasonably visible.

The Hueys finish expending the last of their ammunition for Bailey and return to Holloway. A myriad of tracers eerily crisscross the area at his end, easily visible across the valley from Plei Ko Tu. "Stolen Slipper Four Six, this is Solid Demon Seven Niner, I am Zero Two Mikes from your location, sir, do you have your perimeter marked?" the pilot asked Bailey, across the valley.

"This is Stolen Slipper Four Six, negative on the perimeter marking, Solid Demon," comes Gordon's reply. Intense background noise is heard over his radio. "We're trying, it's hard to coordinate with my RFs. Wait one..." Bailey's team doesn't have the advantage of Major Buhm to help coordinate his men in Bahnaar language. Wagner can only imagine how they could get flares or lights on their corners under heavy attack.

Now the Stinger arrives over Team 46's position,

circling somewhere in the dark sky high above. Wagner and the team are watching and waiting, as small arms tracers race in all directions around Bailey's perimeter. For over eight long minutes the big plane circles. Finally, Bailey calls the pilot to ask if he could verify his corners. He has an RF on each corner, waving flashlights up at a dark sky. "Affirmative," comes the answer. From their position at Plei Ko Tu, Wagner and the team watch and wait for the AC-119 to drop low, to strafe. Surprisingly, it remains at altitude when eerie, silent rays of red pour down from a black sky, looking every bit like a ray gun from an alien space ship. Three hundred rounds every second rake the turf surrounding 46's perimeter, without a single square foot of ground unviolated. Tracer burn-out, at roughly 600 meters, suck the rays into a sponge of blackness a third of the way down. Wagner guesses he is firing from 1800 meters up, surprised they didn't strafe. That wasn't how they worked. Incendiary 20 mm rounds create another red wave front, streaking a swath across the ground, as if it is a reflection of the rays 1200 meters above. The Earth itself seems to explode, ripping a wave of fire across the landscape. Eighteen seconds later, a buzz of high speed chain saws on steroids reaches Plei Ko Tu, a roaring, mythical fire breathing dragon scaring the hell out of the villagers even more, as if they needed it.

Across the valley, all ground weapons ceased firing. Now the Stinger banks to head to Wagner, where incoming rounds are resuming around Plei Ko Tu. He isn't about to turn the Stinger away this time. The Hirsh flares are already burning on their four corners, and Wagner directs the pilot to avoid the entire south side of their rectangular perimeter where the villagers are. Sergeant Stewart dodges three quick mortar bursts, jogging to the north side to throw two incendiary grenades out to add assurance for the Stinger. An error would be a horrific disaster of 'friendly fire', never friendly at all. Wagner tells Kloh to pass the word for everyone in the perimeter to get under any cover available. The Stinger circles twice before again unleashing its incredible firepower, spraying a bright red wave over the entire north and east sides of the perimeter, extending past five hundred meters on each end of both sides. Their task completed, Wagner bestows great thanks and compliments, as the Stinger banks somewhere in the black sky overhead to fly back to Qui Nhon on the coast where they came from, seventy miles away. The night would be one of the most memorable and successful of both team's year. Hell, of their lives.

Early morning Sun had yet to raise the night's 40 degree temperature, but the wind had subsided to a welcome stillness. Two dead NVA sappers were visible in the wire, both shot by the same Montagnard RF soldier. One was shot in the eye, the back of his head blown off. The other through his shoulder as these sapper soldiers crawled under concertina wire. The bullet travelled through his body, exiting just above his knee and severing his lower leg.

At the faintest first light on Christmas morning, a dust-off medical helicopter arrived to take out six wounded RF Montagnard soldiers as well as several villagers. Another eight

RFs were taken out at Team 46's location. All told, two RFs were killed, fourteen more seriously wounded, ten with shrapnel and two from AK-47 rounds.

Checking for damage, the team first looked inside the compound where mortars and RPGs had hit, then into the neighboring border of the village. The villagers were excited, pointing to mortar fins sticking out of the ground. They looked planted there, as if they would grow and produce fruits someday. A few hootches had been hit by shrapnel, including the new shiny metal roofs. Another disadvantage of metal versus grass roofs....they weren't repairable. Several Montagnards were asking them for help with injured in the village. They had been tending to them as best they could, but some were serious. In one hootch, several villagers were crying and wailing. Stewart and Wagner entered to see a woman's torso, hit dead center by a .51 NVA machine gun bullet. The force of the powerful round had dismembered her, separating her arms and legs from her body.

The enemy had a history of dud ammo, unlike American rounds. Assuming the mortar fins were unexploded duds, he looped a small rope lasso around the nearest fin. Kloh told the villagers to get far away and behind cover, while Wagner built a small barrier of sandbags thirty meters away. Blocked by the sandbags, he slowly pulled the rope until it pulled easily. Looking over the bags, he saw the rope only held a harmless tail section with an array of fins. He never saw fins sticking out before. These mortars, fired from farther away, arced higher to reach the distance. That resulted in a higher velocity in its downward flight. A piezo-electric quartz cap in the nose provides an electric charge to ignite the high explosive. It happens so quickly upon impact that the tail section's inertia carried them through the outward blast, drilling the tails into the ground. He repeated this procedure again and again until one round emerged intact. This really was a dud round. It was near one of the new hootches. Simply blowing it in place would destroy the house. Instead, he dug a shallow hole thirty meters away. Having been fired, the mortar could be unstable, sensitive to touch. Very carefully he picked it up, carried it to the hole, placing it softly on its side. With a sandbag ready to tilt down over the round, he pulled the pin on a grenade, carefully laying it alongside. Letting the lever go, he softly laid the sand bag down and sprinted for a small ditch where Blas was watching. Six seconds after letting go of the lever, a muted explosion had Sergeant Blas just shaking his head. "You crazy bastard, sir."

Buhm's tired men were already preparing to sweep the area. Wagner's team joined them, leaving Flanagan behind to help the wounded. Two were serious. Flanagan guided a fast-responding Medevac Huey in to extract them. Twelve villagers were killed, most from the errant RPG.

The area sweep found mutilated and shredded bodies scattered along the north and east sides of their perimeter. In addition, they found innumerable blood and drag marks, and what was left of a mortar location. A crater from one of the 175 mm rounds was only ten meters away, obliterating whatever was there. "Merry Christmas, Chuck," Sergeant Stewart said, grinning. An un-inflated estimate of sixty NVA were killed at Wagner's location, another eighty at Bailey's. Anyone left to find bodies to carry away had to be from a reserve element a safe distance away, as nothing could survive the kill zones. The area that the Stinger hit looked like freshly tilled farmland in Iowa, save for the red color. Nowhere was soil found that had not been cultivated by the onslaught of bullets, turning it into a quilt of small fluffy mounds. Only splinters and leaves lay where there were once bushes and trees. Absolutely nothing survived in the path.

An 'impact award' medal was presented to the soldier who shot the sappers that afternoon, awarded by Major Buhm.

In hopes of adding to the previous night's decisive victory, Major Buhm had his men firing an old 57 mm recoilless rifle across the valley around Team 46's position. He was hoping to kill NVA trying to recover bodies. The M18 57 mm recoilless rifle fired a 2 ¼" round. It was a shoulder fired anti-tank recoilless rifle that was used by the U.S. Army in World War II and the Korean War. A predecessor to a later 75 mm and a Vietnam era 90 mm, recoilless rifles are breech-loaded, single-shot, man-portable crew-served weapons, entirely without recoil. The weapon could be both shoulder fired or fired from a prone position, as well as from a tripod, which the RFs were using today. Wagner had seen a 57 mm in use at Jackson Hole ski area in Wyoming, for avalanche control the previous winter. Rounds were hard to find for the now antiquated weapon, and Sergeant Stewart was working the radio net, trying to find more. A recoilless is designed so the back blast discharge exactly counters the recoil of the round leaving the barrel, hence the name. At no time did the men experience a sharper, more ear-damaging *CRACK!!* then the explosion from the back blast of the relatively small weapon. Hands covering ears weren't adequate in avoiding real pain from each round sent. The RFs firing the weapon had no hearing protection, never realizing the damage they were doing to themselves years later. Given their situation, it seemed irrelevant.

A few hours later, Flanagan, Stewart, Tung, and Wagner stood outside their bunker, as a speck above the horizon grew slowly to a wide silhouette of a B-52, returning from Cambodia to the west. It was the first any of the men had ever seen other than parked on an airstrip. Normally, a 'BUFF' as they were named by G.I.s—*"Big Ugly Fat Fucker"*, might fly at 50,000 feet, unseen and unheard. This one was obviously alone and crippled, flying at only 800 feet, its tan and two-tone green camouflage clearly visible. Wagner looked at Tung, who was staring in awe. "What's the matter, Tung, you no like?"

"Oooh, no like, Trung-uy. Beaucoup noise, beaucoup death," he said in his quiet voice, shaking his head between cupped hands over his ears. Tung *chieu hoi'd* after his entire battalion was decimated in a B-52 raid in Cambodia.

New Year's Eve came and went, and another week went by, giving Buhm time to improve their perimeter defenses. Only a few errant mortar rounds interrupted sleep during the week. A new strong barbed wire fence surrounded the large village in a day, much larger than the existing borders in anticipation of many more villagers coming. Another fence began further out, the space in between strung with zig-zag, ankle high "tanglefoot" barbed wire. Meanwhile, inside the perimeter, bunkers were being built every twenty meters all the way around. Another bunker was being dug for the command post guards. An extensive mortar pit which any American mortar crew would be proud to own was finished in a day. These RFs were amazing. Artillery registration fires were called in around the perimeter in order to speed reaction time and accuracy. Thick vegetation near the water point was cut and burned away.

With more reconsolidation work being assigned to the teams, Wagner had written an aunt in Iowa weeks earlier, who was an ardent member of 'The Sweet Adelaides' singing group, an international organization of women singers committed to a

barbershop quartet style of singing. They enjoyed doing charitable work, and Wagner asked if they would be interested in donating clothing to cold villagers in these Highlands. They responded in spades. Several large boxes arrived with a Chinook. Sergeant Stewart suggested they let the village chief distribute the clothes, which ranged from Tee shirts to heavy women's winter coats. "That might prevent resentment from some who don't get a fair shake, Sir," said Stewart.

"Good idea. Thanks, Sarge. Kloh, can you take care of that?" he said to their interpreter.

The chief distributed all the clothes, to the villagers' delight. One elderly man proudly walked about in a lovely gold wool woman's coat sporting a brown fur collar. Kloh laughed hysterically, knowing it was a woman's. Young Montagnard boys were thrilled with Batman Tee shirts and Chicago Cubs jackets.

Thieu-uy J'Rel was an up-and-coming protégé of his commander Buhm. The team had a mutual respect with Buhm and his men, but J'Rel, one of his company commanders was particularly impressive. He reminded Wagner very much of Krue, the commander of 815 RF Mike Strike Force Company. His demeanor, intelligence, and leadership were remarkably like Krue. He had the same primitive, rugged facial features and a similar intense glare, even when smiling. The date was January 15, 1971. Buhm's men had been reassigned two days before, leaving only an understrength platoon of his RFs to defend Plei Ko Tu, along with MAT 57. The team remained, coordinating supply drops and performing MEDCAP services to the village, which was growing more pathetic every day. The numbers had grown from 2,000 villagers in earlier reconsolidations to over 4,000. In the past, food for this primitive hunter-gatherer society was provided by snares, crossbows, and hand-gathering edibles from the jungle. Farming meager rice paddies and small corn fields augmented their diets, difficult in these mountainous areas, and now they were subsisting on inadequate Chinook loads of rice and other U.S. foodstuffs that were foreign to them. That would come to a halt when U.S. involvement stopped. Plei Ko Tu's population density, as in many reconsolidations, was more like the Bronx. For hundreds of years, these tribal people had never lived in this manner. Disease, always prevalent, was now rampant, evidenced by the plethora of funeral gongs every night. The filth grew worse, animal feces lay everywhere, only the flies were happier. Septic systems amounted to a shallow hole dug beside each hootch, bringing more happy flies. A few more bamboo water pipes were added along the creek bank, but the water was barely flowing out of each, due not only to the dry season but to sharing the dwindling supply by each additional pipe. The water was in danger of being contaminated by the inability of the soil to filter and purify such a dense population. Every reconsolidation the team had been involved with had been attacked by Victor Charles, adding to the suffering and misery. This old village had been a thing of beauty and resources. Now it was an ugly, disease-ridden place of grief and despair. Many of the water buffalo, a valuable agricultural asset and a symbol of wealth, had been left in the move. Now they provided a valuable asset for the enemy to eat. They were lost forever to the tribesmen, stolen from them. All in the name of pacification.

Another Chinook arrived in the morning, with a delivery of 'government provisions', aka, American aid. Wagner had J'Rel with him at the LZ, a new experience for this rocky, relatively tall Montagnard commander. His stern glare focused on the Chinook until they had to bend and look away from a powerful downwash and flying dirt. Long whirling blades gradually gave up their angular momentum, slowed and stopped. Leaving a co-pilot, or 'peter' pilot on board, the crew disembarked to observe up close their first experience with Montagnard tribesmen, true legends in American rear areas. Wagner introduced J'Rel and himself, asking if they wanted to take a quick tour. Taking scores of pictures, they relished the chance to put feet on the ground back in 'the woods'. The pilot, a Captain Jim Hennesy, was a tall, smiling Arizonian with a sandy blonde flat top haircut. All the men were apprehensive, out here in Indian country for the first time. Wagner explained a little about the reconsolidation move, with its associated deleterious effects. They were interested, but not terribly. The plight of these ravaged people meant little to an outsider ignorant of their history and lives. They were far more fascinated in this trip into a National Geographics film.

"Do you have a security force here?" one of the crewmen asked.

"Of course," replied Wagner.

"Where are they?"

Wagner wasn't sure why he asked. The RFs were in plain sight around the perimeter. Some were working on their firing positions, others eating. "There," he said, pointing with a sideways motion.

"How many?"

"Twenty five.., twenty eight, I think. Not sure."

"The Vietnamese?" he asked.

"No, those are Montagnards. Ruff Puffs."

"That's it? No Americans?"

"Pretty much all we need," Wagner said.

After a quick walk through the village and a few hundred pictures, they returned to the Chinook. The pilot, Hennesy, asked Wagner if he wanted to take a ride into the Officer's Club at Pleiku Air Base. It sounded inviting.

"How long?" Wagner asked.

"Couple of hours. We're coming back here with another drop. We can have lunch while they're loading us."

"Can we take J'Rel?" Turning to his counterpart, Wagner asked, "J'Rel, would you like to fly in for lunch?" he asked, slowly, for J'Rel to understand. J'Rel nodded, with an almost imperceptible "Yes".

"Sure," Hennesy replied.

J'Rel walked to his platoon sergeant, spoke a few words, and returned. J'Rel's stride was long, quick, confident. He carried himself upright, stiffly. The intensity of his glare did not change.

Triple blade rotors started slowly, gaining speed as the turbines whined and strained. Soon, twelve tons of technology rose up a few feet, nosed down and banked left to quickly gain altitude and speed. Without cargo, it was surprising how nimble this medium-lift helicopter was. J'Rel, flying for the first time in his life, strained to see the ground falling away through a round porthole window. His eyes opened wide, but the serious glare remained. The ride to the air base took only minutes once the big Chinook left the ground. Landing at the big air strip, Captain Hennesy walked them toward the officers club, a big hand on J'Rel's far shoulder. J'Rel was swiveling his head, staring at a myriad of aircraft and sights around him.

The club was busy, it was almost noon. Wagner had not been in an officer's club since leaving the states. If it was his choice, he avoided them. But he had no idea they could be as big, fancy, and clean as this, in Pleiku, Vietnam. Tables had table cloths on them. And silverware. There were even a few waiters. The place was immaculate. Wagner and J'Rel, on the other hand, were filthy. Their jungle fatigues were caked with red dirt. J'Rel, tall for a Montagnard at 5'-10", sat with rolled up fatigue shirt sleeves resting on bronze rocky triceps. His thick black hair curled over his forehead above dark serious eyebrows. They wore the only boots in the club that weren't shined, and Wagner had not shaved this morning. And they stunk. His last bath from the bamboo pipe was three days before. He hadn't really considered that he might be out of place, totally unprepared for this disparate structure of comfort and refinement. Only when he realized they were the focus of a dozen repugnant stares of senior Air Force officers did it occur to him. Captain Hennesy, an Army pilot, was obviously enjoying the moment; sort of a show of contempt for Air Force highers. Wagner's initial moments of embarrassment turned to anger, then disgust. "These sorry-assed REMFs *dare* to disrespect *me*?" he thought. Sleeping in clean warm sheets, eating fantastic meals of steak and lobster, safe from NVA, V.C., snakes, intestinal worms, hepatitis, leeches, spiders and you bastards are leering at *me*? He was only one scorning comment away from being taken out in handcuffs. Meanwhile, Hennesy was loving it. Luckily for the Air Force and Wagner, they limited their disdain to stares.

Hennesy was telling his story of one of their Huey pilots

getting killed days before. In the Vietnamization effort, chopper pilots were required to fly with a Vietnamese 'peter pilot', or co-pilot. "The American pilot apparently showed a lack of respect for his counterpart and told him he was 'no fucking good, number ten'. The Vietnamese shot and killed him with a revolver, right in the cockpit."

"Holy. Unbelievable. Sad. What happened to the Vietnamese?"

"Yeah. The peter pilot had to report to his commander, a Colonel Luan, or Tuan, something like that. The Colonel shot him right in front of his desk. Dead."

Their meal finished with a huge bowl of ice cream each, which their Montagnard friend relished. J'Rel learned what an ice cream headache was all about.

The Chinook reloaded, and the flight back to the village was quick. Wagner wondered what J'Rel thought of the comfortable wealth of the world he had just visited. J'Rel still had his serious glare.

Another week at Plei Ko Tu, and MAT 57 was pulled out to return to Le Quon, where MAT 46 would work from as well, temporarily. Bailey's RFs at the sending end of the Plei Ko Tu operation had captured some NVA prisoners, who related the devastation the Plei Ko Tu battle had done to their unit, part of an NVA regiment. After a lengthy conversation of the battle, the talk turned to reconsolidation.

"Did you have as many problems with this mess as we did," Wagner asked his friend.

"Damn, it was terrible," began Gordon. Nobody wanted to work. In the first hamlet the people were crying and they didn't want to move. They just sat there. The same thing happened in the one up north, but most of those people were glad to get the hell out of there. The V.C. were just taxing them to death, and they were constantly used as forced labor. They even gave the RFs some pigs and rice, they were so happy."

"Did the Chinook pilots bitch about taking too long?"

"Yeah, at first. But after they saw the mess we had, they

didn't say anything. Those doggone Chinooks are terrible, though. The Montagnards were scared silly of them, and the wind a Chinook kicks up is something else. I turned back-to once, to cover my face from the dirt and pig shit, and the wind pushed me right through the side of a hootch. My head went right through the bamboo. It blew Sergeant Gazzari down into a bunker. Everybody was laughing at us."

"Yeah," Darryl said, laughing, "It was pretty crazy at my end, too. Major Nichols was giving me hell for not keeping an accurate count of the damn rice. Give me a break, it was a zoo."

Wagner and the team awarded themselves a three day stand-down, the men needed a well-deserved break. After hours of writing action and reconsolidation reports plus a slew of 'Pacification Ratings' for who the hell knew who for, Wagner kept to himself, coming out only for chow. He needed some time to himself, a pause to reflect on events of the past month. Finally, he found time to set up the stereo system bought in Hong Kong on leave months before, one of the 'must-do' purchases in a soldier's tour, along with a good camera and a Seiko watch. A few vinyl albums from the last trip to the PX completed the assemblage. Listening to Credence Clearwater Revival, he began the belated task of answering letters from home, leaving out most of the gory details.

On the third day, it was January 28, Wagner's third-year anniversary of entering the Army, earning a boost in pay. As a Private E-1 trainee in 1968, pay was $96 a month. That increased to $106 as an E-2 after Basic Training, and a little more after attaining E-3, or Private First Class (PFC). For the entire year in Vietnam as a commanding officer, his total earnings were just over $6,000. At 3% inflation, that would equate to $26,800 by 2021, 50 years in the future. Combat soldiers and Marines had arguably the most dangerous job and highest responsibilities in the world, yet were paid a fraction what their civilian friends were making, as well as missing 'the climb on the ladder of success'....but with free room and board in beautiful southeast Asia.

Tet was approaching, three years after the Tet of '68. The one the press said "was a psychological victory". Walter Cronkite had backed the U.S. effort previously. He condemned the young journalists, saying "They seemed to be engaged in a contest among themselves to determine who was the most cynical". Indeed, the college students Wagner knew who majored in journalism were anti-everything, not just the war. Commonly regarded as 'freaks', they made it a mission to look and act contrarily in an overwhelmingly conservative school. After the Tet offensive, with a quick and limited view, Cronkite suddenly reversed his view, playing a large part in molding America's opinion, helping to erase efforts of thousands of service men and women who died. In fact, the U.S. military and its South Vietnamese allies were winning at the tactical level, repulsing the Tet attacks, killing tens of thousands of Viet Cong fighters. The communists failed to topple the government in Saigon or persuade the rice farmers in the countryside to join their cause. The Tet effectively broke the enemy's back. Viet Cong who weren't killed were exposed, and later killed or imprisoned. Later offenses would further disappoint the North when their southern relatives failed to rally to their cause, instead handily crushing the NVA, albeit with mighty U.S. air support and equipment. For whatever reasons the war was begun or whatever moralities were right or wrong, the United States did not lose the war. They left.

Wagner and Stewart drove to Headquarters to deliver his reports, dropping Stewart off to spend time with old friends. Heading up QL 14, he swung into the 71st to hopefully see Annelle. He had called first from a telephone in HQ, leaving a message that he would swing by. He lounged by the pool, occasionally swimming laps. The water was refreshing in the 90 degree mid-day sun, relaxing mentally as well as physically.

The 71st pool was a world apart from bunkers, Chinooks, disease, and funeral gongs. Sitting on the pool's edge, he felt his obliques and ribs. Losing 15% of his weight since arrival in Vietnam, there wasn't an ounce of fat left on his body. There were no scales at Le Quon or in the scores of villages Wagner visited, and he had no idea he had dropped twenty five pounds since entering country.

After an hour, Annelle walked out. Her smile was brighter than the sun that glistened off busy ripples in the pool. Weeks of not seeing her and absent a confirmation of requited feelings, he still lacked confidence that he was reasonably welcome. "Absence is the most common reason for break-ups" was a statistic from a required Sociology course in college that entered his mind. Not that they had a relationship to break up in the first place, and this place was full of guys she saw every day. After a few minutes of easy conversation, his confidence rose and the statistic dissolved. They talked about Corrine, who was presently assisting surgery, and Gordon, and letters from home. She said she had written her father about the Ludendorff bridge, and her father would like to meet him. The words wrapped around his mind with a warm rush, delighted that she actually told her family about him. That had to be good for something.

"I heard there was a major battle south of here on Christmas Eve. You weren't involved in that, were you?"

"Yes. Gordon was on the other end of it. We were moving Montagnards again. They hit us every time we have a reconsolidation."

"Oh, my God. Everyone was talking about it. It was the biggest action in the area, all year. And that was you?"

"Well, it wasn't *just* me," he said dryly. "I had some help." Wagner related the gist of the battle, especially the Stinger gunship, and the later trip to the officer's club with J'Rel, which Annelle found hilarious.

"I'd love to have been there," she said, holding her knees under her chin. At the club, I mean." Her smile was captivating.

"It was a trip, a real trip," he said. "They're probably still talking about it. Probably making up a whole new preventive regulation right now." Wagner described a recent trip in a Kiowa helicopter. He was assigned a quick mission alone, to fly to a small remote village near the Kontum border eighteen klicks north in order to pay a Montagnard villager with Vietnamese Piasters, for a cow that got hit with American artillery shrapnel. The cow was already eaten. The villagers were more isolated than any he'd seen, way back in the hills. The men, albeit older, had hair down to their shoulders. "I'd never seen that before," Wagner told her. "Montagnard men always have relatively short hair, within reason. These guys are

like the Montagnard versions of hippies."

"What do they cut it with?"

"Don't have a clue," he replied, raising his eyebrows. "My guess is a machete. Their wives don't chew it off, they don't have front teeth."

"So I remember you telling me," she laughed. "Why did they pick you to pay this guy?"

"I have absolutely no clue. I does whut ma boss tell me ta doo. So the pilot flies me back to Le Quon, and immediately my Major tells me I have to pick up an ARVN body in Pleiku. We have to drive the body of this poor ARVN soldier up into Kontum province, to a small Vietnamese village. So Sergeant Flanagan and Stewart and I hop in the Jeep, pick up this coffin in an ARVN compound just north of Pleiku, and strap it on the Jeep. We took the canvas top off and folded the windshield down, and strapped it down with the head to the front, feet to the rear. Everything was fine until we got behind a Vietnamese civilian truck, about a mile from the village. We weren't going that fast, but he slammed on his brakes, and so did I. This sickening *'clump'* sound told me the body's now fitting into the front 2' of the coffin. So we pull into the village, no idea what to expect. It didn't go well. Vietnamese families are probably closer than Americans, they're all they have. What I assume was the immediate family are clinging all over our Jeep, wailing like crazy. Not just crying....*wailing.* I think it's sort of part of the custom, though certainly real grief."

"So why you, why did they have you do this?"

"Again, no clue. I don't think it was smart, they may associate us.. I mean the team.. with his death. I think it would have been better if the Vietnamese handled it. But with the Cambodian incursion and all, maybe they had no vehicles or men to handle it quickly. Certainly not the craziest thing I've seen in this war."

Three more hours passed. Annelle talked about letters from home, about friends' 'boring' lives, and her unsure plans on returning home and not wanting to be like them. Wagner told her how the war for him was coming down to how the Montagnards fared more than who wins, still confusing as to which side winning would be better, considering the pathetic reconsolidation villages. Then he told her about his Kit Carson Scout, who just got married. Vietnamese marriages were typically arranged by parents, and Tung's bride was no exception. She lived in the Chieu Hoi village a few kilometers northeast of Le Quon, and two teams were invited. Tung was a nice-looking, very mild mannered man of 28. His bride was considerably younger, and extremely shy. The entire village was populated with *Hoi Chans*, enemy V.C. or NVA soldiers who voluntarily surrendered and switched sides. Though simple, the wedding was interesting and pleasant. Rice wine from vases similar to the Montagnards' was included, but the food was quite palatable. It was good, even, and certainly more sanitary. A wife from the Chieu Hoi village may have been the only possibility for Tung, given the communal Vietnamese hatred for the North.

X OUTPOST

"A position on the chess board where a knight is defended by a pawn from its same side."

Saying good bye was becoming more difficult, he wished he could keep her for the night. As per the norm, the danger of driving late forced Wagner to return to Le Quon in the late afternoon, retrieving Sergeant Stewart first. The afternoon winds were picking up again, dust whirling from the shoulders of QL 19. Travelling east on the highway, three miles outside of Pleiku City, a figure stood on the side of the road, arm out, thumb up, hitchhiking. "Not worth the risk," Wagner and Stewart thought simultaneously. Seconds before passing the figure, they realized it was a blonde woman. Wagner slammed on the brakes and threw it in reverse. Wheels grinding to a stop on a coating of sandy dirt, Stewart leaned out the side of the Jeep and asked, "May I ask what the hell are you doing out here, ma'am?"

"Hi. I'm Julia Nickett. I'm a freelance reporter. Are you going to Qui Nhon?" she asked. Julia was fortyish, with sandy-blonde disheveled hair, a rather English face with a thin, pointed nose and eyes that slanted down toward the sides. She wore tan civilian pants and matching shirt, reminiscent of an African safari outfit, complete with a wide-brimmed desert hat, the kind with a flap on the rear to shield sun and rain. She wore G.I. jungle boots as well.

"No ma'am, we're just going to Le Quon, a few miles ahead. You plan on goin' all the way to Qui Nhon? You know this is Indian country, don't you?" Sergeant Stewart continued, surprised.

"Why are you going to Qui Nhon," asked Wagner.

"I'm doing a story on some of the top Vietnamese. I just spoke to a Colonel Bern, and he told me I couldn't come here. I told him I didn't work for him, and I'd go anywhere I please."

"Wow. Tell you what," Wagner said. "You leave our

names out of it, and we'll give you some stories, if you're open to them." In a second, he knew it was the answer he had hoped for. A way to get the word out what was happening to the Montagnards and to what had evolved into their MAT team's purpose, to their war. He knew he couldn't change much himself, even if he refused orders, someone else would simply fill his shoes. Additionally, his men....their opinion....was important. Most reporters stayed in the coastal cities, particularly Saigon. They gleaned their stories from third hand reports back and forth from cities like Pleiku to Saigon. A recent story in Stars and Stripes, a U.S. military independent news source, reported *"PLEIKU AIRBASE OVERRUN BY REDS"*. Subsequent stories gleaned from that embellished lie were reported across America, causing Wagner's very concerned father to immediately write to his son to find out if he was okay, or alive, even. It sounded like another Hue offensive happening in Pleiku, this time with the bad guys winning. In truth, several 122 mm rockets landed inside the Pleiku Air Base perimeter, wounding several and causing moderate damages to a few buildings and aircraft. Not a terribly unusual event and hardly an overrun situation. These reports helped to add career feathers in the caps of reporters who 'bravely filmed the war'. They did not represent all reporters, of course, there were outstanding exceptions. Miss Nickett appeared to be one of those. She was the first reporter of any kind any of the men had seen here in the bush.... and she was an answer.

"Have you heard about village reconsolidations, ma'am?" Sergeant Stewart asked. He was thinking the same thing Wagner was, no discussion required.

"Why, yes, I have. But I'm primarily interested in drug trafficking, would you have anything to share on that?"

Wagner was thinking of the discussions involving General Ngo, and Hanson's recordings, but that was premature, and he had no info himself. Anything else would be hearsay. He had not seen drugs, not even marijuana, not once.

"No ma'am, but I think we all would like to discuss some issues with you. As the Lieutenant says, leave our names out of it, if you please."

"Freelance reporter?" asked Wagner. "What does that mean?"

"I sell my stories to anyone interested. Magazines, newspapers, whatever. Newsweek is my biggest and best. We've got a good working relationship, and I feel they're the most honest." She was smelling a story. If nothing else, she had a safe ride to Le Quon and she could continue her trip to Qui Nhon in the morning if things didn't work out. She probably wasn't entirely aware of the extent of her danger on the road at night, but she certainly had courage. "Balls as big as a sway-back hog," in Stewart's words.

Major Nichols was gone for his week of R&R. Both teams were home at Le Quon, a total of nine men. At first, most were reluctant to talk to this reporter, but one comment drew another, then another. Before long, nobody held anything back regarding conditions of Plei Ko Tu, among others. Sitting around the dining table with Julia Nickett, they described in detail their involvement and discontent. It was getting late when Wagner asked if she could accompany them to Plei Ko Tu in the morning. She was more than eager.

They arrived in the village early, the Sun was over the trees only an hour before. After a relatively cold night it was quickly becoming another hot, dry day, accompanied by wretched red dust. Flanagan was trying hard to impress Julia Nickett with his self-proclaimed encyclopedia of knowledge about the Montagnards, the country, and the war in general. Fidelity meant nothing to him, and he never stopped trying. He was seldom successful without paying, but Julia quickly found him annoying and a bore. Flanagan finally gave up, and conversations were often and plenty between the other team members and Julia. Kir was along this time as the interpreter, laughing and joking with Sergeant Stewart. The large village and bolstered defenses afforded adequate safety to bring him, and he was their best interpreter for Bahnaar Montagnard.

They had hoped for village improvements by now, but clearly things had deteriorated even more. Julia Nickett took pictures and notes constantly. Immediately upon arrival through the village boundary, a shocked expression revealed her dismay for the plight of these Montagnard villagers. Wagner found Major Buhm, who was back with the unit protecting the village. Buhm told him that many of the villagers had already left, choosing the risk of retribution by the NVA, Americans, and Buhm's army over trying to subsist in this horrific village. Turning to Julia, Wagner said, "The government made a bad decision here, and the Montagnards have corrected it with their feet."

Major Nichols returned a week later, spending most of a day at Headquarters. Another hot windy day stirred deeper layers of Pleiku clay. Jungle vegetation from a rainy season months before continued to dry up, sluffing off to leave another layer of composting hydrocarbons, plant food for upcoming summer rains. Deep greens became pastels, taupes and beiges, plainer each day. Dry weather had its advantages, certainly more desirable in the field than constant rain, but the enemy enjoyed it as well. Activity had been increasing all around Pleiku Province and beyond. Dry trails and roads enabled the NVA to move more materiel and faster, from the arteries of the Ho Chi Minh Trail through a myriad of veins winding south and east through Kontum and Pleiku. Several more B-52 raids into Cambodia sent the team house mirrors rattling again, while more intel sifted down to the team level, reporting enemy movement.

When the Major returned to Le Quon late in the afternoon, he called Wagner and Bailey in to talk. He wanted to know more details about Plei Ko Tu and the recent moving operation. Bailey was normally reticent, remaining professional in the discussion. His comments and answers were brief, factual, and objective. Wagner's were factual, not so brief, and subjective. The previous month was growing more disconcerting, wearing on his principles. Scores of deaths and widespread misery at Plei Ko Tu and others were gnawing at his conscience. Now he was torn between duty and decency. He had no qualms about killing the enemy, the mission he signed up and trained for, however arguable it can be deemed decent. That was the contract, the deal, what soldiers do. He knew it going in. Soldiers kill people. Ultimately, it is a military's purpose. Without it, a country has no force, no power, no threat. Nothing to deter Idi Amins, Hitlers, Stalins, Khans, Khrushchevs….and Ho Chi Minhs. This new purpose assigned to them was outside the contract. It was wrong, and he knew it, his men knew it. True, some villages actually wanted the move, happy to be protected from a merciless enemy. In smaller numbers, it might work. Outsized villages resembling Plei Ko Tu clearly did not. Nichols listened to a visibly upset Wagner, who never showed anger, only a strong concern that could best be described as nothing-to-lose. He neglected to mention the reporter. Major Nichols was uncharacteristically quiet. He didn't disagree, he knew the facts as well as the consensus of opinions within his command.

Two weeks passed, Team 57 continuing with previous training and minor PF operations, mostly day time, return-by-dark excursions, while looking for signs of enemy activity. PF units, commonly limited to twenty or thirty men at best, were not equipped to perform Table of Organization & Equipment (TO & E) maneuvers, nor would they be coerced to. Poorly led units couldn't even be coerced to leave their compound.

Back at Le Quon, a constant low frequency humming of the compound generator was silenced for a few hours while the NCOs of Team 46 sliced through trenches of 'soft-soil-giveaways' in the ground with machetes. Every few weeks, Vietnamese 'wire-taps' would have to be cut away from the generator underground feed wire. The Vietnamese would tie in multiple hot connections in order to power AM radios, heaters and cooking gear, endearing them even less to Sergeant Blas.

Among Manual Blas's peeves were the way Vietnamese whistled into their PRC-25 radio handsets before making or answering a call. It was necessary to scare evil spirits and angry ancestors out of mystical airwaves.

Wednesday, February 18, 1971, Wagner was told to report to headquarters. Colonel Bern would see him at 0930 hours. Wagner arrived early, finding Doug Hanson and Jerry Dulane going over reports in Dulane's office. They were collating papers filled with numbers and statistics of body counts, pacified villages and supply inventories, both Vietnamese and American. As they worked they were discussing letters from home when Darryl walked in. "Hey, Darrilla, how's it going?" Hanson asked. "We were talking about you just ten minutes ago."

"Hi sweetheart, dreamin' about me again?" Wagner replied. "It's going well, recently, anyway. Hi Jer, I assume you've got your defensive fires registered around Headquarters."

"Chairborne all the way, our location is secure, fire for effect," he replied. "I didn't realize you two were so close."

"You have no idea. We go back a long way. Torrid." Hanson said, dryly.

"Doug, I thought you were married," Dulane said.

"He is, but he says he's leaving her," Darryl added with a glare at Hanson.

"You know guys," Dulane said, quieter. "I saw Sergeant Akers just walk by, he's going to think you're serious. Can you imagine the scandal? Word is, he's a gossip."

"I *am* serious," Wagner said, still dryly.

"You two want me to leave the room?" Dulane asked.

"Sweetcheeks here said he'd leave her for years. I'm beginning to think he's just lying."

"How long have you been waiting?" asked Jerry.

"Too long. You knew I just turned 26, didn't you? I figured I've got to settle."

"You bastard," Hanson said, with an incredulous look.

"Bitch."

"Bastard."

"Bitch."

"Alright, you two. Just kiss and make up," Dulane said.

"If it weren't for the great sex....."

Hanson walked over to flop onto a ratty upholstered couch left in the building from Viet Minh days. "Darryl, we were just talking about letters from home. Not from home-home, but from friends. Do you think it's weird that nobody gives a damn about the war?"

"Not any more. Everybody's sick of it, nobody gives a shit, I just see apathy. They really could care less. Not even interested in how we're doing, who's winning, or what combat is like. All I get are three questions."

"That's about it, that's what we were saying," Doug said.

"Three questions?" asked Jerry. "What three questions?"

Darryl looked at them both intently, and said, "Is the drug situation really that bad, what do you think of Lt. Calley and the all-time winner-- have you seen many snakes over there."

"And your answers?" he asked.

"Honestly, I haven't seen so much as a joint over here. Not one iota of drugs, nothing. Glad of it."

"And?"

"Number two...Calley. Guys, he went through the same OCS school we did, about a year earlier than us. We were all told in no uncertain terms 'the buck stops with you, the leader'. I mean, I get the frustration and hatred in their situation. But you don't let that crap happen. G.I.s are the same everywhere, every country. Young, macho, tough guy wannabes, whatever. Without leadership, it's gonna happen. They tend to go crazy with weapons and war. Human nature, gang-mentality thing. Shouldn't have let it happen. I read he graduated near the bottom of OCS.

"Okay, what about snakes. Seen many?"

"The all-time winner," said Wagner grinning. Nobody cares what combat is like, about fear, close calls, killing bad guys, or if we're winning or losing. They wanna know about friggin' snakes. Kind of says it all about back home, doesn't it?"

"Okay," Jerry said, laughing. "Have you seen many snakes over here?"

"Three. The first was a black racer, maybe 6' long, greased lightning. That was at Mang Yang Pass. The second, he was a coiled up thing in a foxhole, kind of a copperhead looking thing, I don't know if it was poisonous or not. My interpreter almost took us all out blasting it with his M-16. The third one, though, I was alone with only eleven Montagnard RFs. My sergeant was back at a village, I needed him there for radio relays. We were on a patrol about three klicks from the village, on a bamboo hillside. I was maybe the fourth man back. I could only see the man in front of me and sometimes the man in front of him. The 'Yards didn't talk, they moved low and fast, no noise. This little Bamboo Krait, the one they call the 'two step' for 'you get bit, you take two steps then you die…he was curled around a bamboo branch that stuck out over a narrow hillside trail. Beautiful bright chartreuse green color, only a couple of feet long if that. His little head was very triangular, very tiny neck. He just sat there, his head and neck horizontal, looking at us. Each RF soldier would simply lean back and point as he filed by, so the next man would see."

"You didn't kill it?"

"No, hell no. What for? Besides, that would make noise. We weren't coming back the same way we went. Maybe he'll get him an NVA someday. So that's it, three. I've got the radio, I have the command, so-to-speak. If I get killed, you lose that, so I'm not walking point. So by the time any self-respecting snake sees the first man at point, Mr. snake is gone."

"Wow," Jerry said. "Anyway, my friends are all against the war, but they don't care much about it anymore either. So was I, as you know, Darryl. Now, not so much. I've come to believe we've gotta win this, these people keep telling me they're all gonna die when we leave."

"I know. I hear the same thing. Many times. And as you know, I've come around to a lot of the way you thought. Now, I'm pretty much only concerned how the Montagnards fare. Screw the war," Wagner said.

"You mean that?" Jerry asked.

"About the 'Yards? Yeah. About the war? No, not really. Just not as convinced."

The conversation changed to a recounting of excitement of the last month, and the bizarre meeting with a reporter. Then Doug looked past Darryl and Jerry, got up and walked to the door. Peering left and right down the hall, he closed the door and returned. Speaking in a softer voice, he said, "Darryl, earlier, Jerry and I were talking about Bern.... the stuff we talked about before. Drugs and reconsolidations."

"I thought something was going to break months ago. What happened?" Wagner replied.

"Not much. Nothing I know more about, I mean. But I have absolutely no doubt that money and drugs are involved. I think there are land deals with the Vietnamese going on as well, as you've suspected, Darryl." Picking up a Samsonite briefcase, Hanson continued, "Take a look at these. I had to go to Nha Trang two weeks ago, a one-day trip. I brought these with me, they have a photocopy machine there. I copied several pages, filled with figures.... in American dollars, I think. We were waiting for you. It's in Vietnamese... can you read this?" he asked, holding a batch of papers. Wagner quickly scanned the cover page, printed in a format parallel to U.S. Army official military documents, but in Vietnamese.

1971-Thang Mot

TRU SO CHIEN

QUYỀN CHỈ HUY VIỆN TRỢ QUÂN SỰ VIỆT NAM CỘNG HÒA

Diagonally across the words, a large rectangular stamp

in black ink said "BI MAT".

Trying to recall words not seen since language school, he had problems with tonal signs under and over vowels. They were confusing and outside common vocabulary. It was dated January, 1971. "It says 'headquarters and military something'. Wait... Republic of Vietnam, something, Military Assistance Command... I think. The stamp translates, I think, to 'not the victim of eyes.. uh, okay... secret, or confidential," Wagner told them. Turning the cover sheet, most other words he clearly understood: *Can Sa, Ma Tuy, Cocain, Thuoc Phien*; Marijuana, Heroin, Cocaine, and Opium stood clearly out as top headers. *Tong so tien* at the bottom meant Total Money. Reading further, *tra tien*, 'pay money', and *o ben trong duong ruot khoang* 'location inside intestinal cavity'. The list went on, indicating *kilogam*, or kilograms for each item. Tens of thousands of *do-la*, or dollars were listed under each column.

"I didn't know what any of the Vietnamese meant," Doug said, "but one word caught my eye....*cocain*. If it meant cocaine, I figured there was more to it, based on our bit of *Maxwell Smart* work," Doug said. "I'm no Don Adams, but you realize, we're taking our lives into our hands here, this could be pretty serious. I took a risk just taking these, but Colonel Bern was gone. They were under personnel reports I needed."

"Like messing with the mob," Jerry said.

"You could have called me with your jungle boot heel phone," Wagner said, grinning.

Wagner kept looking, trying to remember words. On the fourth page, there were several columns, each with a header word in Vietnamese.

LANG   MET VUONG   SO NGUOI   PIASTERS

Under the first column was a list of village and hamlet names that were familiar to him. He had physically been there or at least knew them from months of scrutinizing topo maps. On this list, they began with 'Ap' and 'Lang', Vietnamese words for hamlet and villages, but all ending with Montagnard names, including Plei Ko Tu. Wagner read the meanings of the four columns: "Village, square meters, number of people, and piasters...Vietnamese money," he said. Plei Ko Tu had the largest numbers, 92,000,000 under square meters and 4,028 under number of people. "These are all reconsolidation villages. I see '*Nguoi Thuong*' several times in here... Montagnards."

"What's with the piasters," Dulane asked.

"The amounts roughly correlate to the square meters, it looks like," Wagner said. "Am I going out on a limb to say this is a real estate list? Montagnard lands? There are some huge bucks here."

"Looks like it," Hanson added. It's all right here with the pages of drugs. What's Hoang Dinh Tuan, and Phan Van Hai mean?" The words were at the bottom of the list of villages, typed and signed. There were no ranks assigned, probably civilians.

"Vietnamese names, not familiar to me... you?" Wagner asked.

"Nope," they both replied.

"Wait," Dulane said. "Hoang.. wasn't one of Ngo's Colonels named Hoang something? But that's just a first name, doesn't mean anything."

"No, Vietnamese family names are first, given are last. Can I have a copy of this?"

"I only made one copy," Doug answered. "I shouldn't keep it here. This is looking pretty heavy... no, I really shouldn't keep it here. Took a big chance to go this far. Can you imagine if Bern finds out? Or worse, Ngo."

"Okay, it'll be safe in my room at Le Quon, but I'm thinking of mailing it to that reporter," Wagner said. "Confidentiality essential, of course. By the time it's in print, we'll probably be home."

"Probably?"

"Well, they still couldn't connect us."

It was almost time to meet with Colonel Bern. The morning's findings made Wagner nervous, nothing new in nine and a half months of nerves and tension. He didn't know why he was called in to meet with Bern.

Wagner left Jerry Dulane's office towards Bern's and Robichaud's office area, surprised to find Gordon Bailey standing in the hallway outside Bern's closed door. Gordon had no idea what the meeting was for either, having been pulled from the field to attend.

At exactly 0930, Bern opened his door and said to them, "Come in please. " There was no 'good morning, gentlemen', no 'how are you?' "Sit down," he said, taking his seat behind his large French teak desk. His hands were clasped together, fingers entwined, thumbs against his chin. Wagner and Bailey sat in two French cane backed chairs of 1950s vintage. Bern was all business, his dark eyebrows furrowed again. He began by asking about the battle at Plei Ko Tu, interested in details. Action reports had given him overviews weeks earlier, always subject to errors and omissions. Bern was thorough about everything. He had actually visited the site sometime after the battle, but neither Wagner nor Bailey were in the village at the time.

Both lieutenants answered his questions, not offering more than what was asked. Wagner wanted to complain about reconsolidations, but in light of Hanson's copied sheets of drugs, names and numbers only minutes before, he wouldn't begin to. It soon became apparent, however, that Major Nichols had either complained to Bern on his own or relayed to Bern Wagner's 'rant' concerning the reconsolidations two weeks earlier. In any case, Bern appeared to be upset, but was trying hard to contain it, to remain professional. "Hiding his sorry-assed slime bag personal agenda," Wagner was thinking, his eyes fixed in a stare only partially masking disdain. He wanted to confront him. He wanted to jump over the desk and grab him by the throat, spin him into a chicken-wing, pick his sorry ass up and slam his head onto his big ugly desk. Over and over again. Finish by packing hog shit into his disemboweled cavity before sending him home in a body bag. Code his white ass and let his drug cronies in California pull it out. Maybe they can sell it on the street.

"I understand there are some concerns about our pacification efforts, meaning some of the reconsolidations. But they have clearly been shown to be successful. The NVA doesn't like it, it's starving them, food-wise, men-wise. The villagers are usually better off, it's saving their lives.

"Right," Wagner was thinking. "So they can sit in the middle of a shit-covered city with 4,000 other farmers and starve to death, if disease doesn't kill 'em first. They just love it. But we've given 'em metal roofs."

"The fact that the NVA are attacking nearly every effort to move these smaller hamlets proves it's hurting them. There is no other reason they'd be doing that if it wasn't," he continued, now up and pacing behind his desk. His hands were together behind his back in *parade rest* fashion, his eyes on the antique wood floor before him. Some of our RF commanders are beginning to resist these moves. They don't understand the big picture. They've lived in this province all their lives, and they don't see how this is going to win the war for them. "Fact is, in this job, sometimes it takes a boot in the ass. Your responsibility is to keep your team safe and get the job done... whatever. But if you find your counterpart is stalling, won't do his job, I will expect your involvement. Sometimes that gets sticky, but it's essential. You do understand?"

"Yes, sir," Bailey answered. Wagner just glared.

"Fact is, the NVA are taking forty, fifty, even sixty percent of their rice. They can protect that in one village. Divided, they can't." He paused, thinking. "You have any problems with your counterparts, I want to know about it. Your District Senior Advisor, Major Nichols or myself, we want to know about it."

"Yes sir," Bailey answered.

"Another thing. If you find any problems with some of these old NCOs that you don't feel you can handle, you let Major Nichols know about it," pointing his finger at Wagner to make his point.

"Yes sir," Wagner finally answered. He was sure Nichols had relayed something about Flanagan's protracted attitude, nothing else could explain it. It certainly had nothing to do with Blas and Stewart, they were top-notch professional soldiers.

After another twenty minutes of Bern's version of a 'pep talk' schmooze about how well both lieutenants were performing in combat and advising counterparts, he looked at his watch and said, "Wait here for a moment." He walked past them, out the door, returning two minutes later with Colonel Robichaud, the civilian David Friedman, and Friedman's lady friend "assistant", Madam Phung. She smiled at Wagner with the same flirtatious grin that she had when he was first introduced to her months ago. She was wearing the same style dress. Silky, tight, and western style, but this time red with a black leaf pattern. Her long black silky hair was fittingly attractive, like in a travel ad, even in her late 30s. Vietnamese women, at least the ones not working in the fields and rice paddies, looked incredibly young for their age. They took great care to stay that way as long as possible, even holding a paper over their face to block sun rays for a quick crossing of a street.

By this time, Doug Hanson had joined them, summoned by Colonel Robichaud.

"And of course, Lieutenants, you know Mr. Friedman. And this is Madam Phung,.."

"Yes, ma'am, we met you several months ago, I believe," Wagner said, shaking her hand. She was flirting with him again, raising her other hand to twist her hair with a slight head tilt as she shook his hand. Bailey was grinning. Friedman wasn't.

The discussion focused on reconsolidations, with Robichaud and Friedman asking increasingly detailed questions regarding the abandonment end, the small hamlets that were vacated. They were particularly interested, it seemed, in reports of villagers moving back. Colonel Bern grew tense, irritated. More than once he tried to change the course of the conversations. Wagner held his tongue, offering no more than absolutely necessary. Bailey did the same.

Colonel Bern ended the meeting with the lieutenants by

gently guiding them to the door and, thanking them for coming, saying he looked forward to working with them over the coming months. As they exited the room, the Colonel was closing the door and turning to his official company.

XI ISOLATED PAWNS

"Isolated pawns do not have a pawn of the same colour on either of their adjacent files."

Three days later, Wagner and the team were preparing to go back to Plei Ko Tu. It wasn't for training, finding NVA, or advising. The team simply felt a need to provide assistance in any way they could. They never made it. Major Nichols called Wagner into his trailer office. He looked a little older, tired in spite of the early hour. He already had a short cigar burning in the ash tray, unusual for him at this hour, especially without scotch. He looked weary, maybe sad.

"I have a new assignment for you," he said, with a finger pointed at a topo map on his desk. "Your team will be working at a location a klick or two south of the Kontum border, a few klicks west of QL 14, here."

Wagner looked at the remote, desolate area he was pointing to. Something about that remoteness.... another long distance from artillery support; not far from the Cambodian border... a wave of anxiety crept up his back, across his shoulders, into his brain. Each new, remote and unfamiliar area brought with it a shadow of dread, a fear of the unknown, perhaps. Maybe getting 'short', with 79 days and a wake-up left in his tour.. "Sir, isn't that outside our A.O.?" he asked.

"It *was*. That's part of what we need to discuss. Team 46 is being dissolved. Early outs are attritioning teams everywhere, all part of troop withdrawal. Even MAT teams are being affected." Wagner immediately thought of his own time left, still pondering extending, still unsure about leaving the Army. "Your A.O. now covers the entire northern two thirds of Pleiku Province."

Wagner pondered that for a moment. MAT 57's area was already far larger than his team could cover in years. Now he had over a thousand square miles with hundreds of villages.

Relatively few of those were protected by RF or even PF soldiers. Most depended on Peoples Self Defense Forces, PSDFs, or nothing at all. Comprised of old men using World War II weapons, PSDFs were routinely slaughtered if they chose to defend, and often were if they didn't. They may have been occasionally successful against the V.C., but no match for well-equipped NVA units.

"There's an RF company there," the Major continued. "533 Company. A combination of Vietnamese and Montagnards. A Vietnamese captain, Captain Thanh commands it. I don't have much information other than they've been stagnant. Word is, the village chief may be V.C. If he is, the whole village probably is. There's reported enemy movement along these highlands to the west and here," he said, poking a finger to an area three kilometers south of the village. It was an area of small streams connecting to form a larger one flowing west, toward Cambodia. It originated from mountain tributaries four klicks east of the highway, earning the name of Ia Khol before it passed through a large U.S. made culvert under Highway 14. After travelling west another five kilometers, tributaries from more mountains to the south increased its flow to earn another name, Ia Pien. Further westward flow found it meandering snakelike through a flat plain of small intermittent lakes and rice paddies, filling and drying subject to the seasons. This valley area, south towards Plei Mrong, was where the Major indicated enemy movement along 'highlands to the west'. "The village itself is called Plei Krut. It's actually a group of small Montagnard hamlets spread over an area six clicks wide and three plus klicks north-south. About eight square miles. The closest village to this is Plei Mrong, about ten kilometers southwest. There are no roads or trails connecting it. In fact, the dirt road leading into Plei Krut and one into Plei Mrong to the south are the only roads in the northern third of Pleiku Province on the west side of QL14, and none anywhere west to Cambodia, it's entirely unpopulated. Not even Montagnards. There are no longer friendly troops at Plei Mrong either, the RFs who worked out of there have been relocated south."

Wagner studied the village area, comprising eight groups of tiny black squares indicating homes. Each group had its own 'Plei' name, ending with Ya Te, To, O, Op, Preng Het, Prep, Grung Rut, and Pok. All were situated near or along a narrow dirt road leading west from Highway QL 14. Two were located one or two kilometers north and south of the road, which dwindled to a foot trail halfway through the six kilometer span. "Sir, that's out of range for Artillery Hill, they don't have anything that will reach that far," Wagner said, wondering if it was even considered.

"You'll be supported by guns up here, in Kontum," he said, pointing to a fire base on another map. "They'll have 105s and 155s. No 8" or 175s. You'll be at the far end of their range, but they will reach you, max range will be about two klicks south of Plei Krut. Beyond that you'll have nothing." Though comforting to know artillery was available, Wagner had been through that "max range" rodeo several times, nervous about resulting inaccuracies. The 105s and 155s were, however, a plus. They were more accurate and faster firing than long-range 175s, albeit less powerful. He had no experience with the firebase, but its remote, less populated location should mean faster clearances. All of this passed through his mind in seconds while the Major continued. "Your RF perimeter is located roughly here," he said, pointing to a spot four kilometers from the highway. "It's an old Special Forces camp. It was overrun two or three years ago. The north side of your perimeter has tall grass. Don't go in there, it's reported to be a minefield, put there by Special Forces. They haven't been removed."

"Is there a mine card?" Wagner asked, hoping for a map, of sorts to show where the mines were in order to remove them.

"If there was one, there certainly isn't now. My guess is, when they got overrun it was abandoned."

"How long will we be staying there?"

"I don't have that information," Major Nichols replied. "It may be several weeks."

Wagner called the team together to pass on the assignment. They would bring two Jeeps and a trailer, carrying Blas, Stewart, Flanagan, Tung, Kloh, and himself. "Be ready to leave at 0700 in the morning," he said, over Flanagan's derogatory quips. "Sergeant Flanagan, make sure we have triple PRC-25 batteries. And beaucoup medical supplies. We'll likely be pulling MEDCAPS." Flanagan smelled precarious prospects coming, they all did. He protested MEDCAP work more now. Not that he didn't enjoy helping villagers, he just liked to bitch, and stay out of harm's way. Flanagan wasn't the only one to become more wary while getting 'short', including Wagner. He was barely aware of it, but it was there. Flanagan left the room, bitching again. Kir, the young Montagnard boy-interpreter, whispered to Wagner, "Trung-si Flan'gan.... I no'like, no'like," he said, shaking his head. Wagner just looked down at him, then put his arms around him to give him a bear hug.

They were up early, greeted by a dim azure sky, a warming orange glow advancing upward over the mountains of Mang Yang Pass. Packing gear and supplies in one Jeep trailer, they planned to move out right after breakfast. Ammunition, Claymores, extra weaponry, including Blas's 12 gauge shotgun, boxes of fragmentation and smoke grenades filled a quarter of it. Flanagan's medical supplies, mostly for the villagers, filled another quarter. The rest went for food, blankets, cots, etc. Piled on top of this assortment was a large folded Army mess tent someone had scrounged months before, unused. Knowing the stay might be lengthy and no old Special Forces structures remained, it would be handy to store equipment protected from dirt and forthcoming early rains. Sergeant Stewart was teasing Tung again, telling him "Tung, you no good, go back to North Vietnam." Tung smiled, but said little. The two were becoming good friends, this merry black American sergeant and mild mannered, polite-but-still unsure North Vietnamese Army sergeant. Sergeant Blas was also forgetting his bias toward this Vietnamese. Here were three sergeants, laughing and working together, from Georgia, Guam, and North Vietnam... Wagner was a little worried Stewart might be going too far, but said nothing. Tung would just laugh and grin, bright Vietnamese eyes smiling at Stewart. Just before they were ready to leave, Sergeant Blas asked Tung in his Guamanian accent, "Tung. Let me ask you. What you like best, M-16 or AK-47?" For years, the M-16 had been denigrated, AKs praised. Earlier models of M-16s had a history of jamming, resulting in unknown numbers of deaths, hurried into production by a manufacturer where the dollar wins. Later modifications of a chromed bolt, more powder in cartridges, and a bolt-assist mechanism nearly eliminated problems. Meanwhile, the world-wide popularity of the AK was largely based on its heavy, loose clearance parts which allowed it to keep firing when exposed to dirt and mud. A 7.62 mm bullet, with more stopping power than a 5.56 mm M-16, was also an advantage. But an M-16 round, .223 caliber, had a much higher velocity. Energy is calculated in mass times velocity squared, and the little round is capable of creating massive damage in soft tissue. On the other hand, Wagner had seen rounds pass 'through and through', causing relatively little damage. In some cases, men didn't even know they were shot. The question grabbed everybody's attention. Heads swung and work stopped.

Uncharacteristically, Tung opened his eyes wide, spread his arms out to the side, and said, "Oh, Trung-si, M-16! That *fucking* AK-47, it heavy, it jam, ammo heavy..."

The answer surprised everyone, but Tung's exuberant reaction more so. It was the first time anyone had heard him swear. He was learning from Americans.

"It jam?" asked Stewart. "What you mean, it jam? I thought that was why it was so good, it don't jam none."

"Yah, mine jam," Tung said, eyes still wide. "And heavy. M-16 light. No kick. Ammo light."

Wagner had to agree at least to the M-16 being a fine weapon. His had not jammed once, after hundreds of rounds, in adverse conditions. In training, nearly everyone qualified better on the M-16 than the much heavier old standard, the M-14, which, like the AK, shot a 7.62 mm bullet. The manuals said the

M-14 was more accurate to a longer range, etc. etc., but experience said otherwise. A low recoil may have been part of the reason. The M-16's firing rate was also faster on automatic, and rounds in the air often decides battles. Regardless, weight of a weapon and its ammunition was an important matter to an Infantryman.

Just before mounting the Jeeps Sergeant Stewart remarked, "Now don't we have us some fine diversity here. We've got a Pacific island ugly Guamanian who now lives next to a country called Californicate, full of fruits, nuts, and flakes. We got us a handsome fat Irishman from the middle of the Yoo-nited states, a lieutenant from somewhere up north in the middle of Canada, a Montagnard from the jungles of Vietnam, and a North Vietnamese from someplace next to China. And my own black African ass from a place just above another foreign country full of geriatric golfers. How could we possibly lose this war?"

The drive west on QL 19 to Pleiku City and north on QL 14 to an insignificant dirt road leading into Plei Krut took less than an hour, much of it in slow traffic through Pleiku City. Wagner had formed an image what the area would look like. It was based on previous trips up 14, usually only a third of the distance north, but also from his topo map, which he studied for two hours the night before. He wanted to know every hill, valley, stream bed, artillery reaches, and likely avenues of enemy approach. The dirt road was barely wide enough for the Jeep, more a trail than a road. It was open, tan grassy terrain, no trees for 50 to 70 meters to either side. A rise 50 meters ahead hid whatever lay beyond it from the highway. As they topped the crest and began a gradual descent, a dozen abandoned Montagnard hootches sat on stilts close to the right side of the trail. Already the place had an aura about it. All their weapons were pointed toward the structures, a possible ambush location. As yet, they had no guarantees even if an RF contingent was defending the village. Another 50 meters revealed a dozen Montagnard villagers, walking in a typical single file, each evenly spaced two meters apart. It was unusual to see middle aged men among the women and older men. Most had been killed or conscripted into one side or the other. A blatant difference in these people was immediately evident, never before seen... there were no smiles. Only scowling glares. "We're in trouble," Wagner thought.

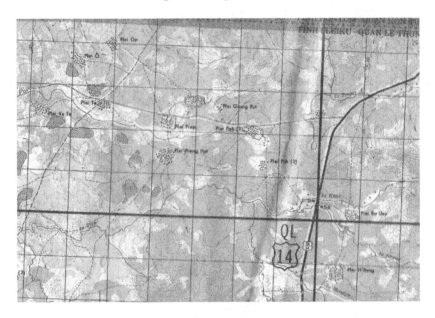

Another 40 meters and the little caravan passed over a nearly dry creek bed. The creek mysteriously meandered from right to left another 700 meters before it looped around a knoll and back into itself, before disappearing into the Earth. Several foot trails radiated away from this loop, "Possibly a water point? Tunnels? Where does the water go?" Wagner imagined, studying his map. It would demand some investigation. Another 2,000 meters brought them to the PF perimeter. It was disappointingly small, and minimally maintained. Triangular in shape and only 50 meters on a side, it bordered the trail, concertina and barbed wire forming its shape, with an 8' door of bamboo and concertina for passage. A dozen small soldiers, wearing filthy red-dirt stained fatigues, jungle boots, and jungle hats sat in three groups near firing positions and small bunkers placed every 10 to 15 meters around the inside of the perimeter. Most positions had no overhead cover and none had rear protection. Their deeply tanned faces watched the American Jeep convoy approaching. A few of the bunkers had small children sitting on top.

The team immediately assessed the defenses, which were meager. A village of forty stilt hootches stood in a cluster due south. Beyond them, seventy meters from the road, the grassy treeless terrain changed to jungle in varying shades of green. This could be an avenue of enemy approach, through the village. From there, the ground sloped gently downward to the Ia Khol stream another 1600 meters south, running east-west. A mountain, 900 feet high, rose as a dark shadow from the trees behind it, adding to a foreboding appearance. Everything east,

the direction they had entered from, was open, cleared years before with Agent Orange. The dirt road continued west as a trail in mostly open terrain before trees, intermittent wetlands, and tall grasses could conceal enemy movement. Worse, but acceptable. The north was another story. Trees began 30 meters from the trail and perimeter. Of greater concern was the extensive tall green grass filling in that 30 meters to a point a third of the way across the north side. It was taller than a man, and strangely green when the dry season paled much of the landscape. Victor Charles could practically have lunch with them and they would not know.

On the northerly inside east edge of the perimeter there was a larger sandbagged bunker, rising three feet above the ground. A Vietnamese soldier wearing a light green beret climbed out of the entrance and walked toward the Jeeps. A wide face absent a smile topped out his 5'-4" height. A pale, untanned face, slightly bulging stomach, and soft, undefined forearms extending from rolled up fatigue sleeves told of an educated, ineffective leader sent here to the badlands of Pleiku. He looked to be in his mid-thirties, and clearly unhappy with his situation. The team read him in an instant as he introduced himself with limited English. A 'pip' of three black five-petaled flowers on his fatigue shirt indicated he was the *Dai-uy,* or captain of the small understrength RF unit. The name Thanh was sewn to his pocket.

Thanh was accompanied by a young second lieutenant and his NCOs. Introductions were made, and Wagner asked where the team would locate. It was part of a counterpart's job to provide a bunker or at least a location, but often not done, particularly with Vietnamese units. Wagner immediately noticed that more than half of this company was Vietnamese, and all of the officers were. Thanh briefly spoke with his lieutenant and returned to his bunker without a word more. The lieutenant, a handsome, tanned young Vietnamese named Nguyen Hai, spoke passable English. Hai was slightly taller than most Vietnamese, at 5'-7", with a hint of European, probably French. He pointed to an area where the team could set up. It was small. Too small. The team discussed the options, and decided to expand the perimeter by setting outside the perimeter on the east side. They would have to scrounge some concertina and tanglefoot wire to add the extra area, but until then be rather exposed in an attack.

The formalities over, the team began to carve out their new temporary home. The main problem was communications: there weren't any. They were too far from anyone, artillery, headquarters, anything. The 292 antenna was needed again, quickly erected by Blas and Flanagan with Tung's help. Without communications, there was little hope for survival in a large attack, but the 33' two-niner-two gave them that commo. Artillery or air support was critical. Their second concern was a complete lack of cover; no bunkers or even foxholes. Sergeant Stewart took Kloh into the small adjacent village to attempt to arrange for some paid digging labor, saving time for advisory duties as well as hurrying their defenses. It was nothing new, MAT teams were expected to pay out of pockets for food and any other items for their existence they couldn't scrounge. Only weapons, clothes, backpacks and a few other basic items were officially issued. Even food and ammunition were supposed to be requisitioned through Vietnamese channels. That never happened, not once.

Meanwhile, Wagner discussed the problem of tall green grass on the north perimeter. "That is minefield," Hai told him. "Mines. Left long ago. No go in there. Number ten." The mines were "Bouncing Betties". When tripped, they bounced 4' in the air before exploding, sending shrapnel sideways for a devastating kill radius.

Within an hour, the mess tent was erected, canvas sides welcome to keep blowing dirt to a minimum. In the flurry of team activity, evening was approaching before they knew it. Flanagan and Stewart concocted a 'team meal' made up of a variety of rations gleaned from the stores of Hoa Khe's kitchen, much to her displeasure. Stews were a usual presentation, easier to cook and portion out among the crew, facilitating minor changes in each meal based on what was on hand. Sometimes village or RF soldier food swaps added to variety, not always universally appreciated. Stewart, growing up in poverty in rural Georgia, was more accustomed to 'chitlins' and farm rations than the rest of the team, and he never complained.

Sleeping on hard ground had grown acceptable, but never a favorite. A semi-permanent position such as this afforded the luxury of cots, but Wagner brought an Army-issue net hammock. "I like the idea of getting off the ground," he said to Tung. "I hate spiders." Tying one end to a Jeep windshield parked against the wall and the other to a tent pole inside, he figured it would be a comfortable improvement. The hammock, capable of being packed into very small spaces in a backpack, seemed a perfect answer. But being small and portable, it had no 'spreader bar' on either end.

Flanagan laughed and said, "Good luck, Lieutenant. You ain't gonna like it." He was right, one night was enough. In the morning, Wagner's shoulders felt 10" wide, squeezed together like a soft, slow vice.

A cool early morning found the team continuing work on defenses and readiness. "What do you think we should do with this grass?" Wagner asked the sergeants.

"We should burn it," Blas suggested.

"Agent Orange?" Stewart asked.

"If that don't work, we could shoot it down," Flanagan quipped, bringing chuckles.

"You know, that's crazy enough to work," Wagner said. "Why not? We don't have Agent Orange. We don't have anything to burn it with. It's green. And I'm not going in there with a lawnmower."

Blas set up his M-60 machine gun on a bipod. From ten feet away, he ripped into the grass, spraying rounds back and forth like a garden hose. It actually worked, to a degree. The barrel began to emit a slight glow, then a dull red, bright red, and finally orange hot. With a standard issue asbestos mitt, he cranked the barrel a third turn and pulled it out, re-inserting another, and kept firing. Twenty five hundred rounds and three grenades later, the grass was ravaged. Not perfect but much better.

"Let's put Agent Orange and gasoline on our list," said Wagner. "And M-4 fuel thickener, to make napalm. That should do it."

The grass removal fielded an audience of RF soldiers, amused at the crazy Americans. But they still did nothing on their own sorry defenses. That was part of the Adviser's job, to change their attitude and energy, if possible. Initial living preparations complete, Wagner, Blas, and Stewart began an inspection of defenses, using Tung as their interpreter. Unsure how the RFs would accept an NVA, they kept him close. Attempts to include Captain Thanh in the perimeter tour proved futile. Thanh delegated Hai instead. Wagner guessed Hai was a good officer, held back in a quagmire of lax leadership. The inspection was nothing new; many times before had the team performed the same endeavors with a wide range of results, depending entirely on leadership of the unit. Routine problems of firing position faults, weapons placements, ammunition storage, weapon cleaning and so on were brought up, met with apparent interest from Hai. He was easy to work with, energetic and receptive to suggestions. As they walked, Wagner saw live M-16 rounds laying randomly in the dirt. Empty cans and garbage occasionally decorated the entrance to bunkers and firing positions. They saw young kids again, sitting on and playing around the tiny bunkers. A beautiful little Montagnard girl, four years old at most, squatted on bent knees on one of the bunkers, wearing a filthy black woven skirt and faded red top. She was alone, her huge brown eyes were spaced wide above a tiny turned up nose. She stared up at Wagner, looking frightened, not daring to move. Tears left little tracks down her dirt-caked face. A dozen baby goats, of varying black, white, and brown fur patterns frolicked around her bunker, gamboling and butting each other's tiny heads. They were no more than 14" head to tail.

"What are these kids doing inside the perimeter," he asked, thinking they belonged in the village.

"They are the soldiers'," Hai answered.

"Where do they live?" Wagner asked.

"Here. In bunker. Family live here."

Wagner turned to his sergeants. "You hear that? They live in this tiny hole? It's what, 5' by 4' in there?" Sergeant Stewart just shook his head sadly.

"What if we get hit? Where would they go?" Wagner asked.

"Probably just hole up in there, sir…sad."

On the south side of the perimeter, the village side which may be the most prone to attack, there were no soldiers. They found that this is where twelve R.D. Cadre were positioned, when they were present. The RD Cadre, or Rural Development Cadre, were young men who were probably better educated than the soldiers and were supposed to be idealistic. They were assigned to go out and bring security and development to the people. It was a way they could get out of being in the army. The men of MAT 57 found most of them useless. Lazy, cowardly, and uncaring. Thanh likely put them on the south side figuring they were the most expendable. Nine were equipped with old M-1 carbines and a total of six grenades. Three had no weapons at all.

Dai-uy Thanh finally joined them, and Hai stayed a pace behind, saying nothing. Wagner finished the perimeter tour with standard questions regarding operational patrols. Most Vietnamese commanders lied about sending patrols out, preferring not to deal with dissenting subordinates who wanted no part of it. Some American units were no different, it all went back to strong leadership. A failure to send out patrols regularly cost many more friendly lives than sitting waiting for an enemy to annihilate them. "Do you go on hainh quan? *Di vao hoat dong*?"

"Oh yes, go operation. Go often," Thanh answered.

"How often? How far?" Wagner was hoping the stream two klicks to the south and areas to the north, under heavier cover, had been combed. That's where they'd be. Valleys, near water and heavy cover.

"Usually go here," he said, indicating a line across the map, halfway to the Ia Khol stream.

"To *nuoc*? To Ia Khol?" Wagner asked.

"Oh yes, sometime," he replied.

"We go on next operation, Dai-uy?"

"Yes. I like you go," Thanh said, a blank look in his eyes.

"When we go?"

"Maybe in two days. Maybe Tuesday we go."

Tuesday came and went, nothing happened. While Blas and he worked on the bunker and artillery registrations, Wagner told Flanagan and Stewart they should go to the village to perform a MEDCAP. He firmly believed that *nothing* was more important than medical care to the rural populace. 'Winning hearts and minds' didn't amount to much from anything else, in his experience. But nothing was more important to these third-world people than their families, and their families were diseased, wounded, injured more than anybody could imagine. Stewart was eager, loving the work of helping needy villagers. Flanagan was not. The area was obviously dangerous, the people unfriendly, almost certainly V.C. The team had never felt the animosity from villagers toward Americans from either Montagnards or Vietnamese that they found here. Flanagan complained every step of the way. He said he didn't have adequate medical supplies for a MEDCAP, and if he wasn't supplied them, he wasn't going to scrounge them. In yet another head-butting contest, Wagner assured him that he would.

When a need for some other supplies arose, Stewart, Kloh, Tung and Flanagan drove in to the 71st for a whirlwind scrounge maneuver, quickly amassing a sizable load of everything from penicillin to tourniquets. Stewart stayed at the 71st, advised by a doctor to treat a minor looking infection that was spreading in his thigh from a minor thorn puncture weeks earlier. They were going to incise it in the morning and ensure it wasn't spreading. An additional scrounge mission to nearby Camp Holloway filled ammunition needs. Kloh was left off to take advantage of transportation to his home village, after a long-delayed leave that he earned.

When they returned to Plei Krut, Wagner repeated his order, putting it on the line. "Sergeant Flanagan, you *will* perform the MEDCAP. You've been stalling with every excuse in the book, and that's going to end right now."

"You lookit, Lieutenant," Flanagan said, humping his shoulders to look bigger and pointing an angry finger at Wagner's face. "You've been pestering me all week to pull a fuckin' MEDCAP without proper supplies, and I just ain't gonna do it. I've had enough of this shit. It's not my job, and there ain't a nun's chance in hell I'm gonna do it."

Wagner had finally had it. He'd put up with this cantankerous bastard for ten months, trying to keep the team together, trying to not fail leadership ability, trying to make Flanagan useful without sending him to another team to pass on a problem child. Blas and Tung were staring, waiting to see how this would pan out. With a controlled breath, he said slowly, "Sergeant Flanagan, I'm really tired of hearing all your complaints. I'm tired of your rotten goddam attitude. And I sure as hell don't want to hear any more of your insubordination. You *will* perform this MEDCAP tomorrow. Starting at 0900."

"I don't give a shit about you or my shitty goddam attitude, Lieutenant. This isn't my job and I'm not gonna do it!"

In his entire two years working with NCOs of all ages and ranks, Wagner never had a serious problem, even with some that weren't too effective. Most were great. This was the first. "Sergeant Flanagan, this good Army is paying you for something, and if this isn't it, I'd sure as hell appreciate your explanation for what it is. You either get your ass out there tomorrow or expect a court martial. *Period*."

Wagner meant it. The Major practically asked him to do it before, knowing Flanagan's history. He had resisted. It was Flanagan's career. He had good medical skills. If nothing else, he wasn't a chicken-shit draft dodger, he was here risking his life like the rest of them. But this was the final straw. Flanagan walked away, inside the tent, pouting. Wagner wanted him relieved then and there. If he had been back in Le Quon with the Major there, he would have been. Wagner was still fuming when he looked back to see Tung and Blas perched on a bunker, grinning with approval and a 'thumbs-up' from Blas. That was important. Very important.

Flanagan was frustrating enough. Thanh, like many Vietnamese counterparts before, was wearing on him. He lied about everything. The operations he insisted he went on weren't happening and probably never did. Wagner asked him one more time before supper that night, and got the same promise. "Two days," Thanh said.

The bunker was almost complete, but not quite. Their paid village help hadn't shown up for the last two days. The team had almost finished one wall, but had a slew of sandbags to fill for the other walls, roof, and entrance tunnel.

The tent worked for cover, but other than defensive foxholes to fall into, they were vulnerable to attack.

At 0530 hours the next morning, a Vietnamese private woke Wagner, asleep on his cot in the tent. "We go now," he said.

"What?"

"We go now. Hainh quan. We go."

Wagner looked out to see two dozen RF soldiers, geared up to go. Dai-uy Thanh was up and ready, decked out in his beret. "Jee-zus, Thanh's moving out," Wagner yelled, waking Blas, Flanagan, and Tung as he swung his feet out to throw on boots and clothes. Luckily, his gear was at the ready, loaded M-16, a bandolier of 7 magazines, three frag grenades, two smoke grenades, a canteen of water, and of course, the PRC-25 radio. There was no time for food. Grabbing his compass and sliding his plastic-sleeved topo map in a leg map pocket, he looked out the tent flap to see the column already leaving. "Okay, Sergeant Blas, I'm going to ask you to stay with the radio here. If we need artillery, I'll need to give you coordinates and adjustments. You've got the call signs and freqs." It was a tough call, made in an instant, to leave alone with the RFs. But after the bitter confrontation of the day before, he wasn't about to change his orders for Flanagan. "Besides," he figured, "Flanagan would be all but useless in the woods," There it was. He and Tung would head out with the RFs, leaving Flanagan to his MEDCAP orders and Blas to radio relay. They quickly caught up with Thanh and Hai, who were positioned halfway back in the column. The point man was already three hundred meters down the path. Thanh was carrying nothing but a walking stick and a holstered revolver. Nothing else. Behind him, an RTO carried his radio. Nothing else. Behind him, a soldier carried a pack with food and water for the two officers and the RTO. Nothing else. At least Lieutenant Nguyen Hai and all the sergeants carried weapons and ammunition. So here they were, heading out with no plan, twenty six men, twenty three with rifles. One RF carried an M-79 grenade launcher, the rest M-16s.

The worn path they were on meandered south to the left of the village. Wagner noticed how the village, unconsolidated, was attractive and lush, houses randomly set, banana trees growing among them. They had gone a thousand meters, well into thick jungle, when the column suddenly stopped. A 'runner' came back to talk with Thanh. It made Wagner nervous, in a single file, on a well-used trail, and no security reacting to the flanks, the men didn't even crouch. They looked like they were waiting for a bus. Wagner moved on ahead, keeping with Thanh to the head of the column. Thirty meters ahead, they reached the lead men and the reason the column stopped. There, in the middle of the trail in plain sight was a 6' wide hole, 5' deep. A simple bamboo mat reinforced with cross pieces of bamboo sticks had been pulled away, exposing the hole filled with ordinance. It had not even been attempted to hide. So much for Thanh making regular patrols.

Security was still little to none. Wagner winced as two RF soldiers jumped into the hole, not checking for booby traps, often placed to kill an unwelcome visitor. They rapidly handed a weapons cache out to their men. Luckily, it hadn't been rigged. They removed American 60 mm mortar rounds, NVA 82 mm mortar rounds, a box of AK-47 ammunition, seven 5" diameter by 15 ½" long shells that looked like artillery rounds, and seven 5" diameter by almost 4' long tubes, with spring loaded fins at one end. The fins were arced, folded in to fit the radius of the tube. Wagner had no idea what they were, until Tung explained they were 122 mm rockets, the largest weapon the enemy commonly possessed. He finally figured out the shells were warheads that attached to their aluminum tube rocket bodies. When the rocket slammed out of a launching tube, the fins sprang out to stabilize its flight. Thanh ordered his men to carry the cache back to Plei Krut, one man to a warhead and two to a rocket body.

The warheads weighed 41 lbs. each, the rocket bodies 88 lb., a lot for small men to carry. Wagner radioed their find back to headquarters, giving numbers and types. The walk was easy back along the same trail, taking under fifteen minutes. They laid their find out in front of the team mess tent for pictures and a count. But now there were only three warheads and six rocket motors. "What happened to the rest?" Wagner asked Hai. Thanh had disappeared into his bunker.

"They threw them away," Hai answered, nervously.

"Why?" asked an incredulous Wagner.

"Too heavy," he answered, with a disgusted look.

The Montagnards all carried their heavy loads back. The Vietnamese did not. Too heavy.

Calling headquarters to report the numbers again, Wagner heard, "What happened to seven each?" from an RTO in Pleiku.

"They threw them away," replied Wagner.

There was a long pause. "Uhh, say again, over."

"I say again, *they-threw-them-away*, over."

Another long pause. "Uhh,...wait one." A long delay and then, "Understand they threw them away. Why, over?"

By now Colonel Robichaud was on the other end. Wagner responded, "Word I get is they were too heavy. They tossed them on the return to base, over." He took the opportunity to ask if Agent Orange was available for his grassy mine field. The Colonel would check.

On Wagner's assertive advising, Dai-uy Thanh ordered a small patrol to head back to retrieve the missing items, but it was a little late for Thanh. A Vietnamese truck with MPs had already been dispatched to pick him up. It arrived an hour later, and Dai-uy Thanh was led away in cuffs and ropes in the back of the truck. A 'tiger cage' barbed wire enclosure awaited him. Worse, he had 'lost face'.

An hour later, Wagner received a call from Major Nichols to report back to Le Quon, he didn't say why. Shortly before he was to leave, two Montagnard villagers ran to the tent area shouting something in Bahnaar. Kloh was still on his leave, making translation difficult through one of the Montagnard RFs who spoke little English. The village chief's daughter was 'wounded' is all they could gather. Flanagan, done with the MEDCAP work in the village, grabbed his bag and the team ran the short distance to the main village next to them. In the village chief's hootch lay a young girl, writhing in pain. Her face, neck, and shoulders were bright red. Again, translation was difficult, but she had been badly burned with steam when cooking in a sealed steel ammunition box. When it blew, she suffered second degree burns outside, but into her airways as well. She was critical. Wagner ran back to get the Jeep, returning with a litter thrown in, while Flanagan poured cool water on her. They loaded her onto the Jeep and strapped her down, bringing her father as well. If she died without her father present, the Americans would be blamed, and her soul might wander if not inside the village or under her father's care. The trip to the 71st hospital was fast. Daughter and father would stay at least overnight. Wagner asked about Annelle, but had no time to see or visit her, it was getting late and they had to return. He radioed the Major to explain the event, and it was agreed he could return to Le Quon in the morning.

After morning chow, Wagner headed back to Le Quon. On the way, he picked up Stewart, his infection cured. Upon arrival, Nichols informed them that Lieutenant Roy Gambor, a first lieutenant from recently dissolved MAT Team 46 would be 57's new assistant team leader, 'Five Seven Alpha', completing the 5-man team. Gambor and Stewart would return to Plei Krut, while Wagner had a different temporary assignment.

"You'll be flying to Nha Trang in the morning, Major Nichols told Wagner, "there's a Colonel Hallard who is going to meet you at MACV Headquarters. He wants you to report to him at 1100 hours. I'll bring you in to the air base."

"Do you know what this is about, sir?"

"Have you ever met Hallard,?" the Major asked.

"Yes, sir. Twice. I believe you were there, not long after I got here."

The Major looked puzzled for a moment, then remembered. "Yes, that was at the Quang Que, Colonel Bern was there, right?"

"Yes, sir."

"I don't know. I was only told to have you report. I assume it has something to do with the activity your team's encountered. You've done well. Outstanding, really. Maybe he wants to discuss your career, or extending? He seems to know a lot about you," the Major said, leaning back in his chair.

"I remember he was thorough, knew a lot the first time I met him. But isn't he an MP Colonel?"

"I believe so. You haven't done anything I don't know about, have you?" he asked, grinning.

"Nothing I'll admit to," Wagner replied. "I claim the fifth. Can you do that in the Army?"

Early, 0600 hours, Wagner, Nichols, and his bodyguard Seht left in the Major's Jeep for Pleiku Air Base. Passing by the 71st, Wagner gazed at the pool, wishing he could visit. He was wearing clean jungle fatigues and handyman Friday-shined jungle boots. As well as a holstered Smith & Wesson .38, he carried his M-16, though most didn't in cities this late in the war. The Major dropped him off, whereupon he was directed to a waiting C-47 tail dragger, painted in camo.

Climbing the wheeled ladder, he entered to find only seven passengers were on the flight. After a thirty minute wait, a pilot climbed aboard and stepped into the cabin with another pilot. Very shortly, the ancient twin engine was taxiing down the runway, passengers sitting back in an unfamiliar 12 degree angle until the tail lifted moments before leaving the ground. "One more neat toy in this good Army," he mused, thinking of the incredible history of this plane, dating back to 1941. He imagined the paratroopers on D-Day, 'stand up, hook up, shuffle to the door' and out into a sky of tracers and anti-aircraft fire over Germany. A military version of the old DC-3 passenger planes, it had a wingspan of 96' and a cruising speed of only 160 mph. The ride took only a half hour from takeoff to touch down, Wagner only needing to find Hallard's office in MACV.

He was early, time enough to drop some letters off at the Nha Trang APO post office before reporting to Hallard. Before he found his office, Hallard recognized him in the hall. "Lieutenant Wagner. Come right in," he said, smiling.

Wagner was anxious, but not overly worried. He was short. Without extending, he would be out in just over two months. Whatever Hallard had in mind, for whatever he might have done wrong, there was nothing to fear compared to combat. In fact, nothing in his life ever would be again.

366

Everything else paled. He was ready for whatever surprise Hallard had in mind, ready to counterattack if necessary. He didn't think this meeting had anything to do with staying in or extending. He said nothing, just waited for the hammer.

"Please be seated, Lieutenant," he said, taking a seat at his desk. "I trust you've found your assignment interesting."

"That would be a good word for it, sir," he answered, dryly.

"I've heard good things. You can be proud of your service. More than proud. You've found the Montagnards to your liking, I believe."

"Absolutely, sir. They are incredible," Wagner replied, in a flat, still suspicious tone.

"That's good. I would guess you're not too sure about some of these reconsolidation moves, that true?"

Suddenly it was becoming clearer. Had Bern been worried he was becoming a liability, an interference with his schemes with Ngo? Was Hallard in with Bern? Was he conniving a legal frame to keep him quiet? What did Nichols know? Did they find Hanson's tapes, or.... oh, shit, the reporter. Nickett.

"I think there are some problems, yes, sir."

"Problems, how?"

"Hundreds…maybe thousands, of Montagnards are dying. We're killing them, sir. Our best allies. We're making enemies, V.C. out of them. We move 'em out of some beautiful jungle home and stick 'em in a goddam city. They're dying from every shitty disease you've ever heard of. They're friggin' starving! Pacification? Bullshit." Months of pent up anger and disgust welled out of him in an instant. He hadn't intended it, it just happened. Nothing else mattered, whatever this Army could do, it was nothing compared to what any one Montagnard was subjected to. And he had become part of the problem.

Hallard said nothing. He just stared, an intense expression in his eyes, his hands folded on his desk.

"I do realize," Wagner continued, a little calmer now, "it's not always bad. Some villages actually want to combine, they're scared, they're tired of these assholes stealing their rice and men. I get that. But these huge megavillages, that's just bullshit. That's when we're worse, worse than the NVA. We just kill 'em a different way. We like to kill 'em slow. And we give 'em friggin metal roofs to die under."

Hallard paused a few seconds to make sure Wagner was done. Then his intense expression morphed into a grin. Without saying anything, he pulled a Newsweek magazine from his drawer and tossed it in front of Wagner. "You seen this?" he asked.

Wagner hadn't. But instantly it made sense. Her story was in there. Did she use his name after all? They all asked her not to. But she did, she must have.

"Page 64," he said.

Wagner picked it up, opened to 64. There, in the upper left hand corner, was a Bahnaar Montagnard woman. Gray stringy hair, parted in the middle, tied behind her head. Green Montagnard cone-shaped cigar hanging out one side of her mouth, traditional hand woven dress in black with gold and red trim. A woven bamboo basket hung on her back.

The article's title was **"THE WAR IN INDOCHINA"** Under the picture it said, "*Montagnard woman: Helpless pawn*"

"My God, she even used my words," he said to himself. Reading down further, he saw the name of two villages they had taken her to.

Above the beginning of the story it said, "***People of Sorrow***". Reading on, it said:

For centuries, the montagnards have been the outcasts of Vietnam. Scorned as moi - "savages"- by the dominant Vietnamese who drove them into the mountains centuries ago, they have suffered endless encroachments on their lands and have seen their tribal societies rent apart. Indeed, it was only when U.S. Special Forces embraced the montagnards for their fighting skills and their abiding loyalty that the tribesmen found any welcome in their native country. But as the U.S. withdraws from Vietnam, the montagnards once again are becoming helpless pawns. Within recent months they have been uprooted by the thousands from their highland homes and placed in resettlement camps under a Vietnamese policy that has forced them into a life of degradation and suffering.

The moving force behind the relocation of the montagnards has been Maj. Gen. Ngo, the energetic commander of the highland region which has long been the montagnards' homeland. Dedicated to the concept of pacification, Ngo has tried to achieve that goal by de-populating rural lands. He has moved nearly 35,000 montagnards from their homes and has defended his policy on the ground that is the only way he can secure the highlands. "How can I bring pacification to the people if I don't have enough troops," he told Newsweek's Blake Smith last week. "I am relocating the population where we can control them." Additionally, says Ngo, the montagnard relocation severely hampers the Viet Cong's operations. "One prisoner told us that because we have moved 24 hamlets near the Cambodian border, a Viet Cong battalion has had to split up because of shortages of food and manpower."

But in his zeal to pacify the highlands, Ngo has packed montagnards into refugee camps that have bred death and despair. In the montagnard village of Plei Ko Tu, some 450 montagnard families, who once lived in lush farmland and owned their own water buffalo and pigs have subsisted for four months on roots, leaves and rice. So far, more than 300 of the original number have died, victims of malnutrition, dehydration and diarrhea. And sadly, Plei Ko Tu is not unique. In a second camp, Plei Blang Ba, 56 people have died and an additional 400 others have run away. "The government made a bad decision moving people here," said one American advisor at Plei Ko Tu, "and the montagnards have corrected it with their feet."
Despite U.S. insistence that the tribal relocation is a Vietnamese project, the fact is that American personnel and equipment were used to move the tribesmen to the camps. And official U.S. evaluation reports of life in the Pleiku Province resettlement camps have never indicated problems. As one U.S. official in Saigon stated with a noticeable lack of interest: "We just kept getting glowing reports."

Recent investigations of the resettlement camps have proved beyond doubt that such reports are wildly misleading. And most informed U.S. officials believe that the montagnards' plight will worsen as Vietnamization proceeds. "I don't see any hope for them," sighed one U.S. Embassy official in Saigon recently. They're just going to be pushed around and trampled upon by the Vietnamese until they expire." And in fact some montagnard leaders have taken the same fatalistic approach. "We're a dying race," said one former tribal official. Indeed, the montagnards' tragedy has been increasingly compared to that of another primitive people who were displaced by a more ambitious race. "They're Vietnam's version of the American Indians," said one of the advisers at Plei Ko Tu. "I don't think that they have any future except sorrow."

The story continued about Ngo's involvement with drug trafficking. Wagner stared, thinking, "She quoted me on almost everything in here. Except the parts about Ngo and drugs. Maybe that part came from Saigon or wherever, from another reporter, this Blake Smith," he thought to himself. "But my name's not in here. They can't prove a damn thing, those bastards." Looking up at Hallard, he said, "Pretty much sums it up, doesn't it."

"I understand your concerns, son. I am aware of the problems. Not all of it is within my control. But some, at least, will be. I won't discuss that now. I am not going to order you, I am going to ask you...because I seriously doubt in your case my order would accomplish much on this subject...to stay out of this, at least for a while. I don't want to see you involved, at least not yet. I need you to trust me on this. I don't want you to discuss it with anyone, not even your men."

Wagner looked at Hallard, trying to figure him out. With almost a sneer, he said, "All due respect for rank, sir, *why-should-I-trust-you*?" He and Hallard both remembered their conversation in May, when Wagner's assignment in Cam Ranh Bay was switched by Hallard.

Hallard paused, grinned, and picked up a shiny white 'White Mice' Vietnamese MP dress helmet resting on his desk. Putting it on, he said, "Because I wear a white hat. I'm one of the good guys."

Wagner tried to put it together. Hallard *probably* was a good guy. He *probably* was going after Bern. He *probably* really needed Wagner out of the picture, in order to make a case and take action. It made sense. If so, how long?

"Alright, sir. I sincerely hope I *can* trust you." Then, stepping way out of line again with a hint of a threat, he added, "I already have one war."

Hallard just grinned. "Thank you, Lieutenant. We won't let you down. I promise. I do want you to continue your reports to Major Nichols. I need to know everything, they're important. Nichols is a good man." Standing up, the Colonel looked Wagner directly in the eye and said, "I picked you. Picked Lt. Bailey, too. And Hanson. I like a good team. That Cam Ranh Bay assignment…had to pull rank to get your MAT switched. I needed a leader, someone who has balls and will fight for the right cause. He reached over and shook Wagner's hand. "Be careful, son, There are hostiles out there." Wagner assumed he was referring to the NVA.

He spent the night in Nha Trang. The next morning, as he waited for his flight outside MACV Personnel Operations, he recognized Lt. Dowery, the replacement green lieutenant of the 54th Security group from Holloway. Dowery was wearing his dress khaki uniform. A duffle bag was slung up on his shoulder as he picked up a packet of forms before heading to a C-130 to Saigon. A full three rows of ribbons adorned his chest, under a Combat Infantryman's Badge. The top ribbon was a Silver Star, the highest award under a Medal of Honor. As Wagner began to speak, Dowery saw his eyes drop to stare at his colorful array of medals. "Hi, good to see you, gotta catch my freedom bird," was all he could say, turning to awkwardly run to his plane.

"That filthy sonofabitch," thought Wagner. "The only time he was in the field was that operation with us. There is no way. And a C.I.B… Absolutely no way. That sonofabitch. Now he's a war hero for the folks back home."

Landing back at Pleiku Air Base in the same C-47, Wagner was surprised to see Blas and Stewart waiting for him with the Jeep. "Happy to have you back, sir," Stewart said, his usual big smile in place.

"We are, sir, you missed a little fun."

"Hi guys. What?"

"We had a brief bit of action at Plei Krut last night. Could have used you, Charlie must have known our fearless leader was gone," quipped Blas in his dry humor. "We had some incoming…mortars and B-40s."

"Wow. What happened?"

"Luckily, sir, we jes' finished our beloved bunker, with a little help from our contractors," Stewart said. "We moved in last night. Damn good thing. One a.m., Victor Charles sent in about twenty 82s. Several B-40s. Shredded our tent! Could've used your help with those guns."

"Anybody hurt?

"Two RFs, one pretty bad. We got a dust-off in the morning."

"Wow, sorry I wasn't there. Did Lieutenant Gorman call in arty?"

"Yes, sir, but it took a while. He could use a little help, I believe. But he did good. He was cool."

"Glad no one was hurt. How's the bunker?"

"Oh, it's jes' fine. The rats thanked us. They always know where to go when the shit hits the fan."

Clouds covered the sky for the first time in months. It was still dry season, but not looking like it. The air was heavy and moist. What little air movement came from the south, bringing with it a souvenir of faint pungent smells of denser jungle north of Ban Me Thuot. Sergeant Blas had his 12 gauge shotgun ready, more for nailing doves that inhabited the entrance road to Plei Krut than for NVA. A MAT team had to adapt to survive, they were told. Actually, he just felt like hunting, the squab was secondary.

Arriving at the perimeter, they saw RF soldiers busy improving positions, finally taking action on advisory work so frustratingly promised by Captain Thanh. As the new commander of RF 533, Lt. Hai was proving himself, aided by the previous night's attack. Several impact craters pocked the ground, mostly outside the perimeter. Stewart and Blas were anxious for Wagner to see their mess tent, where Lt. Gorman was, sorting some damaged food.

"Hi, Roy, everything okay..." Wagner looked up and saw the shredded tent. "That was from one RPG?" he asked. The roof had hundreds, maybe thousands of various sized jagged holes.

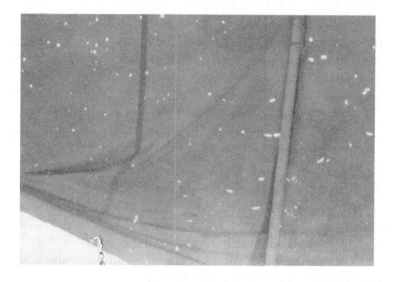

"Just one," Gorman replied." It hit exactly where your cot was,." he said, pointing to a scarfed crater on the red ground. "You would have been shredded, too. Lucky you were in Nha Trang, huh?" *Inches and seconds,*" Wagner reminded himself. "Distance and time."

The village chief and his steam-burned daughter had returned, and a dramatic change was evident among the villagers. Scowls had turned to smiles, not just in the main village, but the satellite hamlets as well. The MEDCAP and subsequent episode with the village chief's daughter made all the difference. Flanagan knew it. His attitude improved. Whether it was self-esteem from his medical contribution or Wagner's threat was unclear. In any case, he did not argue the next few successive medical trips to the side villages. He even did house-to-house medical calls, with Blas or Stewart assisting when they had time. They had won an enemy village over. The chief's word was law.

Kloh had returned as interpreter. It was 1700 hours, the team was joining together to prepare some "montagnard stew"--any stew involving bamboo shoots, rice, and at times, gleaned local additions like squab or even beetles. In the waning sunlight, three RFs approached from the east, one carrying a dark green object. It looked like a wheel, but as they came closer, they could see it was metal, a flat cylindrical shape, a foot in diameter and a half a foot high. It had hand-written letters painted on it. Kloh spoke with the men, turning to address the team. "This...this tank mine. Huge BOOM! " he said, hands up forming a 'Y'.

"Where from?" Wagner asked. The letters looked Russian.

"There." He pointed towards the entrance road from the highway. "Other side of hill." They carefully laid the mine beside the wire by the minefield before walking back to see where it had come from. The RFs were armed with a mine sweeper, assigned to periodically sweep for mines along their dirt access road. They found this one only minutes before. The hole it came out of was no more than a foot from their Jeep track. The narrow dirt road made it all the more unbelievable they didn't hit it. It was an anti-tank mine, capable of blowing their Jeep thirty feet in the air, turning it inside out just as one was on the road to Plei Blang Ba two months before, killing an RF Vietnamese captain. Again, *"inches and seconds,"* thought Wagner. "How many ways can you die over here?" Then he remembered a bizarre story of the unlucky Jeep. "A Vietnamese colonel-- what was his name--he was travelling with a Vietnamese captain driving the Jeep. He told the captain to stop. The colonel got out, and told the captain to drive ahead.

Thirty meters ahead, the Jeep hit the mine. The colonel claimed the little Buddha on a chain around his neck told him to get out, something was dangerous... the Buddha was right. But that name, the colonel, I saw it before, somewhere...Hoang something..."

"Ask them if it had just been put there," he told Kloh. Kloh said four or five words, typically an abbreviation of what they asked to translate. They always wondered what got lost in the process.

"Yeah," Kloh answered. "Knife through. Go through," he said, making a stabbing motion with his hands.

Wagner guessed he meant a bayonet used for prodding passed easily through. "Dirt soft? New?"

"Yeah. Dirt soft. Easy. Jus' do...uhh..new."

Disturbing. He had hoped it had been a dud, put there months or even years before. "Tell them we need the road swept very well every morning."

They would blow the mine in the morning, in a hole next to the perimeter. "We need another foxhole," Blas said. "The lazy man's way. Thank you Mr. Victor Chuck."

Sitting around a small fire for supper, Sergeant Stewart told a story he just heard from Sergeant Fernald, in his words, his 'soul brother' from Holloway. Fernald happened to be the new First Sergeant under Captain Knowles. Seems Knowles and Lt. Dowery, the two officers who had lead the 54th Security team on their joint operations, had a little deal going, putting each other in for medals before DEROSing to the states. Dowery reportedly got a Silver Star for "pulling a man out of a burning Jeep" in front of their headquarters building.

Wagner said, "Oh my friggin' word! I saw that sonofabitch Dowery getting on a plane to DEROS this morning! Three rows of ribbons, the top one a Silver Star. And a C.I.B. You know that was bullshit."

"How in Christ's name do you need to be pulled out of a burning Jeep?" asked Blas.

The talk around the fire bounced around from stories about their kids at home, football, Flanagan's John Wayne, to each soldier's plans after DEROS. Wagner didn't mention whether he was staying in, extending, or getting out. If he did get out, he wouldn't be able to go back to college until Fall, and he had no job waiting, essentially no skills or plans...other than one: touring the west, a long-held dream.

Tung was with them, and Stewart started in on him again, "Tung, you no good, you go back to North Vietnam." Tung just smiled. "You hearin' me? You no good. Damn, man, you just go on back." Stewart wasn't being mean, it wasn't in his nature, and Tung *probably* knew it. But Wagner wasn't sure. Everyone just laughed.

Without warning, Tung said, "Sergeant Stewart."

"What?" Stewart replied.

"You same-same *Con Trau*. Water buffalo. Big, black, ugly."

"What? I oughta whup yo' scrawny little ass."

"Con Trau...you go back Af'ka."

"What?"

"Go back Af'ka. You no good here." Tung was laughing.

"No-o-o-o, man, I been there! They don't want us black folk there!"

A few days later, Wagner got a radio call from Major Nichols. His reconsolidation directive came through. The small nearby satellite hamlets around Plei Krut would be consolidated with the main village on the south side of the perimeter. A collective moan chorused from the men when Wagner relayed the news. It was happening all over again. They didn't know if it was desirable for these villagers or not, in light of recent increasing enemy activity and Americans pulling out. It looked mixed, but hard to tell. Montagnard smiles rarely expressed much displeasure, it was only a guess. It was up to the RFs to tell the villagers to do it, as well as to force them if necessary. The move began one village at a time, one house at a time. A team of sixteen to twenty Montagnard villagers, mostly older men, had to pick up an entire house and hoof it as much as two miles. A typical hootch consisted of a 'post-and-beam' construction of logs, floored and sided with woven bamboo mats, and a thick roof of long grasses. It was a strain for the men to merely lift them, let alone carry them intact for thousands of meters. Most of it was uphill on a gradual rise to the main village, along a grassy foot trail. The MAT team was accompanying a squad of RF soldiers protecting the moves, when the laborers began to falter from the load. Stopping to rest, they were chattering in Bahnaar with one another, obviously complaining of its weight. When they rose from their rest, Wagner and Stewart each stepped under the center sides, bearing a sizable portion of the load, due to a few inches of added height. A loud chorus of the word *"b-r-ronn"*, meaning 'strong' ensued, and the group found renewed vigor, happy to be joined with men they thought they could trust to help. Halfway through the trip, one of the villagers from the rear ran forward to tap

Wagner's shoulder. He was holding a grenade. It had fallen off his web gear when it rubbed against the center column. It was an M-33 'baseball' grenade, round instead of oval like its M-26 predecessor. Filled with 6.5 oz. of composition B explosive, the one-pound round grenade had a square, tightly coiled spring inside the shell, serrated to produce hundreds of 1/8" sharp square fragments. Easier to throw than a 1 ¼ lb.

WW II Mk-2 'pineapple' grenade, it was more effective in wounding more enemy, yet the 70 large external fragments of the old Mk-2 were more lethal, though filled with weaker TNT explosive. He gratefully thanked the man in the marginal Bahnaar he knew. Embarrassed by his carelessness, he replaced it on his belt. "What if this guy was still a V.C.?" he thought. "One more way to get your ass blown away."

So the move progressed over the next two days. The team was successful not only in gaining faith and trust with villagers, but with the RFs. Hai was one of the best Vietnamese counterparts Wagner encountered all year. His company of men had dramatically changed for the better. The compound perimeter was still ragged but improving, and the company's morale was improving with it. He had asked Hai to continue with patrols, difficult for him due to the moving operation and a low head count, which fortunately was increasing. The cripplingly understrength company was growing in numbers, evident by numbers in the perimeter. Lax concerns by Thanh had allowed his men, mostly Vietnamese, to disappear into the city and their villages, but now that was being addressed by Hai.

On the evening of the third day, the skies opened up with a sudden torrent of rain, the first real rain of the season. It rained hard all night, an early monsoon. Water was running into the bunker, in spite of a small moat formed around it. Cots kept them dry, a major improvement over sleeping in wet, muddy foxholes or jungle floors. The rats appreciated the shelter as well, several running over Wagner's poncho liner during the night, followed by a flashlight chase around the ground-level ledge above the cots. One of them bit Blas, who shouted midnight expletives, calling the rat's momma a plethora of bad names. They managed to chew through Wagner's plastic capsule of malaria pills, eating almost all of them. They chewed leather on his jungle boots, ate the jungle hat cord leather slide and for dessert, they ate C-4 plastic explosive chunks placed on the ledge for poison. But they kept coming. "Uncle Ho's breeding these suckers," Sergeant Stewart grumbled.

In the morning, the place looked entirely different. Dry red dirt changed to mud, rivulets of water ran in various paths across the compound. A company of men's boot prints made thousands of muddy mosquito pools in and around the perimeter. First order of the day was to improve drainage and dry out equipment that had been left exposed. They had not had time for breakfast when a call came in from headquarters, calling Gorman into the city for an emergency leave, a death in the family, leaving the team short once more. Moments later, Hai came to tell Wagner "We go now." He had a file of nine men lined up and ready to go, responding to the team's requests for another "Hainh Quan".

"Wish these guys would give me a little advance notice," Wagner said. Stewart's leg was looking re-infected, it was agreed he should take the Jeep back to the 71st, taking Kloh with him. Blas would take radio relay again, leaving Tung and Flanagan. Another 'contest of wills' had occurred the day before with Flanagan regarding another MEDCAP, and again Wagner didn't want to rescind his order. Essentially useless as an infantryman, Flanagan would only be missed as a medic should he need it, but Hai had a Vietnamese medic. It was only a guess at how good he was, mindful of the way the Honda operator had been given 'yank-and-kick' first-aid from uneducated Vietnamese civilians.

With Tung, the patrol numbered twelve. Half were Vietnamese, half Montagnard. They waited the few minutes for Tung and Wagner to throw on weapons and gear, and headed down the same path of the weapons cache. Wagner and Tung both wore 'tiger fatigues', green-beige-black horizontal camouflage striped fatigues obtained on the black market, to look as much alike their counterparts as possible. Hai was an improvement for command, and he had an excellent Montagnard sergeant named K'sor. They worked well together, and the men seemed to respect Hai, who didn't show prejudice if he had any.

The rain had stopped earlier, leaving the grass of the first several hundred meters wet and sparkling, spider webs glistening between blades. The air was clean of dry dust, and smelled different this morning, sweet and oxygenated. The vegetation smelled like it was growing again, in spades, waiting for seasonal monsoons to replenish months of semi-hibernation. Insects enjoyed it as well, tiny ghosts appearing from holes and crevices. Crickets chirped, dragonflies buzzed. Already mosquitos arrived in force, whining in their ears until a late morning Sun would reduce their numbers. The vegetation didn't wait to change into darker and varied greens, it happened overnight.

The small patrol moved through now heavily wooded terrain, quietly and effectively, but Wagner's unease of traveling on a trail was disregarded by his counterpart until they passed the hole that held the cache. From there, Hai directed the file to the left, paralleling the trail by twenty meters. The terrain continued to slope down, gradually at first, then steeper as the Ia Khol stream ran two hundred meters ahead. Trees were taller here, unhindered from drifting mists of Agent Orange of earlier years. Maneuvering through low-lying growth was relatively easy so far after months of dryness, but becoming less so as down-sloping land approached a wetter stream bed.

The column stopped, a soldier pointing to the ground ahead. Each of the five soldiers ahead examined it as they passed. When Hai and Wagner reached the spot, they saw several 6" wide prints in the muddy ground---tiger prints. Wagner hadn't seen a tiger, but one had been killed a few months before he arrived in Le Quon, only two klicks north of the compound. The animal had nearly 4" long claws on it, which were quickly cut off by the Vietnamese for good luck tokens.

Progress was increasingly slow through a now dense underbrush. The stream was only sixty meters ahead. Wait-a-minute vines grabbed at clothing and gear, occasionally poking through thin jungle fatigues with inch-long snake fangs that demanded a halt until picked off. Suddenly Wagner felt his forearms on fire below rolled up tiger fatigue sleeves.

Thinking hornet's nest, his first instinct was to run, but a quick glance down revealed inch-long reddish ants, several of them latched on, oversized Formicidae pincers gripping pinched up folds of skin in a vice grip, injecting their formic acid. Many more ran across his fatigues, attempting to bite through cloth, some succeeding. Brushing frantically and backing away from branches crawling with ants, most of them were off, but stinging like hell. Two had to be pulled off, one leaving its monster pincers still gripping a fold of skin. The rest of the column gave it a wide berth. They turned right to parallel the stream, heading west through even thicker growth.

Wagner always had a keen sense of smell, possibly from never smoking, or maybe that's why he didn't smoke in the first place, he couldn't stand the smell. Now he caught the faint but distinctive odor of a Montagnard cigar. He wasn't sure, with a variety of other jungle odors present. Tapping Hai on the shoulder, he said, *"Khong di. Khong di chuyen."* Do not move. Hai signaled his men to stop.

"I maybe smell a montagnard cigar," Wagner whispered in Vietnamese, pointing into the light air moving from their left. Most of the men grew up in an environment of indoor culinary smoke and cigars, and smelled nothing unusual.

Hai whispered to K'sor, who guided the small file to the left, where Wagner pointed. Slowly, intently they moved, crouched so low they were almost duck-walking. Vegetation grew thicker a dozen meters ahead, obscuring a view of the point where K'sor led. Within a minute, a series of **POP POP POP POPs** from M-16s broke the dreamy stillness of a peaceful jungle. Wagner immediately had his radio handset in his ear, ready to call Sergeant Blas to relay a fire mission. The file moved quickly ahead. Breaking through a light clearing, they saw K'sor and two other soldiers with three shirtless Montagnard men, hands raised. Looking down, Wagner saw another, blood spurting out of his chest, eyes wide open, unblinking, staring at Wagner's boots. One hand still gripped an AK-47. One of the shirtless men was yelling "Chieu hoi, chieu hoi!" K'sor was yelling at the men, grabbing one and slamming him against a tree. Pulling a .45 from his holster, he slammed the barrel into the man's temple. The prisoner had a terrified stare, saying nothing. K'sor yelled again, jamming the barrel hard into his temple. The man said something, before K'sor began to pistol whip him. Blood was coming out of several gushing wounds on his face before Wagner stepped forward to grab K'sor's upper arm. Maybe he should have stayed out of it. Maybe if he had been K'sor, had shared his years of hatred and killing he would do the same. Maybe if it wasn't a Montagnard being beaten to death... *"If I was a Montagnard, I'd be a V.C.,"* he thought again. "K'sor, please.... K'sor...."

K'sor glanced quickly at Wagner, then back to glare at his prisoner. He yelled at him more, but the man just said, *"Innhh, Ooh-ka-butt"* several times, almost crying. (*He didn't know.*) Then he repeated, "Chieu hoi."

Without Kloh, Wagner had to rely on K'sor's limited English to translate, telling him, "'Chieu hoi' only works if you give up voluntarily, not if you surrender." As K'sor slowly relayed the information, the prisoner's face sunk in fear, as if to say, "Oh, shit."

Hai radioed his men at the compound to send another patrol down to retrieve the prisoners, while Wagner radioed Sergeant Blas to relay the activity to Headquarters and to have the Kontum artillery pointed towards his pre-planned fires, where he would adjust if needed.

Noise discipline gone, Wagner worried about their position. K'sor's men searched the dead man, finding nothing but a small silky confederate flag. It was stained with old blood, never washed. Two small holes were almost imperceptible with frayed edges and blood. In twenty minutes, a fast-moving 5-man patrol of Hai's soldiers arrived and escorted the men back, leaving the dead man where he lay, staring into the woods to send a message to his V.C. brothers. The patrol continued down a steeper slope until they hit the Ia Khol. The stream was only two meters wide where a foot-thick log lay across. The night's rain had brought the stream from a narrow, languid creek to a swift stream four feet deep. Normally clear, the water had become a reddish fog of eroded soil and debris. The wet mossy log was slippery, but navigable. The first five men, carrying a minimum of gear were across before Wagner. His PRC-25 radio, water, ammo bandolier, grenades, and rifle made the going precarious. Almost across, his feet flew off the log as if it were ice, hip slamming the log on the five-foot drop into the Ia Khol. Holding his rifle up with one hand and quickly grabbing a limb with another, he quickly sprang out to save the radio, their life line. The others were laughing, especially Tung. Resuming the march west along the stream bank, Tung insisted he walk in front of his American friend, saying, "No trung-uy, I go first...first. It my duty." This was the first of many times Wagner would find his Kit Carson a solid ally, seeming willing to protect him with his life.

Continuing along the southern edge of the stream, they crossed several small tributaries, contributing to the Ia Khol's current by their own rain swollen flows. Mosquitos were out in force, surviving through the dry season in this life-blood source of water. The column stopped, men crouching with weapons pointed into trees. The vegetation was markedly more open on the other side of the stream. Meter-wide holes in the dirt bank were easily visible through sparse growth along the opposite side, a meter higher and three meters from the water. They waited, watching without movement or sound for four minutes, all weapons off safety. The stream was wider here, but still deep, and fast flowing. To cross here would invite disaster if they made contact. Slowly, the file angled away from the bank, heading further downstream in deeper cover. Initially a straight flow, the Ia Khol now snaked and twisted for 500 meters until a deep, narrow section afforded a crossing opportunity. A large tree had bridged what now had grown into a small river. An array of dead branches stretched in all directions where it lay on the opposite shore. One man crossed at a time, the others watching with safeties off. This bridge was no less slippery than the last, the soldiers crossing on all fours, looking like humongous Fuck you lizards crossing a window sill, one leg at a time. Again, it was Wagner's turn, and again, he slid off the log. Fortunately it was on the far end, over water only 2' deep. Even though shallow, he managed to submerse most of his body, but kept his rifle and radio dry. They were laughing again, but quietly.

Now the file moved back up the stream, heading back east toward the bunker complex. Nerves on edge, senses tweaked, safeties off, the men moved slowly and quietly. Wagner radioed Sergeant Blas to call for a fire mission on a pre-planned target, with a "wait one" ending. It would be a PIA for the artillerymen to scramble to the guns, turn them to the target, all for nothing if it wasn't needed, but Wagner didn't care. "There wasn't much of any activity these days, they need the exercise," he was thinking. "If we need it, I want it right now." This was one of the smallest groups he had ever been with, and no Americans with him to boot. And in the worst enemy-active area in the province, maybe in the country, in an artery of the Ho Chi Minh trail. The previous Special Forces camp situated here having been overrun didn't help his confidence.

After four hundred meters, the objective was just ahead. Sergeant K'sor was walking 'slack', or second man from point, when they saw the first bunker, twenty feet from the water. The area was open except for well-spaced trees providing overhead cover. The ground indicated heavy use, hard and well packed from many feet. They remained motionless for a quiet wait of five minutes, Wagner and Hai crouching together twenty five meters back. Seeing no activity, K'sor and two soldiers approached the opening. "The guy has balls," Wagner thought. "Great little soldiers."

K'sor went inside cautiously. Forty seconds later, he came out and waved the patrol forward. He found nothing inside, saying only "they sleep here". They continued on to the next bunker, another dozen meters through more sparse saplings and trees. The procedure was repeated. Nothing. Not one bunker had been attempted to hide, no doors, no camouflage brush, nothing. They had enjoyed seclusion safe from U.S. or ARVN forces for a long time, at least since the Special Forces were here years before. Two more bunkers east along the shore produced nothing before the fifth bunker held five AK-47s and two boxes of magazines, all full of 7.62 mm rounds. Wagner was half expecting an explosion in each one, wired for intruders, but it didn't happen, obviously from their enemy's over-confidence. K'sor seemed to know. The last two bunkers were empty.

The patrol reversed its course, heading back along the river, heading west again along the snaking section. "Never follow the same trail back," Wagner reminded Hai, and he listened. A hundred meters before the tree crossing, Hai luckily directed the file to turn right, up gradually up-sloping but smooth, thinly vegetated terrain heading back toward Plei Krut. Forty meters ahead, a waiting trap of Montagnard V.C. watched as their plans went awry, foiled by the file no longer walking into their L-shaped ambush. Seeing their chance fading, their leader told them to open fire, though their kill zone was far from ideal. Trees and earth received the brunt of their fire, formed centuries before by a previous course of the Ia Khol in an area otherwise unprotected by rises in the ground. Every soldier hit the ground instantly, weapons still off safety and firing toward the sounds. Though the numbers were small, the noise was deafening. Grenades were blowing up twenty meters away, thanks to deficient throwing arms from an enemy who didn't play baseball. Wagner was instantly on the radio, calling Blas for artillery relays. "Taking fire. From X-Ray seven niner, add 400, right 100. azimuth 4400 mils, one round Whisky Papa, will adjust. Danger close. Shot and splash, hurry it up, over."

As Sergeant Blas relayed the order, Wagner found one of the few times he actually used his M-16, usually too busy calling in artillery and coordinating with counterparts. On full automatic, his M-16 was firing in short bursts, three rounds for each simple trigger pull, followed by bursts of seven to ten rounds, emptying 20 round magazines in seconds. He saw no targets, just leaves and bushes blowing from automatic weapons. The last two rounds in each magazine were red tracers, to indicate an empty magazine. Those rounds traced the source as well, answered by several sharp *Craaccks!* overhead and blue streaks of tracers, in turn answered by Hai's men with rounds directed at their tracers' source. Wagner pulled a grenade from his web gear, pulled the pin, and threw it as far as he could, the one-lb. olive drab ball rolling into the trees where the tracers led. The blast was followed by screams, repressing their fire for brief seconds, allowing a suppressing fire from Hai's men. Shortly after he threw another, with the same results from the RFs, and the firing subsided. Wagner asked Hai if he could send men to flank the right, as the enemy had no choice but to depart north and west, the river blocked the south. Hai didn't want to do it, and Wagner couldn't blame him, with only twelve men. One was dead, another badly wounded and bleeding out. After what seemed hours, Sergeant Blas called on the radio to say, "Shot out, sir."

A half-minute later, a 155 round of white phosphorus landed three hundred meters south. "Tell them 'Drop 100, left 100, one round of HE quick. Will adjust, over."

Sporadic rifle fire began to spring up again, answered by rapid firing from Hai's men. When the 155 high explosive round came in, it stopped. Wagner called Blas again, "Five Seven Bravo, tell them 'Drop 100, Right Five-zero, three rounds HE quick, on an azimuth of 1600 mills. Fire for effect, over.'"

Sporadic firing picked up again, and only four minutes later Blas radioed in his Guamanian accent, "Five Seven, this is Five Seven Bravo, shot out.". Three rounds exploded simultaneously in the woods a hundred meters ahead, on target. The firing stopped. Wagner called for three more rounds south of the last target, followed by three more north, trying to catch a retreating enemy.

As soon as he sent the targets to Blas, Hai told him one of his men was shot through his hand. Wagner looked over to see Hai's medic working on him. The soldier didn't talk, he made no noise. Seconds later, traffic on his radio came in from an "Orbit Two Niner". The voice was clearly agitated, complaining "These people on the ground aren't ready, somebody had better get their sierra (phonetic for shit) together."

"Orbit Two Niner, Orbit Two Niner, this is Gray Phantom Five Seven, Gray Phantom Five Seven, over."

"Gray Phantom Five Seven, Orbit Two Niner. What the hell is wrong down there, I've got four Fox-Fours full of ordnance and low on fuel. I need targets and clearance, I need it now," he yelled, obviously irritated. Fox Fours were F-4 Phantom jets, re-directed from a scrapped mission somewhere. They did not like landing with bombs. Wagner had the only activity in Vietnam at the moment, and whatever mysterious powers controlled it, they had redirected this forward air controller and his Phantoms to him.

"This is Gray Phantom Five Seven, over," Wagner answered. "Who the hell are you again, over?"

"Gray Phantom Five Seven, I am a FAC! I've got four Fox-fours low on fuel. I need targets now! I suggest you get your shit together."

It took a second to sink in. After a miserable day and not really appreciating some Air Force Major forward air controller yelling at him, Wagner answered, "Listen, you sonofabitch...I had no idea you were up there. I am tired, wet, scared, and I'm all alone with nine little people down here. You talk to me that way again and I'll shoot you down myself! You just wait a minute and I'll get you some goddam targets!" As angry as the pilot was, it paled compared to Wagner. "Be advised I have arty on the way from our

November. I will cancel that fire mission. Wait." Another first. Wagner had never sworn or outright threatened a senior officer before…but what the hell, he was Air Force.

The Cessna O-2 Skymaster, nicknamed "Oscar Deuce", was a two-engine, push-pull propeller, double-tailed observation plane used for forward air control (FAC). It was an improved replacement for the smaller and slower O-1 Birddogs. Wagner couldn't talk directly to the jets, he had to give the FAC the coordinates and adjust, whereupon the FAC would talk to his jets, and mark the target with white phosphorus rockets for his 'fast-movers' to annihilate.

Calling Blas again, he told the artillery to cancel, needing confirmation. Getting back to the FAC, he said, "Orbit Two Niner, be advised artillery is being cancelled, but through my relay. I have no commo with the arty myself. This may take a minute." After a check of the map, he sent his coordinates to the FAC. "Anything along the November side of the blue line is fair game, to the Whisky of my location. I'm marking with smoke now." The 'blue line' meant a river on the map, November was north of it, and Whiskey west.

Calmer now, the FAC replied that he understood, and apologized. His jets had very limited time in the air, barely enough fuel to return to base.

Finally, the confirmation came across, the FAC hearing it as well, the artillery call was cancelled. The O-Deuce Cessna banked, the pilot clearly visible in a cockpit built for observation. He dropped low, sending a WP rocket slamming into the earth. Thick white smoke bellowed out of the jungle canopy. "Perfect," said Wagner. Now, along the blue line heading to the whiskey of that round." Now he could see the four Phantoms, just small silhouettes in the sky, circling high above. The engines made a faint roar, similar to jetliners, but sharper, crackling higher frequencies. Suddenly, small rounds cracked overhead again, from the same area of the initial ambush, answered again by the RFs. The pace of fire was growing. The faint roar of the Phantoms high above became louder, interspersed with a crescendo of small arms fire. Capable of a payload of 18,650 lbs. and costing 2.4 million each, they had a top speed 2.2 times the speed of sound. Their shape gave them a distinctive and ominous look of a raptor, with upturned wings and downward angling tails. 63' long, and 38' wing spans carried an armament of 500 lb. HE bombs, napalm bombs, and an M61 Vulcan cannon delivering 6,000 rounds per minute, or 100 a second, of 20 mm--3/4"-- lead ball or incendiary rounds. Fully loaded with weapons and fuel they weighed almost 21 tons each. Thirty seconds later, the first camouflaged Phantom came from behind and to the left, like an eagle diving on prey. It banked in a steep sideways turn, condensation trails streaming like white smoke over its wings. It roared over the trees not a hundred meters away, leveling out on a 'dry' run, not expending ordnance. The second Phantom did the same. Circling around for a second pass, they screamed in like a Thunderbirds show over Boston Harbor. But Thunderbirds didn't drop bombs. Big ones. Two 500 lb. cylindrical shadows fell from its wings, sending a concussive wave through chests and heads, felt before it was heard, the jungle blowing away in limbs, earth, and trees. The second jet followed, dropping further west, then the third and fourth, each followed by an enormous crunch of composition B explosive. Small arms fire immediately stopped, not to return. "Beautiful, Orbit Two Niner, beautiful. Looks perfect."

"Roger, understand location is on. Stand by."

The next pass was more impressive. Two shiny cylinders dropped, tumbling in flight....napalm. With a fraction of the noise from the HE bombs, fire exploded skyward from the river banks, cooking tall trees, sending a wave of heat across their small squad. From 50 meters away, they had to turn to shield their faces. Following Phantoms dropped more napalm successively to the west.

"Orbit Two Niner, I have beaucoup bunkers along the blue line, to the echo of your first bombs. Suggest you concentrate on that."

More passes, more bombs. Finally, heavy ordnance expended, the FAC asked Wagner if they could rake the area with 20 mike-mikes. Wagner answered with, "Roger, Orbit Two Niner, but keep it along the river. I don't want any civilians around the paddies or hootches to the November hurt, over."

They banked again, one after another ripping the jungle with 20 mm Vulcans. Each round weighed 3.5 ounces, the recoil of bullets at 22 lb. per second actually slowing the huge jets in flight. Like the Stinger, there was no machine gun noise, just a thunderous roar like a high speed chainsaw. A dark cloud of large brass shell casings showered down from the nose. All firing had ceased, whatever enemy was out there were all dead or scared to death, with good reason. The fighter-bombers had dropped or fired a total of 37 tons of high explosive, high velocity and burning ordnance in a matter of minutes.

The jets left, low on fuel and out of ordnance. The FAC stayed, at Wagner's request. "I can use all the help I can get," he said, now amicable with the spy in the sky. If nothing else, he still had three white phosphorus rockets under his wings. Walking toward the river, An eight foot diameter crater of red, rockless dirt still emitted lazy, white plumes of smoke slowly drifting from the walls of its cone shaped walls. The composition B had a sweet, pleasant smell to it, mixing with chlorophyll of shattered leaves. A lack of rocks had always been the norm, but the crater was evidence that none existed even at depth. Radiating out from the crater sides were saplings and small trees, all pointing out like bicycle wheel spokes. No trees were left standing for 20 meters all around, leaving a carpet of green leaves covering the ground, knocked free from the blast. Trees farther away were splintered in two from shrapnel. Along the nearest standing trees, Wagner found a twisted, quarter-inch thick bomb fin. "Soov'neer?" asked Tung.

More traffic ensued on the radio net, mostly from highers anxious to get involved. "Orbit Two Niner," Wagner said, "we've got a lot of traffic, could you drop down a dime, I'll meet you there, over?"

"Roger, sounds like a winner," came the reply.

"You copy, Five Seven Bravo?"

"Roger, copy," said Sergeant Blas. Dropping 10 Hz to a lower freq, they had the radio net to themselves, and highers didn't interfere.

Walking on, they passed more craters. They crossed the river, wading through a wide spot 4' deep, up the opposite bank through a bamboo thicket. The RFs had a false sense of security after the air strike. They became noisy and careless. Coming to the area of the napalm strikes, they walked between a wide swath of treeless growth thirty meters wide and a couple of football fields long. Only low vegetation and grasses remained, now burned black by thickened fuel. Tall tropical trees bordered the swath on both sides, Wagner looked up and saw what looked like large gobs of gray snot hanging from branches. Smoke was coming from the side of the hill across the stream as well. "Orbit Two Niner, I'm seeing smoke, black smoke, coming from the side of the hill to the Sierra of us, can you tell, over?"

The O-Deuce banked, dropped down, and flipped over, flying upside down *between* the swath of trees. Near the end of the swath, he rolled it right-side-up and rose up, saying, "Aw, yes, just some old Nape that didn't burn." More 'snot' was visible smoldering from high limbs of nearby trees until they exited the open swath area and entered a thick bamboo jungle. The RFs were chattering now, and smiling. "Can't see you now, Five Seven, you okay?"

"Roger, this is getting worse, the RFs are gathering bamboo shoots, wait one."

"They're what?"

"Getting food. Wait one."

Wagner complained to K'sor, who complied with a few harsh words for his men. Further into the bamboo, they saw the devastation from the 20 mm Vulcan cannons. Nearly every tree was splintered and broken from thousands of large, high velocity bullets. The ground was churned and fluffy where they impacted, uprooting small trees in the process. Soon, the FAC radioed he was running low on fuel and had to RTB. The small patrol continued on, quieter now, progressing slowly up a steep hillside. Suddenly, Wagner felt nauseous, faint, a weakness in his thighs. He blamed it on heat and the extra weight he was carrying compared to the rest of the patrol. He was ashamed to show weakness or inferiority, to the RFs and Tung. He was becoming dehydrated, but didn't realize it. In the excitement, fear, and fast pace of the day, he had forgotten to drink. Big mistake. Hai noticed it, but noticed exhaustion in his men as well. He stopped the men on a hillside, covered in chartreuse-leaved bamboo. Still observing noise discipline, they sat and snacked. Wagner recognized his negligence, and drank most of his canteen. It had become oppressingly hot and humid. His clothes were still soaked from the river as well as sweat. Mosquitos found them, whining in droves. Reaching inside his shirt to scratch an itch, he felt a soft wad of gel. Three leeches were attached to his chest and stomach, another in his armpit, swollen with blood. Removing his pants, he found two more. A few drops of insect repellent quickly shriveled them up and they dropped off. He wondered how they could find their way inside clothes in such a short time, probably all from the river. A loud piercing scream broke the jungle quiet. It sounded like someone holding a blade of grass between cupped hands and blowing on it. *"SCCREEEEECH!"* Again and again. Several times. ***"Who the hell is doing that? What the hell?"***

Tung leaned over and said, "Trung-uy---*Con khi*."

He couldn't remember what a Con khi was.

"Mun-ki. Mun-ki," he said as he pointed up. Above them, sitting between the trunk and a branch of bamboo was a medium sized orange-brown ape, half-hidden by bamboo leaves, screaming at them.

"So much for noise discipline. Let's get the hell out of here, Hai." Quickly moving out, they hadn't gone twenty meters before an experience months earlier was repeated as they stepped around another pretty chartreuse-green bamboo krait snake, watching warily from a head-high branch as each soldier passed, leaning away and pointing to it. *"Inches and seconds."*

The patrol headed back toward the ambush location, approaching now from the opposite end, from the west, to encircle and hope to find stragglers, if any. Despite the noise and confusion, Hai and K'sor thought it wasn't a large force, just a 'hit and run' action, though Wagner didn't see a lot of running until the artillery hit. Except for some blood spatters and traces, they found no bodies or pieces, not even blood trails. "If they escape, they prob'ly underground," Tung said. That would be most likely, but the highers wouldn't like it. They wanted body counts.

Almost back to the perimeter, they were met with a ruckus of yelling and screaming, yelling and screaming. Entering the wire, they saw their three prisoners, laying on the ground, hands tied behind their backs and ankles bound, clad only in undershorts. A Vietnamese RF soldier was standing above them, holding a sharp 4' bamboo slat. He yelled, then lashed their backsides. Again. And again. Their legs and backs were bleeding from a score of long cuts. Each lash brought more screams.

Blas, Flanagan, and Wagner stood watching for a moment, wondering who was in charge. This was torture, and Wagner knew it wasn't condoned by the U.S. military, that would be his responsibility. But this was a Vietnamese issue, and not his call. *"Again, maybe if it wasn't a Montagnard prisoner…"*

Wagner hesitated, then walked quickly to the scene, as Flanagan reproached him, "Stay out of it, Lieutenant. It's none of your business." He kept walking, and Flanagan repeated it, "Stay out of it, Lieutenant."

Ignoring Flanagan, he gripped the Vietnamese by the upper arm, telling him to stop, in Vietnamese. The soldier glared at him. Wagner was tired, irritable, and just plain fed up. Fed up with Flanagan, fed up with Vietnamese treatment of 'his 'Yards'. He was yelling now, ordering the soldier to get the hell out of there, disregarding the 'you cannot command' rules of an adviser. Flanagan was still yelling when Wagner turned and yelled back, "That's enough, Sergeant! Time to mind *your* business. Understand? Get your damn medical bag and get your ass over here with it. UNDERSTAND?" Twenty minutes later, a Vietnamese truck arrived from Pleiku to take the prisoners away. They had a rough road ahead. They may well have been better off with the Vietnamese soldier.

As if the day's events weren't enough, that evening the RFs were firing 60 mm mortar rounds outside the perimeter. Each one produced a loud *BOOM* of fast burning propellant, sending 2 3/8" diameter rounds out a half kilometer in a 60 degree upward path. Wagner had just turned to go inside the tent when a hollow *WHUMP* came from the mortar tube. Looking back, he saw a round silhouetted against the sky, forty feet up, just reaching its apex to fall back to earth. The RFs had allowed the propellant bags to get wet in the recent rain, resulting in only the igniter charge inside the tail partially firing. Wagner, well inside the casualty radius with no immediate cover, wheeled and sprinted for the Jeep trailer, several feet away. Barely reaching the backside of the steel trailer, he dove in a belly flop on hard, muddy ground as he heard another, lighter *thump* of the round hitting the ground. A safety device in the detonator, inactive from too few revolutions out of the tube, prevented it from arming itself. "*Inches and seconds*....sort of," he said. "One more way to get killed over here." If that wasn't enough, that night an older Montagnard villager left his temporary "resettlement" tent given him during the house move, apparently to relieve himself. A nervous RF perimeter guard shot him. The M-16 bullet left a tiny mark where it entered, but his backside was blown apart, instantly killing him. *Onehelluvaday.*

The action attracted a lot of attention. There was little happening in other areas of the country by 1971 outside of Cambodia, and news quickly travelled to Nha Trang II Corps headquarters, even to MACV headquarters in Saigon. The stories would grow embellished, even more so by anxious reporters in the cities hoping to add feathers to their career caps. Hai's commanders wanted a body count. They didn't care that he had few men or that he had limited resources and limited reinforcement capability. They wanted numbers, driven by American commanders in Saigon.

Sergeant Stewart returned in the morning, his infection healed and given a clearance from the hospital. He brought with him news that Lieutenant Gorman wouldn't be returning for several days, and that Agent Orange would not be available. It was causing too much notoriety in the states, reportedly causing cancer, seizures, and a variety of other ills, besides ruining Vietnamese civilians' crops. Most didn't believe it, and the men were upset they couldn't protect themselves from enemy crawling through their adjacent minefield because people back in 'the world' were complaining. What harm could a vegetation defoliant do to a human?

The days passed, days mixed with rain and sun, and Plei Krut's resettlement continued. Montagnard men of twenty or more moved larger-than-normal grass roofed homes from surrounding villages. Interesting and confusing at the same time, some groups of homes, or hamlets, seemed to relish the idea of moving to a safer position while others reviled it. The further from the main village, the more the latter prevailed, but even the men from the latter smiled as they carried their homes. It was a Montagnard trait, and it was hard to read. Rain had added significant weight to larger homes, built of larger logs. The team helped carry the enormous weight of some homes, while not one RF soldier helped. One hootch, hoisted on twenty four men's shoulders, creaked and groaned as they hoofed up a slight grade. Suddenly they heard cracking, and twenty four men scrambled as the post and beam roof racked rearward, collapsing on wall columns below.

Early the next morning, Wagner and Hai were called into Pleiku for a debriefing of their previous enemy actions, but the majority of the focus was again on resettlement progress. A Vietnamese colonel was present, along with Colonel Robichaud and Friedman. The meeting didn't last long, and Wagner held his comments to an absolute minimum. Much of the discussion was between 2Lt. Nguyen Hai and the Vietnamese colonel, too fast for Wagner to follow their flow of Vietnamese. Before they left, Colonel Robichaud told them, "A general is going to be visiting with you tomorrow, Major General Charles Green. General Green is the II Corps MACV commander."

After the meeting, Hai wanted to show Wagner a bit of the city and invited him to meet his family. As they walked along the main street of Pleiku, Hai reached over to hold his hand. It was a Vietnamese tradition, friends held hands... they taught it in advisory schools, just part of the custom, drawing a series of entertaining comments from the class. This was the first time it actually happened. Embarrassing, weird, but expected. So here he is, a lieutenant, in red dirt-filthy tiger fatigues, walking with a five and a half foot thin Vietnamese in tigers and a beret, holding hands... as a full deuce-and-a-half truck loaded with American G.I.s passes by, all staring....
With a grin, he waved.

The visit with Hai's family went well. They were polite, soft-spoken, and obviously educated, the reason Hai was an officer. His father was missing his arm from just below the shoulder, a war injury of the Viet Minh war twenty years earlier, not long before Nguyen Hai was born. The family had seen decades of war, atrocities, and hardships. They were extremely proud of their lieutenant son, but understandably fearful for his life, tenuous at best. A family lunch was a welcome respite from the LRRP ration-and-rice team stews of late. Wagner thanked his counterpart's family, arranging to pick up Hai after a swing by the 71st Hospital before returning to Plei Krut.

XII SACRIFICE

"The intentional loss of material to get a more important result. Often the start of a combination."

He had not seen Annelle for six weeks. The same gnawing doubts haunted him. Whatever military confidence he gained through the year didn't much carry over to his social life, not here anyway. Each time he saw her, it quickly returned, only to fade again after days, weeks, even months apart. Would she still like to see him? Has she latched on to some new Jody by now? A doctor, maybe? Entering the pool area, same routine, a quick request to a passing nurse to tell Annelle he was there, and a desperately needed shower and shave in any case, in the pool's men's room. When he walked back in the sunlight, wearing cut-off tiger fatigue shorts for a bathing suit, she was already there. Feeling a veil of relief, he sat by the pool, talking with her as if they were together yesterday. Again, Annelle had heard the news of 'a small battle somewhere north, near Kontum', and again, it was his. He recounted the Phantom strike, the angry FAC, the bunkers and tortured prisoners. "The Phantoms, I think, were the second highest point of the year, so far," he said"

"Sounds exciting. What was the first?" she asked, quietly thinking…her?

"The Cobra. Definitely the Cobra. If I had better eyes, I'd be a pilot, I'd probably make it a career."

"I like your eyes," she answered.

"I like yours," he said, smiling. "Absolutely beautiful."

The pool felt so good, a far cry from leech-ridden swollen waters of the Ia Khol. Sun and security, a nice respite. Sitting on the pool edge, Wagner asked her again when she was DEROSing, what her plans were, had they changed…he wanted to ask her what he'd been thinking about for some time. His decision to get out, extend, or make a career might depend on it. Time was growing short. "Annelle....

"Have you decided what you're going to do back in 'the world?" she said at the same time. "I mean, are you going to stay in?"

"ESP again. I was just going to say, I plan on getting my last year of Engineering done, going back in the Fall. My DEROS date is May 12. My dream for a long time has been to tour the west. I've saved most of what I've been paid, on top of what I got for my '65 Corvair and my bike just before coming here. My plan is to buy a Chevy El Camino, a new Yamaha 650, and a small travel trailer. I can throw the bike in the back of the Camino, and just travel through the west."

A long pause. She just looked into the pool, her hair still wet and clinging to her neck.

Wagner was looking into the pool as well. Turning his eyes to her, and not giving it a snowball's chance in hell, he said, "...Want to come along?" Immediately, she said, "Okay."

Wow. He really had given it little to no chance. Just a shot. She actually said okay, she didn't even think about it. "Now," he told her, a concerned look in his eyes, "you wouldn't have to worry, no commitment, if you don't like it, you're not happy, whatever reason, you want to go home, I'll either get you there or get you a plane or bus ticket, I promise."

She just looked at him and smiled. "I'll be getting out in April. I'll be going to Kansas, I have to see my family first..."

"My aunt lives in Garden City. My Mom will be coming to visit her, probably. You can be with your family for a while, I can extend for a month, I can visit with my mother, then I could pick you up?"

The conversation continued with plan details, where each wanted to see and tour, friends both pre and post-Army to see....though both shared a disappointment in having seen most of their friends grow distant. Marriages and military resulted in vast differences in culture, experiences and life-style; things no longer in common that couldn't be understood by others. They both found that apathy was a factor, forming a veiled rift from friends' inability to comprehend their staggeringly different experiences. Those events couldn't possibly be duplicated, that rift sometimes taking years to overcome, sometimes never.

That was it, the decision-maker. He had been on the fence regarding staying in or getting out and being home in May. If he stayed in, he would immediately make captain on the twelfth of May, simply by signing up for another year. Or he could ETS from the Army and finish school in September. He was leaning toward going home anyway, but Annelle sealed it. It came down to a sacrifice of a military career or an extension. What a great summer it would be, the first in six long years. Strange, though, with never a kiss or touch he had basically committed to a romantic bond with a beautiful girl he had talked to in total hours, not in days or months or years. Crazy. But great.

With tentative plans made, Wagner once again had to leave the 71st. Picking up Hai at his family home, they made the drive back to Plei Krut. His mind was not on war or the heart-wrenching plight of the Montagnards.

In the morning, Wagner's team of NCOs unanimously asked to take the Jeep into Pleiku while the General was visiting. Wagner thought this strange, but they knew of this General Green and wanted no part of it. Many of Hai's RFs were gone for the day as well, others were catching up on sleep in their bunkers. Still others just tended to family affairs, as some lived in bunkers with them, unimaginable as it seemed. So only Wagner and Tung represented MAT 57 when the call came in at 0930. The General was on his way. Two-star Major General Charlie Green, II Corps MACV commander, was flying all the way from Nha Trang on the coast. No doubt the recent enemy activity stirred some interest. There wasn't much more going on elsewhere in the country, at least among the advisory teams which fell under Green's command. Mainly, it was a 'flag showing' from the General.

Outside of the eastern end of the little perimeter afforded the best landing zone with regards to level, open ground and relative safety from snipers. Over the horizon to the east, over QL 14, three small silhouettes grew larger, larger, until Wagner could tell there were three Hueys coming in a line, the second and third slightly to the right of the one in front of them. The ground was damp, a small blessing over 'DDLs', or dry dirt landings. Distinctive *'WHOP-WHOP-WHOPS* of three Hueys became louder as the familiar shape of Bell UH-1 helicopters approached their perimeter. "God, I love those things," he thought. "Beautiful." Popping yellow smoke, he guided the pilot in on his PRC-25 radio. All three circled the village area twice before the middle one banked for a quick drop and flare-up landing. Waiting for the blades to slow, Wagner crouch-ran to the open side, holding his bush hat tight against his head. A portly man, 5'-9" tall with two stars on his helmet climbed out, not without a little difficulty. His collar insignia indicated his branch was Infantry. Behind him stepped another man, 6'-2", slender but solid, with his dark eyebrows and eyes visible below his steel pot helmet. He was wearing full bird colonel cloth insignias and an artillery branch insignia sewn on his collar. Wagner, still in a crouch, said, "Not sure if I should salute, sir, I've been told not to in the field." A salute made officers a sniper target.

"That's fine, Lieutenant, no problem," he said, returning a quick salute while crouched under the Huey rotating blades. The two officers were followed by a short, stocky man Wagner recognized as Colonel Bah-Nah, the highest ranking Montagnard officer he knew of. Bah-Nah's command of II Corps Mike Strike Montagnard Forces included Major Buhm, and Wagner had worked with him before. The General acted surprised that the two knew each other. Colonel Bah-Nah, like Buhm, was a very impressive leader, somewhat quieter and not as well known to the RFs and villagers, but a man to be respected, even revered among his men. The American Colonel was Green's aide, Colonel William Carter.

The Huey never shut down, rotary wings spinning slowly for a quick take-off if needed. The 4-man entourage walked under the 47' diameter blade path in a crouch until they cleared the danger of increasingly drooping blades. The two other Hueys, gunships, kept circling, 180 degrees apart the entire time.

Some small talk, then General Charlie Green wanted to talk a little about the battle and the Phantom air strike. Colonel Carter stood a meter to the side and behind the General, occasionally rolling his eyes as the General talked. The Huey gunships kept circling. "Well, Lieutenant, let's take a walk of the perimeter. Where is your team?"

"They had a bit of a necessary scrounge mission, sir, we needed some supplies after the recent action."

"Now, I want you to tell me if you're alright here, if you think you've been put out on too much of a limb, so to speak?"

"It's okay, sir, I think we'll be alright." Wagner saw Colonel Carter clench his teeth and roll his eyes as if to say, *"What're you, nuts? What does he expect you to say?"*

Walking the perimeter, Wagner had a feeling Colonel Bah-Nah was being led along like a puppy, disrespected. All advisers, the General included, had been trained to advise, not command. Try to respect, and above all, never cause your counterpart to 'lose face'. Now the General was walking the two-foot perimeter berm beside Colonel Bah-Nah, making an official inspection out of the show. Colonel Carter walked behind him, with Wagner. Spying several M-16 live rounds laying in the mud next to a firing position, the General bent over to pick up a round which he thrust in Bah-Nah's face, yelling "What's this, Colonel Bah-Nah?"

Bah-Nah said nothing, just stared with a whipped puppy look. Colonel Carter leaned toward Wagner with a hand covering the side of his mouth, "It's a fucking bullet, you idiot," he whispered. That caught Wagner by surprise, but it confirmed what he thought the Colonel was thinking.

Finding more rounds, he repeated the show, shouting "Do you know how much this costs the American taxpayer, Colonel? Twenty one cents! Twenty one cents each! What are these doing lying around in the mud?"

Carter repeated his move, whispering, "That's gonna break the economy....you think Bah-Nah knows what a taxpayer is?"

Next came the 60 mm mortar pit. It was actually pretty strack after the fiasco with the wet mortar bags, but Charlie Green was yelling again. "Where are the firing stakes for this weapon, Colonel Bah-Nah?" Turning to his aid, he said, "Colonel Carter, you're an artillery officer, shouldn't there be firing stakes for this weapon?" The Vietnamese and Montagnards both commonly used the small 60 mm mortar in a hand-directed mode, without stakes, and were surprisingly accurate from years of practice. It sped up their firing rate considerably, and they rarely used the weapon in an 'adjusting fire' scenario where stakes would improve accuracy. Like horseshoes, close counts. Colonel Carter leaned towards Lt. Wagner again, "The fucking idiot doesn't even know it's not artillery, it's an infantry weapon." Wagner was embarrassed for Colonel Bah-Nah, but now he was stifling laughs at Carter's digs. In front of firing positions, Claymore mines were placed near the wire, per the norm. They were covered with pieces of old ponchos for protection as well as camouflage. "What's this for, Colonel? Why is this Claymore covered?" he shouted at Bah-Nah. Colonel Carter leaned back and whispered, "To keep the fucking thing from getting wet you idiot." On it went, more face-losing reproaches, until the General completed his 'showing of the flag'. Wagner asked him if he wanted a tour of the village where the relocated hootches had just moved, hoping to show him the one that collapsed. The General declined. "Now if you think your highers are putting you in harm's way out here, I want you to let them know."

"Yes, sir, I think we'll be alright... Colonel Bah-Nah's soldiers are great, he replied, looking at the Montagnard commander. I think he's a great leader." Colonel Carter stood behind Green, smiling with an understanding nod of approval.

"One more thing, Lieutenant," said the General. "Do you have any rocks around here?"

Thinking he meant "ROKs", or Republic of Korea soldiers, he said, "ROKs, sir?"

"Yes, I want to send my son a Montagnard love stone."

"Oh,…rocks. No sir, I haven't seen a rock all year, except in stream beds. It's all dirt here."

Before the three men boarded the waiting Huey, Colonel Carter leaned toward Wagner and over the noise of the turbines and blades, said, "Colonel Hallard speaks highly of you. Stay safe." The gunships still circled until they lifted off to return to Nha Trang.

The team returned a few hours later. Wagner hadn't really lied to the General. They actually had made a successful scrounge mission, including the procurement of new jungle boots to replace the second pair issued nearly a year ago, rotting away above the soles. Fresh food for rats.

"Looks like we lost Lt. Gorman, sir." Blas said. "He got switched to another team. Teams are getting disbanded all over. He's been called to a team down south, somewhere near Ban Me Thuot. We're back to a four man team."

Every day it rained. The early rainy season was there to stay. Warm muggy nights were replacing cool, at times cold nights. Mud replaced blowing dirt. Mosquitos replaced…..fewer mosquitos. Leeches replaced fewer leeches. Reconsolidation house moves continued, every day more brutally heavy houses were man-carried to new locations, drawing the attention of NVA human leeches seeing their supplies dwindling.

It was March, the team had been living in and operating out of Plei Krut for nearly a month. Evening was overcoming a hot afternoon and a strong shower just ended, leaving an eerie green glow in a muggy falling sunset over Cambodia to the west. Days of intermittent strong rains left a dank, clammy smell to the days and nights, worse in the bunker. A stench of ratshit-fed mold grew more intense. Sergeant Flanagan was sitting on the bunker, monitoring the radio inside, their 33' antenna enabling commo. A slightly elevated voice called for Gray Phantom Five Seven. "Sir, we got a call for ya," Flanagan snorted. He sounded like it was an inconvenience.

Handset to his ear, Wagner said, "This is Gray Phantom Five Seven, over."

"Roger, be advised, we have reports of red haze moving toward your position from several locations, southwest, west, and northwest of your location, over."

The call curled his gut. Infrared had picked up enemy troops advancing from several directions, a coordinated attack, not a probe or harassment. "Careful Apple Two Niner, Gray Phantom Five Seven, understand red haze headed towards me, give me coordinates and numbers, over."

A lot of static ensued, finally clearing, "Gray Phantom Five Seven, this is Careful Apple Two Niner, be advised, we have no coordinates, they're telling us that many groups are heading toward you, three directions, all I have, over."

Wagner was irate. An OV-10 Bronco reconnaissance plane had flown over, equipped with modern infrared capabilities. It carried on-board computers capable of giving coordinates within 10 meters using triangulation from several towers. That's what they're for. *"You have no coordinates? What the hell are you telling me? I don't want to hear that shit, you get me those coordinates now!"* He had no idea who or what rank he was talking to, and could care less. As with the radio net, every person in the country is there for support of the man in combat at the moment, and some clown wasn't doing his job. Their very lives may well depend on it. The other team members were huddled around the bunker now, knowing something didn't bode well, "Get Lieutenant Hai over here," he told Flanagan, while waiting for a reply from Careful Apple. Finally, he heard, "Gray Phantom Five Seven, this is Careful Apple Two Niner, negative on the coordinates, we don't have that info for you, but the range is now between two and three klicks, over." Wagner was fairly screaming in the handset. Several attempts, back and forth, brought no better results.

Hai came running from his command bunker. Wagner and Tung explained the situation. Hai felt the same gut-wrench that his counterpart did, quickly wheeling to yell to his company. Men popped out of bunkers like ants, running to firing positions and the mortar pit. Others ran through the open wire-and-bamboo gate, the last man wrapping barbed wire around the poles to secure it.

Wagner was on the handset, calling artillery. "Busted Tackle, Busted Tackle, this is Gray Phantom Five Seven, Gray Phantom Five Seven, *Fire mission*, over."

"Roger, Gray Phantom, This is Busted Tackle Two Eight, go."

"Busted Tackle Two Eight, this is Gray Phantom Five Seven, I have bad guys heading toward us from three directions, coordinates unknown at this time. Get your guns pointed my way, have HE Victor Tangos ready, I will send coordinates, wait one." The flat lowlands in the directions the enemy were advancing from were open and wet, much of it wild rice paddies. HE-Quick-Detonating rounds lose killing power in the water and mud. Victor Tangos, 'variable time' fused rounds explode a few meters above ground, yielding a far better killing radius unless in the trees. If there were trees instead, they would explode harmlessly high above, making the standard quick-detonating shells the choice. In just over a minute, Wagner picked several likely avenues of approach on topo map foot trails meandering through recently rain-filled 300 meter wide shallow lakes that laced the area. "Busted Tackle Two Eight, Gray Phantom Five Seven, sending coordinates, Zulu Romeo Seven...."

Elements of NVA soldiers from the K394th Composite Battalion of the 95B Regiment, in green uniforms and pith helmets, carried their AK-47s, mortars and RPGs along the narrow Montagnard foot trails in the dim light of a crescent moon. They were fearful and apprehensive, as every soldier would be, but dedicated and resolute. They wanted very much to kill their enemy, especially Americans, and they knew there would be four there. They had days, weeks to prepare, with an extensive knowledge of their objective: numbers, weapons, locations, perimeter. The element of surprise had been heavily in their favor until the Bronco's infrared spoiled their day. The trek toward Plei Krut was a confident hike at night, nothing more, ending in a surprise attack on a sleeping, unsuspecting enemy. No one could know they were coming, the reason for breaking their unit into small groups, all the way from the Cambodian border. Almost undetectable. Almost. Most of them were very young, some very old, gleaned from the North's heavily attritioned resource of men. Dedicated, but most were young and inexperienced in war. Some were breaking noise discipline, ragging on their buddy ahead of them in the file, more intent on staying on the dimly lit trail than on....

Before he was through, Wagner had a dozen coordinates, with no range or azimuth, telling the fire base to 'spread them around'. "Will you adjust?" asked the other end. "Negative on adjust, I have no visual. More coordinates to follow. Keep'em coming." Ten minutes passed before the first rounds hit, loud crunches breaking the stillness of twilight. Air bursts a few meters above the earth sent a distinctly different sound from ground-transmitting concussions of standard HE-Quick rounds, even at this distance. Hot, humid air transmitted noise faster and louder than weeks before, and less hampered by forests of trees in open areas to the west. Between lakes and above rice paddies, bright instantaneous flashes and concussions sent searing hot shrapnel radiating out at five times the speed of sound, tearing vile paths through anyone unfortunate enough to be in the kill radius. Deadly air bursts sent thousands of ripping fragments, more deadly than bullets, into and through small North Vietnamese bodies. Men were screaming and crying. Commanders ordered them to run, run out of the kill zone, difficult to do without leaving the trail and getting mired in mud and ponds, where more shrapnel rained into them. The kill zone was a misnomer, the entire area was a kill zone, there was no safe place to hide. Wagner had chosen his fires well, and spread them over many klicks. The lakes and ponds were his friend, the enemy's enemy. Men became disoriented and separated, others lay dead or dying, horribly torn apart because of *inches and seconds*. Wrong place, wrong time.

Wagner asked Careful Apple for new infrared info. "Negative, the Bronco left, low on fuel" came the reply from whoever Wagner received the call from. He thought of the idiot at Holloway ordering the Firefly Huey to RTB. He badly wanted that infrared. He was only guessing. How many. Where. Did his artillery have success? Calling many more 92 lb., 2 foot-long 155 mm shells, he mixed some white phosphorus in with the HE-VTs, hoping for more panic and confusion among whatever was heading his way. The bright white smoke, illuminated by burning phosphorus, helped to know the directions of his targets. The enemy could see their own dead and dying.

In the village, older Montagnard PSDF civilian '*Minute men*' crouched in foxholes outside their hootches in the outlying remaining small hamlets comprising Plei Krut. They held M1 Garands and M1 Carbines, standard issue WW II weapons. The Garand was a fine weapon, despite its age, firing a powerful 30-06 bullet. The Peoples Self Defense Force was the same here as everywhere else, old men protecting their immediate village.

In the perimeter, seventy five Vietnamese and Montagnard RF soldiers lay waiting in bunkers and firing positions. Those that had families huddled together. Eight more men waited in listening posts outside the perimeter. The artillery was now down to H & I fires, a few rounds every thirty minutes. Wagner loved spending taxpayers' dollars. There were plenty spent tonight.

Men were on 50% alert, half sleeping, half on guard. The moon was lower in the sky, affording little light. There was no wind, no noise. At precisely 0230 hours, muffled explosions broke the silence off to the west and north, mortars leaving their tubes. Silence, then **CRUMMPP CRUMMPP CRUMMPPs** of 82 mm rounds landing outside the compound, all 50 meters short.

Two LPs outside the perimeter were running back, Hai and Sergeant Rok are yelling to their men not to shoot, always a terrifying risk for a listening post soldier.

Wagner runs the twenty meters to enter Hai's bunker, wanting targets from Hai's listening posts. More rounds are coming in, walking closer, through the wire and into the compound. The two Vietnamese LPs are crazy-excited, yelling in Vietnamese, too fast for Wagner to understand anything but *'phao-binh'*, artillery. Seconds pass, Hai scribbles some coordinates for Wagner, who sprints back to the team bunker, as three more mortars explode across the perimeter. Almost reaching the bunker, exploding shell flashes expose two rats beating him inside as shrapnel kicks puffs of dirt to the left. Barely touching the three steps down, he checks the targets and calls Busted Tackle. The guns are quick, clearances still viable from earlier calls, pointed and ready. For once, no other chatter interferes on the radio. Huge **CARUNNCH!s** of 155s land, blowing trees apart in close support to the north. The west requires more range and accuracy, there are still remnants of one unmoved village there, PSDF and R.D. Cadre soldiers around it in foxholes. *Can't call too close.* Each call requires a *'Danger close'*, close enough now to require Wagner's initials as well, a liability issue for the fire base. Sprinting another trip back to Hai for adjustment fires, two more mortars land off to each side with a flash of light and sounds of shrapnel zinging and panging off bunkers and Jeeps. Something hits his upper back, but it's nothing more than a stinging punch, almost painless under adrenalin. Wagner chases in two more rats, as Sergeant Stewart says, "Even the rats have sense enough to keep their ass in here, sir."

"Tell me about it," Wagner replied. "Quick, look at my back, here," he said, pointing. "Something hit me. Am I bleeding?"

Holding a flashlight, Stewart said, "Don't see anything, sir."

After intermittent fire from the north, the incoming mortars are finally subsiding, squelched by the 155s. The remaining LPs are now running in, with Sergeant K'sor yelling at his men not to shoot. Safely inside, the LPs run to their bunkers and the north side opens up with small arms fire, a few rounds at first, then a crescendo for only seconds, withering and dying. Three seconds of silence before pops and cracks of AK rounds send blue tracers flying slightly high across the compound. Another return sprint to his bunker, Wagner thinks he sees flashes from his artillery in the woods, but he's too hurried to be sure. Tall grass, already regrown from Blas's M-60 'lawnmower' blocks most of his view. Three more round trips to Hai's bunker and subsequent 155 rounds to the north bring the battle almost to a halt. A few RFs fire out of the north side, thinking they might have seen movement, their nerves fried. But soon, no more return fire. Hai yells something to them. Wagner is adding subsequent rounds, targets farther from the north perimeter, hoping to catch retreating NVA while only a small remaining force cover their retreat. The skies are beginning to lighten to the east, sending a hint of solace with it after an exhausting adrenalin drain. There would be no overrunning of the compound on this night. Another half hour sees a faint orange glow over Mang Yang Pass, pushing a light azure blue veil, in turn pushing violet, indigo, blue and black curtains toward the west. The compound grows lighter, light enough to chase the demons of the night into their nooks and crannies. Amazingly, Hai reports only eight light casualties among his RFs, all shrapnel wounds, not even a need for a dust-off chopper. Sergeant Flanagan works with an RF medic, requiring only bandages and gauze. Headquarters is already on the horn, looking for body counts. The team saddles up for a check on the outer village where the PSDFs were.

They accompanied two platoons of RFs, moving rapidly to the small hamlet. On arrival, they saw old PSDF and RD Cadre soldiers, some sitting and some standing, but saying nothing, just staring at the approaching RFs. The enemy had snuck into the village from the south, approached the poorly equipped Montagnards and from as close as fifteen feet fired B-40 RPG rockets and threw satchel charges into their positions. One older Montagnard, wearing nothing but a loin cloth and an old military shirt, was already dead and wrapped in a poncho. Both boots, still laced, had been blown unexplainably off his feet. Another was bleeding from his face, scalp, arm, side, and both legs. His head was wrapped in bloody bandages so that only one agonized eye was visible. Every minute or so he would sit up and emit strange animal sounds. He must have known he was going to die. Wagner saw their face and hands were blackened, as if by creosote. He didn't know that this was the appearance of flash burns. He had seen it before, but didn't know it, they never taught that in training. Another Cadre was shaking uncontrollably from the concussion of a satchel charge, while still another had a bullet wound in the stomach, the bullet passing through his side. Behind a hootch, a woman was crying. Below her lay an older man, another Cadre, with no visible wounds, but dead. Walking back to the wounded men, the RFs were holding up bamboo backpack baskets, soaked in blood, with several small homemade satchel charges in them. The charges were made of sandbag material, held with bamboo ribbon strips. Another backpack basket, soaked in dark drying blood, held two unfired RPG rocket rounds, one of them pierced by a bullet between the explosive canister and piezo-electric firing cap at the nose. The bullet had killed the enemy soldier that carried it. Wagner called for a U.S. dust-off for the wounded men, but they would not comply when he couldn't confirm the LZ wasn't still hot and not U.S. personnel injured. Flanagan did what he could, but it wasn't much, in light of the severity of their wounds. Finally, Wagner

convinced the dust-off chopper pilot the area was secure, and they were headed their way. While the other team members worked on the wounded, Wagner directed the Montagnard RFs in pigeon talk to form a litter out of a poncho and two nearby poles. When the dust-off Huey came in, the pilots insisted it be quick, they emphasized "in and out". They came in hot, flaring up and landing fast. The team ran carrying the other wounded, while Wagner and an R.D. Cadre picked up the burned, one-eyed man on the litter, running to the chopper. Fifteen feet short, one of the rotten poles broke, and the man rolled onto the ground. The one eye looked at him, then rolled up in its socket. Wagner picked him up and ran to the chopper, wishing he had done that in the first place. The rotten pole was his choice, his fault, and it may have killed the poor man. *Strange how those seemingly lesser events in a year of many can stick with you. The man's face would stay in his memory forever.* He didn't know if the man died or not while lifting him in. The

Huey lifted off and was gone, but if he was alive, his chances were slim, indeed.

Returning to the perimeter, the team inspected the damage. None of the other villagers or the RFs' families were hurt. But lying next to one of the bunkers were a half dozen baby goats, the same ones he'd seen playing so happily weeks before. They had no marks, no blood, but they were dead. They, more than most of the human carnage Wagner had seen during the year, conveyed a sadness of innocent beings destroyed by war. He felt like crying, and probably would have if he could be alone.

The Colonel wanted a body count. Wagner had no idea, but simply told him they found nothing but pieces and blood. He figured it was better to let the gooks drag them off, "Gives 'em something to do and it sends a message to Uncle Ho-- you send 'em down, we waste 'em. Don't screw with us, Uncle assHo." He had heard about inflated body counts, but never saw it or was told to do it. If the highers ever created one, he was not involved. If anything, they had a lot of unknown kills never reported.

XIII CHECKMATE

"A move which attacks the opposing king, and which the opponent cannot get out of."

Major Nichols arrived at Plei Krut with Blote, his body guard, the next morning. The team was still assessing damage and planning a resupply ammunition scrounge mission when his Jeep pulled in. After a thorough discussion with the team of the battle, Nichols turned to Wagner and said, "Could you come with me, Lieutenant?" as he turned toward his Jeep. Wagner thought this strange, wondering what he may have done. "I have some news," he said, looking sternly into Wagner's eyes.

After a short delay, Wagner said, "Yes, sir?"

"Sergeant Flanagan is being court martialed. The investigation is complete on the shooting in August. It was his pistol bullet." Wagner just stared, trying to comprehend. "It wasn't just that, Flanagan has a history, well before your arrival. I know he's been a problem, this just finalizes it. It's way above an Article 15."

"What happens next?" Wagner asked.

"There will be MPs here later. Say nothing, to no one. Just make sure he's here this afternoon....and your team will be returning to Le Quon in two days, your job is done here at Plei Krut. Another thing...I'm DEROSing. I've stayed to see this through. I'll be gone in a week. I'll go over it with you. Temporarily, at least, you'll be taking my job. You'll be the new District Senior Adviser. Congratulations."

"Early outs" were the norm in the Spring of 1971, crazy in light of the hundreds of thousands of dollars spent in training men primarily for war. Induction centers through Basic, AIT, Jungle Schools, Officer schools, Airborne, language schools, Command and General Staff schools, to RVN training, all for one purpose: To go to Vietnam and kill the enemy. As with nearly any job, nothing prepares you like OJT: "On-The-Job Training." War is no exception. But instead, after learning the lessons of war, the enemy, the country, Uncle Sam wants to send you packing. When Wagner had attended a mandatory "DEROS or Extend" meeting, he strongly considered extending, but only for a month or two. He would not have a decent job before returning to school, he had nobody needing him home, but he wanted to help the Montagnards. He knew his job as never before, and he had a great team. Two or three months off for the summer would be plenty. He could use another month or two of Army pay for school. Truth be told, the job was exciting as much as it was interesting. If nothing else, the advisory job was exciting. A lot of veterans felt it, a lot of them extended, a lot of them signed up for one or more additional tours. He explained to the Specialist handling the extensions, "I only want to extend one month or two to mid-June or July."

"Yes, sir, but because you're an officer, we can keep you six months."

"That won't work," he answered, thinking of Annelle and school in September.

"Sorry, sir, those are the regs."

With those words, the Army lost an experienced, knowledgeable, dedicated and extensively trained volunteer soldier. All because of a system's 'regs'. Crazy. But not as crazy as their 'Early Out' program, sending experienced and knowledgeable men home well before their one year tour was up.

When the Major left Plei Krut, the men were waiting for some revelation coming from Wagner, but he said nothing, wondering what the team would think. He had nothing to do with Flanagan's arrest, but would they believe it? Their opinions were important, and he despised 'management by fear' as he had seen often in his short career. It didn't matter that they were all growing 'short' in their tours.

Shortly after 1200 hours, a Jeep appeared over the crest coming into Plei Krut. Pulling into the perimeter, the big E-6

Sergeant riding shotgun asked, "Is there a Sergeant William Flanagan here?" Blas and Stewart stood staring in disbelief, saying nothing, as the Sergeant read Flanagan his rights and handcuffed him. Flanagan was still swearing and threatening when they drove off.

"What the hell, sir?" Sergeant Blas said.

"That's what Major Nichols was here for this morning," Wagner said. "I want you both to know I had absolutely nothing to do with this. No knowledge whatsoever, it was as much a surprise to me as to you."

Doug had just finished processing Dulane's, Bailey's and his own early outs. He was wondering whether Wagner would accept one, when the sound of vehicles outside drew him to the window. Outside were two U.S. military police V-100 'Big Wheels', and three MP Jeeps. Several hard-pounding feet entered the building. Outside his door, he watched eight MPs enter, led by Colonel Hallard. Four held CAR-15s and four had side arms, clubs and handcuffs hanging from their waists. Striding swiftly across the orderly room, they stopped at Colonel Bern's office. Bern rose from his desk and walked to where they stood by his door. "Oh my God, they're here. I wish Wagner could see this," Hanson thought. "They're gonna hang the bastard."

Hallard and Bern exchanged a few words, then Bern walked to Colonel Robichaud's continually closed door and opened it. Inside, Robichaud and Friedman were seated in old French upholstered chairs, talking and smoking cigarettes. Startled, they looked up to see Bern with a squad of helmeted MPs behind him. Robichaud rose from his seat, saying, "Colonel Bern," what do we.... then he saw the MPs moving swiftly toward him with handcuffs. Colonel Hallard said, "Colonel Robichaud, Mr. Friedman, you are under arrest for...." as the MPs grabbed and handcuffed them,.....you have the right to remain silent..."

Bern stood smiling, eyebrows furrowed in a deep vee.

"Colonel Robichaud...Mr. Friedman... it's over. It's over," he said.

Doug stood outside the door, his mouth wide open. He had no idea....

Wagner received a radio call from Hanson that evening. Doug didn't go into detail, only that "the issue they had been working on" had come to fruition and he'd like to talk with him. Wagner, receiving a visit only that morning from Major Nichols, told Hanson, "We're vacating Plei Krut, mission's over. See you in two days."

The team left Plei Krut, glad to have made it through unscathed, save for leech, thorn, ant, and rat wounds and only a tender spot in Wagner's back. No question, it had been the hairiest month of the year, with more close calls than the entire rest of the year, and too damn remote. Le Quon was looking good, its showers and food even better. The first surprise was finding Team 46 had been disbanded. Le Quon only had Major Nichols left, and he, too, was DEROSing. His best friend, Gordon Bailey, had already been shipped home with an early out. He didn't have a chance to say good-bye or talk of plans. It was the only thing this Army ever did fast, DEROSing and discharging. After the team settled back into their home at Le Quon, Wagner drove back to Pleiku to meet with Doug Hanson. He had not heard the news of Robichaud's and Friedman's arrest.

"You should have been here!" Doug almost yelled in a loud whisper. "It was unbelievable. You just *had* to see their faces! Cat's ass! Best day of the year. I had no idea."

"It was Robichaud and Friedman all along? What about Bern?" Wagner said, astonished.

"That clever bastard kept it hidden. He was working with Hallard the whole time. It took a friggin' year, but they got them. It was only about drugs. Hallard said he couldn't do much about the reconsolidation lands. That's a Vietnamese thing, 'out of his hands' he said."

"So Robichaud was the drug honcho? The body-stuffing, all that?"

"Yes. Bern was sent here in part to control the whole thing, kind of a sting. He worked with Hallard, the military investigative officer,…

"But Friedman," Wagner said, "….he was CID, right? Criminal Investigation Division. He had jurisdiction over the military who might be suspected…"

"Right, Doug interrupted, "But he was in on the whole thing. He was working with the OSI, Office of Special Investigation. They forged documents that were flawless in sending bodies back with heroin. I'm told the CID has been involved a lot over here. Huge bucks to be made."

"Un-freakin' real," Wagner said, staring at the floor, feeling a little upset for blaming Bern. "Jerry know?"

"Jerry's gone. But yep, he knew just before he left."

"I didn't have a chance to say goodbye, to Gordon or Jerry."

"I'm leaving, too. Two days."

"You bastard!"

"Bitch!"

"Nuts, nothing more about stealing land, though?" Wagner asked.

"Too bad they couldn't do more about Ngo and the reconsolidations, I know how you feel about…"

"I guess I can tell you now, Darryl interrupted. "I was sent to see Hallard early this month. He had asked me to keep this quiet, he said something to the effect it was under his control…to trust him."

"And you did? Trust him, I mean?"

"I thought so. Wasn't sure. But he said 'some of this wasn't under his control. I assume that was regarding reconsolidations, land stealing."

"That's too bad. I thought my recordings might help. After the arrests, I gave those to Bern, by the way. Just left them on his desk. I didn't want him to know where they came from, just in case, before I got the hell out of here. Guess we can't do much for the Montagnards."

"Well, there is one thing. Hallard had a copy of Newsweek. Told me to read it. 'Page 64', he said. It was a full page story on Plei Ko Tu and Plei Blang Ba, two of my villages. That reporter, the freelance reporter woman reporter I told you about? She quoted me on almost everything in her story...except the drug part. I had no knowledge whatsoever about that. There was a lot about General Ngo."

"I had no idea. I'll have to get a copy. Do you think that might help?"

"I hope so. Another thing. Just before I saw Hallard, I dropped some letters off to home. Plus one more. To Newsweek. The report you copied? It's in their hands."

"Oh my God. Fantastic. No names, right? I mean us?"

"Don't worry. No names. But that does bring another name to mind. Hoang Dinh Tuan, one of the two colonels on the bottom of that report? I knew I'd seen that name somewhere, but couldn't remember where. I finally remembered. It was from a story a counterpart at Plei Blang Ba told me, about a Vietnamese Colonel. This Colonel sent his Jeep and captain driver down the dirt path to their village because 'a Buddha around his neck told him something was dangerous'. That sucker's name was Hoang Dinh Tuan. The Jeep and captain were blown to hell from an anti-tank mine. That had to be a murder, as my guess. I just reported that and info from your reports to Colonel Bah-Nah, our highest ranking Montagnard officer. I don't know what will come of it, but the man has ways..."

It was late March, and MAT 57 said good bye to Major Nichols, he was DEROSing home. As District Senior Adviser, he was a good leader, a good person and friend. Nichols truly had the interests of his men, the civilians and soldiers, and the country at heart. It was hard to see him leave. Temporarily, Lieutenant Wagner would serve as the new District Senior Adviser, a position normally held by a field grade officer, major and above. There wasn't much added responsibility, everybody was leaving the country like rats leaving the proverbial ship, adding to a feeling of being deserted and forgotten. Even half of their artillery was leaving, their life-savers. A Sergeant First Class Ronald Kaltz was dropped in via a Huey mail run. The team no longer had a medic, and though Kaltz was an Infantryman, he volunteered to pick up the slack as best he could. Other than every soldier's medical training, he had none, but hopefully the needs would be minor for the remainder of the rest of the team's tour, all coming up soon. Kaltz loved learning the medic trade, loved treating the villagers, loved the interaction. The team liked him immediately.

The team had just finished a Claymore class and MEDCAP at a village not far from Mang Yang Pass. Approaching a mountain turn, an American gun truck came speeding toward them, taking up the center of the road, not far from their road ambush months ago. It was leading a convoy that had hit a mine, got shot at, and were barreling out of the pass. Assuming everything on the road was Vietnamese this late in the war, they were fully prepared to crush anything in sight, like a small Jeep. Sergeant Blas was driving, Wagner riding shotgun. Blas had nowhere to go but the shoulder. The M-151 independent suspension caught the soft dirt and immediately folded the front right wheel. The Jeep rolled, Wagner holding onto the windshield with his left hand, M-16 in his right. It seemed like slow motion. It was all in control, he was bailing out, ready to roll into a grassy bank below. Suddenly, the compressed spring above the axle released its potential energy. It kicked the Jeep like a spooked frog, the windshield frame slamming solidly into Wagner's chin. The M-151 rolled on its side, sending Wagner tumbling through the grass. His vision filled with little bright starbursts blinking like flash suppressors. Looking back he saw a furious Sergeant Blas on one knee, jacking his M-16 and pointing it at the lead gun truck. The one with the quad fifty machine gun. "NO-O-O! Wagner yelled, diving for Blas's weapon. Blas's Guamanian temper was trumping all reason. Wagner would never know if he was actually going to shoot that truck.

The convoy never stopped, and why would they? They just got shot at, it was their job to get the convoy to its location, not to win a firefight. And it was '*only*' a Vietnamese Jeep as far as they knew. The Jeep was easy to right, and had no damage. Wagner said he was fine. That evening, his jaw started to swell. His chin didn't bother him, it was his jaw joint that was becoming painful. Then the radio call came in from the TOC. Timmy, the RTO, came up to tell them, "A report from Saigon...a possible regimental-sized NVA unit is right behind our compound. Part of the K394th of the 95thB NVA Regiment, they said. They're supposed to be cutting off the highway to the coast, and holding Le Quon, the district headquarters as a psychological victory. They're doing the same thing fifty klicks south, down QL 14 near Phu Nhon."

XIV   DEFENSE

"A move or series of moves taken to protect a piece or position which is under attack."

NVA activity had been increasing across I and II corps, and Pleiku Province was a hot spot. MAT 57's village intelligence net, part of the efforts to provide the Cobra pilot info in August, confirmed the report from Saigon: "a large body of troops were heading west, toward Le Quon, about fifteen kilometers out." Another source told them "a possible battalion sized force was seen moving through the mountains, travelling west, now eleven clicks out." The team quickly began coordinating with their RF company defending Le Quon, when an American convoy pulled in to the gate. One of their trucks had hit a mine, blowing half of its front end away, causing several hours delay, and were late getting to Holloway in Pleiku. It was almost 1800 hours. Someone told them they had Americans at Le Quon, so erring on the side of caution, they decided to pull in for the night.

"Very happy to have you," Blas told them. "We like your gun trucks."

They had four, armed with single, double, and quad-.50 machine guns, along with M-60 machine guns and mortars. After explaining the current enemy situation and their four-man American numbers, the transportation unit looked stunned. They weren't as pleased as the team was. "We could have made it to Holloway in fifteen more minutes," complained a young driver. "So shit, we pull into this compound where it'll be safe and find we got half the fucking North Vietnamese Army outside the door."

Wagner slept on his stretcher on the tower, staying awake until 0100, scanning the perimeter with his big starlight scope, seeing no movement. A single shot an hour later had him rolling off and into position in one fluid move. He felt no grogginess, no cobwebs, instantly alert, senses tweaked. The shot came from their Vietnamese command post guards, 60 meters away. He heard Vietnamese yelling, some automatic fire from an M-60…then *Boom! Boom! Boom!* Three RPGs exploded almost simultaneously. He already put Blackhawk on notice, their guns were pointed towards them, clearances done. Enemy mortars began falling like rain, walking from the Vietnamese end toward him. "Sandy Panther Two Five, this is Gray Phantom Five Seven, *fire mission*, over."

"Roger, Five Seven, go."

"I need three rounds on Delta Tango Lima seven niner, azimuth 3200 mils, space 'em out 100 meters, over."

The gun trucks were positioned around the quadrants of the American end of the compound by the team house, latrine, and volleyball court. The berms were too high to fire over for the gun trucks, they could only help if the perimeter was breached. Wagner watched from his lofty perch as a mortar blew up behind the back end of the nearest gun truck, 30 meters to his left rear, sending shrapnel pinging off the team house metal roof below him. The blasts from incoming and outgoing kept shutting down the overload feature on the starlight, rendering it useless trying to spy enemy sappers coming through the wire. He called Holloway, hoping to find his Cobra friend, who had unknowingly DEROSed to the states, along with much of Camp Holloway. Wagner had a sick feeling that the intel for once was right, this was no small attack. Blackhawk had not yet fired, but called back, "Gray Phantom Five Seven, this is Sandy Panther Two Five, should have a shot in about one mike, over."

"Roger, understand one mike. Give me shot and splash, over." While waiting, a bright white incendiary flare ignited from the left north corner. It was attached to their corner Hirsh flare. It lit the thickened fuel in its bottom pan, heating the M4-thickend fuel inside the canister. In twenty seconds, the cigarette filter plugging a quarter inch hole in the top blew out, sending a stream of boiling napalm ten feet in the air, lighting the perimeter corner. More firing erupted from that corner, indicating there might be sappers coming through the wires.

The Hirsh flare killed any chance of seeing through his overloaded starlight scope. It also lit the tower where he stood. He sank a little lower, peering over his sandbag wall. Now the RFs are pumping out big four-deuce mortar rounds, strangely silent until now. Their outgoing blasts are adding to the noise and confusion, mixed with small arms fire. Enemy tracers indicate the enemy is firing from the far tree line, mostly high with several rounds searing near his tower. From excitement and adrenalin, he forgot about his jaw, swollen like a chipmunk. It had swollen more, a bulging target for a radio handset swinging into it when Blackhawk calls back. He hears "Shot out, over", and bangs the phone into his jaw, sending a wave of pain through his temple while he waits a half minute for the rounds to hit.

"Splash" comes the call, as bright flashes light the trees to the north, trailed by rustling, cracking sounds through the air, finished with faint booms from their source to the east. A subsequent call for "Drop 100" brings several more rounds in an array closer to the perimeter, walking closer, as close as he dares unless they have enemy in the wire. He prays that won't happen, more afraid of an errant shell than the enemy. A call comes through from Headhunters, the helicopter assault company at Holloway. "We are on our way to your Lima, over."

Wagner calls Blackhawk to hold fire, birds on the way." Two Huey gunships arrive, seeing all four corner thickened fuel Hirsh flares marking the perimeter with brightly burning 10' high streams of thickened fuel. Miniguns blazing, sounding like chain saws, they annihilate the east, north and west sides of the compound, some 7.62 mm rounds hitting close enough to be in the wire. Red burning tracer ricochets are bouncing wildly in crazy directions off the ground in a brilliant display. A huge explosion of thickened fuel and white phosphorus blows out of the north berm directly north of Wagner's tower, causing the pilot of an approaching gunship halfway through his last run to bank his chopper wildly to his right, panicked by a ball of fire almost enveloping his path. "What the hell was that?" he yelled into his headset.

"I believe one of our RFs just popped a perimeter barrel, you okay?" As happened in the past, the house-sized ball of fire stopped both sides from firing for a minute.

"Jee-zus, what are you trying to do to us?"

"Sorry, shit happens. I had no idea. I'll..." Another explosion rocks the tower, a bright blast directly below Wagner and an acrid smell of dirt and TNT permeates the air around him. The radio is going wild with chatter. Phu Nhon, fifty clicks south, is getting hit. The frequency is alive with another MAT team calling for support. Phu Nhon sits right on QL 14, the village Tim had just passed the intel about. The attack is quickly dwindling on Le Quon, the real attack is at Phu Nhon. Le Quon was the diversionary target. Occasional mortars and B-40 rockets are still coming in, but far fewer. In Phu Nhon, pandemonium and yelling mixed with serious, but calm voices fill the net. Their MAT team is doing its best to coordinate artillery, RFs, ARVNs, U.S. gunships, and finally four American dusters and tracked armored personnel carriers (APCs). They are receiving heavy fire from a large force of the same K394th of the 95B NVA regiment. These are well-equipped regular North Vietnamese soldiers, in large numbers. Travelling from mountain tunnels and strongholds several klicks to the east, they managed to mostly escape detection to mount their attack. Several attempts to gain an upper hand at Phu Nhon only results in pull-backs by American artillery groups. As the battle at Phu Nhon rages, resupply is difficult due to a fountain in the landing pad, solved by the men blowing it away. Heavy enemy mortar and 122 mm rocket fire is devastating the compound. Wagner is still calling in artillery at Le Quon while gunships are sent to Phu Nhon. A Huey gunship pilot is looking for targets, guided by men on the ground in the dark of night. When they finally begin firing, another voice yells at them to stop, "You're shooting up the tracks," he screams. The pilot is furious that he had been directed to shoot friendly APCs and dusters, oblivious to the mass confusion the men on the ground face. Another pilot answers a call from somebody that "The gunnies are pissed off and going home." Medevacs are called in for several wounded and one American KIA, a handsome 38 year old Sergeant First Class from New Hampshire, serving with the MACV group stationed there.

The tracks are receiving heavy fire. Three M42 dusters, light tanks weighing 24.8 tons and equipped with twin M2A1 40 mm automatic anti-aircraft guns and an M-60 machine gun, level a village they are taking fire from. The NVA used the Montagnard village for a shield, and few villagers are spared. When daylight comes, confusion and chaos still reign, but the friendlies are gaining with heavy firepower, if not numbers. A1-E Skyraiders, single engine bombers with a top speed of 320 mph, are capable of slower, more accurate bombing in close support than jets. They carry a large payload with extended 'time over target'. The pilots are Vietnamese Air Force, or VNAFs. Wagner listens between his own hectic radio calls to hear a Chinook pilot yelling in a strong southern accent at the advisers on the ground, *"One of your VeeNAF pilots tried to baawmb me."*

The adviser on the ground says, "Say again, over?"

"I said one of your VNAF pilots tried to baawmb me. Get those bastards out of here!" Again, it seems to be the MAT team, who had only second hand knowledge of their counterparts' coordinations, that is causing all the problems. The men in the sky have no idea…

Wagner had only short naps since the action began, staying each night in the tower. In the early morning hours of the third day, he grabbed a Sony cassette radio recorder to bring up with him. For fifteen minutes, he recorded radio traffic for part of the battle, a short reminder of what chaos and difficulties occur in a battle involving several units. The battle lasted for five days, the brunt of it at Phu Nhon. But Le Quon suffered as well. It was a decisive victory despite overwhelming enemy numbers. Over 387 NVA were killed at Phu Nhon, with an unknown amount at Le Quon. Other than four men in MAT 57, there were no American troops to sweep the area for enemy dead, and their Vietnamese counterparts weren't interested. Neither was Wagner. Total friendlies killed at both sites combined were eighty two ARVN and RF KIA, and one American. One hundred and eighty three were wounded, including twenty one Americans at Phu Nhon.

Wagner, his jaw swollen so badly he couldn't eat, was hurting. The danger over, he drove the Jeep alone to the 71st hospital in Pleiku to find what damage had been done. Refusing pain medicine from Kaltz, he was wondering if that had been a mistake, as he pulled into the 71st. "You look like a damn chipmunk," the doctor said, an Army Major. "Let's get some X-rays."

Wagner asked the doctor if he knew Annelle. "Of course, I think she was sent to the 85th in Phu Bai, not sure. You know her?"

The news hit Wagner hard. She's gone? How to reach her? Did she try to contact him? There were no means to. Nobody seemed to know where each staff member was sent.

After X-rays were taken and agreeing to some pain medicine, he drove to Pleiku Headquarters where he was surprised to see Doug Hanson still there. "I thought you were gone by now," Darryl said. "What the hell happened? Wait..you love it too much, you just couldn't bear..."

"Jesus, you look like a chipmunk. What the hell happened to you?" Doug asked.

"Heroic war injury. There I was...surrounded,"

"We're gonna read about you. What happened, really?"

Wagner told him the Jeep story, and about his portion of the battle.

"Did you hear about Colonel Hallard?" Hanson asked. His grin turned into a serious look.

"Oh-oh, what?"

"He was in a chopper, flying up to Qui Nhon. It blew up five minutes after takeoff. Just fell out of the sky."

Wagner stood in disbelief. "Dead?" he asked.

"Oh, yeah. Nothing left. I heard the explosion was big.

"Do you think..."

"Yes, I do," Hanson interrupted. Glad we're getting out of here. I guess you didn't want your early out."

"Nobody offered it. But no, I wouldn't take it. I was going to extend."

"You *are* crazy." What's wrong with you?"

"It's not my fault. Inherited."

Wagner tried to call the 85th from Headquarters to find Annelle. No luck, they didn't know her there. Later, he returned to the 71st. The doctor said, "Your jaw looks fine. Your chin, however, is shattered. Some pieces floating around that should come out."

"My chin? Won't that look funny?"

"Shouldn't. They'll either fill it in with silicone or leave it for scar tissue. Let's set you up for surgery in Qui Nhon. It'll be simple. In and out." They arranged for Wagner to fly to Qui Nhon on the coast, hopping a flight out of Pleiku Air Base. Arriving at the Air Base, they told him, "Planes aren't flying. Too much enemy activity. But you might wait for something to spring up."

He drove back to Le Quon instead. Two days later, the planes still weren't flying, and the pain hadn't stopped in his jaw joint. He still looked like a chipmunk. Finally, Sergeant Kaltz, with a severe hemorrhoid problem, offered to drive with him for surgery of his own. The 70 mile drive in a roughly sprung Jeep on a less-than-perfect road was tough on Wagner's jaw, every bump a shock through his temporal lobe, but it played hell with Kaltz's asshole. Arriving in Qui Nhon, they were surprised to be met with a fast, efficient process, and both of them escaped alive after a quick procedure from Army 'doctors-in-training'.

"Wasn't as bad as my episiotomy," Kaltz said.

"You know, Sarge, I wish the hell we had you on the team all year. You coulda replaced a *real* asshole," he said. The ride back was better, Kaltz had a sweet whoopee cushion, and Wagner, a stronger pain pill. Kaltz insisted on driving.

The next two days were a whirlwind. Planes were flying again, and Wagner and Hanson were each handed a surprise three-week early out, with no choice in the matter. There was barely time to pack belongings to send home. It was bitter-sweet, leaving his team who became family, brothers, and friends. Professional and skilled soldiers, Blas, Stewart, and now Kaltz. They had spent a lifetime together in one short year. Thirty nine months of service and war was suddenly over for Wagner. Three weeks before their year's scheduled tour was up, Wagner and Hanson were together for a simultaneous DEROS and flight 'back to the world' on a World Airways 707. Out of a team 'family', out of Vietnam, out of a war and out of a job, back in the states all in one twenty one hour day. Arriving in Oakland, California he bought a ticket to Denver, where three later minor surgeries would correct a flawed repair in Qui Nhon.

Loose-fitting Khakis on a shrunken body, decked with standard ribbons and medals, he boarded the Continental Airlines jet, surrounded by an alien world of civilians. Gauze wrapped his head and jaw, the healing incision itching underneath. He sat near the rear, next to a window, wondering how he could ever find Annelle. He couldn't remember the name of her town. A thin, tall man with gray hair, tan pants, white shirt and red suspenders sat down in the seat next to him. Turning his head to Wagner, he said, "I see by your uniform you're in the service?" he asked, in a stuffy tone.

"No, not anymore. Just got out today."

"Have you been to Vietnam?" he asked, head tilted back, looking down a long thin nose.

"Yes. Just got home."

To express his disdain, the man said nothing. He simply turned away with his book, one leg folded over the other in a feminine nut-crushing pose, as though the soldier beside him was diseased.

THE END

AUTHOR'S NOTE

My first writing of Pawns of Pleiku was in the Spring of 1971 after returning to the states. I was receiving surgical repair in Denver, Colorado from an ambush-related Jeep accident shortly before being sent home. Copies of my action reports during the year were vital to recount a myriad of events as accurately as possible. It was never published, and reviewing it many years later, I saw just how poorly written it was. However, it succeeded in keeping the memory alive of those unique experiences, mainly involving the fascinating Montagnard people. Forty eight years later, a 'winter of inactivity' following a hockey injury added motivation to finally re-write this story.

I never experienced post-traumatic stress, at least not knowingly. No doubt a relatively 'old age' at 26 helped, as did my voluntary choice of Infantry. Also, I never saw an American killed. That may be surprising, but there were none in the field other than team members and two brief joint operations. Counterintuitively, the majority of cases of P.T.S.D. occurred in soldiers who were never 'in the field'. They often experienced a sudden and unexpected violence, such as a barrage of mortars or a sapper attack in a relatively safe post. Soldiers in the field were trained, ready, and expected violence, reducing the potential of mental trauma.

Years later, I would often hear "My uncle was there, but he doesn't like to talk about it". Not always, of course, but that often translated to a non-combat role. Through most of this war, only a small percentage were combatants. Personally, I found most combat veterans are eager to talk, particularly with other vets or if anyone has interest, which is uncommon.

I experienced events that could never have been predicted or duplicated. *"I'm glad I did it, but I wouldn't want to do it over again"*, has been echoed by millions of warriors before and since. Out of tensions, fears, filth, disease, sadness and horrors, there are always positives and negatives…that unforgettable year, unique, complicated, confusing….impacted me in a variety of ways:

That *"How To Study Guide"* paperback book the helicopter dropped into our compound so long ago….so seemingly inconsequential at the time, proved pivotal. The book was key in elevating a 0.89 Engineering grade point to a 3.81 out of 4.0….probably a record change of some kind. It helped produce a career and a future.

Four years after returning, I acquired a rare type of epilepsy. Thousands of temporal lobe seizures plagued me for thirteen years, finally fading away forever. At the onset, I didn't know if I needed a psychiatrist, neurologist or an exorcist. Several tests were made to determine if it was epilepsy, encephalitis or a brain tumor. One of those tests was a barbaric, excruciating pneumoencephalogram, now replaced by MRI technology. It was by far the most physically painful experience in my life. Through a spinal tap, air is pumped up the spine into the brain to separate layers in order to see a possible tumor. Years later, the internet would provide the information to finally identify the cause as the defoliant *Agent Orange*. Its toxic ingredient, Dioxin, causes seizures. It usually occurs years later and at a time of stress. The government and Veterans Administration never recognized it, though an inordinate number of Pleiku veterans suffered the same rare disorder. Resulting medical bills exceeded all my pay in Vietnam, never reimbursed. But even after epilepsy, hepatitis, and a broken jaw, I healed and am virtually unscathed. I was lucky. So many others were not.

I carry no regrets about the war save for one: following orders to move Montagnard villages.

Searching for my soul mate, four years after coming

434

home, I found and married her. She was beautiful, with big, captivating blue eyes. We have been married for life.

.......she was a nurse.

And finally, forty eight years after leaving Vietnam, at age seventy four... almost a half century later.... I wrote a book.

PAWNS OF PLEIKU is written as historical fiction. In order to protect individuals' confidentiality, names have been changed, both U.S. and indigenous peoples, as well as some village names. Combat, patrol missions, reconsolidation moves, interactions with villagers, and most conversations were from my action reports and memories of actual events, and are factual. Stories of drug trading were gleaned from media reports and later the internet, and not actually experienced by the author.

The book is neither an advocate nor a protest of the war or any war. It is not intended to be an argument for or against reasons we were in that war at all, there are far too many confusing factors to re-hash what has been argued ad nauseam. Most agree, as do I, it was a mistake to enter it, but I believe it was worse to abandon our allies. I do have a problem with men who say, "Let's go get 'em" whenever the news reports an offensive violation or conflict in the world. What they are really saying is, *"Let you or your son go get 'em, not me or my son."* Those not in harm's way are too quick to want others to act, not understanding the waste, horrors and grief that follow.

What I *would* argue is that militarily, we won.... then we left. With a lack of supplies, the South Vietnamese lost. Yes, corruption, poor leadership in many cases, and other factors contributed. But there were excellent leaders and fighters as well in both Vietnamese and Montagnard ranks.

My belief is based on several factors:

1. In the 1970s, no other Americans saw the perspective of the war that advisers did, including the progress or lack thereof from both civilian and military standpoints.

2. By 1971, only 2% of the remaining 130,000 U.S. troops, or roughly 2,600 U.S. soldiers were actually 'in the field'. South Vietnamese soldiers, or ARVNs, and RF/PFs were doing well when equipped and supported, arguably with U.S. air support. Pleiku Province was, at the time, considered the 'least pacified' in the country, yet I was surprised how safe most areas were to travel and reside in, particularly near Pleiku City. I expected every day to be a war. Instead, most areas this late in the war seemed peaceful and normal.

3. Friends and classmates from advisory and language schools with the same MAT assignments in the Delta "never heard a shot fired all year in anger". They could travel to villages on motorcycles at night with little fear.

4. During the course of my tour, our team had two Kit Carson Scouts, surrendered NVA enemy soldiers, who had a strong contempt for their homeland leaders. They had thought they were "coming down to free the people, but instead were coming to kill them." Their conditions and poor expectations were a convincing argument the North was losing when the U.S. was still involved and supporting. The enemy's hopes resided on our predisposed media, their greatest ally.

5. A dozen years later, I befriended an ex-ARVN soldier who told me stories of his brother, a South Vietnamese Airborne commando, who had been dropped into North Vietnam. He told of the people there "issued with white pajamas and flags" for when the Americans would invade as they anticipated.

With a few violent exceptions, the cities were the first to be cleaned up in the 60s. Soldiers didn't routinely carry weapons in cities by 1970. The coastal countryside was next. The Delta was well under control. The central and northern rural jungles and mountains were the last, but growing safer. Finally, thanks to the Jane Fondas and Tom Haydens, and later Walter Cronkites of the world, the U.S. stopped supplying our allies weapons, ammunitions and support systems. Meanwhile, China and Russia ramped up their supplies. There were South Vietnamese units literally fighting without bullets at the end of the war, against top grade weapons and equipment. We didn't lose, we left. Most post-1969 *combat* vets agree. We deserted our allies, Vietnamese and Montagnards. They were left to be slaughtered in a genocide the American public never considered or cared about. The biased media didn't stop with the end of the war. Four and a half decades later, Ken Burns would do his documentary of the Vietnam War. The bulk of his interviews were with North Vietnamese and Viet Cong soldiers and U.S. anti-war protesters, who weren't about to provide anything positive. I knew the accent immediately between North and South Vietnamese, and most were from the North. One exception was a U.S. Army adviser who spoke truthfully and accurately. But Burn's extensively done production will likely remain the 'bible' of the war forever in history.

I hope not.

PICTURES AND MAPS

438

About the Author

Monty Vogel grew up in Portland, Maine. In January 1968, a week after the Tet offensive began, he had been an Engineering student at the University of Maine when he enlisted. Assigned as an E-2 Private in the Army Fire Department, a letter to his congressman was necessary to enter Infantry Officer Candidate School to be commissioned as an Infantry Lieutenant. Returning to the University to graduate after 39 months of military, he worked as an engineer for a major plastics manufacturer in Maine. Retiring in 2004 at 59, he started a part time one-man diving business, providing boat moorings and other services. After six years, that business was sold to provide time for him and his wife to build a unique solar home on a small bridgeless island on the Maine coast, a seven year project. Monty and his wife Beth live by Sebago Lake in Maine, where they raised their two daughters, Tammy and Laura. All three became nurses.

Made in the USA
Columbia, SC
25 April 2022

59436419R00251